To Paul

Africa, London, New
York .... your life is
a quest with enterprises
at every step!

Heres to you

at Reshing fy

Oct 2010

Advance Praise for *The World that Changes the World*

The World that Changes the World provides a unique and timely window into the global forces that shape our world—and that we can shape for the better. The multifaceted, multinational, multisectoral insights in this volume offer inspiration, ideas, and opportunity for action and impact.

Dr. Melissa A. Berman
President and CEO, Rockefeller Philanthropy Advisors, Inc.

The philanthrocapitalism movement—in which the winners in our capitalistic society make doing good a core part of their personal and business strategies— now needs to effectively mobilize and impact the nonprofits, social activists, capacity builders, regulators, and broader community. *The World that Changes the World* puts together the pieces of this puzzle by explaining how these varied actors of the social ecosystem function and interact with each other, and how philanthrocapitalism and other forces of change can bring about a better world.

Matthew Bishop
Co-Author, Philanthrocapitalism*: How giving can save the world*

The World that Changes the World is a veritable *tour de force* of the individuals, organizations, and leading-edge thinking that are driving this convergence across the sectors. It is a compendium of essays that span the broader sustainability spectrum; from post-CSR business approaches through to transformational change within NGOs and capital markets. It is as rich in its diversity of thinking as it is its diversity of authors . . . [It] should become the pocket guide for changemakers of the world in the same way that *The Lonely Planet* is for travelers of the world.

Gib Bulloch
Founder and Executive Director, Accenture Development Partnerships

The World that Changes the World has put together, for the first time, a holistic and comprehensive map of and insights into the social world. It is a unique effort by 21 authors located across the globe who have managed to put their thoughts in a structure and manner that flows seamlessly from chapter to chapter. If there is an X PRIZE for collaborative thought leadership of the social ecosystem, this book would get it.

Dr. Peter H. Diamandis
Chairman and CEO, X PRIZE Foundation

This is a comprehensive primer representing the diversity of perspectives that comprises the evolving global social ecosystem. Its most important contribution is the wide net it has cast to draw upon Asian, Australian, British, and American contributors.

Dr. Pamela Hartigan
Director, Skoll Centre for Social Entrepreneurship,
Saïd Business School, Oxford University
and Co-Founder, Volans Ventures

This is a path-breaking book. It is the first holistic overview of the major forces such as volunteerism, philanthropy, and social enterprises that are transforming our globalized world.

Tommy Koh
Ambassador-at-large, Singapore
and Chairman, SymAsia Foundation

The World that Changes the World is, itself, a catalyst for change. It presents a landscape of the things that matter most in the nonprofit world as seen through the eyes of the changemakers themselves, who sit not on the periphery but who eat, live, and breathe change in the nonprofit world.

Wherever we are in the social ecosystem, *The World that Changes the World* has something for us. It nudges us to learn about the other stakeholders in our space. The more we know about them, the more we know how to engage with them, learn from them, and work together with them to have a greater and greater impact over time.

Wendy Kopp
Founder and CEO, Teach For America

This book is timely. It captivates for its directness with information and for its well-illustrated and uncomplicated charts and maps that make it all so painless to understand the complexity of the changes that are underway.

As we struggle to meet the ever-changing needs of the people that we in the social sector have dedicated our lives to helping, we also need to know what we can do, and connect better with the friends who share the same drive. This book helps us to achieve this task and to see how we are all connected with the same mission. The book helps us to reflect that *we* are, in the end, the greatest change there is.

Braema Mathiaparanam
President, South East Asia and Pacific Region,
International Council of Social Welfare

What a terrific resource!

This book is a priceless cache of information and inspiration for every stakeholder of the social sector. The 21 diverse and well-researched chapters, with analysis and examples written by the changemakers themselves, provide the reader with both the framework to organize their own thoughts and the stimulation to take action.

The World that Changes the World is a must read for social sector practitioners as well as private and public sector leaders who can benefit from the experiences of the social purpose organizations and the insights of their leaders.

Usha Menon
Executive Chairman, Management Centre Asia

What is clear is that there are tremendous opportunities to break the silos between the different actors in order to share knowledge and ideas, identify synergies, and explore new methods.

Imagine my excitement when a big-picture book such as this comes along to explain and break those silos. Now, in one place, we have a valuable one-stop resource for the many players in, and observers of, the social ecosystem: for the philanthropists who would like a quick yet comprehensive understanding of the social space; for the progressive charities who are exploring innovative means of generating and using resources and capital; and for the government authorities who are trying to figure out how they may best spur the sector.

Doug Miller
*Honorary President, European Venture Philanthropy Association
and Founder, Asia Venture Philanthropy Network*

The World that Changes the World is a solid primer for those interested in social change. Cheng and Mohamed bring together a selection of wise thinkers and authors to explore the challenges we face collectively in the social sector—lack of accountability, dependency, and the need for innovation. You will be challenged to turn your ideas into action, which is what the world needs most today.

Jacqueline Novogratz
*CEO, Acumen Fund
and Author,* The Blue Sweater

The good news is that today, there are passionate groups of people everywhere looking for and working on solutions to these issues. They are part of what is called the social sector.

The bad news is that the social sector is messy and fragmented . . . In fact, some parts of the social sector are messier than toilets.

It's great to know that there is now a book that makes sense of all the crap that moves around in this sector. *The World that Changes the World* has created a framework by which all the disparate, fragmented pieces of the social sector are made understandable and coherent. It gives us more credit than we may deserve, but, nevertheless, the book reinforces the hope and spirit that drives many of us.

Jack Sim
Founder, World Toilet Organization

Congratulations! The contributors have captured the dynamic environment in which third sector organizations are now operating—that space between the market, government, and communities. *The World that Changes the World* is thought leadership at its best—envisioning the future through reflection and analysis of past trends and contemporary challenges . . . a volume to be dipped into at each reader's entry point to the sector.

Senator the Hon. Ursula Stephens
Australian Parliamentary Secretary for Social Inclusion and the Voluntary Sector

Publisher's Note:

Several of the endorsement quotes above are abridged from longer commentaries and reviews provided. The full text can be viewed at the book website (www.worldthatchangestheworld.com).

The World that Changes the World

How philanthropy, innovation, and entrepreneurship
are transforming the social ecosystem

The World that Changes the World

How philanthropy, innovation, and entrepreneurship
are transforming the social ecosystem

Edited by

Willie Cheng
and
Sharifah Mohamed

JOSSEY-BASS™
An Imprint of

This edition is published by John Wiley & Sons (Asia) Pte. Ltd., 2 Clementi Loop, #02-01, Singapore 129809 on behalf of Jossey-Bass, A Wiley Imprint.

989 Market Street, San Francisco, CA 94103-1741–www.josseybass.com

Jossey-Bass books and products are available through most bookstores. To contact Jossey-Bass directly call our Customer Care Department within the U.S. at 800-956-7739, outside the U.S. at 317-572-3986, or fax 317-572-4002.

Jossey-Bass also publishes its books in a variety of electronic formats. Some content that appears in print may not be available in electronic books.

The Lien Centre for Social Innovation seeks to inspire ideas and innovations, foster new alliances, and facilitate solutions to strengthen the nonprofit sector. It is located at the Singapore Management University Administration Building, 81 Victoria Street, #09-03, Singapore 188065, website: www.lcsi.smu.edu.sg.

Library of Congress Cataloging-in-Publication Data

ISBN: 978-0-470-82715-4

Typeset by MPS (A Macmillan Company)
Printed in Singapore

10 9 8 7 6 5 4 3 2 1

Contents

Overview

Beneficiaries

Social Purpose Entities

Capacity Builders

Community

Government

Change Enablers

Macro-Trends

Acknowledgments

It started off as a simple idea: produce a book that takes a holistic look at the global social ecosystem, its issues, and where it is going; but we never quite anticipated the many logistical and creative challenges that were involved. For while the creation of this book did not take a cast of thousands, certainly, a lot more people than we envisaged were involved in this ambitious and worthwhile undertaking.

There are, therefore, many we would like to thank, and we apologize, in advance, to those we may have inadvertently left out along the way.

First, of course, are our co-authors (in order of the chapters): Tan Chi Chiu, Gerard Ee, Jon Huggett, Chris Cusano, Sara Olsen, Thomas Menkhoff, Rob John, Paulette Maehara, Laurence Lien, Stephen Young, Alan Webber, Peter Shergold, Stephen Lloyd, Maximilian Martin, Robert Chew, Jed Emerson, Kumi Naidoo, Geoff Mulgan, and John Elkington.

They did not all come on board the project at the same time. We started with a framework of 18 chapters. We ended with 21 chapters and adjusted the chapter topics and sequences as we went along. We are grateful to the few authors who came on board late in the day but who still worked valiantly to tight deadlines.

We want to thank all the authors for their patience, for putting up with creative differences and multiple turnarounds, and for sharing their wealth of knowledge in an unprecedented collaborative mapping of the social ecosystem.

We and, for that matter, each author, were helped by a group of friends and committed professionals who provided ideas, critiques, research, edits, and even rewrites of portions of the individual chapters. Several of them helped out on multiple chapters. We list them (in alphabetical order) and the chapters they helped with:

- *Halimah Chew of the National Volunteer & Philanthropy Centre:* Chapter 11 (Volunteerism)
- *Lindsay Driscoll of Bates Wells & Braithwaite:* Chapter 15 (Regulator)
- *Roger Frank formerly of Developing World Markets:* Chapter 18 (Social Finance)

- *Allen Gunn of Aspiration:* Chapter 17 (Technology)
- *Lee Poh Wah of the Lien Foundation:* Chapter 8 (Philanthropy)
- *Gabriel Lim of the Lien Foundation:* Chapter 8 (Philanthropy)
- *Patsian Low of Serenity Associates:* Chapter 5 (Social Enterprises), Chapter 9 (Venture Philanthropy), Chapter 14 (Government), Chapter 18 (Social Finance), and Chapter 19 (Global Civil Society)
- *Farheen Mukri of the Lien Centre for Social Innovation (the Lien Centre):* Chapter 2 (Unmet Social Needs)
- *Michael Nilsen of the Association of Fundraising Professionals:* Chapter 10 (Donor Management)
- *Suzanne Ooi of WordCraft:* Chapter 8 (Philanthropy)
- *Bindu Sharma of the International Centre for Missing and Exploited Children, Singapore:* Chapter 12 (Corporate Social Responsibility)
- *Mark Surman of the Mozilla Foundation:* Chapter 17 (Technology)
- *Tan Tze Hoong of Gnosis Consulting:* Chapter 1 (The Social Ecosystem), Chapter 2 (Unmet Social Needs), Chapter 4 (Charities), Chapter 8 (Philanthropy), Chapter 16 (Culture and Leadership), and Chapter 17 (Technology)
- *Cheryl Tang of ApVentures:* Chapter 2 (Unmet Social Needs), Chapter 3 (Charity Definition), Chapter 8 (Philanthropy), Chapter 10 (Donor Management), and Chapter 11 (Volunteerism)
- *Jared Tham of the Lien Centre:* Chapter 12 (Corporate Social Responsibility), Chapter 13 (Media), and Chapter 19 (Global Civil Society).

There were pit stops along the way to make sure that the language of our world would make sense in the wider world. For this, we thank our two copyeditors: Daven Wu and Robyn Flemming from whom we learned much about the *Chicago Manual of Style Online*, serial commas, and many other mysterious rules of English grammar.

We also want to thank Cheryl Tang, Vadivu Govind, and Professor Steven Miller, Dean of School of Information Systems at the Singapore Management University for reviewing all the chapters.

We want to express our deep appreciation to the several individuals who gave generously of their valuable time to review an early version of the book and provided us with their endorsements: Melissa Berman (Rockefeller Philanthropy Advisors), Matthew Bishop (co-author of *Philanthrocapitalism*), Gib Bulloch (Accenture Development Partnerships), Peter Diamandis (X PRIZE Foundation), Pamela Hartigan (Skoll Centre for Social Entrepreneurship, Saïd Business School, Oxford University), Tommy Koh (SymAsia Foundation),

Wendy Kopp (Teach for America), Braema Mathiaparanam (International Council on Social Welfare), Usha Menon (Management Centre Asia), Doug Miller (European Venture Philanthropy Association), Jacqueline Novogratz (Acumen Fund), Jack Sim (World Toilet Organization), and Ursula Stephens (Australian Parliamentary Secretary for Social Inclusion and the Voluntary Sector). We are especially grateful to Bill Drayton, founder of Ashoka: Innovators for the Public, for his foreword.

There were many who helped oil the wheels of this book's production. The following provided the much-needed liaison with some of the authors: Kevin Teo and Sam Lakha of Volans Ventures, Sharon Mealy of Greenpeace International, Christine Norgrove of the Centre for Social Impact, and Manish Joshi of the Global Campaign for Climate Action. Two of our colleagues at the Lien Centre, Prema Prasad and Daphne Lim have been at the heart of the administration and coordination of all the parties involved.

The book's graphics are the work of many creative minds. Daphne Lim of the Lien Centre helped with enhancing several of the diagrams, while Alicia Tan of Hot Fusion created several cover designs for the book. The book's website (www.worldthatchangestheworld.com) was developed by Kok Tien Nee, Jamie Kok, Troy Toon, and Wong Meng Fei of Thinkingcouch Interactive, with support from Jared Tham of the Lien Centre and Royston Loo and Choo Meng Yong of the Singapore Management University's (SMU) Integrated Information Technological Services team. The graphics for the individual chapters were developed by Jamie Tan and his team at Revid.

We are particularly grateful to John Wiley & Sons for undertaking to publish this book. The people we worked with are testimony to the quality of a premier book publisher: Joel Balbin, Cindy Chu, CJ Hwu, Cynthia Mak, Nick Melchior, and Janis Soo.

We have had much support from various departments of SMU in producing this book. We are especially thankful to Jonathan Chen, legal manager, for his patience and resilience in helping us navigate the multiple and complex contractual arrangements for a project with 21 authors. We also want to thank Professor Howard Hunter, president of SMU, for his overall support of this venture.

Finally, this book would not have come about if not for the support of the Board of the Lien Centre. Several of the board members (Robert Chew, Gerard Ee, Laurence Lien, Thomas Menkhoff, and Tan Chi Chiu) contributed chapters to the book, but all of them—including David Chan, Cecilia Chua, Lee Poh Wah, Steven Miller, Zaqy Mohamed, and Yeoh Chee Yan—have been with us from the beginning, providing us with counsel and encouragement.

And if the analogy is not already clear, you could say that, true to the spirit of a thriving ecosystem, this book has been made possible through the critical and varied contributions of many players, all working toward a common vision of a better social landscape and future.

Willie Cheng and Sharifah Mohamed
The Editors

Foreword

Many people sense that society's problems are multiplying faster and faster—and that they are outrunning the solutions.

The answer lies in the hands of two groups of people.

The first group consists of social entrepreneurs. Social entrepreneurs can only be satisfied in life if they *have* changed one of society's major *systems* significantly and for the good of all. They intuitively know they would never be satisfied with anything less. (By contrast, most artists and scholars come to rest when they express an idea; professionals when they solve a client's problem; and managers when they make their organizations work well.)

As a result, social entrepreneurs are not distracted by local successes that could easily be achieved because of local personalities and circumstances, or by solving a symptom or a part of the problem.

They relentlessly focus in on the root causes of issues. They *have* to find and develop and refine and drive home groundbreaking approaches. They *have* to transform the patterns and systems of their field, be it human rights or health, in such game-changing ways that the problem dies.

The faster society changes, the more often and more extensively its systems must be reformed—and the more essential social entrepreneurs become. Not only because they are entrepreneurs, but because their north star is to change the world's systems for the good of all of us.

Democratic governments uniquely represent everyone (no one elected either Steve Jobs or Muhammad Yunus), but governments, typically structured as bureaucratic monopolies, desperately need social entrepreneurs to imagine and develop the future.

The second group the world needs is changemakers. As the rate of change continues to accelerate exponentially, every part of society—every company, religious house, school, citizen group, city, family, country—must constantly and in many ways also be adjusting. That will not be possible unless the people in that group spot, engage with, and contribute value to all the change around them.

That is why Ashoka's goal is an "everyone a changemaker" world.

The world that is upon us can only work if everyone functions in society like a smart white blood cell would in the body. Those who are not changemakers do not want to see problems because if they did, all that would happen is that they would feel badly about themselves.

Changemakers, quite to the contrary, are delighted to spot problems—because a problem is an opportunity to help others, be powerful, and exercise and strengthen their changemaking skills.

Both groups need one another. Indeed, social entrepreneurs typically spread their innovations by enticing people in one locality after another to adopt and champion them, i.e., by mass recruiting changemakers. These changemakers, in turn, are role models for their neighbors and also recruit them. Some of these changemakers, in turn, will become future entrepreneurs.

These two groups are both accelerating change and essential to staying ahead of it.

Willie Cheng is very much a part of this extraordinary, magical world.

He brings to it the rigor of his years as a partner in Accenture, where he headed the firm's Singapore office and led its communications and high-tech practice. Over the last seven years he has, while remaining a leader in business, thrown himself actively into many dimensions of the citizen sector. He has charmed us, challenged us, and helped us think and act more clearly. He has also learned who among us is especially thoughtful.

This book benefits from all this.

Willie and his colleague, Sharifah Mohamed, have attracted an extraordinary group of contributors, and they have enabled them to think together and produce true insights into our field at this historic inflection point.

This accomplishment mirrors one of the field's greatest—if often little understood—strengths: We work together within and between organizations, people, and movements with increasing skill and ease.

How did the world get the International Criminal Court a few years ago? Certainly not because the nation-states welcomed it: They had blocked it since the 1940s, no doubt because it is the first break in their monopoly of sovereignty. This profoundly historic breakthrough came because 2,000 citizen groups across the world worked together and made it happen.

This book understands the forces at play—the challenges of a world accelerating toward a future defined by change, and the equally rapid emergence of social entrepreneurship and changemaking.

All of us, and all of those about whom we care, must give ourselves permission to be entrepreneurs and changemakers. And we must develop the skills to do so. This book will help.

Bill Drayton
Founder & CEO, Ashoka: Innovators for the Public
August 1, 2010

Abbreviations

Abbreviations

The following abbreviations are used in this book.

CEO	Chief Executive Officer
CSO	Civil Society Organization
CSR	Corporate Social Responsibility
GDP	Gross Domestic Product
NGO	Nongovernment organization
NPO	Nonprofit organization
UK	United Kingdom
UN	United Nations
US	United States

All abbreviations, including the above (but with the exceptions of UK, UN, and US), are usually introduced with the full term the first time they appear in a chapter.

Currencies

All amounts are usually stated in US$. Where another currency is used, the US$ equivalent at exchange rates prevailing in mid-2010 is provided.

Overview

Chapter 0

Introduction

Navigating the Social Ecosystem

WILLIE CHENG AND SHARIFAH MOHAMED
The Editors

There are over three million social purpose organizations around the world, employing more than 48 million people, with a limited budget of US$1.9 trillion annually.[1] It is a growing, but hugely fragmented, complex, and often confusing sector—with very diverse, at times divisive players—that is largely oriented toward the mission of changing society for the better, though not always in the ways of working with each other to achieve this goal.

What makes this world and its players tick? How are they likely to tick differently in the future? What would change the way they tick?

This book seeks to answer these questions.

A key reason for writing this book is that we have not found another that frames and describes the issues and trends of the social sector and its component parts in a holistic and complete manner. Of course, we realized that we, at the Lien Centre for Social Innovation,[2] are vastly inadequate to address these issues ourselves. This is why we have brought together a distinguished group of thinkers, leaders, and experts in the various aspects of the social space to contribute to this undertaking.

As is evident from the book's subtitle, we have used the paradigm of an ecosystem to frame the social world. In our view, a dynamic, interdependent, and sustaining ecosystem of living organisms provides the perfect model with which to analyze this ever-changing world. We have asked each author to provide his or her perspective on the status of a particular facet within the social ecosystem, and to highlight the issues, trends, and future scenarios that affect that facet. Figure 0.1 provides a skeleton of the social ecosystem framework and shows how the individual chapters map onto it.

Figure 0.1 Book Map

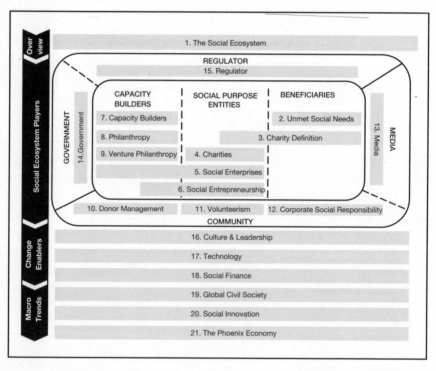

Chapter 1 describes the social ecosystem framework while highlighting key issues and trends. This is followed by 14 chapters that detail the specific core players of the ecosystem (the Beneficiaries, Social Purpose Entities, and Capacity Builders) and the supporting roles played by the Community, Media, Government, and Regulator.

The next three chapters of the book examine the enablers of change in the ecosystem—namely Culture and Leadership, Technology, and Finance. Finally, the last three chapters explore the macro-trends of growth (Global Civil Society), social innovation (Social Innovation), and fusion of the sectors (The Phoenix Economy).

A consistent theme that emerges from these thought-provoking essays is the acute sense of change and vibrancy that infuses the social sector. This feeling of urgency has been with us throughout the gestation of this book—even as we began scouring the social smorgasbord to find kindred souls who were willing to share their passion, ideas, and thinking.

For all of us at the Lien Centre, producing this ambitious book has been a fulfilling, humbling, and exhilarating ride. We hope you will find the journey through the social ecosystem to be an equally enjoyable and invaluable experience.

Endnotes

1   The figures provided in this paragraph are drawn from several sources. A fuller discussion of these numbers and their data sources can be found in the subsection on "Global Civil Society" and endnotes 42 and 43 in Chapter 1, "The Social Ecosystem: Transitions within the ecosystem of change," by Willie Cheng.

2   The Lien Centre for Social Innovation is a partnership of the Lien Foundation and Singapore Management University. Its mission is to inspire ideas and innovations, foster new alliances, and facilitate solutions to strengthen the nonprofit sector. See www.lcsi.smu.edu.sg.

Chapter 1

The Social Ecosystem

Transitions within the Ecosystem of Change

WILLIE CHENG

Chairman, Lien Centre for Social Innovation

The ecosystem paradigm provides a framework for understanding and influencing the forces of change facing the nonprofit sector.

At the core of the social ecosystem are the social purpose organizations and individuals who are helping their beneficiaries, and the capacity builders who seek to help the helpers. Around them are the individuals and corporations in the community, the media, and the government (including its role as regulator) who collectively provide the resources, support, and scrutiny to ensure that the core players function as intended.

Four key enablers of change—culture, leadership, technology, and finance—have resulted in three broad macro-trends in the social sector: the rise of global civil society and its attendant issues; the acceleration of social change through innovation; and the fusion of ideas, models, and practices of the social and enterprise sectors.

W e live in an age of transition.

The big transition, which has been playing out for decades, has been the move to a global knowledge economy. Momentous events have rippled alongside this shift: the fall of communism, the rise of capitalism, and the growth of civil society. In turn, smaller transitions such as changes in a currency's value and society's values may be felt more immediately in our daily lives. Yet, in many ways, all these smaller waves of change are really part of the larger ones.

To place these transitions in context, it is useful to have a framework to anchor ourselves, to be able to understand the forces of change, and to determine how we can respond to them.

One such useful framework is derived from biology. Framed by the study of living organisms, the term "ecosystem" describes a self-sustaining community of interdependent organisms interacting with one another in their local environment. The beauty of the ecosystem paradigm is the way it applies systems thinking to a complex environment.

For our purposes, an ecosystem is defined as a system whose members benefit from one another's participation via symbiotic relationships. And just as systems can comprise subsystems, an ecosystem can comprise sub-ecosystems that interact with, and benefit, each other. Thus, the ecosystem of a country is composed of three interdependent sub-ecosystems: the enterprise ecosystem (the private sector), the state ecosystem (the public sector), and the social ecosystem (the people sector).

In a sense, the social ecosystem plays a unique role relative to the other two: Its function is to fill the gaps and pick up the pieces left behind through the misdeeds, negligence, or oversight of the state and enterprise ecosystems. It is, indeed, the ecosystem of change—change to a better society and change for a better world.

The Social Ecosystem

By applying an ecosystem approach to the social sector—the subject of this book—we obtain a holistic and integrated perspective about how the different players can and should interact with one another to create a more effective sector (and, *ipso facto*, a better world).

A picture of what the social ecosystem and its players might look like is shown in Figure 1.1.

Figure 1.1 The Social Ecosystem Framework

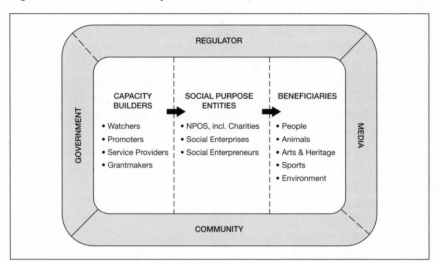

At the core of the social ecosystem are the social purpose entities that seek to positively impact their beneficiaries, and the capacity builders that facilitate the missions of these social purpose entities. Around them are the community (individuals and corporations), media, and government (including one of its distinctive roles as the regulator) who collectively provide the resources, support, and scrutiny to ensure that the core players function as intended.

A description of the nature, key issues, and major trends for each group of players follows in the ensuing subsections:[1]

- Beneficiaries
- Social purpose entities
- Capacity builders
- Community
- Media
- Government
- Regulator.

Beneficiaries

Beneficiaries and their causes are the *raison d'etre* for the existence of civil society. However, we sometimes lose sight of this vital group because they have the least voice.

We would expect social causes to be specific to geography and time. Yet, at a high level, there is a great deal of commonality in unmet social needs across the globe. The basic needs of food, water, and health have existed since time immemorial, and are today, much related to poverty and the developing world. Economic progress, however, has brought with it other social issues, chiefly human displacements (refugees and migrant workers), environmental challenges (climate change and natural disasters), and developed society issues (income disparities, aging population, mental health, and breakdown of the family structure).[2]

Unfortunately, the resources that are allocated to social causes may not necessarily be proportionate to the actual needs. Many factors influence this allocation, but a significant consideration is whether the cause officially counts as a "charitable cause" whereby tax benefits accrue to the nonprofit organization and the donor.

There is a surprising disconnect between what different people see as constituting a "charity" and its beneficiaries. If you ask the man in the street, the common response you will get is that charity is simply about helping the poor and the needy of society. Implicit in this answer is the notion that charity is about redressing the gap between the rich and the poor.

However, the legal definition of charity in most jurisdictions is usually much broader than that. Often, the scope of what legally constitutes charity extends beyond the poor and the disadvantaged to cover the general community good—sports, the arts, the environment, heritage, and even animals.

While there may be nothing wrong with this broadened definition in itself, the result is that when the same support mechanisms (tax breaks, community mobilization, etc.) are made available generally for the community good, then the preferential option for the poor is diluted and sometimes lost. Also, the level of accountability to which some of these "community causes" may otherwise have had to adhere is usually more relaxed for charitable projects than for commercial or public sector projects.[3]

Social Purpose Entities

At the very heart of the social sector are the social purpose organizations and socially motivated individuals who seek to make a difference to society.

Social purpose organizations have gone by different labels depending upon the country and how they have evolved in those locations. The most common acronyms are "NPOs" (nonprofit organizations), "NGOs" (nongovernment organizations), and "CSOs" (civil society organizations). The terms are often used interchangeably, although there are nuanced differences among them. The term "NPO" connotes that an organization is fundamentally nonprofit in nature, while "NGO" and "CSO" emphasize that the organization has no participation or representation by the government. In many countries, NPOs can be funded and directed by the government.[4]

A large number of NPOs qualify as "charities." In most jurisdictions, a charity is legally defined by either income tax law or charity law. In Commonwealth countries, an organization becomes a registered charity under a Charities Act or equivalent legislation. In the United States, a charitable organization needs to satisfy section 501(c)(3) of the Internal Revenue Code; they are often simply referred to as nonprofits or 501c3 organizations.[5] Apart from the beneficial image of having charity status, being a charity carries with it attendant tax benefits: usually, its income is tax exempt and donations to it are tax deductible for the donors.[6]

While most social purpose organizations are nonprofit in nature, a new form of hybrid social–business organization has emerged to bridge the social and enterprise world. These "social enterprises" are, essentially, businesses with a social mission. Grameen Bank, Cabbages & Condoms, and *The Big Issue* are examples of outstanding social enterprises.[7]

Most social enterprises are set up to provide funding support to related NPOs and/or to provide employment opportunities for beneficiaries. While their numbers are mushrooming in many countries, their success rate appears to be lower than that of their commercial counterparts. Most, it seems, are hampered by the multiple bottom lines (financial, social, environmental, etc.) that they have to deliver.[8]

Organizations are driven by people. All NPOs (including charities) and social enterprises are invariably peopled by socially motivated individuals, and helmed by social leaders. In the last few years, a special breed of social leaders called social entrepreneurs has emerged either as part of formal organizations (often founded by them) or operating as individuals.

The term "social entrepreneur" was first coined by Bill Drayton who went on to form Ashoka: Innovators for the Public,[9] the world's largest association of social entrepreneurs. In essence, social entrepreneurs effect systemic, large-scale social change through innovative pattern-changing approaches.

Despite the surfeit of literature on the two subjects, there is still some confusion in equating social enterprises (organizations) with social entrepreneurs (individuals). Not all social enterprises are run by social entrepreneurs (only those that are in the category of pattern-changing), and not all social entrepreneurs run social enterprises (in fact, few do).

But there is no question that social entrepreneurs are role models for the rest of us. Ashoka believes that ordinary citizens from all walks of life can be inspired and instructed by these role models to become "changemakers" and that, in time to come, the wider world will be transformed by the "empathetic ethics of the citizen sector."[10]

Capacity Builders

Even as NPOs and social entrepreneurs directly help their beneficiaries, there is a group of intermediary organizations that seeks to help these helpers. Called capacity builders, they help, as the name suggests, build the capacity of the social sector.

The role of and need for intermediaries may not always be well appreciated. The fact is that all ecosystems need intermediaries to facilitate the core activities and oil the wheels of the marketplace.

A good analogy is the public commercial market. Think of NPOs as public listed companies. They need funds from their investors—the donors. But for donors to know who to invest their limited funds in, they require independent analysts (the watchers) to evaluate and rate the charities. Instead of donating directly, they could actually do so through grantmakers, the equivalent of fund managers in the public markets. Just as the commercial companies service each other, there are NPOs that are service providers to other NPOs. There would also be the equivalent of promoters—the organizations and networks (e.g. the security traders association)—that seek to grow and develop the marketplace or aspects of it.

The range of intermediary organizations needed in the social sector can thus be grouped as watchers, promoters, service providers, and grantmakers.

Watchers facilitate informed giving[11] by providing relevant information about NPOs so that donors and other stakeholders can make better choices. The well-known ones are broad-based rating agencies such as GuideStar, Charity Navigator, and Charity Watch; these provide performance ratings, mainly based on financial analysis, that are similar to the Standard & Poor's of the commercial world. Other watchers are more specific to the activities they are monitoring; examples include MAPLight.org (political funding) and NGOWatch (NPO impact on public policy). Watchers tend to emanate from the US and, thus, their measurement systems reflect the cultural preferences of the Western world.[12]

Promoters seek to grow and develop the sector, or a specific segment within the sector. They could be associations of NPOs coming together, or independent NPOs established for that purpose. An example of an association promoter is the National Council for Voluntary Organizations, which comprises 5,700 organizational members representing more than half of the nonprofit sector's workforce in the United Kingdom. Its mission is to provide the voice and support for a vibrant voluntary and community sector in the UK. An example of an independent NPO is the Institute for Philanthropy, which was established to increase effective philanthropy in the UK and internationally.[13]

Service providers provide services to charities in areas that can be generic to any organization (e.g. premises) or specific to the nonprofit sector (e.g. consulting). The range of services includes strategic advice (e.g. Bridgespan), training (e.g. Social Service Training Institute), professional development (e.g. Compass Point), human capital matching (e.g. BoardnetUSA), brokering (e.g. Charity Choice Goodwill Gallery), and technical services (e.g. Hackers for Charity). Most of these service providers are NPOs themselves. There are also many regular commercial service providers who provide their services to charities at discounted rates. For example, Computer Troubleshooters, billed as the world's largest computer service franchise, has a Charity Service Program that provides discounted or donated computer services to charities.[14]

Grantmakers traditionally comprise foundations (e.g. The Rockefeller Foundation) and funds (e.g. United Way).[15] They take money from donors, big and small, and give it out as grants to the charities. They typically do so through a rigorous process that ensures the money is given for the right purpose and is properly used to achieve the desired result.

Among the grantmakers, a new class called venture philanthropists stands out. The roots of modern-day venture philanthropy lie in the successful tech-entrepreneurs of Silicon Valley employing their newly minted wealth to change the social world through the use of venture capital-like approaches. At the heart of venture philanthropy is a highly engaged partnership that offers development finance coupled with nonfinancial advice that NPOs and their ventures need in order to grow sustainably. The financing options provided by venture philanthropists are more familiar to Wall Street bankers than NPOs.[16] The purpose of the financing—often for the capacity-building needs of the investee organizations—further distinguishes venture philanthropists from traditional foundations.

The venture philanthropy movement is small, but global and impactful. There are about 150 venture philanthropy funds in the US, Europe, and Asia. Joining the successful entrepreneur pioneers are now players from the private equity community, traditional foundations who are changing their grantmaking approaches, and even governments, all seeking to apply market principles to philanthropy for maximum social impact.[17]

Capacity builders thus seek to increase the social sector's impact by building up its capacity. Recent trends show a focus on increasing the impact of capacity builders themselves. These include efforts to incorporate new market-based approaches in their operational models, exploiting advances in information technology, managing the increasing information overload, and improving impact-based social interventions and measurements.[18]

Community

The community provides the underlying support for NPOs and their work by providing resources, especially money, time, and legitimacy. The last element, legitimacy, is seldom thought of, but some NPOs—in particular, charities—have learned the hard way that relevance to the community is critical to their survival.[19]

Within the community, there are several distinct groups of players: individuals, corporations, the media, and government. The media and government have multiple and complex roles in the ecosystem and are covered in the subsections below.

Historically, the role of individuals and corporations has been to give money (donations), time (volunteerism), and general support to the NPOs. In recent years, donors and volunteers have been increasingly asked to do more, and to be more informed and discerning amid calls for greater NPO accountability. The rising tide of the informed giving movement, coupled with the continuing need for funds and volunteers from the community, has led the nonprofit sector to develop strategies, practices, and skills for managing volunteers and donors.

Volunteer management involves the whole process of recruiting, inducting, developing, and retaining volunteers. It is like human resource management for paid staff, but is more complex given the fluid and dynamic process of volunteering. NPOs will do well to understand that the value of volunteerism goes beyond the manpower savings of volunteers to encompass a mutually beneficial engagement with the community. To effectively mobilize volunteers, NPOs also need to understand the nature of the 21st century volunteer, who tends to be less committed, more demanding, and more cause-driven. Some NPOs have responded to this volunteer market reality by adopting an episodic volunteering model where volunteers can sign up for flexible time slots without necessarily being committed to a fixed volunteering schedule.[20]

Donor management, on the other hand, is the systematic process of building relationships with existing and prospective donors to achieve impact giving. The key to effective donor management is understanding what donors want from NPOs: ethical behavior, meaningful and impactful programs, efficient and effective management, good communications, and appreciation. Emerging issues in donor management include the use of third party fundraisers and the privacy of donor information, while new opportunities for fundraising are arising with online giving and the new rich.[21]

For corporations, corporate giving is only one facet of what has come to be known as corporate social responsibility (CSR). Other aspects of CSR include environmental responsibility, good corporate governance, ethical behavior, and enlightened human resource practices. CSR suffers from the conviction by many corporate executives that their primary, indeed exclusive, accountability is to their shareholders and not other stakeholders. In such a "business is only about business" approach, CSR is only practiced when it makes business sense. The alternate view is that environmental, social, and governance (ESG) responsibilities are fundamental and, if necessary, CSR should be mandated through regulations. The field of CSR is evolving as governments, the corporate sector, and the nonprofit community seek to draw out a more compassionate form of capitalism and discourage what may be called "brute capitalism." In particular, the focus on providing ESG reporting to the investment community and the call to quantify nonfinancial CSR variables holds great promise for institutionalizing CSR into corporations.[22]

Media

The power of the media lies in its disproportionate influence over its audience. In this regard, the media needs to be responsible in its multiple roles of news communicator, advocate, watcher, and participant in the social ecosystem.

As news communicator, the media is generally expected to keep the public informed on the happenings and issues within the social sector. Hopefully, as advocate, it will promote the work of NPOs and the nonprofit sector. There has been discomfort in the nonprofit sector about the media's role as a watchdog, or even a bloodhound at times, as it exposes the wrongdoings—perceived or real—of charities. There is a further question about whether media organizations, with their partisan interests, should be a participant in the process to use their influence to shape public opinion other than in an objective manner.

The emergence of alternative media (online news, blogs, and social media) can be both a challenge and a boon to NPOs. Alternative media provides new delivery channels, requires brevity of content, allows user-created content, and creates new leveraged opportunities for viral marketing, crowd-sourcing, and new ways to raise fund.[23]

Government

The government is a unique player in the ecosystem. It has multiple and, sometimes, conflicting roles and functions: regulator (covered in the next subsection), funder, promoter, and participant.

Governments are a major funder of the social sector; on average, they contribute about 35 percent of the sector's revenue through grants and contracts to NPOs. Governments can promote the social sector through initiatives and platforms that enhance the viability and capacity of NPOs and the social sector. As participant or player, governments can directly provide the social services that some in the nonprofit sector may consider their domain.

How each government actually carries out these functions depends heavily on its history and relationship with the social sector. Governments can take three attitudes toward the social sector: as friend, filler, or foe.

Government as friend will actively build the capacity of the social sector and treat NPOs as partners in providing social services while promoting the sector's growth and capacity. It will fund NPOs while restraining itself from being a direct provider of social services, and its regulations are the most enabling for the sector's growth.

Government, in treating the social sector as filler, exercises its prerogative over which services it wishes to provide, leaving the social sector to fill the gap. It may provide supplementary funding for those social services it is not directly funding. In other words, its promotion of the social sector is narrower.

Government as foe sees its primary function as watchdog over the social sector—and vice versa. Here, the government tends to be a major player in social service provision and seeks to rein in the sector through heavy regulation. It pays little attention to promoting the sector and funds NPOs only to the extent they are subservient.

The approaches taken by governments across the world have evolved through time, circumstances, and ideological leanings. There are times when "filler" and "foe" relationships are appropriate, although "friend" seems to be what most enlightened governments now seek. After all, both governments and the social sector have the same ultimate objective: the well-being of citizens.

Therefore, enlightened governments, though wielding immense power and authority, should seek to harness the power of the nonprofit sector through an affirmative approach that recognizes the mutuality of objectives. Such an affirmative government is marked by a whole-of-government and citizen-centric approach to decisions and interactions, an agenda of social inclusion for citizen empowerment, and collaborative governance of the community and its constituents.[24]

Regulator

Some level of order and order-keeping is always necessary in any ecosystem, and as befits its (top) position in the ecosystem diagram, the regulator is an important player in the social world.

The reason is simple: While NPOs are legally owned by select individuals or organizations, the community from which they draw their resources and support is the moral and true owner. The regulator ensures that NPOs, especially charities, operate for the public benefit and not private advantage, and are accountable to the community.

The regulatory function is often seen as a role played by the government. In practice, charities in most jurisdictions are faced with multiple regulators: those that govern their legal structure, the tax authorities, one or more charity-specific regulators, and other government bodies. Certain jurisdictions employ the commission model, a key feature of which is independence from the government, although independence is never absolute. The Charity Commission for England and Wales is a leading example of this model.

Charity regulations ensure that charities exist for genuine charitable purposes and behave themselves, so that there is public confidence in charities. The law, however, usually plays catch-up with reality and situations as they unfold. In the last decade, charity reforms have taken place in many jurisdictions around the world in response to the changing needs of the social sector and demands by the community for greater accountability. Some of these reforms have gone back to basics to look at the role of the regulator, its functions, and its approaches.

Meanwhile, charity regulators continue to grapple with the demands of a fast-changing social sector. Increasing public service delivery by charities has also raised questions about how charities can retain their independence when they are receiving most of their funding from the government. Social enterprises and the like are pushing regulators to create new legal forms to accommodate these hybrid social–business organizations. Regulators are also under pressure to prevent charities from being a conduit for international terrorism financing, especially as they begin to work across borders to support growing global philanthropy in a global economy.[25]

Change Enablers

Figure 1.1 shows neat and well-demarcated compartments housing the different players of the social ecosystem. A more representative depiction would have been an animated video that shows the dynamism of interactions as players push and influence each other within each component and across components of the ecosystem. Indeed, the shape and the nature of the ecosystem will continue to morph even as it is being discussed and understood.

That "change is the only constant" is a truism of our age. But what is also increasingly recognized is that the speed of change is accelerating. So it has been with respect to the transitions that the social ecosystem and its players are experiencing.

Several key factors have enabled and driven the changes in the social sector in the last two decades:

- Culture
- Leadership
- Technology
- Social finance.

Culture

Culture is the set of ideas, beliefs, and customs that a community has evolved over time. It provides that community with its identity, a socially cohesive bond, as well as a special control over the standards and behavior of its people.

The culture of the social sector may be easier to understand by comparing it with the other two sectors. In simplified terms, the main value driver in the private sector is the love of money; in the public sector, it is the love of power; and in the social sector, it is simply love (for our fellow man).

The prevailing culture of the social ecosystem is thus this notion of "doing good." The basic intent of social purpose organizations is to do good for beneficiaries, to change the world for the better. Since the focus is on helping others and improving society, good feelings often result for all the participants in this common mission.

Flowing from this culture of compassion are practices and values that have come to be associated with the relative shortcomings of the social sector compared to its sister sectors. These include, for example, a penchant for handouts, a lack of accountability, and a lack of pace and drive.

Donations and grants are the staple diet of a social sector that prides itself on doing what it does with minimal money. Its needs are satisfied by the actions of generous donors. Unlike the commercial world, with its focus on competition and self-interest, there is not that sense of the survival of the fittest in the social sector. Yet, it should exist; both competition and collaboration are integral to any ecosystem.

Enclosed within this cocoon of doing good and feeling good, corporate practices of good governance, organizational effectiveness, and high performance tend to be eschewed by NPO boards and staff because such concepts come from a world with a largely different culture.[26]

The importance of culture from a change perspective is its impact on the participants' behaviors. In most human endeavors and organizations, culture often accounts for strong resistance to change. Such resistance may perhaps be less so for NPOs because the sector itself is about changing the larger world and so, it is less hampered by monolithic organizations and rigid practices.

Even so, changing the culture of a community, let alone the culture of the entire social sector, is widely recognized as a mammoth and uncertain task. The good news is that noticeable changes have seeped in, among them a push for less donor dependence, greater accountability, and higher performance on the part of social organizations. Interestingly, these changes, as will be described later in this chapter, are the result of the influences of the private and public sectors.[27]

Leadership

It is leaders that drive change, leaders that drive excellent organizations, and leaders that will drive a vibrant social sector. In his studies of enduring "great" organizations, Jim Collins concludes that the best possible impact on organizations and society is achieved by having enough "of the right people on the bus, especially the right bus drivers."[28]

The last few years have seen a debate about whether there are enough "bus drivers," or what is known as the "leadership deficit" of the social sector. A 2006 report by the Bridgespan Group identified the need for some 640,000 new senior managers for the US nonprofit sector, an increase of 2.4 times the current pool, within a decade.[29] This led Collins to conclude that the number one constraint on the effective growth of the nonprofit sector will be the ability to attract, retain, and develop enough of the right leaders.[30]

Proposed solutions to the leadership deficit include increasing capacity and capability through new sourcing models (e.g. idealistic youths and sector-shifters), understanding and catering to the generational shifts, and providing educational and developmental support to NPOs.[31]

What is significant is that the forces of globalization, innovation, and technology are allowing much greater leverage than before for social change. And many leaders are emerging from within, as well as from the fringe of the social sector. Chief among these are the social entrepreneurs engaged in pattern change, and the business leaders who are crossing over with their approach of problem-solving philanthropy.[32]

Technology

Today, technology is probably the most powerful driver of change, especially disruptive transformational change; but while the social world has benefited from the use of technology, it has generally lagged behind in its adoption compared to the other sectors.

Four clusters of technology have the greatest potential to transform the social world: environmental technologies—in particular, clean energy (solar power, wind power, and hydro power) and clean water; health and medical technologies, which have significantly improved mortality rates and the quality of human living; robotics, which help the disabled and aged to function at an optimal level of physical, mental, and social well-being; and infocomm technologies—the combination of computing, information technology, and communication technologies—which have enabled the information age and an interconnected globalized world.

Unfortunately, technology also has its ugly side, and can create social injustices even as it fixes them. At the end of the day, technology is but a tool that must be properly harnessed for the social good. To maximize its value, the application of technology must be integrated with considerations of organizational strategy, the operational processes, and people management.[33]

Social Finance

Money makes the world go round. It is no different in the social world, although NPOs generally make do with what little they have. With the greater ambitions of the sector and the social problems that need to be addressed, financial resources are more critical than ever.

Traditionally, the financing needs of NPOs have been provided through a mix of "free" money by way of donations, grants, and sponsorship; revenue from the provision of products; and commercial loans where possible and appropriate. In recent years, new creative ways and vehicles have emerged to fund, and even to seek the financial sustainability of, NPOs and their ventures.

Many of these new financial options—such as program-related investments, social bonds, and quasi-equity—are a combination of grants, debt, and equity instruments that have been adapted from the financial industry but offered at near, or below, market rates to NPOs.

To assure financial sustainability, some NPOs have, as mentioned, set up social enterprises. These vehicles have more financial options for their capital and operating needs, as they generate revenue and thus allow capital to be returned to lenders and investors. The growth of the social enterprise movement has led governments to create new legal structures such as the Community Interest Company in the UK, and the Low-profit Limited Liability Company in the US, to accommodate the needs of these hybrid social–business organizations.

The sources of these new financing options range from traditional foundations that are exploring new ways to be effective with their grants, to venture philanthropists who, with their business background and creativity, seek to change the way the social world impacts the world at large. A new class of social investors is also willing to receive a lower than market return on their investments, in order to support their social causes. Even regular financial institutions and companies have been drawn in to support the packaging of these new financial instruments.

On the horizon are several financial innovations. Social stock exchanges—pioneered in Brazil—which can lead to secondary social markets, are growing in popularity.[34] Technology-enabled platforms for aggregated giving such as Kiva,[35] and the aggregation of long-term, growth capital by the likes of the Edna McConnel Clark Foundation, will increase the level of philanthropic resources.[36] Socially responsible investing and impact investment products have transitioned, from being of interest to only a select few, into the mainstream. Investors and investees are coming under pressure to account for their work, and new performance metrics are being developed to ensure this.

All in all, the field of social finance has changed the social capital markets for more impactful investment and sustainable change.[37]

Macro-Trends

As the forces of culture, leadership, technology, and finance impact the different players of the social ecosystem, the players impact each other as well. Collectively, this has created a much larger transition: the transformation of the social ecosystem. Lester Salamon calls it a "veritable global associational revolution,"[38] John Elkington talks of an emerging "new economic order,"[39] while Bill Drayton sees the citizen sector as "the most vital, fast-growing sector because it's become entrepreneurial and competitive."[40]

Taken together, these shifts suggest three macro-trends[41] for the social ecosystem as a whole:

- The rise of global civil society and its attendant issues
- The acceleration of social change through innovation
- The fusion of ideas, models, and practices of the social and private sectors.

Global Civil Society

Civil society is on the rise globally. There is widespread agreement on this point even though there is not a great deal of clarity about how big civil society has become.

The Johns Hopkins Comparative Nonprofit Sector Project, which looks at the scale of nonprofit activity across the world, shows an aggregated US$1.9 trillion in annual operating expenditure, 48.4 million full-time equivalent jobs, and about 4.6 percent of the economically active population for the nonprofit sectors in 40 countries.[42] In relative terms, the study indicates that if the nonprofit sector was a country, it would be the fifth largest in the world. It also found that the average annual growth of the nonprofit sector is nearly double the growth of the total economies of five major countries.

Estimates of the total number of NPOs worldwide range from 3 million to 10 million.[43] Most operate within national borders. However, increasing numbers are operating across borders. The likes of Médecins Sans Frontières, Oxfam, and World Wildlife Fund have made their mark and are growing in strength and influence globally.[44] The Union of International Associations (UIA) has more than 21,400 active international NPOs on its register, up from 15,100 a decade earlier.[45]

NPOs worldwide are networking and working on common agendas. The UIA reports that in 2008, over 11,000 international meetings were held across the globe.[46] One of the most prominent meetings is the World Social Forum, a rival convention to the annual World Economic Forum in Davos,[47] which takes on different formats each year. At its height, over 150,000 participants from 135 countries participated in 2,500 activities at one location. Other global forums are also being established for specific segments of the nonprofit world, such as social entrepreneurship (World Skoll Forum), social investments (Social Capital Markets), and volunteers (International Association for Volunteer Effort World Volunteer Conference).[48]

As the global civil society grows in number and strength, it is flexing its muscles. In 1998, global civil society actors working in unison successfully killed the Multilateral Agreement on Investment, a draft agreement negotiated by the Organization for Economic Co-operation and Development countries.[49] The international campaign was celebrated as the first-ever successful mass-activism campaign to utilize the internet to gather information and communicate among activists.

Multinational companies have often been the target of international NPO activity. Campaigning against Nike sweatshops, PepsiCo's venture in military-controlled Myanmar, and Nestlé's marketing of breast milk substitutes are examples of civil society players taking on powerful corporate conglomerates and forcing changes to business decisions which the NPOs consider detrimental to society at large.[50] Meanwhile, NPOs such as CorpWatch investigate and expose corporate violations of human rights, environmental damage, fraud, and corruption around the world.[51]

Notwithstanding its growing base and power to improve the world, global civil society is not without its own set of problems. It has always faced, and will continue to face, the challenges of limited resources while working against the status quo and vested interests. It often finds itself having to depend on governments and enterprises for funding and support even as it seeks to change them.

What's more, some of the issues that global civil society faces—the rich/poor divide, motivation, and accountability—are, ironically, the same issues it champions against the state and enterprises in society at large.

The much-championed rich/poor divide issue also besets the NPO world. International NPOs are overwhelmingly concentrated in the developed world and exercise their power over local NPOs and the developing world. These NPOs have been variously accused of compensating themselves well with aid funds, poaching talent from the developing countries, and serving the "imperialistic agendas" of the developed world.[52]

The motivation for civil society should be generosity and altruism. Charity scandals and cases of NPO misconduct have led to the questioning of their values and agendas. Added to this, businesses and governments have sought to impose their values and approaches on the NPOs.[53]

While civil society has been vociferous in its push for accountability by governments and companies, it has, in turn, been accused of not practicing what it preaches. The generally smaller size and voluntary nature of NPOs and their work often mean less structure, organization, and discipline compared to governments and companies. Questions have arisen over the effectiveness, transparency, and value of their work.[54] In recent years, voices of concern regarding NPO accountability have grown louder. In 2004, for example, NGOWatch was established to highlight "issues of transparency and accountability in the operations of NPOs and international organizations."[55] In a sense, NGOWatch mocks the "watch-style" NPOs[56] that monitor the actions of corporations and governments.[57]

Social Innovation

Innovation can accelerate change. In fact, its power to scale change is such that many businesses and governments have pursued innovation as a primary means of attaining their next level of growth.

The social sector has also generated and implemented many world-changing "new ideas that meet unmet social needs."[58] These include distance learning, fair trade, citizen ecological movements, microfinance, and human rights advocacy.[59]

More significantly, social innovation has become a mini-industry of sorts within the social sector. Organizations such as the Young Foundation[60] and the Lien Centre for Social Innovation are dedicated to fostering the cause of social innovation. The industry is nascent but vibrant with players coming together in networks. The Social Innovation Exchange fosters mutual learning alongside joint initiatives such as a Global Academy for Social Innovation.[61] As the industry develops, we are also seeing the creation of dedicated social innovation incubators that provide funding, mentoring, and hands-on implementation support for new ideas. Also emerging are "social Silicon Valleys" where related institutions involved in social innovation are co-located.[62]

The interest created by the social innovation industry has led governments and grantmakers to provide large-scale funding and to create initiatives and programs that contribute to the industry and foster social innovations. Innovation tends to occur at the intersection of disciplines and sectors. The participation of the private and public sectors in social innovation will see the development of more, and better, ideas for social change. Systemic change—the ultimate goal of social innovation—is usually also dependent on collaboration and changes in all sectors of the economy.

Thus, inasmuch as social innovation is about accelerating social change, these developments in the social innovation industry and increasing cross-sector collaborations are leading to the acceleration of social innovation. In other words, what we are seeing is the acceleration of the accelerator of social change.[63]

Fusion

The three interdependent sectors of the economy—the public, private, and social sectors—have traditionally coexisted but functioned quite separately, each with its own purpose, basis, and culture. Of late, they have become increasingly fused, particularly between the social and private sectors.

This fusion is taking place at several levels.

At a basic level, it takes the form of the copying and adaptation of ideas, models, and practices, primarily from the corporate world to the nonprofit world. Since the dawn of foundations and professional grantmaking, NPOs have increasingly become more attuned to the need for transparency, accountability, and measurable outcomes.

In recent years, successful businessmen-turned-philanthropists such as Bill Gates, Jeff Skoll, and Mario Morino have pushed the envelope on the use of business and market approaches in the social world.[64] The term "philanthrocapitalism," first coined by author Matthew Bishop to describe this phenomenon,[65] is now used to loosely cover a gamut of models and approaches including social enterprises, venture philanthropy, and new forms of social finance.

Perhaps a more subtle aspect of this sector fusion is the cross-pollination of thinking that is seeping into, and slowly altering, the cultures of the social and market economies. Certainly, it is accepted that the social economy is not always efficient, and that the adoption of business principles can lead to increased accountability and reduce waste. It is also recognized that a modicum of enlightened self-interest can create the incentive structures needed to increase the sector's performance.

For the market economy, the campaigning by social activists for compassion for the poor, the disadvantaged, and the environment has resonated. A new and growing demographic of the consumer market has been identified as LOHAS (Lifestyles of Health and Sustainability) customers. Even as businesses debate the basis and merits of CSR, its rate of acceptance and uptake is growing. Hopefully, the financial crisis of late 2008 has increased the willingness of corporate leaders to do well by doing good. Their reflections will help them understand that their long-term interests lie in a balanced, enlightened approach toward all stakeholders. In turn, capitalism is reshaped, and for the better.

A report by Volans[66] concludes that the paradigm shift toward a more equitable and sustainable future is already underway in the larger world. It points out that a new generation of innovators, entrepreneurs, and investors is accelerating the changes for delivering scalable sustainable solutions to the world. The report identifies 50 pioneers of this "Phoenix Economy," a mix that includes not only outstanding social purpose organizations, but also mainstream commercial companies and even government bodies. More significantly, the report collates a set of concerted actions that governments, business leaders, and educators can take to rapidly achieve this "new economic order."

The highest level of fusion can be achieved by the integration of the social and market economies. A key focus of the social economy has been the poor and needy at the "bottom of the pyramid."[67] This group represents, in global terms, about 2.7 billion people who survive on less than US$2 per day.[68] Yet, this socio-economic group has largely been ignored by big businesses because it is perceived to not be able to afford even the basic necessities, while depending on handouts from governments and donors. However, microfinance, pioneered by Grameen Bank in the late 1970s, has shown that adapting the right business model for bottom-of-the-pyramid customers can, in fact, make serving the poor a viable business.[69] Today, microfinance is a vibrant industry that economically empowers many in the developing world who would otherwise have been excluded from mainstream financial services. The model is now even being adapted for developed countries.[70]

In the past few years, a growing group of academics, market practitioners, and social entrepreneurs has actively pursued "inclusive capitalism" whereby organizations sell goods and services to low-income people while embracing poverty alleviation strategies to improve their nutrition, health care, education, employment, or environment.[71] Muhammad Yunus of Grameen Bank, for example, has created a joint-venture social enterprise with the multibillion-dollar commercial yogurt maker, Groupe Danone.[72] The mission of Grameen Danone Foods is to bring affordable nutrition to malnourished children in Bangladesh using fortified yogurt.

Ashoka is also taking a proactive and scaled approach to similar social–business opportunities. Its Hybrid Value Chain model[73] leverages the Ashoka network to bring together players from both the social and enterprise sectors to collaborate on new products as well as new industries that can serve low-income populations on an unprecedented scale. For example, Ashoka brokered a commercial partnership between Amanco, a leading multinational water system company, and two of its Ashoka Fellows who work with small farmers in Mexico. The 35 million small-holder farmers in Mexico earn less than US$2 per day, but they can double or triple their income with irrigation technology. Before Ashoka came onto the scene, only 12 percent of agricultural land was irrigated. Amanco reengineered its products and business model to produce affordable irrigation technology to create a new and profitable market for itself. The NPOs involved were the key market enablers who promoted and mobilized the farmers. They earned a commission on sales that covered their operational expenses while helping to advance the NPOs' social programs.[74]

Forward the Ecosystem of Change

In summary, the social ecosystem framework can be a useful tool for shaping the changes in the social sector. Only by first understanding the players, the change enablers, and the trends in the social ecosystem, and then influencing the role, motivations, and behavior of the different players, can policy makers, sector leaders, and indeed all of us, seek to move this ecosystem forward.

As noted earlier, the social ecosystem is uniquely positioned as the catalyst of change for the state and enterprise ecosystems. Its role is to change the wider world for the well-being of all living on this planet.

Yet, even as players in the social ecosystem seek to change the world at large, they must realize that they need first to cope with the change drivers and trends occurring in their own sector. In other words, the ecosystem of change has to change itself for the better—at the same time as it goes about its mission of changing the rest of the world.

Endnotes

1   This chapter seeks to be both an overview of the social ecosystem as well as a high-level summary of the other chapters in the book. As such, many of the key issues and trends of the individual components are drawn largely from the relevant subsequent chapters. In order to provide a seamless read, I have not always identified the authors of the individual chapters in the main text. Instead, I have sought to do so via commentaries and references in the endnotes. It is also useful to note that the book map shown in Chapter 0, "Introduction: Navigating the social ecosystem," provides an easy way to see how the individual chapter topics map into the ecosystem framework and how the book is organized.

2   These unmet needs are elaborated in Chapter 2, "Unmet Social Needs: Scanning the world's social issues," by Tan Chi Chiu.

3   The different definitions of "charity" and their implications are explored in Chapter 3, "Charity Definition: Different kinds of kindness," by Sharifah Mohamed.

4   For a discussion on the various labels, see "Difference Between NGO and Non-Profit Organizations," DifferenceBetween.net, www.differencebetween.net/business/difference-between-ngo-and-non-profit-organizations.

5   The US Internal Revenue Code (IRC) describes more than 30 types of tax-exempt organizations, including charitable organizations, social welfare organizations, labor unions, trade associations, fraternal societies, and political organizations. The largest category is known as "charitable organizations," defined under section 501(c)(3), and they include charities, religious organizations, hospitals, and educational institutions. Every 501(c)(3) organization is classified as either a "public charity" or a "private foundation." Public charities have broad public support and tend to provide charitable services directly to the intended beneficiaries. Private foundations often are tightly controlled, receive significant portions of their funds from a small number of donors or a single source, and make grants to other organizations, rather than directly carry out charitable activities.

6   Depending upon the tax jurisdictions, the tax exemption for the organization and tax exemption/deduction for its donors can be combined or separated. For example, in Singapore and many Commonwealth countries, a Registered Charity has income tax exemption on its surpluses, but it has to be separately recognized as an Institution of a Public Character (IPC) for it to provide tax deduction receipts to its donors. Some organizations are Registered Charities but not IPCs, some are IPCs and not Registered Charities, and some are both. In the US, a 501(c)(3) entity has tax exemption for itself and for its donors.

7   Grameen Bank, www.grameen-info.org; Cabbages & Condoms, www.pda.or.th/restaurant/; *The Big Issue*, www.bigissue.com.

8   The subject of social enterprises and their challenges is covered in Chapter 5, "Social Enterprises: Fulfilling the promise of social enterprise," by Jon Huggett.

9   www.ashoka.org.

10 Social entrepreneurship is further covered in Chapter 6, "Social Entrepreneurship: Of pattern changers and changemakers," by Chris Cusano.

11 The subject of informed giving is further explained in the subsection below on "Community" and is also covered more extensively in Chapter 10, "Donor Management: Closing the funding gap," by Paulette Maehara.

12 Guidestar, www.guidestar.org; Charity Navigator, www.charitynavigator.org; American Institute of Philanthropy's Charity Watch, www.charitywatch.org; MAPLight.org, www.maplight.org; NGOWatch, www.globalgovernancewatch.org/ngo_watch/.

13 National Council for Voluntary Organizations, www.ncvo-vol.org.uk; Institute for Philanthropy, www.instituteforphilanthropy.org.uk.

14 The Bridgespan Group, www.bridgespangroup.org; Social Service Training Institute, www.ssti.org.sg; Compass Point, www.compasspoint.org; BoardnetUSA, www.boardnetusa.org; Charity Choice Goodwill Gallery, www.goodwillgallery.co.uk; Hackers for Charity, www.hackersforcharity.org; Computer Troubleshooters, www.computertroubleshooters.org.

15 Rockefeller Foundation, www.rockefellerfoundation.org; United Way, www.unitedway.org/worldwide/ and www.liveunited.org.

16 The new forms of social finance employed by venture philanthropists are covered further in the subsection below on "Social Finance," under the main section "Change Enablers."

17 Grantmakers and foundations are described further in Chapter 8, "Philanthropy: Powering philanthropic passions," by Thomas Menkhoff. Venture philanthropy is more fully covered in Chapter 9, "Venture Philanthropy: Venturing into entrepreneurial philanthropy," by Rob John.

18 The subject of capacity builders is more fully explored in Chapter 7, "Capacity Builders: Making value visible," by Sara Olsen.

19 Usually, this issue comes to the fore in the wake of a scandal and these charities, no matter how well endowed and resourced, can find that they are unable to function properly when the public support for them and their mission diminishes or disappears.

20 The subject of volunteers and volunteer management is further covered in Chapter 11, "Volunteerism: Matching the supply and demand of volunteers," by Laurence Lien.

21 Donor management and fundraising is further covered in Chapter 10, "Donor management: Closing the funding gap," by Paulette Maehara.

22 CSR is further covered in Chapter 12, "CSR: Toward moral capitalism," by Stephen Young.

23 The subject of media is explored further in Chapter 13, "Media: Amplifying the social beat," by Alan Webber.

24 The functions, relationships, and vision of an affirmative government are further covered in Chapter 14, "Government: Affirmative government for social good," by Peter Shergold.

25   The subject of regulation and the regulator is covered in Chapter 15, "Regulator: Love, law, and the regulator," by Stephen Lloyd.

26   The culture of compassion in the social sector and the attendant consequences on pay, pace, and performance are dealt with more fully in Chapter 4, "Charities: No charity for charities," by Gerard Ee.

27   See the subsection below on "Fusion" under the main section "Macro-trends."

28   Jim Collins is the bestselling co-author of *Built to Last: Successful habits of visionary companies* (New York: HarperBusiness, 2004) and author of *Good to Great: Why some companies make the leap and others don't* (New York: HarperCollins, 2001). He has written an accompanying monograph to the latter, *Good to Great and the Social Sectors: Why business thinking is not the answer.*

29   Tom Tierney, "The Leadership Deficit," *Stanford Social Innovation Review*, Summer 2006.

30   Jim Collins, "The Who Thing," *The Nonprofit Sector's Leadership Deficit: Commentaries* (Boston: The Bridgespan Group, March 2006).

31   Frances Kunreuther and Patrick Corvington, *Next Shift: Beyond the nonprofit leadership crisis* (Baltimore, MD: Annie E. Casey Foundation, 2007). Also, several of the commentaries in *The Nonprofit Sector's Leadership Deficit: Commentaries* (Boston: The Bridgespan Group, March 2006) highlight various solutions.

32   The subject of culture and leadership is further explored in Chapter 16, "Culture and Leadership: Transformative leaders wanted," by Maximilian Martin.

33   The subject of technology is covered in Chapter 17, "Technology: Rebooting technology for society," by Robert Chew.

34   Other social stock exchanges either already exist or are being planned in South Africa, Portugal, Canada, London, and Kenya. Brazil: Social and Environmental Stock Exchange, www.bovespasocial.org.br/institucional/home.aspx; South Africa: Social Investment Exchange, www.sasix.co.za; Portugal: Social Stock Exchange, www.gulbenkian.pt/section154artId2022langId2.html; Canada: Green Stock Exchange, www.greensx.com; London: Social Stock Exchange, http://rockpa.org/impactinvesting/profiles/social-stock-exchange/; Kenya: The Kenya Social Investment Exchange, www.ksix.or.ke.

35   Kiva (www.kiva.org) facilitates micro-lending by individuals to small businesses via the internet.

36   Other groups raising growth capital include New Profit Inc., Sea Change, the Nonprofit Finance Fund and Growth Philanthropy Network. For the Edna McConnell Clark Foundation's Capital Aggregation Project, see www.emcf.org/how/growthcapitalpilot/index.htm.

37   The subject of new forms of social finance is covered more fully in Chapter 18, "Social Finance: Financing change, changing finance," by Jed Emerson.

38   Lester M. Salamon, S. Wojciech Sokolowski and Associates, *Global Civil Society: Dimensions of the nonprofit sector, Volume Two* (Bloomfield, CT: Kumarian Press, 2004).

39   John Elkington, Alejandro Litovsky, and Charmian Love, *The Phoenix Economy: 50 pioneers in the business of social innovation* (London: Volans Ventures, 2009).

40   "Interview between Bill Drayton and Michael Febek," on the occasion of the Essl Social Prize award ceremony at the Weiner Hofburg, May 4, 2010, www.esslsozialpreis .at/uploads/media/Interview_Drayton-Fembek_engl.pdf.

41   The significant trends impacting the various players of the social ecosystem as well as the change enablers have been briefly summarized in the earlier sections and will be described in further detail in the subsequent related chapters of this book. These three "macro-trends" seek to abstract the higher-order, system-wide changes occurring across the social ecosystem.

42   The data cited in this paragraph is from a 2008 presentation made by Lester Salamon based on the Johns Hopkins Comparative Nonprofit Sector Project, a study of nonprofit activity across some 46 countries. Note that the data does not always refer to the 46 countries due to limitation of the data in some countries. The aggregate data to depict the scale of activity is for 40 countries, and the comparison of average annual growth rates is for 5 countries (US, Japan, Canada, Belgium, and Czech Republic). Current information and data on the Johns Hopkins study are available online at www.ccss.jhu.edu/index.php?section=content&view=9&sub=3. The latest book summarizing the results of the study is: Lester M. Salamon, S. Wojciech Sokolowski and Associates, *Global Civil Society: Dimensions of the nonprofit sector, Volume Two* (Bloomfield, CT: Kumarian Press, 2004). Volume One (published in 1999) and Volume Two of the ongoing study cover separate countries.

43   Estimates of the number of worldwide civil society organizations (CSOs) have ranged from 3 to 10 million.
(1)   The President of the Center for Alternative Development, Nicanor Perlas, estimates in "Civil Society—The third global power," *Info3*, 2001, that there are over 3 million NGOs.
(2)   There are 8 million .org registrations in the Public Interest Registry, not taking into account the number of .net and .edu registrations which could be CSOs; we should also bear in mind that there will be .org registrations that are not purely CSOs. See, www.pir.org/news/pr/2010/25years.
(3)   Author Dr. Timothy Schwartz's estimate of 10 million CSOs is based on data from Société Générale de Surveillance, as indicated in his blog entry: "How to save the NGO sector from itself," http://open.salon.com/blog/timotuck/2010/03/10/ part_i_how_to_save_the_ngo_sector_from_itself#_edn15.

44   Médecins Sans Frontières, www.msf.org; Oxfam, www.oxfam.org; World Wildlife Fund, www.wwf.org.

45   Union of International Associations, www.uia.be. Data is based on the year 2007/08 and is available at www.lse.ac.uk/Depts/global/yearbook07-8.htm.

46   Joel Fischer, "Press release: UIA International Meeting Statistics for the year 2008," by Union of International Associations, June 2009, www.uia.be/sites/uia.be/files/documents/ statistics/press/press09.pdf.

47   www.forumsocialmundial.org.br.

48   World Skoll Forum, www.skollforum.com; Social Capital Markets, or SOCAP, www .socialcapitalmarkets.net; IAVE World Volunteer Conference, www.iave.org.

49   Nicanor Perlas, "Civil Society—The third global power," *Info3*, 2001; Stephen Kobrin, "The MAI and the Clash of Globalizations," *Foreign Policy*, Fall 1998.

50   Nike sweatshop: http://depts.washington.edu/ccce/polcommcampaigns/Nike.htm, www.globalexchange.org/campaigns/sweatshops/nike; Pepsi venture in Myanmar: www.thirdworldtraveler.com/Boycotts/Hx_PepsiBurmaBoy.html; Nestlé baby milk boycott: www.babymilkaction.org/pages/boycott.html.

51   www.corpwatch.org.

52   References on the rich/poor divide (some authors allude to a north/south divide) and NGO imperialism: Alejandro Bendaria, *NGOs and Social Movements: A north/south divide? (Civil Society and Social Movements Programme Paper Number 22)* (UN Research Institute for Social Development, June 2006); James Petras, "NGOs: In the service of imperialism,"*Journal of Contemporary Asia*, 29(4), 1999, www.neue-einheit.com/english/ngos.htm; Joseph Mudingu, "How Genuine are NGOs?" *New Times*, August 7, 2006, www.globalpolicy.org/component/content/article/176/31491.html.

53   See discussion in the section "Fusion" below regarding philanthrocapitalism and the impact of business values and approaches on NPOs. The readings on NGO imperialism (see prior endnote) discussed how Western governments use NGOs to effect their agendas in the developing world.

54   References on accountability: Jem Bendell, *Debating NGO Accountability* (UN Non-Governmental Liaison, August 2006); "Civil Society Accountability: 'Who guards the guardians?'" a speech by Kumi Naidoo, CEO of Civicus at the United Nations on April 3, 2003, www.gdrc.org/ngo/accountability/ngo-accountability.pdf; Jon Entine, "Why 'Progressives' Oppose NGO Transparency," *Ethical Corporation Magazine*, August 2003.

55   www.ngowatch.org. NGOWatch was launched by the American Enterprise Institute for Public Policy and the Federalist Society for Law and Public Policy Studies, two influential and well-funded think tanks serving the US administration. See Jim Lobe, "Bringing the War Home: Right wing think tank turns wrath on NGOs,"*Foreign Policy in Focus*, June 13, 2003, for background on the formation of NGOWatch.

56   Examples of such watch groups are www.wombwatch.org, www.judicialwatch.org, www.governmentwatch.org, www.corpwatch.org, and www.transnationale.org.

57   Global civil society and its issues are covered more fully in Chapter 19, "Global Civil Society: Rallying for real change," by Kumi Naidoo.

58   "New ideas that meet unmet social needs" is the Young Foundation's broad definition of social innovation. See Geoff Mulgan with Simon Tucker, Rushanara Ali, and Ben Sanders, *Social Innovation: What it is, why it matters and how it can be accelerated* (Oxford: Saïd Business School, 2007).

59   The world-changing social innovations identified here and several more are listed in Geoff Mulgan with Simon Tucker, Rushanara Ali, and Ben Sanders, *Social Innovation: What it is, why it matters and how it can be accelerated* (Oxford: Saïd Business School, 2007).

60   www.youngfoundation.org.

61   SIX, socialinnovationexchange.org.

62   Incubators include Social Fusion, http://socialfusion.org/about.html; CAN Mezzanine, www.can-online.org.uk; The Hub, www.the-hub.net; and Launchpad, www.launchpad.youngfoundation.org. The first social Silicon Valley is the Social Innovation Park in Bilbao, Spain. See also Allison Benjamin, "Small is Powerful," *The Guardian*, January 7, 2009; Gorka Espiau, *The New Social Silicon Valley* (DenokInn, 2010), www.euclidnetwork.eu/data/files/resources/the_social_innovation_park.pdf.

63 Social innovation is further described in Chapter 20, "Social Innovation: Stepping on the accelerator of social change," by Geoff Mulgan.

64 Bill Gates: Bill & Melinda Gates Foundation at www.gatesfoundation.org; Carol Loomis, "The Global Force Called the Gates Foundation," *Fortune*, June 25, 2006; "Crafting partnerships for vaccinations and healthcare—The Bill & Melinda Gates Foundation," *Global Giving Matters*, December 2003–January 2004 feature, www .synergos.org/globalgiving matters/features/0401gates.htm. Jeff Skoll: Skoll Foundation at www.skollfoundation.org; Tom Watson, "Skoll at Oxford: A changing time for philanthropy," onPhilanthropy, April 2, 2007 at www.onphilanthropy.com. Mario Morino: Venture Philanthropy Partners at www.vppartners.org; "Venture Philanthropy: Leveraging compassion with capacity," an address by Mario Morino for the Northern Virginia Technology Council, March 2001, www.efooting.org/NewSite/documents/MorinoInstitute03.08.01.pdf.

65 Matthew Bishop and Michael Green, *Philanthrocapitalism* (New York: Bloomsbury Press, 2008), www.philanthrocapitalism.net.

66 John Elkington, Alejandro Litovsky, and Charmian Love, *The Phoenix Economy: 50 pioneers in the business of social innovation* (London: Volans Ventures, London, 2009). This report is covered in Chapter 21, "The Phoenix Economy: Agenda for a sustainable future," by John Elkington.

67 The term "BOP" has been popularized by authors such as C. K. Prahalad, *The Fortune at the Bottom of the Pyramid* (Upper Saddle River, NJ: Wharton School Publishing, 2005) and Stuart L. Hart, *Capitalism at the Crossroads: The unlimited business opportunities in solving the world's most difficult problems* (Upper Saddle River, NJ: Wharton School Publishing, 2005).

68 www.globalissues.org/article/26/poverty-facts-and-stats.

69 The model of microcredit pioneered by Muhammad Yunos, founder of Grameen Bank and recipient of the 2006 Nobel Peace Prize, is as follows: a group of five villagers is loaned a very small sum of money and the whole group is denied credit if one person defaults. See www.grameen-info.org/bank/GBGlance.htm.

70 Microfinance references: Microfinance Gateway, www.microfinancegateway.org/p/site/m/; Julian Evans, "Microfinance's Midlife Crisis," *Wall Street Journal*, March 1, 2010; Nimal Fernando, *Microfinance Industry: Some changes and continuities* (Manila: Asian Development Bank, May 2007); *Industry Insight: MicroFinance* (Hyderabad: Cygnus, September 2008).

71 While the term "inclusive capitalism" has been used earlier, it was popularized in recent times by C. K. Prahalad and Allen Hammond, the Vice President of Special Projects and Innovation at the World Resources Institute, an environmental think tank. See Allen Hammond and C. K. Prahalad, "Selling to the Poor," *Foreign Policy*, May 1, 2004.

72 Reaz Ahmad, "Grameen Teams up with Groupe Danone to Set up Food Plant," *The Daily Star*, 5(636), March 13, 2006; "Grameen Danone Foods Launched," *Grameen Dialogue*, April 2006, www.grameen-info.org/dialogue/dialogue63/regularfl2.html.

73 www.ashoka.org/hvc.

74 Valeria Budinich et al., *Hybrid Value Chains: Social innovations and development of the small farmer irrigation market in Mexico* (Arlington, VA: Ashoka, 2009).

Beneficiaries

Chapter 2

Unmet Social Needs

Scanning the World's Social Issues

TAN CHI CHIU
Consultant and Managing Director,
Gastroenterology & Medicine International

The work of the social sector has been to identify and seek solutions to unmet social needs, primarily from the ground up. Macro approaches to identifying these needs are few and far between. The UN's Millennium Development Goals represents the most coherent global strategy thus far for tackling worldwide poverty.

Looking holistically at global human needs through history, we can identify two broad levels of needs. The traditional basic needs of food, water, and health are intertwined with the causes and consequences of poverty. Higher-order needs are those that affect human prosperity and well-being, principally modern-day needs arising from human displacement, environmental challenges, and the problems of developed societies.

T he social sector exists to foster the well-being of society. An essential condition of human well-being is that people's needs are met. When needs are not met, they could lead to socially recognizable harm or suffering, or societal disorder or dysfunction. Identifying unmet social needs and seeking to address them is thus the primary and critical function of the social sector and its organizations.

What, then, are the unmet needs of society?[1] The answer to this question is a function of time, place, and circumstances—and it is relative to the perspective of the party answering the question. Throughout history, different individuals and organizations have sought to answer the question at different levels of society.

Identifying Unmet Social Needs

Taking a fundamental approach to total human needs, Abraham Maslow's 1943 theory on human motivation can be instructive.[2] His model of a Hierarchy of Needs (see Figure 2.1) is a simplified pyramid with the most fundamental needs at the base extending to the most esoteric at the top. Maslow's theory is that bottom-of-the-pyramid physiological needs such as food and water have to be fulfilled before people will progress up the pyramid to seek fulfillment of higher-order needs, such as aesthetic needs and self-actualization. It is generally recognized that addressing needs sequentially from the bottom of this pyramid upward is, in reality, far too simplistic. Maslow's pyramid, however, is useful in putting in perspective that human needs should be approached from a holistic standpoint.

In practice, most of the identification of unmet social needs around the world has been done in a ground-up fashion by civil society organizations (CSOs). As needs are identified, socially minded individuals or CSOs who deem it within their scope and calling will respond to address those needs. That, indeed, is the strength of civil society: its nimbleness of response and grassroots-based approach in dealing with society's needs.

However, a more macro approach that looks holistically at the problems of society in a country or the world, and identifies unmet social needs and supporting actions, should yield more complete and enduring solutions. Yet, this has not often been attempted, especially by the social sector, whether at the national or global level.

Figure 2.1 Maslow's Hierarchy of Needs

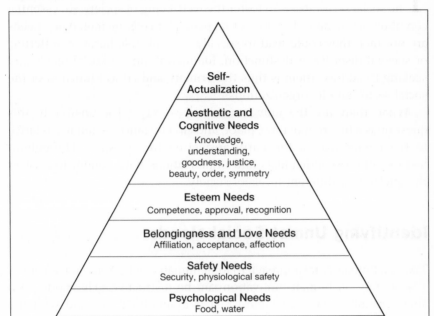

There are two known ongoing country-level initiatives in this respect. The Young Foundation's Mapping Emerging and Unmet Needs project is an ambitious two-year research program that aims to develop insights into how Britain's unmet and emerging needs can be prioritized and met.[3] In the same vein, the Lien Centre's Unmet Social Needs project seeks to identify vulnerable groups alongside the broader social needs of Singapore.[4] Both projects are works-in-progress.

Much of what has been done at the global level has looked at social needs from an economic cost-benefit standpoint.

The Copenhagen Consensus[5] is an international think tank that seeks to establish priorities for global welfare using methodologies based on the theory of welfare economics. Critics, however, have pointed out that its approach prioritizes solutions based on resource optimization and cost efficiency, rather than prioritizing problems by importance. While pragmatic, the objective view is that the Copenhagen outcomes may not be truly impactful. For example, malaria eradication was deemed highly cost-effective compared to ameliorating climate change, which, although more complex and expensive, has greater potential to save lives and livelihoods.

The most comprehensive and ambitious global agenda for dealing with the world's greatest socio-economic problems is contained in the UN's Millennium Development Goals.[6] Adopted by world leaders, these goals are related to poverty, primary education, gender equality, child mortality, maternal health, diseases, environment, and development (see the box, "The Millennium Development Goals"). These goals address mainly basic needs, but also include higher-order needs. Although criticized for being detached from the political and economic realities of countries, the Millennium Development Goals remains the most coherent global strategy to date that tackles worldwide poverty.

There is no universally accepted or practically satisfying method of classifying social needs. However, there are two broad levels of needs that humankind is facing:

- Traditional basic needs of food, water, and health, which are much related to poverty and the developing world
- Higher-order needs, which are those that affect human prosperity and well-being; they are principally modern-day needs arising from human displacement, environmental challenges, and the problems of developed societies.

Traditional Basic Needs

Since Man first appeared on earth, his basic needs for survival have revolved around food, water, and health. Sadly, despite centuries of civilization, these needs are still dire, especially in poorer countries.

It is impossible to consider "poverty" in isolation, because it is multi-faceted and sustainable solutions need to be developed at the national and international levels, rather than at just the local level. The causes and consequences of poverty are intertwined and constitute a vicious circle. Poverty leads to hunger, unsuitable living conditions, lack of water and sanitation, disease, malnutrition, failure of education, gender inequality, lack of economic opportunities, lack of access to health care, and shortened life-spans. The poor are also disproportionately affected by conflict, disasters, and other consequences of global warming and economic fluctuations. Alleviation of poverty must therefore address every element in the matrix.

The World Bank estimates that 2.7 billion people live on less than US$2 a day.[7] That is about 40 percent of the world's population; collectively, they account for less than 5 percent of global income.[8] Happily, poverty rates

The Millennium Development Goals

The Millennium Development Goals were developed out of the eight chapters of the UN Millennium Declaration, signed in September 2000. There are eight goals with 21 targets and a series of measurable indicators to be achieved by 2015.

Goal 1: Eradicate extreme poverty and hunger
Target 1A: Halve the proportion of people living on less than US$1 a day
Target 1B: Achieve decent employment for women, men, and young people
Target 1C: Halve the proportion of people who suffer from hunger

Goal 2: Achieve universal primary education
Target 2A: By 2015, all children can complete a full course of primary schooling, girls and boys

Goal 3: Promote gender equality and empower women
Target 3A: Eliminate gender disparity in primary and secondary education preferably by 2005, and at all levels by 2015

Goal 4: Reduce child mortality
Target 4A: Reduce by two-thirds, between 1990 and 2015, the under-five mortality rate

Goal 5: Improve maternal health
Target 5A: Reduce by three-quarters, between 1990 and 2015, the maternal mortality ratio
Target 5B: Achieve, by 2015, universal access to reproductive health

Goal 6: Combat HIV/AIDS, malaria, and other diseases
Target 6A: Have halted by 2015 and begun to reverse the spread of HIV/AIDS
Target 6B: Achieve, by 2010, universal access to treatment for HIV/AIDS for all those who need it
Target 6C: Have halted by 2015 and begun to reverse the incidence of malaria and other major diseases

Goal 7: Ensure environmental sustainability
Target 7A: Integrate the principles of sustainable development into country policies and programs; reverse loss of environmental resources
Target 7B: Reduce biodiversity loss, achieving, by 2010, a significant reduction in the rate of loss
Target 7C: Halve, by 2015, the proportion of people without sustainable access to safe drinking water and basic sanitation.
Target 7D: By 2020, to have achieved a significant improvement in the lives of at least 100 million slum-dwellers

Goal 8: Develop a global partnership for development
Target 8A: Develop further an open, rule-based, predictable, non-discriminatory trading and financial system
Target 8B: Address the special needs of the Least Developed Countries
Target 8C: Address the special needs of landlocked developing countries and small island developing states
Target 8D: Deal comprehensively with the debt problems of developing countries through national and international measures in order to make debt sustainable in the long term

have fallen globally over the last two decades.[9] However, wide regional disparities persist, the poorest regions of the world being in East Asia, South Asia, and Sub-Saharan Africa.

While governments and CSOs seek solutions such as microfinance to alleviate poverty in general, other solutions are needed to address the basic needs of food, water, and health.

Food

The number of hungry people has been increasing for more than a decade.[10] Today, more than a billion people, about one in six people in the world, are undernourished. Two regions, South Asia and sub-Saharan Africa, account for the bulk of the food deficit.

The situation is set to worsen with rising populations, a shortage of arable land, decreasing yields, water scarcity, and increasing droughts and floods. At the same time, urbanization creates demands for higher-value and resource-intensive food such as meat, thus driving up prices and reducing affordability. The supplanting of food agriculture by biofuel production to feed the world's insatiable energy needs is a recent and worrying trend.

Yet, some experts point out that the world actually produces enough food to feed everyone adequately. This is especially so when techniques of multi-cropping, cloning of high-yielding crossbred grains, and, controversially, genetically modified or transgenic strains have helped to boost food production. The problem, they say, is not scarcity, but the grossly imbalanced distribution of food. Developed nations have a surfeit of food, while many developing countries languish, a consequence of the economic realities of the global food market that cannot be easily overcome. This unequal distribution is also caused by food consumption patterns. North America, for example, consumes on average 800,000 kilograms of grain per capita annually but mainly as meat, poultry, eggs, and milk; whereas India consumes less than 200,000 kilograms per capita, mostly as a direct food source, leaving little for conversion to meat protein.[11]

Food security—the availability of food and access to it—has thus become a concern to the UN and national leaders. For example, more than half of the planet's population lives in urban areas; any disruption to farm supplies may precipitate an urban food crisis in a relatively short time. Food security is a complex issue, linked to health and malnutrition, but also to sustainable economic development, environment, and trade.

The difficulties of ensuring food security in national terms are illustrated by the modern trend of "farming abroad." According to the UN, some 30 million hectares of the developing world have been tapped by farming companies from the developed world. The UK, the US, China, South Korea, and Saudi Arabia are leasing land in Africa and Asia to grow food primarily to preserve the price stability and security of their own food requirements. Farming abroad, despite the promise of local employment and technology transfer, also smacks of neo-colonialism with all its negative connotations, with the potential for socio-political upheavals. Riots broke out in the Philippines when the public learned that land had been leased to China, and the same happened in Madagascar with respect to South Korea.[12]

Water

Water problems affect half of humanity, and water continues to be one of the most challenging unmet needs today.

Some 1.1 billion people in developing countries have inadequate access to water and 2.6 billion people lack basic sanitation. Close to half of all people in developing countries suffer at any given time from a health problem caused by water and sanitation deficits; some 1.8 million children die from diarrhea each year.[13]

To these human sufferings can be added the massive economic waste associated with the water and sanitation deficit: health spending, productivity losses, and labor diversions. For example, millions of women spend several hours each day collecting water. This economic waste is greatest, unfortunately, in the poorest countries where the economic cost of water shortages is staggering. Sub-Saharan Africa loses about 5 percent of gross domestic product (GDP)—or some US$28.4 billion—annually, a figure that exceeded total aid flows and debt relief to the region in 2003.[14]

The demand for water is increasing. Water use has been growing at more than double the rate of population increase in the last century. Agriculture represents about 70 percent, industry 22 percent, and homes the remaining 8 percent of freshwater use worldwide. By 2025, water withdrawals are predicted to increase by 50 percent in developing countries and by 18 per cent in developed countries. It is also forecasted that by 2025, 1.8 billion people will be living in countries or regions with absolute water scarcity, and two-thirds of the world population could be under water-stress conditions.[15]

Environmentalists have warned of impending "water wars," with increased competition for water resources due to climate changes and increasing populations, as well as tensions over privatization of water supply and territorial rights.[16]

Over the last decade, there have been a number of international conflicts over water. When China launched a political crackdown in Tibet in 2008, some observers noted the importance of the water supply in Tibet to China, although the political complications between the two went beyond water. In 2007, the Kajaki Dam in Afghanistan was the scene of major fighting between the Taliban and North Atlantic Treaty Organization forces. In 2006, Israel and Lebanon damaged each other's water treatment facilities and systems.[17] Water resources are also potential "weapons" of conflict. For instance, Amnesty International has accused Israel of preventing Palestinians on the West Bank and the Gaza Strip from having access to enough potable water.[18] India fears that China may dam the Brahmaputra River, which originates on the Tibetan plateau, because of a dispute over Arunachal Pradesh.[19] Analysts point out that more than 50 countries on five continents could be caught up in water disputes unless they are able to establish agreements on how to share reservoirs, rivers, and underground water aquifers.[20]

Additional issues of water include diminishing ground water, a problem of particular importance in northern India,[21] and the contamination of aquifers by toxins such as arsenic in places such as Bangladesh and Ghana.[22]

Health

Despite the tremendous advances in medicine, several countries still experience declining life expectancy, while health disparities between rich and poor countries continue to grow.

The critical global health areas are maternal and child health, infectious disease, and chronic disease.

The majority of maternal and infant deaths occur in the poorest places where health services are inaccessible or nonexistent. Consider that the number of infants in the developing world dying in their first month of life equals the total number born in the US in a year. A woman in sub-Saharan Africa has a 1 in 16 chance of dying in childbirth, while a woman in North America has only a 1 in 3,700 chance of facing the same fate. Research shows that the majority of maternal and infant deaths result from preventable causes.[23]

The three most deadly infectious diseases are HIV/AIDS, tuberculosis, and malaria, with influenza being an outsider.

HIV/AIDS results in nearly three million deaths a year, the majority of them in sub-Saharan Africa. In fact, 6 percent of sub-Saharan adults are infected with HIV, the next closest being the Caribbean at 1.2 percent. The majority of those living with HIV/AIDS in the developing world do not have access to treatment, due to the fragile health systems and the high cost of medication. Children orphaned by AIDS victims face discrimination, neglect, and adverse social circumstances. More than 15 million children under the age of 18 have lost one or both parents to HIV/AIDS.[24]

Tuberculosis kills two million people a year. The regions most affected include Southeast Asia, Eastern Europe, and sub-Saharan Africa. Fighting the disease is complicated by the lack of control measures, the spread of HIV/AIDS, and the emergence of multidrug-resistant tuberculosis.[25]

More than a million people die from malaria each year, and almost half of the world's population is at risk of acquiring the disease. This is because of deteriorating health systems, growing drug and insecticide resistance, climate change, and war. The majority of cases occur in sub-Saharan Africa, and most of those who die in this region are children under five.[26]

The problem of pandemics is exemplified by Influenza A (H1N1). Pandemics are harder to prevent in this age of globalization with the massive movements of people across borders. This was how H1N1 quickly spread following its emergence in Mexico in 2009. It was fortunate that less than a year after its emergence, H1N1 waned in prevalence worldwide with no evidence of increased virulence in the strain.

While infectious diseases receive much attention, chronic diseases represent 60 percent of the global disease burden. Heart disease, diabetes, stroke, cancer, and other conditions killed 35 million people in 2005.[27]

Global health problems do not result merely from the *de facto* existence of diseases that require treatment. They are largely to do with the political and economic choices of governments, the widening of the rich/poor divide through globalization, conflict, climate change, and environmental degradations.

Higher-Order Needs

The traditional basic needs of food, water, and health, intertwined with poverty, while not unique to the poor countries of the world, have primarily been their burden.

As society and countries industrialize and progress economically, they are beset by other problems. These higher-order needs can be those that affect human prosperity and well-being, principally modern-day problems arising from:

- People displaced due to war, crisis, disasters, and economic situations
- Environmental challenges, in particular, climate change and natural disasters
- Developed societal issues including the aging population, mental health, and breakdown of the family structure.

Human Displacements

Human displacements can be voluntary or involuntary. When voluntary, it is often referred to as economic migration. When people are forced to flee their homes due to political discrimination, disaster, or war, they are referred to as internally displaced persons (if they remain in their countries) or refugees (if they cross international borders).

In 2010, there was an estimated 214 million displaced people in the world, covering the full spectrum of labor migrants, refugees, and internally displaced persons. This is more than double the number in the 1960s. Representing about 3.1 percent of the total global population, there is also a wider diversity of ethnic and cultural groups affected than ever before, with the number of women increasing significantly.[28]

Migrant workers are a new social phenomenon accompanying globalization. While the economic crisis may have temporarily forestalled migrant outflows, the underlying causes of economic, social, and demographic disparities, as well as environmental factors, continue to create powerful pressures and incentives for people to move. However, the lower economic status of migrant workers can result in issues of marginalization, rights, discrimination, and stereotyping in the host countries. In some parts of the world, migrant workers face appalling working conditions. Some of them become victims of human trafficking and sexual exploitation.

Although migrant workers are generally economically beneficial to both their home and host countries, rampant migrations from low-income countries leave a talent vacuum, creating economic impoverishment at home. This is apparent, for example, in the Philippines and South Africa, where the outflow of doctors and nurses deprives their native populations of essential medical services. Such a "brain drain" accounts for an estimated 1.5 million skilled expatriates from developing countries being employed in higher-income countries, with the number set to rise.[29]

Refugees and internally displaced persons are a sad fact of modern strife, persecution, and discrimination. The UN High Commission for Refugees reports that forced population displacement has grown in size and complexity in recent years. In 2008, there were some 42 million forcibly displaced people, including 16 million refugees and asylum seekers, and 26 million internally displaced persons.[30]

War creates refugees. In 2008, half of all refugees were from Afghanistan and Iraq.[31] While there has been a sharp slowdown in repatriation, more prolonged conflicts have resulted in protracted displacements. For the first time since 2005, the total number of refugees dropped by 8 percent in 2008. However, the number of internally displaced persons has increased steadily over the last 10 years.

Ethnic discrimination such as that faced by the Sri Lankan Tamils,[32] the Rohingas,[33] the Karen tribe of Myanmar,[34] the Tibetans, and the Uigurs of China[35] has also resulted in many of them becoming refugees. Humanitarian efforts on behalf of these people have been challenging in the face of the ruling regimes' xenophobia and paranoia.

Environment

The two major concerns related to the environment across the world today are climate change and natural disasters.

Global warming and climate change came under the spotlight with Al Gore's film and book, *An Inconvenient Truth* and the conclusions by the UN Intergovernmental Panel on Climate Change that "the warming of the climate system is unequivocal" and that human activity is causing it.[36]

A 2005 World Health Organization (WHO) study indicated that 150,000 people every year will die from the effects of global warming, and that the number could double by 2020.[37] The poor, as usual, are disproportionately affected. The Red Cross found that global warming and climate change, when superimposed on the already vulnerable, poor, and rapidly urbanizing communities, create "super disasters."[38] Rising sea levels will destroy habitable low-lying territories such as the Maldives and Carterets Islands[39] while threatening important coastal territories, especially in Asia.[40]

Climate change has a major impact on food security when drought and flood reduce the amount of arable land, particularly in the vulnerable deltas of rivers such as the Yangtze, the Nile, and the Mekong.[41] If Himalayan glaciers melt, water supplies to two of the world's largest grain producers, China and India, will be at risk, with a tremendous impact on food prices and food security everywhere.

Amelioration strategies for global warming are contentious. Even if there are to be carbon dioxide emission curbs, any possible strategies may suffer reversals as the world's most polluting economies focus on revving up their carbon-spewing engines of growth to overcome the economic depression, while deflecting disproportionate responsibility to developing nations that are still struggling to progress, something greatly resented by poorer countries represented by the Group of 77.[42]

It is no surprise, therefore, that the long-anticipated UN Climate Conference in Copenhagen in December 2009, which held out the hope of a global treaty to replace the Kyoto Protocol, degenerated into chaos and resulted only in a largely symbolic Copenhagen Accord that was long on rhetoric but short on tangible and legally binding commitments from member countries.[43]

Climate change is also blamed for an increasing number of natural disasters,[44] with the number attributable to climate change increasing by nearly a third in the last four decades. In the last 20 years, the number of recorded disasters has doubled—from about 200 to more than 400—per year. Disasters caused by floods are more frequent—up from about 50 in 1985 to more than 200 in 2005—and floods damage larger areas than they did 20 years ago. From 1988 through 2007, over 75 percent of all disaster events were climate-related and accounted for 45 percent of deaths and 80 percent of the economic losses caused by natural hazards.[45] Oxfam estimates that the number of people affected by climate-related disasters will rise by about 50 percent, reaching 375 million a year by 2015.[46]

We are all too familiar with accounts of the different disasters resulting from earthquakes (e.g. the Peru earthquake of 2007 and the Haiti earthquake of 2010), tsunamis (e.g. in Papua New Guinea in 1998 and the Asian Tsunami of 2004), landslides (e.g. the Shanxi, China landslide in 2008 and the St. Bernard, Philippines mudslide in 2006), typhoons and hurricanes (e.g. Typhoon Nina in 1975 and Hurricane Katrina in 2005), and volcanic eruptions (e.g. Mount Pinatubo, Philippines in 1991 and Eyjafjallajökull, in Iceland, in 2010).

The positive side of natural disasters is the overwhelming global humanitarian response to each disaster. The Asian Tsunami, for instance, raised an estimated US$13.6 billion in humanitarian aid.[47] However, this is also where disaster preparedness, mitigation, and long-term developmental assistance find a nexus that presents both opportunities and risks to the resilience and independence of the affected communities.

Disasters must be understood in the context of socio-economic, demographic, and political forces, and even climate change factors, that determine the vulnerability of societies. Disaster preparation, and amelioration, must be grounded in development with a long-term view, rather than a short-term view, of surviving a disaster.[48] The Haiti earthquake is a prime example of a nation suffering the consequences of the worst possible combination of factors: poverty, social problems, unstable governments, corruption, slipshod building standards, environmental degradation, and situated on a hurricane track as well as a major tectonic fault line. Already having suffered six catastrophic killer hurricanes and storms from 2002 to 2008, Haiti had neither the defenses nor the capacity to withstand its epic earthquake in 2010.

The unevenness of aid response to different types of humanitarian situations has caused concern. For example, US$1,800 was spent on each victim of the Asian Tsunami, compared with just US$23 per person for the humanitarian crisis in Chad resulting from its civil war.[49] Aid must be impartial if it is to be effective and credible.[50] A World Bank study shows that donors from Organisation for Economic Co-operation and Development (OECD) countries tend to give bilateral aid and cash if the recipient country has reserves of oil, is a trading partner, and has sound institutions, whereas non-OECD countries are less motivated by self-interests but tend more to address the degree of real need.[51] The Central Emergency Response Fund of the UN goes some way to providing equitable and quick responses to humanitarian emergencies around the world.[52]

Recipients of humanitarian aid, on their part, must ensure that donors have confidence that cash and resources are not lost through corruption and misuse. The Asian Tsunami, for instance, left a trail of destruction that has yet to be comprehensively rebuilt, due to inefficiencies and corruption.[53]

Developed Societies

Better-developed and more economically successful societies have needs related to development that give rise to significant pathology in segments of society.

Rich nations grapple with issues that come with globalization, beyond their obvious vulnerability to global markets. The Gini coefficient is widening as the benefits of globalization are spread unequally throughout society, disproportionately affecting already marginalized groups such as the physically or mentally infirm, dysfunctional families, the elderly, the unemployed, the lowly educated, and the poor.

Non-infectious diseases ("diseases of civilization") will pose increasing challenges in more developed countries where hypertension, diabetes mellitus, obesity, and a variety of cancers become epidemics in their own right. Universal health care is not a given in all developed countries either, the most stark aberration being the US.[54]

At the turn of the 21st century, there were approximately 600 million older persons (60 years or older). This was triple the number recorded 50 years earlier and will triple again in another 50 years. In the more developed regions, about one-fifth of the populations were older persons in 2000; this is expected to reach one-third by 2050. Population aging arises from two demographic effects: increasing longevity and declining fertility rates.[55]

Aging populations place increasing demands on health care and social support structures.[56] The potential support ratio (the number of persons aged 15–64 per one older person aged 65 years or older) fell from 12 people in 1950 to 9 people in 2000 and will fall to 4 people in 2050. This will ignite debates around intergenerational equities and transfers, especially in systems where current workers pay for the benefits of current retirees. Social services, pensions, and health systems creak under the strain unless this is mitigated by people also staying healthy and active in their later years, something forward-looking nations such as Singapore encourage.[57] From a social standpoint, an aging population affects family and community support structure, family composition, and living arrangements.[58]

The aged may face challenges of declining health, mobility, intellectual stimulation, activity levels, and also discrimination and stereotyping. Health care needs to be rational and affordable to retirees, a concept recently dubbed "slow medicine."[59] There also needs to be a sensitive and comprehensive system for the community to help the elderly with "end-of-life" issues.

The drive for both economic survival and affluence has its costs. About 450 million people around the world suffer from a mental or behavioral disorder. Nearly one million people commit suicide every year. The highest recorded rate of mental illness is found in the US. A WHO study found that the impact of mental illness on overall health and productivity in the US and throughout the world is profoundly under-recognized. In established market economies, mental illness ranks with heart disease and cancer as a major cause of disability.[60] In addition to health and social costs, those suffering from mental illness tend to be victims of human rights violations, stigma, and discrimination, both inside and outside psychiatric institutions. The burden on their families, who are often the primary caregivers, is significant. One in four families worldwide has at least one family member with a mental disorder.[61]

Education and independence of women, coupled with fertility control methods delinking sex from procreation, have led to the institution of marriage coming under threat by "modern" variant lifestyles: alternative families (cohabitation or gay marriages), having children outside of marriage, and single parenthood.[62] One in two marriages in the US, Sweden, Finland, and Belgium ends in divorce—homes are broken and children are the biggest casualties.[63]

With the institutions of marriage and family at risk in many countries, quality upbringing of the next generation is a challenge. Children suffer from the consequences of hyper-competitiveness, making a "normal" childhood increasingly rare.[64] This, coupled with parental neglect and emotional deprivation from overworked parents, has led to such psychological vulnerability that the rate of youth suicides has risen alarmingly, especially in Asian societies such as Japan,[65] Korea,[66] and India.[67] This is exacerbated when family influence is supplanted by a new and often risky social interaction order for youth mediated through the internet. Childhood delinquency, eating disorders, premature sexual experimentation, smoking, and drug abuse among the young are on the rise.[68]

Perhaps the main cause of these social issues is changing social values. Modern society is generally more liberal and self-centered in its outlook, with less emphasis on families and communities.

Finally, are developed and richer societies actually happier? Studies doubt this, and economists believe that beyond a per capita income of US$20,000, there is a diminishing or even negative return. The GDP, for decades hailed as the indicator of a country's progress, says nothing of the less measurable aspects of societal happiness. Factors such as income distribution, education, healthy life expectancy, work–life balance, environmental sustainability, and mental health are not measured by the GDP. The Young Foundation identified a sizable segment of the British population that is dissatisfied with life on a high income because of childlessness, isolation, poor health, purposelessness, chronic disability, and separated spouses.[69] One country, Bhutan, in the wisdom of former King Jigme Singye Wangchuck, has eschewed the traditional way of measuring prosperity by adopting its unique Gross National Happiness index that includes pollution, noise, illness, divorce rates, cultural preservation, and democratic freedoms in its assessment of its social progress.[70]

"Imagine"

Imagine there's no heaven, it's easy if you try
No hell below us, above us only sky
Imagine all the people, living for today.

Imagine there's no countries, it isn't hard to do
Nothing to kill or die for, and no religion too
Imagine all the people, living life in peace.

Imagine no possessions, I wonder if you can
No need for greed or hunger, a brotherhood of man
Imagine all the people, sharing all the world.

You may say that I'm a dreamer, but I'm not the only one
I hope someday you'll join us, and the world will live as one.

John Lennon's enigmatic song seems to call for a new world order in which all of humankind's needs according to Maslow's hierarchy have been met and there are no more social divisions, no more conflicts, and everyone is living in harmony with one another and with nature.[71] It is a utopian ideal, perhaps, but an admirable aspiration that we might well learn from Lennon and the Bhutanese.

Perhaps a new era of social consciousness is nigh, at a time in history when a shattering economic downturn has severely dented our faith in capitalism and financial markets and showed up the hollowness and soullessness of society's single-minded but ultimately mindless pursuit of material wealth and its trappings. This may be a good time for a fundamental reevaluation of life's values, and of how those who are well-off can come together to help the less fortunate of the world attain a level of self-actualization that even richer societies crave.

Endnotes

1   This chapter, as part of the lead-in to the rest of the book, seeks to answer the question, "What are the unmet needs of society?" from a holistic standpoint. By necessity of space, the needs and problems of the world can only be looked at from a very high level and the solutions to address the many problems are not covered.

2   Abraham H. Maslow, "A Theory of Human Motivation," *Psychological Review*, 50, 1943, http://psychclassics.yorku.ca/Maslow/motivation.htm.

3   An interim project report is available: Dan Vale, Beth Watts, and Jane Franklin, *Receding Tide: Understanding unmet needs in a harsher economic climate* (London: Young Foundation, January 2009), www.youngfoundation.org/our-work/research/themes/ social-needs/mapping-needs/mapping-emerging-and-unmet-needs.

4   www.lcsi.smu.edu.sg/unmetsocialneeds.asp.

5   The Copenhagen Consensus Center is a think tank based in Denmark that seeks to inform governments and philanthropists about the best ways to spend aid and development money, www.copenhagenconsensus.com.

6   www.un.org/millenniumgoals.

7   "Overview: Understanding, measuring and overcoming poverty," The World Bank, http:// web.worldbank.org/WBSITE/EXTERNAL/TOPICS/EXTPOVERTY/0,,contentMDK: 20153855~menuPK:373757~pagePK:148956~piPK:216618~theSitePK:336992,00.html.

8   Nearly 50 percent live on less than US$2.50 a day and 80 percent live on less than US$5.15 a day. See "Poverty Facts and Stats" at www.globalissues.org/article/26/poverty-facts-and-stats.

9   Poverty rates are estimated to have fallen from 52 percent in 1981 to 42 percent in 1990, and to 26 percent in 2005. See Mestrum Francine, "Global Poverty Reduction—A New Social Paradigm?" *Development*, 49(2), 2006.

10   *The State of Food Insecurity in the World 2009: Economic crises—impacts and lessons learned* (Rome: Food and Agriculture Organization of the United Nations, 2009). The FAO holds that "undernourishment exists when caloric intake is below the minimum dietary energy requirement (MDER). The MDER is the amount of energy needed for light activity and a minimum acceptable weight for attained height, and it varies by country and from year to year depending on the gender and age structure of the population." The words "hunger" and "undernourishment" are used interchangeably by the FAO in its report and in this section.

11   References for the debate on scarcity versus distribution: "Hunger: Scarcity or distribution," Well-fed World, http://awellfedworld.org/issues/scarcity; Stephen Zimmermann, "We Grow Enough Food to Feed Everyone in This World, So Why Don't We? (Part 1 & Part 2)," Citizen Economists, August 1 & 6, 2008, www.citizeneconomists. com/blogs/2008/08/01/we-grow-enough-food-to-feed-everyone-in-this-world-so-why-dont-we-part-1; "Food Security," World Health Organization, www.who. int/trade/glossary/story028/en/.

12   "Chinese Debate Pros and Cons of Overseas Farming Investments," *African Agriculture*, May 11, 2008, http://africanagriculture.blogspot.com/2008/05/chinese-debate-pros-and-cons-of.html; Mark Rice-Oxley, "Food Raid," *The Sunday Times*, August 2, 2009.

13   "Poverty Facts and Stats" at www.globalissues.org/article/26/poverty-facts-and-stats.

14   Ibid.

15   "Statistics: Graphs & maps," UN Water, www.unwater.org/statistics_use.html. "Water stress" occurs when the demand for water exceeds the available amount during a certain period or when poor quality restricts its use. Water stress causes deterioration of fresh water resources in terms of quantity (aquifer overexploitation, dry rivers, etc.) and quality (eutrophication, organic matter pollution, saline intrusion, etc.).

16   "Water Wars," SourceWatch, www.sourcewatch.org/index.php?title=water_wars.

17   These three situations (China/Tibet, Afghanistan, and Israel/Lebanon) are examples from Dr. Peter Gleick, "Water Conflict Chronology," Pacific Institute for Studies in Development, Environment, and Security, November 2008, http://globalpolicy.org/images/pdfs/Security_Council/conflictchronology.pdf.

18   "Palestinians Denied Water," *BBC News*, October 27, 2009, http://news.bbc.co.uk/2/hi/middle_east/8327188.stm.

19   "India Opposes China Dam on Brahmaputra," *Outlook India.com*, October 15, 2009, http://news.outlookindia.com/item.aspx?667839.

20   "Water in Conflict," Global Policy Forum, http://globalpolicy.org/the-dark-side-of-natural-resources/water-in-conflict.html.

21   Ravi Velloor, "India's Groundwater Supply Running Dry," *The Straits Times*, August 15, 2009, www.indiawaterportal.org/channels/groundwater; Sameer Mohindru, "Growth Challenges India Water Supply," *The Wall Street Journal*, August 23, 2006.

22   "Arsenic Contamination of Groundwater," British Geological Survey, www.bgs.ac.uk/arsenic.

23   "Global Health: A gordian knot?" Medical Education Cooperation with Cuba, www.medicc.org/ns/index.php?p=0&s=13.

24   Ibid. Data is based on year 2006.

25   Ibid.

26   Ibid.

27   Ibid.

28   "World Migration Report 2010—the Future of Migration: Building capacities for change," www.iom.ch/jahia/Jahia/policy-research/migration-research/world-migration-report-201.

29   "Global Trends 2015: A dialogue about the future with nongovernmental experts," National Intelligence Council, December 2000, www.dni.gov/nic/NIC_globaltrend2015.html#link8b.

30   *UNHCR's 2008 Global Trends: Refugees, asylum-seekers, returnees, internally displaced and stateless persons* (Geneva: UN High Commissioner for Refugees, June 2009); www.unhcr.org/4a375c426.html.

31   Ibid.

32   Paul Tighe, "Sri Lanka Accelerates Settlement of Civil War Refugees in North," *Bloomberg News*, October 28, 2009, www.bloomberg.com/apps/news?pid=20601091&sid=aUxL.TA0vT.I; "Australia Refuses Tamil Refugees," *BBC News*, October 28, 2009, http://news.bbc.co.uk/2/hi/asia-pacific/8329420.stm.

33 "Thailand Says No to Refugee Camp for Rohingas," *Radio Australia News*, February 4, 2009, www.radioaustralianews.net.au/stories/200902/2482488.htm?desktop.

34 "Junta Intensifies Anti-Karen Persecution," *AsiaNews.it*, November 24, 2006, www.asianews.it/index.php?l=en&art=7840.

35 "Deadly Uigher Riots May Force Policy Debate in Beijing," *Reuters*, July 11, 2009, www.reuters.com/article/topNews/idUSTRE5690TN20090711.

36 *An Inconvenient Truth*, www.climatecrisis.net; Intergovernmental Panel on Climate Change, www.ipcc.ch. There continues to be skeptics, including among scientists, who do not believe that global warming and climate change are as bad as they are made out to be, but this is the minority opinion.

37 Juliet Eilperin, "Climate Shift Tied to 150,000 Fatalities: Most victims are poor, study says," *The Washington Post*, November 17, 2005, www.washingtonpost.com/wp-dyn/content/article/2005/11/16/AR2005111602197.html.

38 *World Disasters Report 2004* (Bloomfield, CT: Kumarian Press, International Federation of Red Cross and Red Crescent Societies, 2004), www.ifrc.org/publicat/wdr2004.

39 "Maldives Cabinet to Go Underwater," *BBC News*, http://news.bbc.co.uk/2/hi/8291487.stm; McLaren Warren, "World's First Climate Change Refugees to be Rescued in 2009," *Business & Politics, Treehugger*, October 11, 2008, www.treehugger.com/files/2008/11/worlds-first-climate-change-refugees-to-be-rescued-in-2009.php.

40 Richardson Michael, "Stakes High for Port Cities," *The Straits Times*, September 15, 2008.

41 Michael Blum and Harry Roberts, "Drowning of the Mississippi Delta Due to Insufficient Sediment Supply and Global Sea Level Rise," *Nature Geoscience 2*, June 28, 2009, www.nced.umn.edu/system/files/blum_roberts_09.pdf.

42 Kevin A. Baumert, Tim Herzog, and Jonathan Pershing, "Navigating the Numbers: Greenhouse gas data and international climate policy," *World Resources Institute*, December 2005, http://pdf.wri.org/navigating_numbers.pdf; Natalia Costa, "Climate Talks Go Through Difficult Moment: Brazilian negotiator," *Xinhua News Agency*, October 17, 2009.

43 "Copenhagen. Hopenhagen. Nopenhagen," *The Straits Times*, December 20, 2009.

44 There is contention, though, as to whether global warming is principally caused by human activity, although the link is widely accepted. See Jason Anderson, *Climate Change and Natural Disasters: Scientific evidence of a possible relation between recent natural disasters and climate change* (Brussels: Policy Department Economy and Science, European Parliament, January 2006).

45 "Climate Change Now the Main Driver of Natural Disasters," *Environment New Service*, December 2, 2008; *Climate Change and Food Security in Pacific Island Countries* (Rome: Food and Agriculture Organization of the United Nations, 2008), www.fao.org/docrep/011/i0530e/i0530e00.HTM.

46 *A Science Plan for Integrated Research on Disaster Risk: Addressing the challenge of natural and human-induced environmental hazards* (Paris: International Council for Science, 2008); "Climate Change Now the Main Driver of Natural Disasters," *Environment New Service*, December 2, 2008, www.ens-newswire.com/ens/dec2008/2008-12-02-01.html; "Oxfam Warns of Climate Disasters," *BBC News*, April 21, 2009, http://news.bbc.co.uk/2/hi/science/nature/8009412.stm.

47   Karl Inderfurth, David Fabrycky, and Stephen Cohen, "The Tsunami Report Card," *Foreign Policy Magazine*, December 2005, www2.gwu.edu/~elliott/assets/docs/research/ reportcard.pdf.

48   Euston Quah and Suman Kumari Sharma, "When Disasters Can Help Development," *The Straits Times*, July 8, 2009.

49   "Oxfam Warns of Climate Disasters," *BBC News*, April 21, 2009, http://news.bbc. co.uk/2/hi/science/nature/8009412.stm.

50   Tan Chi Chiu, "Overseas Giving: Should charity begin at home?" *Social Space*, 2008.

51   Paul Raschky and Manijeh Schwindt, "On the Channel and Type of International Disaster Aid," Policy Research Working Paper, The World Bank, June 2009.

52   "Record $590m Pledge for UN Fund," *The Straits Times*, December 11, 2009.

53   Anup Shah, "Asian Earthquake and Tsunami Disaster," *Global Issues*, January 7, 2005, www .globalissues.org/article/523/asian-earthquake-and-tsunami-disaster; *Asia's Tsunami: The impact* (London: The Economist Intelligence Unit, January 2005), http://graphics .eiu.com/files/ad_pdfs/tsunami_special.pdf.

54   "News Conference by the President," July 22, 2009, www.whitehouse.gov/the_press_ office/News-Conference-by-the-President-July-22-2009.

55   *World Population Aging: 1950–2050* (New York: UN Department of Economic and Social Affairs, Population Division, 2009).

56   "Half of Today's Babies Will Live to 100," *The Straits Times*, October 3, 2009.

57   www.c3a.org.sg.

58   Ibid.

59   Dennis McCullough, *My Mother, Your Mother: Embracing "slow medicine," the compassionate approach to caring for your aged loved ones* (New York: HarperCollins, 2008). The term "slow medicine" was introduced by Dennis McCullough of Dartmouth Medical School, in the US, who advocates a family-centered approach to the care of the elderly which preserves patient dignity, acknowledges the limitations of medicine, and advocates a more rational approach to the care of the elderly without bankrupting them.

60   *Investing in Mental Health* (Geneva: World Health Organization, 2003); "Global Study Finds Mental Illness Widespread," *MSNBC*, July 7, 2004, www.msnbc.msn.com/ id/5111202.

61   Ibid.

62   "Major Trends Affecting Families," UN Programme on the Family, Division for Social Policy and Development, UNDESA, www.un.org/esa/socdev/family/Publications/ mtrendsbg.htm.

63   "Divorces per 100 marriages (most recent) by country," NationMaster.com, www .nationmaster.com/graph/peo_div_per_100_mar-people-divorces-per-100-marriages.

64   Michael Czinkota and Thomas Czinkota, "Learning: Less can mean more," *The Straits Times*, November 2, 2009.

65   "Editorial," *The Japan Times Online*, June 15, 2007, http://search.japantimes.co.jp/cgi-bin/ed20070615a2.html.

66   Yoav Cerralbo, "Failing Grades Cause Suicides in Japan and South Korea," *CBS News Viewpoint*, May 27, 2004, www.cbc.ca/news/viewpoint/vp_cerralbo/20040527.html.

67   "The Epidemic of Student Suicides in India," *It's India Time*, March 17, 2008, www.indiatime.com/2008/03/17/the-epidemic-of-student-suicides-in-india.

68   Farheen Mukri, "Hide & Seek with the Birds and the Bees," *Social Space*, 2009.

69   *Sinking or Swimming—Understanding Britain's Unmet Needs* (London: The Young Foundation, 2009).

70   The Gross National Happiness index is the idea of former King Jigme Singye Wangchuck of Bhutan. His view is that economic growth does not necessarily lead to contentment. Gross national happiness focuses on four pillars: promotion of sustainable development, preservation and promotion of cultural values, conservation of the natural environment, and establishment of good governance. See Nadia Mustafa, "What about Gross National Happiness?" *Time Health & Science*, January 10, 2005, www.time.com/time/health/article/0,8599,1016266,00.html. Similar attempts at an alternative to GDP are the Happy Planet Index (by the New Economics Foundation), the Satisfaction with Life index (by Adrian White of the University of Leicester), the Human Development Index (by the UN), and Gallup's poll of well-being.

71   For a sample of various interpretations of the lyrics of *Imagine*, see www.lyricinterpretations.com/John-Lennon/Imagine.

Chapter 3

Charity Definition

Different Kinds of Kindness

SHARIFAH MOHAMED
Manager, Lien Centre for Social Innovation

Charity has come to mean different things to different people.

At its core, charity is about kindness and providing for the poor and needy. However, over time, this idea of kindness has been stretched to cover all aspects of community good, leading to some unintended results in closing the rich/poor divide.

At the same time, charity work has not often been sufficiently extended to deal with the root causes—rather than just the symptoms—of social issues. For charity work to be effective, it must draw more on the head, rather than rely merely on the heart. In addition, a more hands-on approach will connect the giver more to the cause and the real needs of charities.

In a world of inequalities, the kindness we show through our charitable acts holds a special place in our hearts. For those who are helped, charity provides temporary relief from life's burdens. For those who help, it can be meaningful and feel good for the soul.[1]

Philosophers have mused at length about the meaning of kindness and charity.[2] To the common man, however, charity is simply a universal virtue that manifests itself in different forms of alms-giving.[3] In simple terms, charity is about the rich helping the poor and the strong helping the weak. In physical terms, it can be about providing shelters for the homeless or soup kitchens for the poor.

However, over the years, the concept of charity has evolved and taken on a life of its own. It has grown in size and into forms that not many would easily identify as charity. A charity today can be a large, hierarchical organization of several hundred full-time staff working in a swanky office, raising funds professionally from foundations and corporate donors. Or it can be as humble as a group of friends working from makeshift premises, forking out their own money to sustain their work. Or it can also be an intermediary, such as a trust that manages wealth and applies it, on behalf of the donor, toward charitable purposes.

Over time, the expanding legal definitions and interpretations have stretched the kinds of issues that charities address. For example, it is now commonplace to have "charities" that promote and support cultural activities such as orchestral groups and museums, which are primarily the preserve of the rich. With state-subsidized national education and health care, boarding schools and hospitals—which used to exist for the poor—have evolved into service providers for more privileged groups. Indeed, such support goes against the mission of charity as it was originally conceived, which was, and still should be, bridging the rich/poor divide.

One may then ask: How can something as simple and intuitive as charity turn out to be so complicated and contradictory?

The Definition of Charity

A good starting point is to look at the current legal definition of charity. For many countries, this has its roots in the *Statute of Charitable Uses 1601* of Elizabethan England. In turn, this definition links, through the common law system which originated in England in the Middle Ages, some 60 nations of the world that trace their legal heritage to England.[4]

The preamble to the *Statute of Charitable Uses 1601* provides the foundation for legitimate charitable purposes and is still, sometimes, relied upon by modern courts to determine what purposes are, at present, valid charitable purposes. The preamble provides an indicative list of charitable purposes which can be broadly categorized as for the poor and for public works.

It is important to note that before the passage of this Act, helping the poor was regarded as the religious duty of the English church. However, after a series of social and political upheavals, charity became an administrative tool for the ruling English monarchy. The social care system started by the church became one that the rulers sought to extend and manage. The objects of charity henceforth became more secular, as legislation—among them, the *Statute of Charitable Uses*—nationalized public care and introduced laws to rein in charity abuses.

Over the next two centuries, the list in the preamble to the statute was used to determine what constitutes charitable purposes. One of the key questions which case law then sought to determine was whether use for public works—say, education and religious purposes—was sufficient in itself to be deemed charitable, or whether this had to be accompanied by a requirement that the end user was poor. In 1891, in the landmark *Pemsel* case, Lord Macnaghten classified charitable purpose into four main categories:[5]

- The relief of poverty
- The advancement of education
- The advancement of religion
- Other purposes beneficial to the community not falling under any of the preceding heads.

Since then, legislators and courts in many jurisdictions have used these four heads as a convenient basis for determining what constitutes charitable purpose.

This expansion of charitable purpose beyond mere relief of poverty was a practical decision to include other activities that serve the public benefit. The last heading was meant to accommodate new forms of activities that were emerging to meet community needs, as long as they stayed within the "spirit and intendment" of the rule and passed the public benefit test.

Too Broad a Definition

Thus, over time, the broadened legal definition of charity has expanded beyond helping the poor to include education, religion, and other areas beneficial to society. And it has not stopped there.

After all, the breadth (wider social needs) and depth (upstream activities) of social intervention have increased as society has progressed, and new modes of intervention have been required to keep up with more complex needs. Responding to these new community needs, governments and regulators across the world have come to regard many new social causes as charitable by using the fourth catch-all clause of "beneficial to the community not falling under any of the preceding heads." For example, in 2005, the Singaporean government announced that "the advancement of sport, where the sport advances health through physical skill and exertion" will be within the ambit of "other purposes beneficial to the community."[6]

In the UK, the classification of "charitable purposes" under statutory law has been extended to include the advancement of health, community development, amateur sport, human rights and equality, environmental protection, relief of various disabilities, animal welfare, promotion of the efficiency of the armed forces, and the advancement of the arts, culture, heritage, and science.[7] Other Commonwealth countries have formed their own systems to accommodate the diversity of causes. Meanwhile, the US lists over 30 types of not-for-profit activities to determine charitable status and tax exemption.[8] The details may vary among countries, but the direction is the same: Increasingly, more causes are being deemed to be for the community good and, therefore, charitable.

This broadening of the legal definition of charity is not without confusion. The average layman—still with his mindset of charity being for the poor and needy—has a difficult time understanding the inclusion of many public institutions and utilities such as bridges, art galleries, schools, and concert halls as charities. A 2009 poll of over 2,000 UK adults revealed that only 19 percent could correctly identify that Eton College is a charity, while 22 percent mistook the government body, the Equalities and Human Rights Commission to be a charity.[9]

The widening of the definition of charity should not be taken lightly. Charity status provides an organization with many support structures from both the government and the community. The government provides charities with tax breaks, and it follows that its revenues are depleted every time it grants a (broadened) cause the status of a charity. In other words, the government loses money that it could otherwise have used to provide social services.[10] It has been argued that this is justified, as charities do what the government would otherwise have to do. But in cases where the state is already providing this service (hospitals and schools), or where private hospitals are providing services that are no different, then tax breaks for such "charities" can become contentious.

In the US, a 2006 report by the Congressional Budget Office estimated that nonprofit hospitals were exempted from paying US$12.6 billion in taxes a year, adding on to what analysts have estimated to be "US$32 billion in federal, state, and local subsidies [that] the hospital industry as a whole received annually."[11] While a portion of the nonprofit hospital services does get directed to charitable purposes, detractors contend that some provide less in charity care than the tax breaks that they receive. At least one hospital has paid the price for not providing enough charity care.[12] But the fate of about 5,500 nonprofit hospitals in the US still hangs in the balance, as attempts are underway to make their operations more transparent.[13] This is just one example of the perceived unfair advantage that certain services may receive by operating with the status of a charity.

For charities serving the poor, having more organizations that are not really serving the poor but are competing with them under the same umbrella of tax breaks and government support makes it more difficult for them to get their fair share of the pie. The net consequence is that charities for the poor and needy become less visible amid the drone of other fundraising activities and the glamor that is sometimes attached to these other causes.

The tussle for a piece of the UK National Lottery's[14] "good causes" pie is illustrative. Following the UK's winning bid to host the 2012 Olympic Games, about £2.2 billion (US$3 billion) of Lottery funds was diverted from existing good causes toward Olympics projects.[15] This has upset sports grassroots associations and other charities, who believe that this amount should, instead, be used for more urgent and valid needs. Even amid strong lobbying by the national umbrella body of charities to not let good causes "bear the burden of Olympic funding," especially when a budget overrun meant a second dip into the good causes fund, the government went ahead, insisting that the "benefits [that] the Games will bring to the cultural sector, to the nation generally, to sport and to regeneration will outweigh the money we are taking from the Lottery."[16] Whether intended or not, the expanding notion of the community good is questioning the sense of equity and parity in the distribution of resources toward charitable causes meant truly for the poor and broadened causes which are for the community good.

Too Narrow a Definition

While the legal definition of charitable causes may be too broad in some respects, it is also too narrowly defined or interpreted in other respects.

First, the common man's understanding of charity emanates from either religious faith or altruism. Here, charity is a reaction, more than an intervention. It is guided by the heart, and less by rational thought. Consequently, charity is simply about giving to the needy. For the very virtuous, anonymous giving is strongly urged to signify purity of intent. In such a traditional understanding of charity, the donor–recipient relationship tends to be less engaged and interactive since, in the first place, the donor would not want to be seen or known.

Secondly, such forms of help may have sufficed in traditional closely knit societies where needs and social structures were much simpler. However, today's society is made up of more substructures than in the past—among them, labor, family, community, government, and civic groups. And all these units are interdependent. To effect sustainable change in a beneficiary's life, it is not enough just to feed the person. It is as important to help change the individual's environment and equip them to be able to engage constructively with these groups in order to survive and thrive in life.

One way by which changes to an individual's environment can be achieved is through advocacy—campaigning for changes to mindsets, rules, and structures that inherently limit the beneficiaries. To be sure, advocacy is hard. However, some of the more sustained solutions to social issues historically have come from long years of advocacy. For example, the campaign against slavery took 46 years before the *Slavery Abolition Act 1833* was passed in England.[17] Similarly, the campaign for women's right to vote took 70 years before the 19th Amendment to the US Constitution was passed in the US Congress in 1919.[18] Providing shelters, support groups, and other balms for the victims of injustice might have made them feel better and, perhaps, taken care of their immediate needs, but it was the advocacy of making the environment right for the beneficiaries that led to enduring change and avoided creating more victims. If the protagonists of these lobbying movements were given more support and recognition for their work, society may not need to wait a generation or more for positive changes to occur. Yet, advocacy is not often supported as charity even if it does lead to solving a social ill in the long term.

If a charity is expected to alleviate poverty, it should be its place to address the root cause of poverty through advocacy. Unfortunately, advocacy is often deemed to be politically related or motivated, and common law does not recognize an organization as a charity if it has a "political purpose" such as when it seeks to change social policy or law.[19] The 1977 case of Amnesty International,[20] which campaigns for internationally recognized human rights, is illustrative. Explaining why

Amnesty's application for charity status in the UK was denied, the ruling judge said that the organization imposed "moral pressure on governments or governmental authorities" outside the UK with its efforts to release prisoners of conscience (people who have been unfairly imprisoned on the basis of race, religion, or lifestyle).[21] Even though Amnesty sought to remove the barriers to employment—and thus alleviate poverty—its advocacy role against predatory structures was deemed "political." This is an example of a restrictive legal interpretation that limits charity to a reactive role.

To be clear, common law does not put a blanket ban on advocacy work by charities. In the UK, organizations such as Amnesty, Greenpeace, and Friends of the Earth were advised to set up separate charities in parallel to the main organization to carry out educational and research activities; these charity arms can still qualify for tax breaks. In an attempt to clarify the gray area between campaigning and political lobbying, the UK's Charity Commission specified the kind of advocacy work that is allowed; this includes providing political leaders with nonpartisan information and reasoned arguments for their causes.[22]

In the US, by default, charities may have their tax-exempt status revoked if they engage in extensive lobbying to influence the legislation or formulate propaganda, but they can exercise influence in nonlegislative matters such as the administrative agency's regulations or the executive decisions of the president or governor.[23] In other instances, a 20 percent cap can be put on the lobbying proportion of a charity's expenditure if the charity chooses to be assessed under the expenditure test.[24] While options are available for the charities to exercise their right to lobby, a survey of some 1,700 charities shows that most hold themselves back from too many of such activities for fear of crossing the line.[25]

In the face of these limitations and challenges, it is not surprising that advocacy bodies form only 4 percent of civil society on average, while service-function organizations in social services, education, housing, and health form 64 percent in terms of manpower.[26]

Beyond Charity

Charity is important. But charity on its own is not enough. The path of a Good Samaritan[27] can be strewn with structures and mindsets that either entrench the problem at hand or magnify it. World issues have grown to such a magnitude that the do-gooders are forever playing catch-up.

It is no longer enough just to help the beneficiary. Equally important is the question of how one delivers that help. Indeed, charity has gone through several phases. It started with a focus on giving to the poor. Then, in the 15th century, it expanded to address the environment in which the poor—as well as other members of the community—lived. In the 19th century, and with the influence of business minds and principles, the focus was on helping the poor help themselves.

This progression of thinking and approach in charity work led to one conclusion: Being kind does not mean just showing kindness. For example, a social service body may reject an unemployed man's request for monetary handouts and suggest training instead. While this gesture may seem unkind to a depressed man, the counter-argument is that the economic right of the man and his long-term sustainability through enrichment programs is more valuable than a one-off handout. In other words, society's understanding of charity has matured to a level where kindness is not mere form or faith but also includes elements of strategy.

However, many more paradigms still need to change if charity is to be effective in solving society's problems. Three of these worldviews point to the tensions between:

- Heart and head
- Symptoms and sources of problems
- Hands-off and hands-on approaches in helping.

Heart versus Head

In charity, people are driven more by their hearts than by their heads.

Ridiculous sums of money (and countless pages of media space) can be given to just one victim of a random tragedy. For example, the Texan baby, Jessica, who fell into a well, received as much as US$1 million in donations.[28] Imagine how much more impact this amount could have achieved for the five million children who die of malnutrition every year.

In a controlled experiment by the University of Pennsylvania, researchers found that when faced with a choice between helping Rokia, a seven-year-old Mali girl who was desperately poor and hungry, and millions of nameless victims dying of food shortages in Zambia, potential donors were more inclined to give to Rokia because the details were more vivid and personal. What is more surprising was that the more statistical evidence respondents received regarding the situation of depravity, the less generous their giving would be.[29]

It seems that the head does not work too well in the realm of giving; but on the flipside, this actually speaks of the power of intuition and emotions (the right brain over the left brain) in giving. After all, it seems that human beings are hard-wired to give. A study on spending and happiness by the University of British Columbia concluded that happiness does not depend on how big a bonus one gets; rather, it depends on how much of that bonus the individual spends on another.[30] The researchers observed an increase in happiness among those who spent even as little as US$5 of their bonus on someone else in the course of a day.

However, taken to the other extreme, giving may be a result of selfish love: for reasons of tax exemption, for a cause that relates to personal interest, and for personal benefit. Another study by the University of Chicago demonstrates the appeal of self-benefit when helping others: It found that raising funds by selling lottery tickets was much more effective than asking for money in door-to-door fundraising.[31]

No matter how one interprets these findings, the power—even indulgence—of the heart is hard to avoid. In deliberations of charity, strategies are needed to channel this positive energy into a fruitful outcome.

Symptoms versus Sources

In addressing social problems, charities tend to focus on the immediate welfare of the victims, rather than on the root cause of their problems. This is perpetuated by the common perception of charity as being one of merely helping, instead of empowering, the beneficiary.

In pursuing a social mission, a charity can choose to address the symptoms and provide relief through services. Or it can look deeper to address the sources of the problem, and advocate for changes in problematic norms or laws.

To illustrate, there are two ways of dealing with the abuse of low-income migrant workers in many countries. The first is to provide shelters and counseling services to alleviate the workers' plight. The second is to preempt abuse by educating employers on fair employment practices and by engaging policy makers on the creation of legal frameworks to deter offenders. The first approach is important; the second one is even more so for long-term enduring solutions.

More social movements are recognizing the importance of interventions that marry immediate relief for beneficiaries with long-term sustainable solutions that address the root causes. One example is GOONJ, a charity that provides recycled and other basic amenities to millions in far-flung villages in India. GOONJ collects discarded clothes from the well-off and provides them to the poor. However, it does not do this free of charge. Instead, the philosophy of its founder, Anshu Gupta, is that the clothes should be given in exchange for work by the recipients in its development or community projects. This not only provides meaningful engagement and employment for the poor but also preserves their dignity in not receiving handouts.[32]

Anshu Gupta is a social entrepreneur. The good news is that there are more like him who are emerging on the scene. These are the individuals who seek game-changing approaches to address the root causes of society's problems.[33]

Hands Off versus Hands On

Some donors have a common—perhaps misplaced—perception that they have discharged their responsibilities once they have given a proportion of their income to charity. Even though donors nowadays are more involved in making decisions on giving, this process is mostly dominated by a calculative and distant analysis of whether charities are more prudent with their operational spending.[34]

It is because of this lack of engagement with the charities that donors, and indeed the general public, fail to understand the unique problems that charities face in operating with multiple stakeholders and limited resources. Thus, charities continue to face the problem of inadequate manpower and skills, limited attention to capacity-building efforts, and the lack of focus on strategic interventions that can reap more long-term returns.

Two positive trends will hopefully result in more hands-on engagement by donors with charities.

The first is the rise of the volunteer–donor. Increasingly, good volunteer management and donor management practices are recognizing the value of, and developing strategies for, cultivating the volunteer–donor.[35] Many studies have shown that people who volunteer tend to donate more money to charity than those who do not. A recent US survey found that volunteers donate, on average, 10 times the amount donated by non-volunteers.[36]

The second trend is that the personal engagement of donors with the charities is not confined to grassroots volunteers, but is the mark of a new breed of businessmen–philanthropists. These neo-philanthropists are giving of their money, time, and ideas—all in large measures—to help charities be more effective. They are implementing approaches adapted from their business background, including leading-edge capital venture tools, which are making a collective impact on the charity scene.[37]

Charity in Spirit and Substance

Charity has long been about kindness.

The common man sees kindness as being applied to the poor. However, the law has expanded the scope of charity recipients to include a multitude of community causes. By being kind to these community causes, we may be unkind to the poor who now have to compete for the preferential treatment and support structures available to all charities.

Being kind should not just mean taking care of the immediate needs of the beneficiaries. Being kind may require being unkind in the short term, while doing the hard work of addressing their long-term plights. Being kind may also require one to be courageous in standing up to social inequities.

There are, indeed, different kinds of kindness; but no matter which kind we settle on, the best ones engage the heart, the head, and the hands.

Endnotes

1   There are, of course, many benefits to the person who performs charity, ranging from the intangible (those related to the soul and sense of well-being) to the material (tax benefits, naming rights, etc.). Many studies and writers have analyzed these. Examples: Fiona Macrae, "Charity Makes You 'Stronger and More Popular'," *mailonline*, April 21, 2010, www.dailymail.co.uk/news/article-1267609/Charity-makes-stronger-popular-studies-find.html; Cait Genereuse, "The Benefits of Giving to Charity," internetseer, www.internetseer.com/services/article.xtp?id=26323.

2   See Richard M. Titmuss, *The Gift Relationship: From human blood to social policy* (London: Allen & Unwin, 1970) for a seminal work on the relationship.

3   Tzedekah in Judaism; alms-giving in Christianity; *sedekah* in Islam; *thamtaan* in Buddhism; and *datra datrtva* in Hinduism, among others.

4   These 60 nations are former colonies of the British Empire, including the US. They also include Commonwealth countries such as the UK, Australia, Canada, and New Zealand; and the small, less-developed nations of the Seychelles and Tonga. Common law is law developed by judges through decisions of courts, rather than only through legislative statutes or executive branch action.

5   *Income Tax Special Purpose Commissioners v. Pemsel* [1891] AC 531.

6   *Budget Speech 2005* (Singapore: Ministry of Finance, 2005), www.mof.gov.sg/budget_2005/budget_speech/downloads/FY2005_Budget_Statement.pdf. See definition of charity by the Commissioner of Charity at the Charity Portal: www.charities.gov.sg/charity/index.do.

7   *Charities Act 2006,* www.opsi.gov.uk/acts/acts2006/ukpga_20060050_en_1.htm.

8   *Illinois General Not for Profit Corporation Act,* §103.05 lists 33 purposes, including some
that are clearly not charitable in the common law sense. This law is available on the
website of the Illinois General Assembly at www.ilga.gov/LEGISLATION. See Kerry
O'Halloran, Myles McGregor-Lowndes, and Karla Simon, *Charity Law and Social
Policy: National and international perspectives and functions of law relating to charities*
(Brisbane: Springer, 2008) for more details on how different countries deal with the
expanding range of social organizations and with the question of public benefit.

9   "Perception Gap between Public and Charities Threatens the 'Special Relationship' says
ACEVO," Press Release on survey by the Association of Chief Executives of Voluntary
Organisations, August 10, 2009, www.acevo.org.uk/Document.Doc?id=249.

10 For instance, in the US, charitable deductions cost the government US$40 billion in
lost tax revenue in 2006. According to the Joint Committee on Taxation, this is more
than what the government spends altogether on managing public lands, protecting
the environment, and developing new energy sources. Data cited from Stephanie
Strom, "Big Gifts, Tax Breaks," *The New York Times,* September 6, 2007, www.nytimes
.com/2007/09/06/business/06giving.html?pagewanted=2&_r=1.

11 Data cited from: Barbara Martinez, "Senators Consider Curtailing Hospitals'
Tax Breaks," *The Wall Street Journal,* July 10, 2009, www.online.wsj.com/article/
SB124718085849920111.html. Also, refer to "Nonprofit Hospitals and Tax Arbitrage,"
prepared by the US Congressional Budget Office for the Committee on Ways and
Means, US House of Representatives, December 6, 2006.

12 This refers to the widely known case of Downstate Provena Covenant Medical Center
in the US, which had its tax-exempt status revoked in 2003. Officials cited as the reason
the 210-bed hospital's US$831,724 spent on "charitable activities" in 2002, saying it was
less than the medical center's US$1.1 million in property taxes. The state's Department
of Revenue upheld that decision in 2010. Illinois law now requires hospitals to provide
charity care to poor people to qualify for their tax exemption, but it does not specify how
much. Data cited from Lorene Yue and Mike Colias, "Illinois Supreme Court Upholds
Ruling against Provena in Tax-Exempt Case," *Chicago Business,* March 18, 2010, www
.chicagobusiness.com/cgi-bin/news.pl?id=37496.

13 The *Patient Protection and Affordable Care Act* (Pub. L. No. 111-148) includes four
primary adjustments to the federal income tax exemption requirements for nonprofit
hospitals. Under the Act, tax-exempt hospitals must take a series of actions, including
the conduct of a community health needs analysis at least once every three years; make
widely available their financial assistance policies and, for discounted care, how they
determine amounts that are billed to patients; notify patients of financial assistance
policies through "reasonable efforts"; and restrict charges of uninsured, indigent patients
to those amounts generally charged to insured patients. All these measures are intended to
improve transparency about how the hospitals fulfill their charitable mission. Under
this Act, the exempt status of hospitals is reviewed every three years. Extracted from
Michael W. Peregrine, "New Requirements for Tax-Exempt Hospitals," Healthcare Law
Reform: Insights from Washington, DC, March 29, 2010, www.healthcarelawreform
.com/2010/03/articles/hill-developments/new-requirements-for-taxexempt-hospitals/.

14 The National Lottery was meant to provide a funding channel for good causes that are
unfunded but desirable, and its underlying principle was that, for one, funds raised
for good causes from the operation of the Lottery should not be subsumed into public
expenditure. Since the inception of the National Lottery, nearly £21 billion (US$31

billion) has been given to good causes, with grants ranging from £12 (US$18) (for a cycling award) to £604 million (US$895 million) (given to the Millennium Dome), with the highest average grant value going to millennium projects, and the lowest to charitable expenditure. Data and analysis cited from: Paul Bickley, *The National Lottery: Is it progressive?* (London: Theos, 2009).

15   The contribution from the Lottery to the Games was originally £1.5 billion, but in March 2007, this rose by £675 million to £2.2 billion due to a revised increased budget. The increased contribution represents 20 percent of Lottery proceeds due to go to good causes from 2005 to 2012/13. "2012 Games: Impact on lottery funding in London," london.gov.uk, www.london.gov.uk/media/press_releases_london_assembly/2012-games-impact-lottery-funding-london.

16   Brendan Carlin, "More 'Good Cause' Lottery Cash to Help Pay Soaring Olympics Bill," *Telegraph.com*, November 18, 2006, www.telegraph.co.uk/news/uknews/1534495/More-good-cause-Lottery-cash-to-help-pay-soaring-Olympics-bill.html; Paul Jump and Helen Warrel, "Charity Coalition Rallies Opposition MPs against Lottery Raid to Fund the Olympics," Third Sector Online, April 23, 2007, www.thirdsector.co.uk/channels/Finance/Article/652248/Charity-coalition-rallies-opposition-MPs-against-Lottery-raid-fund-Olympics/.

17   www.wilberforcecentral.org/wfc.

18   "Women's Rights Movements in the US," Infoplease, www.infoplease.com/spot/womenstimeline1.html.

19   Kerry O'Halloran, *Charity Law and Social Inclusion* (New York: Routledge, 2007). According to the public benefit rule, charities must not have a primary purpose which is political, because it is not possible to judge whether a proposed change in the law will, or will not, provide a benefit to the public. A "political purpose" means any purpose directed at promoting the interests of any political party; or securing or opposing any change in the law or in the policy or decisions of central or local government, whether in the local country or overseas.

20   Amnesty International was founded as a nonprofit in 1961 with the general objective of ensuring, throughout the world, the observance of certain provisions of the Universal Declaration of Human Rights, which was proclaimed by the General Assembly of the United Nations in 1948. The organization works on censuring detention, and securing the release, of prisoners of conscience who have neither used nor advocated violence. It also opposes the infliction of the death penalty, torture, and other cruel, inhuman, or degrading treatment of detained persons whether or not they have used or advocated violence. See www.amnesty.org.

21   "Case Comment: McGovern vs. Attorney General, Maurice C. Cullity, Member the Ontario Bar, 1981," accessed from *The Philanthropist*, www.thephilanthropist.ca/index.php/phil/article/viewFile/420/420. Also see: *Speaking Out: Guidance on campaigning and political activity by charities* (Liverpool: Charity Commission, 2008).

22   *Oxfam: Report of an inquiry submitted to the Charity Commissioners* (London: Charity Commissions, April 1991).

23   More details available in: "Introduction to Lobbying by Public Charities," Nonprofit Law Blog, July 22, 2006, www.nonprofitlawblog.com/home/2006/07/introduction_to.html.

24   Referred to as section 501(h), a charity may fill up a simple form 5768 and conduct lobbying activities within the cap specified, as long as they submit their expenditure

for assessment. Also see Elizabeth J. Reid, "Advocacy and the Challenges it Presents for Nonprofits," in *Nonprofits and Government: Collaboration and conflict*, ed. Elizabeth T. Boris and Eugene Steurle (Washington, DC: The Urban Institute Press, 2006).

25   Jeffrey M. Berry, "A Needless Silence: American nonprofits and the rights to lobby," *The International Journal of Not-for-Profit Law*, 6(2), January 2004, www.icnl.org/knowledge/ijnl/vol6iss2/special_6.htm.

26   Lester M. Salamon, S. Wojciech Sokolowski and Associates, *Global Civil Society: Dimensions of the nonprofit sector, Volume Two* (Bloomfield, CT: Kumarian Press, 2004). This data is based on manpower in organizations where the principal activity is stated as advocacy as a percentage of total manpower in the nonprofit sector. Although advocacy is the principal activity in these organizations, not all manpower will be devoted to advocacy; there will be support functions such as finance and human resources, and other service functions in this organization. At the same time, for those other organizations classified as non-advocacy—for example, service-based organizations—there could also be advocacy-based functions within these organizations, but their manpower will not be counted.

27   "The Good Samaritan" is the Biblical story of the Samaritan who helps a complete stranger in distress notwithstanding that the stranger is a Jew, a tribe unfriendly to the Samaritans. The colloquial phrase, "Good Samaritan" has come to mean someone who helps a total stranger.

28   Baby Jessica was trapped in the well for two-and-a-half days. An image of Jessica's bandaged face as she was pulled out of the well won a Pulitzer Prize. Frances Romero, "Top 10 Miraculous Rescues: Baby Jessica," *TIME*, April 6, 2010, www.time.com/time/specials/packages/article/0,28804,1977927_1977934_1977866,00.html.

29   Deborah Small, George Loewenstein, and Paul Slovic, "To Increase Charitable Donations, Appeal to the Heart—Not the Head," *Organizational Behavior and Human Decision Processes*, March 2007, www.faculty-gsb.stanford.edu/aaker/documents/smallloewesteinslovic.pdf. The 2005 study was conducted by Deborah Small and her colleagues from the University of Pennsylvania, using a series of four field experiments involving ordinary citizens. The researchers gave each person five US$1 bills. They were then instructed to read a letter containing a charity request, after which they were asked to donate a sum of money, ranging from zero to five dollars, anonymously in an envelope. According to the researchers, people gave most in the field experiment where they were asked to make a donation to an identifiable victim in the absence of statistics or "rational" thought.

30   Michael Norton, Elizabeth Dunn, and Lara Aknin, "Spending Money on Others Promotes Happiness," *Science*, March 21, 2008.

31   Craig Landry, Andreas Lange, John A. List, Michael K. Price, and Nicholas G. Rupp, "Toward an Understanding of the Economics of Charity: Evidence from a field experiment," East Carolina University, University of Chicago, University of Maryland, University of Nevada-Reno, NBER, and RFF, August 27, 2005, www.chicagocdr.org/papers/listpaper.pdf#search=%2522towards%20an%20understanding%20of%20the%20economics%20of%20charity%2522.

32   www.goonj.org. Lee Siew Hua, "He Gives the Poor Dignity," *The Straits Times*, October 24, 2009.

33   The subject of social entrepreneurs is covered in Chapter 6, "Social Entrepreneurship: Of pattern changers and changemakers," by Chris Cusano.

34   Patrick Newton, "Charity: Head not heart?" Yougov, June 1, 2010, www.today.yougov .co.uk/consumer/charity-head-not-heart.

35   For example, see Susan J. Ellis, *From the Top Down: The executive role in successful volunteer involvement* (Philadelphia: Energize, Inc., 2010).

36   "Fidelity Charitable Gift Fund and VolunteerMatch Form Alliance and Release Landmark Study on Volunteering," Fidelity Charitable Gift Fund, December 3, 2009, www.charitablegift.org/learn-about-charity/news/12-03-2009.shtml.

37   These neo-philanthropists and their approaches are covered in more detail in Chapter 8, "Philanthropy: Powering philanthropic passions," by Thomas Menkhoff; and in Chapter 9, "Venture Philanthropy: Venturing into entrepreneurial philanthropy," by Rob John.

Social Purpose Entities

Chapter 4

Charities

No Charity for Charities

GERARD EE
Chairman, Council for Third Age

Charities exist to help the poor and the needy. However, well-run charities are few and far between.

The key reason is that the same compassion that drove the formation of charities and their work can result in poor governance, low performance, poorly paid workers, and a narrow focus on the needs of the poor that leads to suboptimal outcomes.

To solve this, we need to remove the element of compassion when it is not necessary or appropriate in the workings of charity. Only then, will we have high-performing charities that can effectively deliver on their mission.

Charities are the "gold class" of the nonprofit sector. In most jurisdictions, a charity is an officially recognized nonprofit organization with tax and other benefits.[1]

Charities are growing across the world alongside the rise of the nonprofit sector. In the US, there were more than one million public charities in 2010, up from 633,000 a decade ago.[2] In the UK, the number has been rising by 5,000 new charities a year, stabilizing at nearly 181,000 in 2010.[3] Even in the island-state of Singapore, the charity sector grew from 400 charities in 1983 to nearly 2,000 in 2008.[4]

More than just growth in numbers, the strength of charitable organizations is growing. While the number of US charities grew by 60 percent in the last decade, both their annual expenditures and total assets grew by 79 percent.[5] The top charities are expanding annually by more than 35 percent in terms of revenue, programs, and services.[6]

Indeed, the charity scene is a good one to be associated with. After all, it is about doing good. However, from time to time, charities and the charitable sector come under fire.

The occasional charity scandal—whether for outright theft by charity workers, extravagant spending by its leaders, or questionable political involvement beyond their cause—gets the press and the public hot under the collar. Some scandals have led to major charity law reforms.[7]

A 2007 Harris survey showed that 32 percent of US adults had less than positive feelings toward charitable organizations, and the same number thought that the nonprofit sector was headed in the wrong direction.[8] Another survey showed that less than half of Canadians believed that charities are transparent in their business dealings.[9] Businesses also take issue with the tax breaks that charities enjoy, saying that this gives them an unfair advantage for providing services which businesses can also provide.[10]

While concerns may be triggered or exacerbated by scandals, the greater issue for charities has been the broader one of accountability and performance versus financial wrongdoing and regulatory compliance. The call for greater corporate governance which is so prevalent in the corporate and public sector is, increasingly, being directed at the charity sector.[11] The question being asked is: Why are charities not able to hold their own and operate as well as corporate and public sector organizations?

High-Performing Charities

Recognizing these concerns, various parties, especially in more mature nonprofit sectors such as the US and the UK, seek to help charities become high-performing organizations.

Among them are Charity Navigator, GuideStar, and Charity Watch, which monitor, analyze, and rate charities.[12] In their evaluation criteria, they usually apply a set of financial ratios similar to those for commercial organizations that have been tailored for the charity sector. For example, a key benchmark is the program ratio: the percentage of total expenditure that a charity spends on its core programs (as opposed to its administrative overheads). However, financial-based ratios and ratings have been criticized by some for being too rigid and not reflective of the nature of charities that do not have a single and common bottom line like commercial organizations.[13]

An emerging group of analysts and consultancies such as New Philanthropy Capital[14] takes a broader approach and considers financial and nonfinancial factors to help donors evaluate charities while also helping charities become more effective. Other consultancies, such as The Bridgespan Group,[15] help charities with strategy development and implementation.

To promote excellence, league tables and awards are sponsored by various media organizations (e.g. *Fast Company*'s Social Capitalist Awards), foundations (e.g. The Nand & Jeet Khemka Foundation's India NGO Awards), corporations (e.g. Citibank's Asia Pacific NGO Awards), and nonprofit organizations (e.g. the World Association of NGOs Awards).[16] These awards are often supported by a combination of players. For instance, the *New York Times* Company Nonprofit Excellence Awards is organized by the *New York Times*, the Nonprofit Coordinating Committee of New York, and Philanthropy New York.[17]

Three winners of such awards—Teach for America,[18] Prisoners Assistance Nepal,[19] and Habitat for Humanity[20]—are described in the box, "Award-Winning Charities." Such exemplary organizations can be both a source of inspiration, and a source of learning, in terms of what makes for a well-run charity.

Indeed, this spirit of excellence is what Crutchfield and McLeod, the authors of *Forces for Good*, sought to showcase with 12 of the most successful charities in the US.[21]

Award-Winning Charities

Teach for America

Teach for America (TFA), a US-based charity, was set up to deal with the "national injustice" of the achievement gap between students from low-income communities compared to their higher-income peers. Not only has it been able to inspire and recruit some 24,000 of the nation's best graduates from the Ivy League to teach at hard-to-staff poor school districts, but the results also show that the students who were taught by TFA teachers had improved test scores.[22]

In doing so, the charity does not need extraneous fundraising other than grants for general administrative support. Rather, fresh and outstanding graduates yearning to contribute and thirsting for new challenges are the ready social capital that it leverages to deliver its mission.

TFA only asks its participating graduates to teach for two years. It expects its 17,000 alumni to be a force in the community to improve outcomes and opportunities for low-income students, and to fight for systemic reform in the education system.

Prisoners Assistance Nepal

Prisoners Assistance Nepal is a Nepalese grassroots organization that takes an integrated approach to providing for the basic needs and human rights of prisoners and their families. Its ethos centers on keeping families in contact while ensuring that innocent children do not need to endure the traumas of their parent's imprisonment. In its attempt to provide for the complete care of these children, it has set up a children's home and school, a youth center, and programs for farming skills. Its housing program has benefited 300 children.

The organization also engages prison authorities in reforms and has a number of programs to support male and female prisoners in Nepal's under-resourced prison system. It also has educational and community programs both inside and outside prison to help prisoners reintegrate into the community.

Habitat for Humanity

Habitat for Humanity is an international charity that builds basic and decent housing for the poor in the developing world with volunteer manpower.

After the houses are built, Habitat sells them at no profit to the beneficiaries. However, it is not just a simple buy-and-sell transaction of a down payment and monthly mortgage. Depending on the locality, the beneficiaries are also expected to put hundreds of hours of their own labor—what it calls "sweat equity"—into the building of the house. To ensure sustainability, Habitat conducts checks to make sure that the houses can be paid for, and that payments are always channeled back into the funds for the building of more houses.

To date, Habitat has built more than 350,000 houses around the world, providing more than 1.75 million people in 3,000 communities with safe, affordable shelter.

High performance, according to their findings, is not just about perfect systems and processes, or about successful fundraising, or finding a new breakthrough idea. In fact, a few of their impactful charities scored only one or two stars out of a total of five on the Charity Navigator's scale. Instead, high performance was to be found in how charities work "outside the boundaries of their organizations" while still creating impact. They identified six practices of these 12 high-impact organizations:

1. Work with government and advocate for policy change (e.g. Self-Help).
2. Harness market forces and see business as a powerful partner (e.g. Environmental Defense with Walmart).
3. Create meaningful experiences for supporters (e.g. Habitat for Humanity).
4. Build and nurture nonprofit networks to collaborate (e.g. Exploratorium).
5. Adapt to the changing environment (e.g. Share our Strength).
6. Share leadership to empower (e.g. Heritage Foundation).[23]

Jim Collins (the author of *Good to Great*), who has studied both the business and nonprofit sectors, feels that business principles still hold in the social sector but that their application needs to take into account the differences between the two sectors. The distinction is not between business and social, but between good and great. He notes that nonprofits have their own set of unique problems such as resource constraints, talent dearth, and lack of prestige, but great charities are those that have the discipline to lead even through a diffused power structure (e.g. Girl Scouts of the USA) or to think of an alternative economic engine in the absence of the profit motive (e.g. Teach for America).[24]

In these studies and in debates on excellence in charities, questions arise about whether, and which, business principles are valid and applicable for charities. Those who are against the application of business approaches to charities will cite the differences between the two sectors. It is worthwhile looking at the root cause of these differences.

The Culture of Compassion

The fundamental difference between the business and charity sectors is their very basis for existence, and this is reflected in their cultures. As Willie Cheng has pointed out, business is about market economics and the bottom line, while charity is about doing good and expressing compassion (see Figure 4.1).[25]

Figure 4.1 Commercial versus Charity Environment

	Commercial	Charity
Mission Focus	Economic	Social
Market Basis	Economic value	Generosity
	Survival of the fittest	Doing good
Funding	Market rate capital	Donations and grants
Workers	Staff at market-based compensation	Volunteers and staff paid below market rate
Recipients of Goods and Services	Customers pay market rate	Beneficiaries pay nothing or subsidized rate
Suppliers	Charge market rate	Charge subsidized rate and give donations-in-kind

Source: Willie Cheng, *Doing Good Well: What does (and does not) make sense in the nonprofit world* (Singapore: John Wiley & Sons, 2009).

In other words, the commercial world is results-driven and the people in it are driven by self-interest. On the other hand, the charity world is mission-driven and its people are driven by compassion.

However, the consequences, unintended perhaps, of this culture of compassion are that:

– Charity workers are poorly paid.
– Governance is generally weak.
– The pace, process, and outcomes in charities fall short.
– There is a narrow focus on the needs of the poor that suboptimizes outcomes.

Poorly Paid Charity Workers

It is a universally accepted fact of life in the charity world that charity workers are poorly paid; or, at best, they are paid below their commercial counterparts.

Most studies have validated this income disparity. The only point of dispute is how big the disparity is, and that would depend on the location and timing of the surveys.[26]

The public and donors expect charities to be"run by highly motivated but relatively modestly paid people."[27] And, charity workers have come to accept this.

There are two reasons for this state of affairs. The first is that in meeting the goal of operating at minimum costs, staff costs also have to be kept low. The second is that charity workers are asked to be aligned, and show their alignment, with the charitable nature of the organization they are working for by taking a wage less than what they might have been entitled to elsewhere. The wage subsidy is thus a partial donation to the cause. Interestingly, this moral argument of contributing to the cause ignores the morality of paying a man less than he is worth; even if, at times, he is paid below-subsistence rates.

The consequence of such a wage policy is that charities will, often, not get the talent they need to be high-performing organizations. Worse, those who are paid less will drift into a mood and state in which their performance reflects their pay scales.

Weak Governance

Charities are generally governed by volunteer boards, most of whom are there for compassionate reasons. They want to help out, to do good. Many do so by lending their networks and names to fundraise and elevate the organization; others help with the specific programs of the charity.

Few are there to truly govern. Most board members realize and accept that governance is part of their job scope. But then, the sector is about compassion, trust, and goodness. So, they reflect these values in their approach to governance.

They create a forgiving environment, giving scope to the management and staff to perform—or not perform. They are not likely to make too many demands of outcomes. Indeed, any outcome is a victory and a joy, a windfall, but not a necessity. Their focus is on the beneficiaries and the charity programs; that is what they came in for, not the back office, the processes, and the operations.

In this environment, there tends to be little in the way of checks and balances. What neglect or inactions there are in management may go undiscovered. Equally, abuses of power may go unreported. In a US survey of over 3,400 nonprofit employees, a good 55 percent had witnessed one or more acts of misconduct in their organization and 66 percent said that they would stay silent out of fear or futility.[28] In Canada, it was found that errant charities continued running for up to five years before complaints about their mismanagement were investigated by the regulator.[29]

Lack of Pace, Processes, and Outcomes

The day-to-day operations of a charity are performed by full-time staff; the work is often supplemented partially, or even wholly, by volunteer labor. Those who have come into the social sector from the business sector often attest to the spirit of compassion that drives the work and the workers in charity. They would also often attest to the lack of pace and processes that can ensure optimal outcomes for the mission of the charity.

There are several reasons for this. First, as mentioned above, the directions and demands for driving outcomes are not quite forthcoming from the top. Secondly, charity workers may not be fully qualified given the poor pay situation. Thirdly, there is little clarity about what the outcomes should be and what steps are needed to achieve those outcomes in most charities.

The fact is that charities in their current form are more complex organizations to manage than commercial organizations. Without a single clear bottom line, what constitutes good outcomes for a charity, and how they can be achieved, is a matter that requires a substantial investment of time and effort on the part of the board and management of charities to determine and implement. In most cases, these people are unwilling or unable to do so. Blame it on the culture of compassion and a work environment that prizes forgiveness for lackluster charity outcomes.

Often, there is also not a great deal of outside pressure for the organization to perform. Regulators and many donors are primarily concerned with ensuring no financial shenanigans and extravagant use of their money. Beyond that, what gets delivered—and something will get delivered—is fine.

Preference for the Poor

Charities have a preference for the poor and the needy. This is what many people associate with charities: a provision for the poor that is almost akin to almsgiving. Consequently, most charities are geared exclusively toward serving the poor and needy, or bias their operations in favor of them.

There is nothing wrong in itself with this approach. The issue is that in the process of skewing their work toward the poor, many charities sub-optimize the quality of their offerings. Much of this is done in the name of cost savings. The logic is this: The poor cannot afford to pay anyway, and lower-quality outcomes are still better than what these beneficiaries would be able to get for this low price (or for free).

Some charities provide differentiated pricing based on means testing—that is, those who can afford, say, kidney dialysis pay more, with the top-end being comparable to market rates. The problem is that since the quality offered is lower, more well-heeled clients will be unwilling to take up these services. What follows is a much smaller source of income for the charities. And what also follows is a lack of demand for better services, leaving the charities to continue on their cycle of tolerance for poor quality and low investment in upgrading efforts.

Removing Compassion

Charity is fundamentally about compassion—and it should be. But since compassion is the cause of many of the fundamental problems in charities, the instinctive answer would be to remove this emotive quotient from those places where it has an inappropriate effect. Indeed, compassion should not factor in several critical areas where charities can be high-performing organizations: the pay of charity workers, the governing role of the board, the management of the organization, and the quality of its offerings to beneficiaries.

First, charity workers should be paid what they are worth. This is entirely consistent with the tenet of justice, an important value in charity work. Charity workers should have a heart for the cause, but that is a mutually exclusive issue from whether they themselves are rich or poor. Who is to say that the rich or the well-paid cannot also be compassionate? Asking charity workers to be paid less than their worth so that they exhibit the important quality of compassion is to lose out on otherwise qualified workers who are unable to afford to survive on the poor wages.

Secondly, the board has to function as any governing board, whether of a charity or a commercial organization, would. Again, volunteer board members should have compassion, but their talents and their drive—the reasons these volunteer board members were recruited in the first place—are also much needed. They came because of their hearts, but they are not asked to check their brains at the door when they join the charity. They should be able to make (reasonable) demands of the charity to perform and to help the charity perform by developing the appropriate strategies and impact measurements.

Thirdly, management needs to rise to the challenge of making the organization effective. It has to work with the board to identify the desired outcomes, and then instill the management discipline and processes to drive these outcomes. There should be compassion in how the beneficiaries are being served, but not compassion in the expectations of processes to be followed and the results to be achieved.

Finally, there should be a separation between the quality of the offerings and the people being served. The former should not take into account the fact that some of the beneficiaries who may have to pay for them may be unable to afford them. Rather, it should befit the dignity of all humans. A simple approach applicable to those charities providing services that cut across beneficiary classes is to have differentiated pricing based on affordability. This means that all beneficiaries of the charity receive the same-quality offering, but those who can afford to pay more do so. Obviously, some kind of means testing has to be put in place to ensure that there is equity in the charges.

There are charities today that follow this approach. These include the National Kidney Foundation Singapore, VisionSpring, and Aravind Eye Care System.[30] Aravind, for one, is known to provide world-class eye treatment for free or at below cost to 75 percent of its patients, while charging a premium price for its well-to-do clients. Being a charitable organization has not been an excuse for advocating substandard treatment to either its patients or its staff.

Toward High-Performance Compassion

For too long, charity has been blindly about compassion.

Yes, there should be compassion: compassion for beneficiaries, and compassion from those who serve these beneficiaries (the board, staff, and volunteers).

But compassion should not stretch to the workings of the charity: in how the board governs the organization, in determining outcomes, in operating the charity to achieve those outcomes, in fair wages for charity workers, and in the quality of its offerings to the beneficiaries.

Instead, high performance should be the goal of charities. Everyone, whether a donor, board member, staff, volunteer, or beneficiary, should demand that a charity performs as well as it can. In other words, there should be no charity for the charities themselves.

Endnotes

1   In the US, charities are those registered under section 501(c)(3) of the US Internal Revenue Code. These organizations are subclassified as either a "public charity" or a "private foundation." The term "nonprofit" is used quite interchangeably in the US to refer to these organizations, although it can also cover 30 other types of 501(c) organizations such as trade unions, business associations, etc., which also qualify for tax exemption.

2   Data of public charities in the US obtained from National Center for Charitable Statistics (NCCS) Public Charities Table Wizard (www.nccsdataweb.urban.org/tablewiz/pc.php) as follows: *December 1999:* (1) No. of public charities: 633,000; (2) Total revenue reported: US$785 billion; (3) Total assets: US$1.45 trillion. *January 2010:* (1) No. of public charities: 1,007,384; (2) Total revenue reported: US$1.408 trillion; (3) Total assets: US$2.59 trillion.

3   Alison Benjamin, "Too Many Cooks?" *The Guardian*, November 8, 2000, www .guardian.co.uk/society/2000/nov/08/guardiansocietysupplement5; UK Charity Commission Register, www.charity-commission.gov.uk/showcharity/registerofcharities/registerhomepage.aspx?&=&.

4   Statistics from Wong Sher Maine, "Small Charities Fight for Bite of the Pie," *The Straits Times*, April 7, 2004; and *Commissioner of Charities Annual Report for the Year ending 31 December 2008* (Singapore: Commissioner of Charities, 2009).

5   Computations from figures in endnote 2.

6   "Top Ten Charities Expanding in a Hurry," Charity Navigator, www.charitynavigator .org/index.cfm?bay=topten.

7   Some of these scandals and the charity reforms are covered in Chapter 15, "Regulator: Love, law, and the regulator," by Stephen Lloyd.

8   "Nonprofits Developing a Bad Reputation," Fundraiser Help: Fundraising Ideas and Tools, data extracted from a survey conducted by Harris Interactive between January 11 and 17, 2006, www.fundraiserhelp.com/nonprofits-bad-reputation.htm.

9   "Muttart Foundation releases 'Talking about Charities 2006,'" Press Release by Canadian Association of Gift Planners, October 30, 2006, www.ncpg.org/igpa/Muttart%20Foundation%20releases.pdf.

10   "Charity Chain Stores have Unfair Advantage," *Startups*, March 8, 2006, www.startups .co.uk/6678842909728717972/charity-chain-stores-have-unfair-advantage.html; John Carreyruo, "Nonprofit Hospitals, Once for the Poor, Strike it Rich," *The Wall Street Journal*, April 4, 2008, www.wsbt.com/news/consumer/17296354.html.

11   See Chapter 19, "Global Civil Society: Rallying for real change," by Kumi Naidoo for a more in-depth discussion on the issue of accountability in the nonprofit sector.

12   A further discussion of charity watchers is in Chapter 7, "Capacity Builders: Making value visible," by Sara Olsen.

13   Mark Hager and Ted Flack, "The Pros and Cons of Financial Efficiency Standards," The Nonprofit Overhead Cost Project. Brief No. 5, Center on Nonprofits and Philanthropy of the Urban Institute and Center on Philanthropy of the Indiana University, August 2004; Paul Niehaus, *Rating the Charity Raters* (Washington, DC: Capital Research Center, October 2003).

14   www.philanthropycapital.org.

15   www.bridgespan.org.

16   *Fast Company* Social Capitalist Awards, www.fastcompany.com/social/; The Nand & Jeet Khemka Foundation's Indian NGO of the Year Award (together with Resource Alliance), www.khemkafoundation.org/awards; Citibank's Asia Pacific NGO Awards, www.highbeam.com/doc/1P2-10411469.html and www.citigroup.com/citi/citizen/assets/pdf/apccr2006.pdf; World Association of Nongovernmental Organizations, www.wango.org/awards.aspx.

17   www.npccny.org/info/awards.htm.

18   Teach for America, www.teachforamerica.org, was seventh in the prestigious *Business Week* annual list of best places to launch a career, sixth among Top 10 Employers of Recent College Grads, and one of the 45 companies that received *Fast Company*'s Social Capitalist Awards in 2008. For these and other awards, see www.teachforamerica.org/newsroom/awards_and_recognition.htm.

19   Prisoners Assistance Nepal, www.panepal.org, won the 2009 Asia Society–Bank of America Merrill Lynch Asia 21 Young Leaders Public Service Award; see www.asiasociety.org/media/press-releases/nepal-ngo-wins-asia-society-bank-america-merrill-lynch-asia-21-young-leaders-pu.

20   Habitat for Humanity, www.habitat.org, received the Kahlil Gibran Spirit of Humanity Award in 2006, www.habitat.org/newsroom/2006archive/04_26_2006_Arab_American_Award.aspx.

21   Leslie Crutchfield and Heather McLeod, *Forces for Good: The six practices of high-impact nonprofits* (San Francisco: John Wiley & Sons, 2008).

22   "Making a Difference? The Effect of Teach for America on Student Performance in High School," National Center for Analysis of Longitudinal Data in Education Research, Urban Institute, Working Paper 17, April 2007, www.urban.org/UploadedPDF/411642_Teach_America.pdf.

23   Self-Help, www.self-help.org/; Environmental Defense, www.edf.org/home.cfm; Habitat for Humanity, www.habitat.org; Exploratorium, www.exploratorium.edu; Share Our Strength, www.strength.org; Heritage Foundation, www.heritage.org.

24   Jim Collins, *Good to Great and the Social Sectors: A monograph to accompany Good to Great* (New York: HarperCollins, 2005).

25   Willie Cheng, "Profits for Nonprofits," in *Doing Good Well: What does (and does not) make sense in the nonprofit world* (Singapore: John Wiley & Sons, 2009).

26   Cecilia A. Fong, "The Nonprofit Wage Differential," a thesis submitted to the Faculty of the Georgetown Public Policy Institute in partial fulfillment of the requirements for the degree of Master of Public Policy, April 8, 2009, posits a 15.89 percent difference after keeping constant other possible interfering factors such as years of experience; Christopher J. Ruhm and Carey Borkosi, "Compensation in the Nonprofit Sector," *The Journal of Human Resources*, 38(4), Autumn 2003, posits an 11 percent difference.

27   Steve Davies, *Third Sector Provision of Employment-Related Services: A report for the Public and Commercial Services Union* (London: Public & Commercial Services Union, June 2006).

28 Aliah D. Wright, "Survey: Many non-profits fall short on ethics," Society for Human Resource Management, March 4, 2008, www.shrm.org/hrnews_published/articles/CMS_025196.asp#P-8_0. In the same survey, 57 percent observed misconduct in the corporate world, while 56 percent observed misconduct in government.

29 Kevin Donovan, "Charity Scams Bust Public Trust," *The Star*, June 2, 2007, www.thestar.com/news/article/220756.

30 National Kidney Foundation Singapore, nkfs.org; VisionSpring, www.visionspring.org/home/home.php; Aravind Eye Care System, www.aravind.org.

Chapter 5

Social Enterprises

Fulfilling the Promise of Social Enterprise

JON HUGGETT

Visiting Fellow, Skoll Centre for Social Entrepreneurship,
Oxford University

Social enterprises are in vogue. The promise of delivering both social impact and financial sustainability has excited many within and outside the social sector. The social enterprise movement is also bringing together the social and business sectors in new ways.

However, to date, most social enterprises have floundered. It is hard to meet more than one bottom line at the same time. Business and social sector leaders have come to social enterprises underestimating the challenges of the other sector. And capital for scaling has been scarce.

Tackling these challenges with the right strategies, the right people, and the right capital will, hopefully, result in a new generation of successful social enterprises.

S ocial enterprises are in vogue. The promise of generating both financial and social returns has excited many across the social sector as well as the business sector and governments.

There is a wealth of blogs, articles, conferences, and books about this phenomenon, while business schools are adding the subject to their curricula.

Many charities are now looking to social enterprises for fresh sources of earned income. Over 700 social enterprises are listed on ClearlySo, the self-styled "global hub for social business, social enterprise, and social investment."[1] The UK Social Enterprise Coalition lists about 300 members.[2] The US-based Social Enterprise Alliance lists over 100 members.[3]

Foundations, social investors, and businessmen are providing seed capital and other funding.

Even governments are looking to social enterprise for solutions. President Obama's Office of Social Innovation and Civic Participation created a Social Innovation Fund to help social enterprises scale.[4] The British government created a Social Enterprise Strategy, a Social Enterprise Investment Fund, and a Social Enterprise Day.[5] Similarly, the Singaporean government has a Social Enterprise Fund and recently kicked off a Social Enterprise Association.[6]

However, beneath the boom—and what some call hype[7]—of social enterprises, there is confusion about what they are and whether they are, in fact, delivering the goods. To fulfill the promise, we need a clearer understanding of social enterprises and the framework within which they work.

Framing the Social Enterprise Space

Beyond the notion that social enterprises are about delivering financial and social impact, what constitutes a social enterprise is not well understood or agreed on—this, despite an abundance of conferences and literature that seek to explain what social enterprises are or should be.

Basic definitions such as "a business with a social mission" or "a nonprofit with earned-income strategy" can include a large range of charities and businesses. And, some social enterprises are for-profit entities while others are nonprofits.

The Social–Business Hybrid Spectrum

Kim Alter's magisterial typology[8] places social enterprises at the "intersection of business and traditional nonprofit" with a "balance of mission and market," and lays out a "Hybrid Spectrum" as shown in Figure 5.1.

Figure 5.1 The Social–Business Hybrid Spectrum

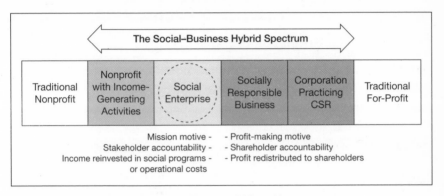

Organizations are arrayed on the hybrid spectrum according to their motive, accountability, and use of income. On the left of the spectrum are nonprofits, some with commercial activities to fund social programs, but whose main motive is to accomplish their social mission. On the right of the spectrum are for-profits that may create social value, but whose main motive is making profit for shareholders.

On the far left of the spectrum are Traditional Nonprofits funded almost entirely by donations and grants. Examples of such charities are Médecins Sans Frontières and the Juvenile Diabetes Research Foundation.[9]

Nonprofits with Income-Generating Activities get paid for some of their goods and services by their beneficiaries (perhaps at discounted rates) or third parties (for goods and services that may or may not be related to the mission of the nonprofit). Oxfam UK, for example, receives over half of its revenue from contracting and trading, not donations. Its famous shops have annual revenue of over £77 million (US$113 million).[10]

On the far right of the spectrum are Traditional For-Profits, whose main or sole purpose is to make a profit.

Corporations Practicing CSR (corporate social responsibility) implement good environmental, social, and governance practices.[11] Most large public companies such as Shell, Walmart, and Vodafone report on their CSR activities.

Socially Responsible Businesses go beyond CSR to make the world a better place. For example, Ben & Jerry's claims a "progressive, nonpartisan social mission" and its profits go to its shareholders.[12]

At the center of the spectrum are Social Enterprises, which aim for social impact with programs that pay their own way.

Levels of Social–Business Integration

Alter's typology also sorts social enterprises by the level of integration of their social and business activities. As shown in Figure 5.2, enterprise activities may be "embedded," "integrated," or "external" to the social programs.

Figure 5.2 Levels of Integration between Social and Business Activities of a Social Enterprise

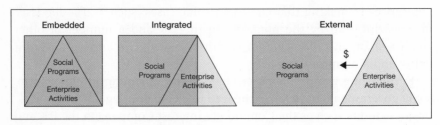

Source: Kim Alter, "Social Enterprise Typology," Virtue Ventures, www.4lenses.org/setypology.

"Embedded" social enterprises have the same activities for both social and business goals. Examples include NURCHA, which has financed the building of over 250,000 homes for a million people in South Africa,[13] and Juma Ventures, which provides jobs and training to disadvantaged youth.[14]

Embedded programs can develop impressive scale. BRAC is a US$0.5 billion nongovernment organization (NGO) in Bangladesh that operates a wide range of social enterprises, including a microfinance institution serving 8.5 million borrowers and schools educating over a million children. BRAC has expanded operations to other countries in Asia and to Africa. Only 27 percent of its revenue is contributed by donors.[15]

"Integrated" social enterprises have different social and business activities which share capabilities. For example, Girl Scout Cookies has supported Girl Scouts in the United States for over 80 years while, at the same time, providing a large and free distribution system for the cookies.[16] Oxfam shops compete with lower costs of labor and goods from volunteers and donations.[17]

"External" social enterprises separate the business and social aspects and often lack synergy. For example, some philanthropic business leaders have pledged profits to charity. Newman's Own is a US for-profit co-founded by the late actor Paul Newman that makes and sells food products and, to date, has contributed over US$300 million to various charities.[18] The Children's Investment Fund Foundation is a UK charity that supports a range of causes in the developing world; its annual funding of over £300 million (US$441 million) comes from the hedge fund of one of the founders of the charity.[19]

For-Profit or Nonprofit Entities

Most legal jurisdictions distinguish for-profit from nonprofit entities, with different legislation governing each. Social enterprises can choose either side or straddle both. The box on the next page, "Choosing between 'For-Profit' and 'Nonprofit'," describes the considerations by many social enterprises in making that choice. In some cases, such as *The Big Issue* (a magazine sold by the homeless in the UK and a number of other countries), organizations embrace both by having two arms: a for-profit entity and a nonprofit entity.[20]

Recognizing the problems of identity and operating in either form, some governments have taken the lead to create new legal hybrid social-business forms such as the Community Interest Company in the UK and the Low-profit Limited Liability Company (L3C) in the US.[21]

Hype and Reality

The wave of interest in the social enterprise movement is whipping up frothy language of "new paradigms," "magic bullets," and "innovative models" that echoes the hype and false hopes at the height of the dot-com boom a decade ago.

Skeptics have raised many questions about whether social enterprises can deliver on the twin promises of financial sustainability and social impact.

A 2007 study by Seedco finds that "the notion that nonprofit social ventures can be purely self-sustaining has not been borne out by real world experience."[29] Instead, the report points out that "the oft-cited success stories are less cut-and-dried than they appear [and there is] a collective tendency within the field to gloss over the difficulties and limitations of social purpose businesses."

Choosing between "For-Profit" and "Nonprofit"

Social enterprises straddle the boundary between nonprofit and for-profit. Some choose to be a nonprofit organization (NPO). Others prefer to be a regular commercial for-profit. A few started out as NPOs and transformed themselves into for-profits, or ended up with both commercial and nonprofit entities.

Social enterprises can choose to be NPOs to help with their strategy for impact and open the doors to philanthropic capital. For example, Kiva, the first online peer-to-peer microfinance marketplace, has chosen to be a 501(c)(3) nonprofit (a charity under the US Internal Revenue Code). Despite offers from venture capitalists to turn it into a for-profit, it has remained a nonprofit. Its status has brought it donations from users, *pro bono* employees, and free advertising from YouTube, Google, Yahoo, and others.[22] Similarly, Nicholas Negroponte, the founder of One Laptop Per Child, remarked that the organization's nonprofit status had opened doors to over US$40 million worth of philanthropic support.[23] The Bridgespan Group, a spin-off of consulting powerhouse Bain & Company, chose to be a nonprofit to help the social sector as an insider.

Other social enterprises choose to be for-profits to raise private capital or to simplify business. They may distinguish between their commercial customers and their "silent clients"—the end beneficiaries.[24] Examples include Calvert Investments (a leader in socially responsible investments), Cafédirect (a premier Fairtrade company), and Virgance (a venture fund/incubator for early stage mission-driven companies).[25] Tony Barclay of DAI, a US$300 million international consulting firm for development projects, argues that its for-profit structure has helped DAI do more for the developing world by allowing it to work with both public and private sector clients, as well as to compete on a commercial basis.[26]

Some social enterprises start off as NPOs and convert to for-profit entities in order to scale. For example, India's SKS Microfinance grew from an NPO serving 2,000 borrowers in 2001 to a for-profit organization with 4.7 million customers in 2009.[27] Compartamos, a Mexican nonprofit, converted from an NPO to a for-profit in 2000 to raise private capital; in 2007, it raised US$467 million in an initial public offering.

Microfinance offers good examples of how social enterprises can flourish as NPOs or as for-profit organizations. Muhammad Yunus, founder of Grameen Bank, has kept the bank a nonprofit. He argues that it is immoral to make money off the poor. Michael Chu of ACCION counter-argues that the way to meet the financial needs of the poor at consumer-friendly rates is to bring in well-funded competition.[28]

Another study by The Bridgespan Group concluded that "despite the hype, earned income accounts for only a small share of funding in most nonprofit domains, and few of the ventures actually make money."[30] The study found that 71 percent of the ventures that received philanthropic funding were unprofitable, 24 percent reported profits, and 5 percent stated they were breaking even. Even then, "of those that claimed they were profitable, half did not fully account for indirect costs such as allocations of general overhead or senior management time."

Even supporters are cautious. Jim Schorr, who started Juma Ventures, a social enterprise to help provide jobs and training to disadvantaged youths, admitted that "the first generation of social enterprise has failed to create both social and financial value."[31]

Why Social Enterprises Fail

Running a social enterprise is not easy and it can be hard to scale. Many fail to overcome the three big challenges of strategy, people, and capital.

The challenge of strategy for social enterprises is the challenge of multiple bottom lines. Like any business, a social enterprise has to make its financial numbers. And like any nonprofit, it must deliver on its mission. Social entrepreneurs hope to do both at the same time. In practice, strategies for different goals can conflict. Larry Summers, Director of the White House's National Economic Council, commented that "[i]t is hard in this world to do well. It is hard to do good. When I hear a claim that an institution is going to do both, I reach for my wallet. You should too."[32]

Social enterprises need people who can drive both business success and social impact; however, leaders coming to social enterprise from either business or nonprofits can underestimate the challenges of the other sector.

What nonprofit leaders often fail to appreciate is how hard it is to make money in business. Many naively look to social enterprise as an easy way to bring in money and avoid fundraising.

Equally, people coming from business are often disappointed at the lack of commercial acumen in their counterparts coming from the nonprofit world. They often fail to appreciate what it takes to drive and scale social impact. Many naively see social enterprise as an easy way to "give back." Some social entrepreneurs have shared with me that the businesspeople on their board "check their brains in at the door." As Jim Collins has noted, in the social sector "business thinking is not the answer."[33]

Social enterprises are businesses and thus require capital. Depending on their legal status, social enterprises may have access to three different kinds of capital: philanthropic capital (like any nonprofit), equity capital (like any business), and debt. However, despite the range of sources, in practice, social enterprises find it hard to raise capital, especially to scale.

Business investors may shun social impact goals, which they may see as hurting financial returns or distracting management. Nonprofit accounting can seem like a "looking-glass world"[34] to regular financial investors.

Philanthropic capital can dry up if a social enterprise is seen to be "making money." And any investor with a clear focus, whether financial or philanthropic, may prefer "pure plays"—simple organizations that are not trying to meet multiple bottom lines.

Making Social Enterprises Work

As the dot-com boom and bust has passed, some internet start-ups such as Google, eBay, and Amazon have not just survived but have gone on to become great businesses. Similarly, while most social enterprises have struggled to make both social and business ends work, some are already scaling as they deliver on the dual promise of social and financial returns. Programs such as Breakthrough are helping social enterprises scale.[35]

These experiences provide valuable clues about what will make social enterprises work well and how they should scale. The themes that emerge echo the fundamentals for other successful organizations: the right strategies, the right people, and the right capital.

Right Strategies

Social enterprises need strategies to deliver both social impact and business success.

A strategy for social impact enables a social enterprise to fulfill its core mission. Founded on a clear mission, and "intended impact," it can win support from beneficiaries, employees, philanthropists, and even regulators.[36]

A strategy for business success enables a social enterprise to create value in a market against competitors that are there purely for profit. Social enterprises can draw on decades of thinking—for example, from strategy firms such as BCG, Bain, and Monitor.[37]

Moreover, social enterprises have a further strategic challenge—to ensure that these two sets of strategies work in harmony and not in conflict. It is not enough to balance the sometimes conflicting needs of the two strategies; the social enterprise needs to integrate them.

Integrating the two sets of strategies requires minimizing any trade-offs and maximizing the synergies. Figure 5.3 illustrates how high-performing social enterprises should achieve this.

Figure 5.3 Stakeholders Value Options

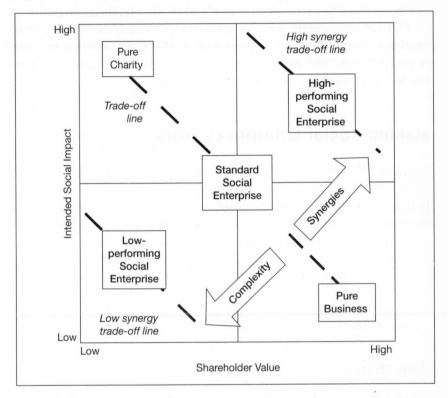

Strategies for social impact and business success can get in the way of each other. A social impact goal of giving jobs to disadvantaged people puts the social enterprise at a disadvantage in competition with for-profits that do not have such hiring restrictions. A financial goal of profitable lending might divert a microfinance institution from where it can have the most social impact. Worse, the complexity of trying to do well while doing good can push up overhead costs.

Social enterprises can seek synergies between social and business strategies among:

- Social impact clients, who are the beneficiaries being served
- Business customers, who pay for services and programs

- Social impact constituents, the supporters who volunteer, advocate, and donate
- Capabilities or shared costs
- Capital and its sources.

Synergies can be within categories—such as overhead that can support both the business strategy and the social impact strategy—or between them. For example, supporters of a social enterprise can help lower costs for the business strategy by volunteering their time. Business customers may prefer to buy from a social enterprise that supports a cause they admire. Good branding can help in all categories: It can help build trust with clients, attract business customers, cement constituent commitment, attract better or cheaper resources, and secure capital.

Right People

To develop and execute an integrated strategy, social enterprises need leaders that can lead in both social and business sectors.

Finding people who are fluent in the language and workings of both the business and social sectors is tough. There is, however, an emerging new cohort of socially minded entrepreneurs that have both sets of skills. Even if many of today's social enterprises fail, their leaders will learn, grow stronger, and live to lead again.

Such entrepreneurs often assemble a team of people from across the spectrum: businesspeople without much experience of the third sector, and activists with little experience of business. If both business and social skills cannot be embedded in each leader, they can be distributed among the team. In many global NPOs, leadership is already highly distributed.[38]

A coherent leadership team needs clear agreement on impact goals, so each member of the team can then make decisions. Without this clarity, focus is lost or too many decisions bottleneck on too few people. Worse, managers forget impact goals and default to budgets, so the social enterprise fails in its mission. Achieving clarity on impact can take time: It is not uncommon to have 20 or more iterations. Yet, the time invested is paid back with good decisions made quickly and efficiently.

While there are few people who are yet fluent in both business and social languages, recruiters often find "hidden talent" for social enterprise. Many businesspeople have experience of the social sector outside of work; for example, through volunteering on a board. Many social sector leaders have managed budgets much tighter than successful businesspeople have. Social enterprise is a great place for people to develop all of their talents.

A coherent team will develop all of its members: businesspeople learn how to be effective in the social sector, and activists develop commercial acumen. The risk is that neither seeks to learn from the other, but tries to convert the other. When businesspeople and activists focus only on their narrow perspectives, they can end up engaged in a dialogue of the deaf.

Right Capital

Even though social enterprises can, in theory, access the three different kinds of capital—philanthropic, equity, and debt—in practice, it can be hard to secure each.

While philanthropic capital can appear to be "free" as it does not require a return, in the strict sense of the word, it can often be expensive to secure. Fundraising can take up well over half of the time of a nonprofit leader. Donations from foundations can come with more onerous reporting requirements than shareholders might demand.

For-profit equity investment requires returns and accountability. Responsible investors may demand lower returns but more accountability.

Debt can be tricky to secure if banks, for example, see an enterprise with a thin base of equity, or find the entity hard to analyze.

To build the right capital base, social enterprises need to meet the needs of each investor. They do not always get a free lunch for being a social enterprise. When looking to scale, many face a funding gap.

Fortunately, hybrids of patient capital are emerging as new forms of social finance. Philanthropists have set up funds with the flexibility to make a range of investments, such as the Soros Economic Development Fund.[39] Governments have set up funds for scaling social enterprises. And a wave of innovation is creating new investment vehicles to help scale social enterprises.[40]

The Bottom Line

Social enterprises promise both social impact and financial sustainability, while socially minded entrepreneurs bring together both business and social sectors, learning from each and helping to transform both.

The next generation of social enterprise can build on the lessons of the first generation. With the right strategies, the right people, and the right capital, they can deliver, at scale, the promise of social and financial returns.

Endnotes

1   www.clearlyso.com.

2   www.socialenterprise.org.uk.

3   www.se-alliance.org.

4   www.whitehouse.gov/blog/What-Is-the-Social-Innovation-Fund.

5   www.cabinetoffice.gov.uk/third_sector/social_enterprise/social_enterprise_day.aspx.

6   The Social Enterprise Fund is now called the Comcare Enterprise Fund and has an annual budget of S$3 million (US$2 million) for grants to seed social enterprises, www.mcys.gov.sg/web/serv_E_CEF.html. Singapore Social Enterprise Association, www.seassociation.sg.

7   Mike Shoemaker, "Is Social Enterprise Over-Hyped?" *Social Earth*, September 12, 2009, www.socialearth.org/is-social-enterprise-over-hyped.

8   Kim Alter, "Social Enterprise Typology," Virtue Ventures, www.virtueventures.com/setypology.

9   Médecins Sans Frontières, www.msf.org; Juvenile Diabetes Research Foundation, www.jdrf.org.

10   From Oxfam's 2008/2009 annual report: £65.7 million (US$99 million) from trading sales of donated goods, and £12.0 million (US$18 million) from trading sales of purchased goods. See www.oxfam.org.uk/resources/downloads/reports/annualreview200708.pdf.

11   See Chapter 12, "CSR: Towards moral capitalism," by Stephen Young.

12   Ben & Jerry's Mission Statement at www.benjerry.com/activism/mission-statement/.

13   NURCHA in South Africa has financed the building of 250,000 homes for the poor, and created many jobs for people who had been disadvantaged under apartheid, by funding small entrepreneurial builders, www.csi.edu.au/uploads/31642/ufiles/Lecture%20Series%20No.%206%20-%20Inaugural%20John%20B%20Reid%20Lecture.pdf; http://sedfny.org/portfolio/companies/nurcha.html.

14   Juma Ventures, www.jumaventures.net; Jim Schorr, "Social Enterprise 2.0," *Stanford Social Innovation Review*, Summer 2006.

15   BRAC Annual Report, 2008, www.brac.net/useruploads/files/BRAC%20Annual%20Report%20-%202008.pdf.

16   www.girlscouts.org/program/gs_cookies/cookie_history/early_years.asp.

17   www.oxfam.org.uk/get_involved/volunteer/shop.html.

18 www.newmansown.com.

19 Ian Wylie, "The New New Philanthropists," managementtoday.com, October 1, 2007, www.managementtoday.co.uk/news/741088/the-new-new-philanthropists.

20 *The Big Issue* in the UK"offers homeless and vulnerably housed people the opportunity to earn a legitimate income" and it is both a limited company and a registered charity, www.bigissue.com.

21 Further details of the various new legal organizational forms being created are provided in the box on "Hybrid Social–Business Organizations" in Chapter 18, "Social Finance: Financing change, changing finance," by Jed Emerson.

22 Bethany Coates and Garth Saloner, "The Profit in Nonprofit," *Stanford Social Innovation Review*, Summer 2009.

23 Negroponte made this comment in a speech at the Social Enterprise Conference organized by Harvard Business School and Harvard Kennedy School in February 2010, www .socialenterpriseconfernce.org.

24 Henrik Skovby, the head of Dalberg Global Development Advisors (www.dalberg .com), suggested to me that a for-profit structure enabled his firm to act more effectively globally for the "silent client"—the end beneficiary of Dalberg's work in the developing world.

25 Calvert Investments in the US makes sustainable and responsible investments, www .calvertgroup.com; Virgance, a San Francisco for-profit, organizes environmental activist campaigns such as "One Block off the Grid" and "Carrotmobs." See "Change We Can Profit From," *The Economist*, January 29, 2009.

26 Tony Barclay, "DAI's Focus on Sustainability in Development Projects" (presentation), October 31, 2008, www.sais-jhu.edu/bin/i/c/SAISPresentationTonyBarclay.ppt#256.

27 Shloka Nath, "At the Crossroads," *Forbes India*, September 27, 2009, www.forbes .com/2009/09/25/crossroads-vikram-akula-sks-microfinance-suresh-gurumani-forbes-india.html.

28 Richard Rosenberg, "Muhammad Yunus, and Michael Chu debate commercialization," Private Sector Development Blog, October 14, 2008, www.psdblog.worldbank.org/ psdblog/2008/10/mohammed-yunus.html.

29 Seedco is a US"national intermediary dedicated to advancing economic opportunities." The report on social enterprises is prepared by Seedco Policy Centre, a research unit connected to Seedco. See *The Limits of Social Enterprise: A field study and case analysis* (New York: Seedco Policy Center, 2007).

30 William Foster and Jeffrey Bradach, "Should Nonprofits Seek Profits?" *Harvard Business Review*, February 2005.

31 Jim Schorr, "Social Enterprise 2.0," *Stanford Social Innovation Review*, Summer 2006.

32 Larry Summers is the Director of the White House's National Economic Council for President Barack Obama. His comment was widely quoted. See Kevin Drum, "The problem with hybrids," *CBS News*, July 17, 2008, www.cbsnews.com/stories/2008/07/17/ politics/animal/main4267791.shtml.

33 Jim Collins, *Good to Great and the Social Sectors: A monograph to accompany good to great on nonprofits* (New York: HarperCollins, 2005).

34 For example, Clara Miller pointed out the many ways that nonprofit accounting can mislead investors, especially if they are not familiar with the sector. See Clara Miller, "The Looking-Glass World of Nonprofit Money," *Nonprofit Quarterly*, Winter 2005, www .store.nonprofitquarterly.org/lowoofnomoma.html.

35 Breakthrough was founded by Permira and CAN to offer financial investment and business support to established social enterprises so that they can overcome obstacles to growth. It was launched in 2005. It first invested in four social enterprises with a combination of equity-like capital and mentoring from private equity and social sector professionals. All four achieved significant growth in revenue (more than 20 percent a year) and social impact (more than 30 percent a year) over the first two years of the fund's life. Its Breakthrough Fund II showed that for an average investment of £142,000 (US$200,000), there is an average 29 percent increase in social impact and 22 percent increase in revenue (versus 8 percent average for charities). See www.breakthroughfund .org.uk.

36 For articles on social strategies, see Susan Colby, Paul Carttar, and Nan Stone, "Zeroing in on Impact," *Stanford Social Innovation Review*, Fall 2003; and Jeff Bradach, Tom Tierney, and Nan Stone, "Delivering on the Promise of Nonprofits," *Harvard Business Review*, December 2008.

37 Books on business strategy include Bruce D. Henderson, *Henderson on Corporate Strategy* (New York: HarperCollins, 1979); Michael E. Porter, *Competitive Strategy* (New York: Free Press, 1980); and Chris Zook with James Allen, *Profit from the Core* (Boston: Harvard Business Press, 2001).

38 Jon Huggett, Katie Smith Milway, and Kirk Kramer, "Increasing Effectiveness in Global NGO Networks," *Bridgespan*, June 3, 2009.

39 www.sedfny.org.

40 These new forms of social finance are explored in Chapter 18, "Social Finance: Financing change, changing finance," by Jed Emerson.

Chapter 6

Social Entrepreneurship

Of Pattern Changers and Changemakers

CHRIS CUSANO

Change Leader, ASEAN, Ashoka: Innovators for the Public

Over the last 30 years, social entrepreneurship has evolved from an arcane concept recognized by a few thought leaders to a widespread phenomenon embraced by people worldwide.

What distinguishes social entrepreneurs from other social leaders is their pursuit of pattern change. They seek to change the rules, systems, relationships, economics, incentives, and behaviors in order to uplift the lives of their specific clientele in society.

Inspired and instructed by these social entrepreneurs, people from all walks of life are becoming changemakers themselves. Such a vibrant citizen sector will ensure that society distills its highest empathetic ethics into the real hard stuff of social change.

Y our child is falling behind in school and his teachers either do not seem to care or do not have sufficient resources to deal with him. The river that runs through your town has gone from clear to caustic in one generation. Farmers and fisher-folk seem to get poorer every year, even as they supply more food to a hungry population.

Nothing in this litany of individual and societal woes is new. In one form or another, such problems are ubiquitous in modern life. What is new, however, is that a growing number of people are dedicating their careers to finding innovative solutions that tackle society's challenges in new and promising ways.

Increasingly, the world is recognizing that these people—who are called social entrepreneurs—are among the best resources for improving life on Earth. Yet, as recently as 1980, this term was known only to a handful of people. How did the term originate, and how has it been applied?

Origins of the Social Entrepreneur

In 1923, the *New York Times* asked mountaineer George Mallory why he wanted to climb Mount Everest. His pithy retort—"Because it's there"—has become a stock rationale for taking action that one sees as so obviously necessary and compelling that it needs no further explanation. Mallory was a pioneer. His sense of what was obvious, what was necessary, and what was possible, was ahead of his time.

Another pioneer, Bill Drayton, was in a similar position in 1980 when he founded Ashoka: Innovators for the Public.[1] As a student of history, he knew that social entrepreneurs—though, of course, that was not what they were called—had existed in all societies throughout the ages. Individually, their positive contributions to the quality of life were well known and well documented. However, no one had ever recognized people such as Florence Nightingale, Mahatma Gandhi, Rowland Hill, Jean Monnet, and John Muir as a social phenomenon in and of itself.[2]

To Drayton, however, it was obvious. There was an unrecognized personality type that seemed to occur naturally, and rarely, in every society. Every once in a while, a person emerges who assigns himself or herself the responsibility of helping an entire society improve its quality of life in some fundamental way. They spend their lives in a relentless effort to change the way their society works in concrete and practical terms. They organize others, propose new strategies, rearrange resources, start new professions, found institutions, lobby political decision makers, build popular support, and endure all the vagaries and hardships of struggling against the status quo.

Eventually, the efforts of these people prevail as drastic steps forward in social progress: the profession of nursing and the sanitary revolution (Nightingale); nonviolent social movements for human rights and justice (Gandhi); the postage stamp (Hill); the European Union (Monnet); and wilderness conservation (Muir).

Drayton coined the term "social entrepreneur" to describe such a person. Business entrepreneurs envision new possibilities for producers and consumers, change people's expectations of themselves and others, and create new value by introducing products, services, and transactions that make the economy more productive. Social entrepreneurs do essentially the same thing, but their goals are not commercial.

The currency of social entrepreneurship, and its "profit," so to speak, is social change. To social entrepreneurs, change means a fundamental shift in how society deals with an issue. Change must always go beyond raising awareness of a problem, or offering services to a finite number of clients; these may be necessary steps in building a social solution, but they are not sufficient to ensure lasting change.

Recognizing the Social Entrepreneur

All those involved in the social sector are concerned with social change. What distinguishes social entrepreneurs from other social activists and leaders is their pursuit of "pattern change." They want to change the rules, systems, relationships, economics, incentives, and ethical values that underpin human behavior insofar as that behavior relates to the social entrepreneurs' particular area of concern. This, of course, is an immensely complex and difficult set of tasks, which is why social entrepreneurs are rarely found and are often misunderstood.

What is pattern change? In its work searching for social entrepreneurs worldwide, Ashoka identified five general kinds of pattern change that characterize the vision and the efforts of most social entrepreneurs who are elected to be Ashoka Fellows.[3] The nicknames for the five types of pattern changers are:

- Architects
- Master Organizers

- Matchmakers
- Maverick Reformers
- Invisible Hands.

These five categories are meant to be descriptive in nature, rather than normative. They are not the criteria for selecting social entrepreneurs, nor are they necessarily the only ones that exist.

Architects

The first kind of social entrepreneur, the Architect, has a vision that entails creating an entirely new field of social work. The Architect's vision for pattern change requires the birth of new professions, new institutions, and new economic transactions.

Architects often stand out for the remarkable insight of their core innovation. For example, Ron Layton founded Light Years IP to promote the idea that intellectual property could be a powerful tool in creating international trade that would alleviate poverty in some of the world's poorest countries.[4] Just as corporations earn money through the sale and license of their intangible assets—brands, trademarks, designs—the world's poor farmers and small producers can also benefit from owning and protecting such assets.

In the past, cooperatives of Ethiopian coffee farmers, despite growing some of the world's best coffee, were forced by market dynamics to sell their beans at very low prices to the long chain of middlemen who would eventually deliver the beans to European and American consumers. The coffee retailed at a premium, touting its origins in Harar or YirgaCheffe, two of Ethiopia's famous coffee-growing regions. Layton asked: Why should not the farmers actually control the use of those geographical designations as their unique intellectual property?

To pursue his idea, Layton started recruiting the participation of professional marketing and branding specialists, initially on a *pro-bono* basis. He recognized the importance of major development institutions in incorporating intellectual property into their agendas. So he began advising the World Bank on this issue. However, the idea was so new and different that there was an immediate need for examples. Thus, Layton set up Light Years IP to develop and showcase a range of successful cases from around the world.

In 2004, the World Bank published Layton's arguments for reducing poverty through intellectual property protection, giving a platform—and stamp of approval—to his ideas.[5] The real test came only several years later when Ethiopian farmers challenged the purchasing policies of global coffee empire Starbucks. The farmers were earning between 60 cents and a dollar for coffee that was being retailed at US$26 per pound in Europe and the US. Aside from the argument of equity, what leverage did the farmers have in asking for a bigger slice of the pie? A very public confrontation took shape with Ethiopia pursuing a trademarking initiative to compel Starbucks and other distributors to pay a licensing fee for the regional names associated with fine coffees. Starbucks was initially prepared to mount a legal battle, but the image of a major public company fighting with desperately poor African farmers would have been a potential public-relations disaster. In 2007, Starbucks and the Ethiopian government reached a licensing agreement that gave Ethiopia greater control of how Starbucks used the regional brands.

Ron Layton is an Architect with a vision for pattern change on a global scale: his concern—inequity in international trade—is global by nature and therefore demands a global solution. An Architect of a new field of social work has to work on many aspects of the system at once, educating, reforming, demonstrating, and spreading the word in order to stimulate a variety of institutions to change at the same time, thus supporting and reinforcing one another. Architects take on enormously large and difficult challenges that might require a lifetime or longer to complete.

Master Organizers

The scope of the vision of the Master Organizer is quite different from that of the Architect. Master Organizers focus on helping to bring true citizenship to a segment of the population that has suffered from systematic discrimination. This could mean an ethnic or religious group, or a gender group, or anyone who is otherwise unable to take an equal place in society.

While Architects devote themselves to developing new systems at the macro level, Master Organizers are completely focused on the lives of their particular clients and the structural obstacles they confront. For example, Elango Rangaswamy is a social entrepreneur from Chennai whose work in developing the governance, self-reliance, and political representation of Dalit villages has earned him widespread acclaim.[6]

Rangaswamy's work is not focused on a single penetrating idea or solution—the problems confronting the people he serves are too complex and intractable to be cured by any magic formula. Instead, through a variety of activities, he is strengthening his clients' ability to respond to the many obstacles they face. The Dalits, also known as the Untouchables, are a class of Indian citizens who have historically been excluded from the caste system, meaning that they are considered to be below even the lowest-caste manual laborers. They suffer crippling discrimination from this social prejudice.

Rangaswamy started by running training programs for newly elected village *panchayat*, or village council heads from Dalit villages, and selecting the most promising ones as model leaders. He trained them to create and implement successful development projects in their villages, such as improving housing conditions, combating illegal moneylenders and alcohol vendors, improving roads and irrigation, and providing education and job training for the young.

Rangaswamy's work has made a tangible impact.[7] In 2007, the group of villages in his home district declared themselves to be "hut-free," meaning that all traditional poor-quality grass-and-mud huts had been replaced by sturdier and cleaner brick houses. Under the leadership of Rangaswamy's village heads, roads have been constructed and irrigation trenches dug without the customary draining of budgets to local middlemen and bribery. Rangaswamy's groups saved as much as 60 percent on public-works budgets; they then plowed the savings back into more community projects. In a comprehensive village development program, he had developed more local production and value-adding processes for local produce, creating local jobs and helping money to circulate among a small cluster of villages. As a result, skilled labor in the village has increased from virtually none to 15 percent of the total workforce.

Essentially, Rangaswamy is an innovation machine, churning out and implementing solutions to whatever problems his clients have, delivering these solutions through a carefully assembled network of honest, well-trained local leaders. Yet, this responsiveness to real conditions does not mean that Rangaswamy is not pursuing a larger vision. Significant pattern change emerges from the cumulative effect of a whole series of improvements that take place in people's lives. These improvements are not just economic; they also change the identity and dignity that people develop from being full participants in their society.

Matchmakers

While Architects stand out for the innovativeness and enormity of their vision and Master Organizers for their deep identification with a disadvantaged group, Matchmakers are distinguished by the particular cleverness of their approach to problem solving. Essentially, what Matchmakers do is to bring the resources and participation of one group in society to bear on the problems and suffering of another group. In a flash of insight, Matchmakers see affinities that others have not yet seen, and they are able to build organizations and movements based on alliances between groups of people who may never have recognized their potential to work together.

One great example of Matchmaking is Mothers Against Drunk Driving (MADD).[8] In the 1980s, drink-related traffic deaths in the US increased to the point where the number of people killed on American roads each year was equal to the number of American soldiers killed during the entire Vietnam War. Yet, no amount of law enforcement or public-service messaging seemed to help.

One woman, Candy Lightner,[9] whose 13-year old daughter had been killed by a drunk driver, recognized that in their common grief, it was the mothers of the victims who had the strongest drive to combat the problem. She started MADD, which began advocating for stricter enforcement of existing laws, as well as new laws prescribing tougher penalties on drunk drivers. It built student-run programs in high schools and colleges to recruit volunteer sober drivers to shuttle peers who had been drinking. It became a leading advocate for a nationwide minimum drinking age of 21. As MADD grew, it became a partner to the police, to schools, to the courts, and to legislators across the country. MADD is a grassroots movement *par excellence*. It focuses the efforts of a few citizens—outsiders to the system—to mobilize broad support and essentially completely change the way that the society views and deals with a hitherto intractable social problem—in this case, drunk driving.

MADD's Matchmaking strategy and efforts have had a huge impact. The organization reports that since 1980, the year MADD was founded, alcohol-related traffic fatalities have decreased nearly 50 percent, from over 30,000 to under 15,500, and that MADD has helped save over 383,000 lives.[10]

Maverick Reformers

Unlike many of the other categories, Maverick Reformers often take on a challenge in which they have complete professional and technical expertise. True to their name, Maverick Reformers take on a dysfunctional public system or service and make it perform better, more transparently, or more justly.

Reformers often spend the earlier part of their careers within the system, and then step outside it in order to improve it, using their intimate knowledge of the bureaucracy and their personal relationships to maintain access while working from the outside. A classic Reformer is Arvind Kejriwal, a former tax examiner who left India's civil service to spearhead a national movement, and then an international movement, for the right to information.[11]

As an insider to one of the world's largest and sometimes most inscrutable bureaucracies, Kejriwal knew first-hand how citizens were put at a disadvantage when dealing with the machinery of the state. Thus, when a citizen applied for a building permit, once the application was lodged, all subsequent steps were in the purview of the government alone; to the applicant, the file had fallen into a deep black box. Such a lack of transparency creates ideal conditions for corruption. Kejriwal saw the opportunity to combat the corruption by arming citizens with the legal rights and procedural tools to unlock the black box and open it to the daylight.

When the Indian federal *Right to Information Act* was passed in 2005, Kejriwal and his colleagues scored a major victory for Indian democracy. In 2008, of 51,000 cases filed with the courts seeking access to information, 70 percent were ruled in favor of the citizens. This number represents a dramatic change in the relationship between the people and the bureaucracy.

The right to information goes beyond individual cases. How government contracts are awarded, how public services are delivered, and how social welfare benefits are distributed are all areas of collective public concern that can be made more transparent with the right to information. In a sense, all Maverick Reformers are in the transparency business, turning the black boxes of institutional systems into citizen-oriented service providers.

Invisible Hands

The fifth kind of social entrepreneur, the Invisible Hand, is someone who changes the dynamics of an economic system to address structural inequities. These people tend not to be widely known, preferring to focus their energy on a few calculated interventions with the potential for enormous social benefit.

One such Invisible Hand is Sasa Vucinic, a Serbian journalist who left his native country during the outbreak of war in the 1990s. Horrified by how the press was being manipulated, he began thinking about how the independence of media was being compromised worldwide. Eventually, he founded the Media Development Loan Fund (MDLF)[12] to correct what he perceived to be a fundamental flaw in the media industry: the trend toward consolidation of ownership, and therefore a homogenization of news. Unlike other products for public consumption, Vucinic felt that news is not just a commercial good, but a fundamental element of democracy. When media is monopolized by one or two giant companies, the public suffers. But how do we deal with the real market forces of the media industry while safeguarding the public interest in having diverse, independent sources of news?

MDLF provides financing to small media outlets around the world, such as radio stations, newspapers, and independent printing presses. By offering soft loans and patient capital, drawn from philanthropic funds and for-profit investors, MDLF helps small media outlets remain commercially viable in an otherwise hostile marketplace.

Vucinic and other Invisible Hands create pattern-changing solutions that benefit people who will never know that they are benefiting from such investments. Newspaper readers in Moscow and radio audiences in Jakarta will never have heard of MDLF, or of Vucinic himself. Nevertheless, the Invisible Hand is not simply an economist or nice-guy investor; he has the citizen in mind at all times, and has the patience and capacity to deliver pattern change by working with intermediary organizations which, in Vucinic's case, are the media, a daily fixture of the citizen's life.

MDLF measures its impact through the success of the independent media outlets it supports. The results suggest that Vucinic's intervention is key to helping these companies survive. According to MDLF: "In 2008, more than 32 million people in developing democracies got their news from 37 MDLF clients [and] after five years with MDLF, current clients on average have increased their sales by 370 percent."[13]

The Patterns of Pattern Changers

While these few kinds of pattern change represent some of the trends in social entrepreneurship, the categories should carry a warning label: They should not be applied too literally or with too much zeal. One mistake would be to declare that only these five kinds of pattern change exist, to the exclusion of other promising forms of social entrepreneurship that might emerge in the future.

Another would be to see them as mutually exclusive. Can an Architect also be a Matchmaker? Can a Master Organizer have elements of the Maverick Reformer? Why not? While the categories may be useful as descriptors of the kind of action needed to produce various forms of pattern change, they also depict a complex and messy world that is always overlapping, evolving, and adapting.

Despite these cautions, from these five categories, we can draw a few general conclusions about social entrepreneurship.

First, each social entrepreneur is clearly working with, and working on behalf of, an identifiable clientele. Social entrepreneurs, therefore, are not activists-at-large who appear in the public eye to advocate or protest whatever the issue of the day might be. While their activities may be diverse, they have a clear focus.

Secondly, pattern change is always an iterative process that can be measured in concrete milestones toward large, ambitious goals. Architects, Organizers, Matchmakers, Reformers, and Invisible Hands build their social impact one piece at a time. Elango Rangaswamy did not declare victory when he opened his *panchayat* academy—it was a step on his path. Ron Layton did not pack up Light Years IP when he managed to persuade Starbucks to enter into fair trade agreements with Ethiopian farmers; he added that success to his case file and kept working toward his vision. In fact, the first common quality of social entrepreneurs—their commitment and responsiveness to people—is what determines this second characteristic of iteration.

Finally, a true social entrepreneur's primary dedication is not to his own idea or vision, but to the people he seeks to serve. In other words, the focus is the citizen, not the solution.

Beyond the Social Entrepreneur

The rise of the social entrepreneur and the growth of the changemaking organizations that they create are all currents in a dynamic, evolving citizen sector that is changing the very fabric of society at large. The impact of social entrepreneurship goes beyond the social entrepreneurs themselves, to the citizens of society, and even beyond the social sector.

From Persons to People: Everyone a Changemaker

As innovators with pattern-changing social solutions, social entrepreneurs not only drive the sector forward through their own work, but they are also becoming role models for other citizens who wish to improve the world. Inspired and instructed by social entrepreneurs, people from all walks of life are finding their place in the emerging citizen sector. This is another fundamental, if subtle, trend that is underway: a transition from focusing on the remarkable contributions of individual social entrepreneurs to an understanding of social innovation as a mass movement itself.

An analogy may be in order. Regardless of the sport, all societies love their professional athletes. India has its cricketers; Brazil, its football heroes; America, its baseball and basketball stars. They are virtuosos at the top of their game, and their impressive ability to run, jump, throw, hit, catch, and kick has earned them their place in popular culture. But a love of sports and admiration for well-tuned athletes are essentially phenomena of observation, of spectacle. A spectator would not enjoy the physical and certain social benefits of exercise by watching others play sports, but rather by heading out to the field or the court or the roadway, and taking part.

However, the popularity of professional sports, personified by world-class athletes, has created the impetus for an enormous amount of amateur participation. Youth sport leagues, midnight basketball programs, company teams, senior Olympics, and local mini-marathons have all evolved as expressions of the general public's love of sport, encouraged by the place that professional sports and athletes occupy in their culture. This is not to say that people exercise because they want to emulate a particular athlete or professional sporting team. Instead, the existence and recognition of professional sports helps create a space in society for participation in athletics, for which people may cite a whole range of additional causes: health, fun, discipline, etc. In the social phenomenon of sports, relatively few famous faces are one catalyst for mass participation.

The same thing is happening with social entrepreneurs. One function of the citizen sector is to identify social entrepreneurs and bring them to public attention. This is an important and necessary educational activity, particularly because the basic ideas and terms for social entrepreneurship are relatively new. By understanding the vision, efforts, struggles, and achievements of individual social entrepreneurs, the world can make more space for them. Thus, the efforts, in recent years, of many organizations such as Echoing Green, the Skoll Foundation, and the Schwab Foundation for

Social Entrepreneurship[14] to promote and support social entrepreneurship are acknowledged as being useful and necessary.

But more important than simply admiring or supporting the work of leading social entrepreneurs, a wide cross-section of society is beginning to emulate them. Social entrepreneurs are becoming role models, and in the expanding light of their public recognition, other citizens are finding their own space in the social sector. More and more, social entrepreneurship is broadening from an interest in persons—the virtuosos—to an interest in ordinary citizens and the role they play in making or amplifying the pattern change started by social entrepreneurs.

An example of how this change is taking place is the emergence of Changemakers.org.[15] The organization came about several years ago as Ashoka sought to understand how it could better use social entrepreneurs and their brilliant innovations to inspire others. One question underpinning the discussion was how citizens can be inspired to see themselves as important actors in improving the world without simply labeling everyone a social entrepreneur, thereby robbing the term of its essential value. But more important, what did society really need? Would a handful of social entrepreneurs be enough to respond to the never-ending onslaught of social problems? Clearly not.

We need a world full of changemakers, a world where all people are empowered with knowledge and skill and opportunity to take action on an issue that they care about. Just as providing the identity "social entrepreneur" allows all those Architects, Matchmakers, and Reformers to explain who they are and what they do, creating the identity "changemaker" helps a much broader group of people not only to identify themselves individually, but to reach out to one another on a common platform.

This is the opportunity Changemakers.org provides. As an online platform, it offers people working on social issues all around the world an opportunity to present their work, learn from each other, and seek partners. To some extent, it is a self-organizing community in which members vote for each other's ideas in competitions and offer comments on what does and does not work. It is also a clearinghouse for people who want to fund social-change work but do not know where to begin sourcing innovations.

Changemakers.org's competitions on preventing domestic violence, improving sanitation, protecting the health of mothers, using sports for social change, nutrition and development, ecotourism, and other topics have leveraged US$40 million for citizen-sector organizations worldwide. Changemakers.org has provided a new arena and a more level playing field for organizations to be rewarded based on their innovation and impact, rather than on their access to traditional funding sources.

From People to Society: Empathetic Ethics

A hundred years from now, how will the emergence of the citizen sector during this period of history be interpreted? Perhaps a better way to ask the question is: How would we like it to be understood?

It is undeniable that social entrepreneurs are taking their place in society and serving as role models for others. An increasing number of citizen-sector organizations are coming into existence. New structures for social finance, including social enterprise, are also being developed. But all these developments are internal to the citizen sector.

Taking a step back, the larger question is: So what? What, if anything, does the emergence of the citizen sector mean in the context of history and the evolution of social life?

The citizen sector's great contribution to society is its ability to translate particular ethical values into concrete action. If government exists and serves society as a way to organize people to live together, and business serves society as a way to manage resources and productivity, then the citizen sector's role is to ensure that the social systems in which we live reflect certain universal values—the desire for justice, dignity, respect, security, peace, well-being, and the fulfillment of human potential.

In fact, even at this early stage of its evolution, the citizen sector deserves credit for a number of impressive advancements in human life, namely: dramatic improvements in the status and equality of women; advancement and pursuit of human rights worldwide; protection of consumers; the non-violent social mobilization that won India its independence; enacted civil rights and anti-discrimination laws in the US; and enormous advancements in health and education.

What all these movements and achievements have in common is the citizen sector's unique ability to change social patterns by drawing on empathy as a tool for change. If simple charity is a response based on sympathy, then pattern-changing social innovation, aimed at correcting society's systemic flaws, is a response that is empowered by the fundamental principle of empathy. If business operates on the principle of efficient allocation of resources, and government on the rational distribution of power, then the citizen sector operates on the productive use of empathy.

Linking all the different kinds of social entrepreneurs together— Architects, Master Organizers, Matchmakers, Maverick Reformers, Invisible Hands, and others yet to be named and described—is their ability to pinpoint where social systems are failing because of a deficit in empathy, and then to create solutions that patch those holes with empathetic ethics. So, Ron Layton's response to the inherent unfairness of international trade is to employ the tool of IP protection, the fairness of which is taken for granted in wealthier consumer countries. Elango Rangaswamy knows that honest and capable village leaders will earn the respect and support of the outside world. MADD simply put a human face on the statistics of avoidable traffic deaths. Arvind Kejriwal elevated the individual citizen's struggle with bureaucracy to a matter of national concern. Sasa Vucinic translated the average citizen's need for independent press into an opportunity for enlightened investors. And Changemakers.org opens up a platform and community for people who aspire to change the world.

So, what is the answer to the great historical "so what?" question of the citizen sector? People will continue to live and die, confronting and doing battle with all the dangers and vagaries of the human condition. But this period of history, in which we are witnessing the rapid growth and development of the citizen sector, ought to be understood as the moment in which society learns to distill its highest empathetic ethics into the real, hard stuff of social change.

Endnotes

1 www.ashoka.org. The story of Bill Drayton, Ashoka, and several social entrepreneurs can be found in: David Bornstein, *How to Change the World: Social entrepreneurs and the power of new ideas* (New York: Oxford University Press, 2004).

2 References abound for each individual. One selected online reference for each is provided here: Florence Nightingale, www.spartacus.schoolnet.co.uk/REnightingale.htm; Mahatma Gandhi, www.mkgandhi-sarvodaya.org; Rowland Hill, www.filahome-stamps .com/stamps/rowland-hill.htm; Jean Monnet, www.biography.com/articles/Jean-Monnet-9411987; John Muir: www.ecotopia.org/ecology-hall-of-fame/john-muir/biography.

3 An Ashoka Fellow is a leading social entrepreneur who has been selected through a rigorous search and qualifying process. There are more than 2,000 Ashoka Fellows around the world.

4 www.lightyearsip.net, www.ashoka.org/node/2987.

5   J. Michael Finger, "Poor People's Knowledge: Helping poor people to earn from their knowledge," World Bank Policy Research Working Paper 3205, February 2004.

6   "The importance of Rangaswamy Elango," *GoodNewsIndia*, May 1, 2003, www .goodnewsindia.com/index.php/Magazine/story/elango-kuṭhambakkam; "Real Heroes: An IITian's pursuit of a stronger India," *IBNLive*, February 24, 2009, www.ibnlive .in.com/news/real-heroes-an-iitians-pursuit-of-a-stronger-india/86160-3-1.html.

7   See www.modelvillageindia.org.in.

8   www.madd.org.

9   www.bookrags.com/biography/candy-lightner.

10   www.madd.org/Victim-Services/Victim-Services/Statistics/AllStats.aspx#STAT_8.

11   www.parivartan.com/home.asp, www.ashoka.org/node/2529.

12   www.mdlf.org.

13   www.mdlf.org/en/main/about/.

14   Echoing Green, www.echoinggreen.org; Skoll Foundation, www.skollfoundation.org; Schwab Foundation for Social Entrepreneurship, www.schwabfound.org.

15   www.changemakers.com.

Capacity Builders

Chapter 7

Capacity Builders

Making Value Visible

SARA OLSEN
Founder, SVT Group

In a commercial marketplace, prices paid for goods are generally accepted as the signal of whether or not value is being created. Imperfect though this signal is, it is a much clearer indication than can be found in the social economy. In the social sector, the prices that beneficiaries pay (if any) are not usually a full reflection of the actual value being provided. In the absence of prices, a great deal of engineering is required to ensure that value is created, recognized, and supported. This is the role capacity builders play in the social sector; yet, they are often its unsung heroes.

Capacity builders seek to increase the impact of individual nonprofit organizations and the social sector as a whole by performing roles as promoters, service providers, industry watchers, and grantmakers. They make efforts to incorporate new business models, technology, and information to improve the impact of social interventions. Recent trends suggest a focus on increasing the impact of these capacity builders themselves.

T he attention of the social sector is invariably on the beneficiaries and those who have made these beneficiaries their calling: the social activists, social entrepreneurs, charities, and other social purpose organizations. At times, the sector turns its attention to volunteers and donors[1] who contribute to social causes. These, then, are the core players making up the supply (donors and volunteers) and demand (social purpose organizations and beneficiaries) sides of the social sector equation.

There is, however, a group of organizations and people that functions as an intermediary to match and balance the supply and demand sides, seeking to increase the overall effectiveness of the players and the sector as a whole. Yet, the role and presence of this group receive disproportionately less attention.

The importance of these intermediaries should not be played down. Intermediaries in the social sector have the unique job of facilitating transactions and outcomes based on many key players' opinions of value—opinions that may differ widely.

An example is in the value perception of programs versus organizational overheads. For a long time, nonprofit organizations (NPOs) have been rightly admired for their passion and financial selflessness in serving their beneficiaries. They go about their mission of addressing society's problems often against heavy odds and with very limited resources. The common approach—mostly not by choice—of NPOs to focus on their programs and on keeping administrative costs low has consequently led to a lack of focus on building the organizational capacity necessary to achieve their aspirations sustainably and effectively. This is reinforced by donors who prefer to fund programs rather than administrative costs. This preference is gradually shifting, with growing numbers of funders recognizing that "excellence in programmatic innovation and implementation are insufficient for nonprofits to achieve lasting results."[2]

This explains why, over time, an industry of capacity builders—intermediaries who seek to build the organizational capacity of individual NPOs, as well as the capacity of the sector itself—has sprung up.

The Intermediaries

Capacity builders are therefore intermediaries who seek to build better structures, discipline, and support among NPOs so that this can translate into better services for the end beneficiaries and a more effective sector overall.

The number and diversity of capacity builders grow in tandem with the development of the social sector. What is present now is a complex and diverse set of players that makes categorization difficult.[3]

For our purposes, a classification based on the roles that these capacity builders play is:

- Promoters
- Service providers
- Watchers
- Grantmakers.

Promoters

Promoters advocate the work of NPOs and the social sector. In the course of performing this duty, promoters also end up being facilitators, and some actually provide broad-based services, although often they do not charge the NPOs for these services directly. This category of actors includes national and international associations and industry advocates for the social sector's development.

Associations are one type of promoter. They are usually membership-based groupings of NPOs that provide visibility, credibility, and networking opportunities; many are broad-based and national in nature. For example, the National Council for Voluntary Organisations and the National Council of Nonprofit Associations are the representative bodies for nonprofits generally in the UK and the US, respectively. Several international federations of NPOs of various kinds have also been formed. The International Council of Voluntary Agencies, for instance, is a global network that brings together humanitarian and human rights groups as an advocacy alliance for humanitarian action.[4]

Associations can also be formed around a narrower constituency of players, such as the American Association of Museums and the Council on Foundations (also in the US); or around a headquarter nonprofit, such as United Way; or around professions and management topics, such as The SROI Network (for the advancement of Social Return On Investment methodology) and the SPM Network (for the advancement of Social Performance Management by microfinance and other social purpose organizations) (both based in the UK but with international purviews).[5] Such groupings provide common platforms for the development and promotion of a common agenda that cuts across organizational boundaries. These organizations seem to be more numerous in the US and the UK, due to the availability of local funding for NPOs registered in these countries.

Industry advocates include the work of applied research centers such as the Abdul Latif Jameel Poverty Action Lab (J-PAL) in the US and the Lien Centre for Social Innovation in Singapore.[6] These centers seek to play an objective role in assessing effectiveness and promoting best and leading practices in the nonprofit sector and beyond.

Service Providers

In the modern economy, all organizations need products and services from other organizations in order to maintain their competitive edge. Many of these are core to the functioning of the organization, such as premises, accounting, and other office support services. Others, such as management consulting and technological support, are more optional but nevertheless can be important.

These services are available to NPOs through service providers in various categories. In some cases, the services are generic (e.g. premises) whether they are used for commercial purposes or by NPOs. In other cases, the services (e.g. consulting) need to take into specific account the nonprofit context.

Some of the service providers are commercial, some are nonprofit, and some have a third hybrid designation which is gaining legal ground in many countries: that of the "social business."[7] Those who are set up as nonprofits to provide the services to other nonprofits do so because they want to be industry insiders aligned with the philosophies and workings of the nonprofit sector. The Bridgespan Group and CompassPoint, for example, are two nonprofits that provide strategy and other consulting support specifically in the nonprofit sector.[8] By contrast, Salesforce.com is a for-profit cloud-based application company which commits 1 percent of each of its product licenses, equity, and employees' paid time to charitable causes.[9]

Service providers can provide their services at full, discounted, or fully subsidized rates, depending upon their funding model and charging philosophy. For example, Computer Troubleshooters, which bills itself as the world's largest computer service franchise, has created a Charity Service Program to provide discounted or donated computer services to NPOs.[10]

As with service providers in other industries, nonprofit service providers can be variable in the quality of their work, especially when they are themselves focused on containing costs. In its survey of the needs of capacity builders, the Conservation Company observed that while a few capacity builders offer excellent services, "a larger number provide services of mixed quality and, like their nonprofit clients, have more work to do to strengthen their own organizational capacity."[11] Capacity builders are not immune from social sector capacity constraints.

Watchers

Watchers critique and rate nonprofit organizations, and set formal and informal benchmarks for nonprofit intervention. More than just monitoring and measuring standards, they also interpret and seek to shape the activities within the dynamic social sector.

Watchers can be very specific to the activities they are monitoring. MAPLight.org, for example, is an NPO that traces the money of political lobbyists and subsequent votes in the US Congress and the state of California. NGOWatch's stated goal is to monitor the activities of NPOs and their impact on public policy.[12]

The more well-known watchers, however, are broad-based rating agencies of nonprofit organizations. They include Charity Navigator, Charity Watch, and GuideStar. They aggregate information about NPOs in their respective countries, and provide performance ratings loosely analogous to the Standard & Poor's of the commercial world.[13]

To date, such ratings entities have focused largely on financial measures rather than social performance, with metrics such as the ratio of overheads to total expenditures. This particular ratio is considered problematic since administrative overhead costs are not correlated with effectiveness strongly, if at all. More recently, these organizations have begun to introduce other qualitative information about performance.

The appearance of these watchers is uneven across the world. Most of them are based in the US, perhaps because the government there plays a less conspicuous role in solving social sector problems or in governing the efficacy of a social purpose activity; and because a relatively entrepreneurial culture exists in the country alongside material and cultural incentives that can subsidize nonprofit activities. The UK is also fostering its own charity analysts such as the New Philanthropy Capital, alongside US-headquartered watchers such as GuideStar.[14]

These charity watchers are seen to reflect certain cultural references and priorities that may not be universal. The unintended consequences of this may be that the ratings systems will perpetuate the definitions of value that those on the money side of the developed world frequently articulate, and overlook value that individuals and social sector organizations on the ground would define.

Grantmakers

Grantmakers provide critical resources to fund the work both of capacity builders and the end-beneficiary NPOs.[15]

Grantmakers can take many forms. They can be a coalition of NPOs, such as the United Way, which are set up to aggregate annual donations for a particular constituency of nonprofits. More often, they are thought of as the traditional family or corporate foundations, with longer-lasting endowments provided by philanthropic individuals or corporations, respectively.

A newer form of grantmaking is the venture philanthropy organization that seeks to support its investee organizations, not just with larger and longer-term grants, but also with advice, both of which are aimed at enhancing organizational capacity and the creation of measurable social value.[16]

Philanthropic giving has long been the supplementary resource base that supports the work of NPOs. Even though philanthropic and donor dollars are much smaller than government funding, these private dollars are valued for their targeted impact and autonomy in supporting a nonprofit organization's pursuit of its cause, free from political and commercial constraints.

Increasing the Impact of Capacity Builders

Capacity builders exist to increase the impact of NPOs and the social sector. It is thus not a surprise that recent trends in the capacity-building industry show a focus on increasing the impact of capacity builders themselves.

These efforts to increase impact can be seen in four key areas:

– Incorporating new business models
– Exploiting advances in technology
– Managing more information
– Improving social interventions based on impact.

Business Models

Many NPOs and nonprofit service providers are adapting market approaches in their product offerings even if they may be for those who are hard-pressed to pay market rates. Their belief is that to prove their worth, excellent services should be validated by the market. International Development Enterprises (IDE), for example, specifically subscribes to the "market oriented development model to increase the income of the rural poor by improving market access, increasing agricultural production, and creating sustainable local businesses." IDE designs and sells affordable productivity-enhancing tools for the developing world. This service provider combines design principles and services that are appropriate to developing world markets and thus help to develop the entrepreneurial capacity of the end-beneficiaries.[17]

This market philosophy is commonly manifested in social enterprises or hybrid social–business organizations. Often, these enterprises are businesses aligned with the social missions of specific NPOs, such as the employment of the NPOs' beneficiaries.[18]

In the search for new business models, new forms of capacity builders are being created. The stock exchange and secondary markets is one area. Brazil's Bovespa created the first Social Stock Exchange in 2003, and the South African Social Investment Exchange soon followed.[19] The premise is to sell for a price the number of "shares" that would be needed for an organization to complete a specific project. Once the project is fully funded, it is implemented. Once the project is completed, a service provider (in South Africa, GreaterCapital) develops a Project Performance Report articulating how the money was spent and "what its impact was, analyzing the project outcomes compared to those forecast, as well as the lessons learned."[20] SocialMarkets.org has prototyped a donor platform where donations are given on the basis of quantified "social return on investment."[21]

Technology-Based Models

Technology—in particular, infocomm technology—is providing a source of innovation for nonprofits and service providers that are seeking new and creative models that can scale.

Web-based matchmaking platforms and "markets" are mushrooming to help funders and social sector organizations find and engage with each other.

For example, MicroPlace, an outfit owned by internet giant, eBay, leverages both eBay's user base and the infrastructure created by numerous microfinance institutions (MFIs).[22] eBay's users become lenders as they place microloans through MicroPlace's online platform. MicroPlace sends the funds to MFIs such as Oikocredit GC which, in turn, loans the money to individuals running small businesses. The MFIs pay a return to the individual eBay donors for the funds they invest.[23] Wokai is a similar platform that matches microfinance borrowers in rural China with donors, most of whom are from other countries.[24]

Platforms also exist to combine human capacity building with technology to reduce the cost of gathering, analyzing, and sharing information about social and environmental needs, impact, and value in places the internet alone cannot reach. Mobile Metrix, an NPO with operations in Brazil, conducts market research on the needs of the "invisible poor" and shares their situation with the world. It seeks to provide accurate data for social service bodies and policy makers to use when creating solutions for a particular social issue, as well as market intelligence to inform businesses with products that would be desirable to residents of these communities.[25]

Another innovative service provider is Polecat, whose MeaningMine tool competes with traditional high-cost global strategic management consulting firms to map the information landscape within which organizations operate, and hence to provide organizations, including NPOs, with a better sense of public perception and feedback.[26]

More advanced technologies are creating new, previously inconceivable applications. For example, online geo-spatial mapping and data visualization using inexpensive or free web-based tools can reveal situations that have been invisible, hidden, or ignored by those familiar with or close to the situation—for better and for worse.

On the one hand, the values of parties who have previously been far removed from the local context may be projected onto local situations in ways the locals do not want, such as when online political organizers enable activists in one state to make calls to voters in other states in an attempt to influence local elections. On the other hand, those who have lacked identity or power are now able to connect with distant others who appreciate or share their values and can work with them to effect desired changes—or to prevent unwanted changes. One example is the coalescing of adults with Aspergers (a form of high-functioning autism) into online support groups, such as GRASP (The Global and Regional Asperger

Syndrome Partnership),[27] where members not only form friendships, but also share experiences and tactics for how to cope with a world that does not understand their unique talents and sensitivities.

Information Management

Given the flood of information now available in the global economy, one major challenge is how the public and, in particular, players in the social sector can make sense of it all. To be sure, there is a dearth of data on the social sector, on the new forms of business models which are emerging, the activity of the social sector in the developing world, and other topics. However, the opposite problem, that of too much information, is also big and getting bigger. In this dynamic and exciting information world, some capacity builders are emerging to facilitate the convening of interest groups to aid discovery of who and what is going on, articulate a common language, and agree on standards of practice.

The internet can be used both to increase transparency and to manipulate perception. While new insights into major emergencies (e.g. pandemics and disaster response) as well as slower-moving challenges (e.g. climate change) are enabled by the information infrastructure and emerging human capacity of the sector, at the same time there are as yet no universally trusted authorities to assure accuracy and objectivity regarding claims of social impact.

Over the next few years, the sector is likely to see the emergence of both private and public sector entities that assert the authority to interpret the avalanche of information about performance. Just as financial accounting involves both certain standard metrics (such as Return on Investment or Earnings Before Interest, Depreciation, Taxes, and Amortization) and standard procedures (such as the steps any organization should take to calculate these metrics), so too will "impact management" involve agreement within sub-industries about not just the standard metrics all players agree to report, but also standardization of processes by which certain aspects of social performance will be captured.

The importance of both technical and legal frameworks in maintaining freedom of internet information while protecting individuals' right to privacy will be a central policy and corporate law issue over the next few decades. Governments are sure to play an increasing role in determining what information social sector organizations report publicly, as well as what processes they use.

Impact-Based Interventions

The ability of organizations to deliver on their social missions in the most efficient way requires a special kind of skill. Managers must have the ability to generate real outcomes while keeping operations adequately resourced. This ability cannot be divorced from the skills funders need in order to understand what actions drive outcomes, and how best to allocate philanthropic resources. If either manager or funder lacks skills in these areas, the social capital marketplace becomes dysfunctional.

Yet, the predominance of program-based funding in the social sector means that cost-cutting measures surrounding human resource management and infrastructure investment are not uncommon. Many capacity builders, especially grantmakers, are recognizing such deficiencies in the operations of NPOs.

Some grantmakers are now offering grants that cater specifically to the NPOs' capacity-building functions. Three hundred and fifty grantmakers with such aspirations came together in the Grantmakers for Effective Organizations (GEO), which is committed to discretionary grantmaking that will strengthen NPOs and help them cultivate better results.[28] Still, a recent GEO-funded survey of grantmaking in the US found that "less than one-quarter of foundations say their grants often or always include appropriate overhead," and "fewer than four out of ten respondents reported soliciting feedback from grantees through surveys, interviews, or focus groups."[29]

To create a greater impact in the social sector, more services have emerged to cultivate sustainable grantmaking and professional services. For example, LGT Venture Philanthropy, an arm of the wealth and asset management LGT group, supports organizations with financial, social, and intellectual capital. It advises wealth managers and makes grants, loans, and equity investments; any profit is channeled back into the fund and used for additional investments.[30] LGT also has a fellows program that supplies professional talent to social sector organizations.

One of the most repeated axioms in management is: "What gets measured gets managed." Yet, professional training in how to measure or manage social and environmental value creation is, at best, in its infancy. New management disciplines and innovation in canonical ones will be needed to meet the demands of the future.

More importantly, the focus on impact is setting the stage for a healthy competition among service providers, promoters, and watchers to ensure quality or to accelerate the extinction of nonperforming organizations.

Making Social Impact Mainstream

For far too long, the social good has been about obligation or sympathy. Therefore, it is measured more often in terms of its giving and less in terms of its impact. Trends in the nonprofit sector are changing this predisposition.

Accounting for the value created by NPOs and for-profit organizations, as well as managing and communicating this social and environmental value, will emerge as a cornerstone of tomorrow's sustainable economy. Debates about the consequences of objectifying social value will wax and wane, as people struggle to reconcile their empathies with efficient resource allocation in the information age. Meanwhile, capacity builders committed to supporting effective NPOs will continue to provide lifelines for nonprofit operational development, and advocate for more impactful NPOs.

Endnotes

1   The term "donors" refers to individuals or groups who practice smaller, perhaps random, forms of giving, as compared to the disciplined and structured giving of the grantmakers through organizational set-ups.

2   "Effective Capacity Building in Nonprofit Organizations," report prepared by McKinsey & Company for Venture Philanthropy Partners, August 2001, www.vppartners.org/learning/reports/capacity/capacity.html.

3   For one example of classification, see Paul Connolly and Peter York, "Building the Capacity of Capacity Builders: A study of management support and field-building organizations in the nonprofit sector," prepared by The Conservation Company, supported by funding from the David and Lucile Packard Foundation, with additional assistance by The Alliance for Nonprofit Management and Grantmakers for Effective Organizations, June 2003.

4   National Council for Voluntary Organisations, www.ncvo-vol.org.uk; National Council of Nonprofits, www.councilofnonprofits.org; International Council on Voluntary Agencies, www.icva.ch. Listings of international federations and networks of nonprofits can be found at Union of International Associations, www.uia.org.

5   American Association of Museums, www.aam-us.org; Council on Foundations, www.cof.org; United Way, www.liveunited.org; Social Return On Investment Network, www.sroi-uk.org/; Social Performance Management Network, http://spmconsortium.ning.com.

6   Abdul Lateef Jameel Poverty Action Lab, www.povertyactionlab.org; Lien Centre for Social Innovation, www.lcsi.smu.edu.sg.

7   The coining of the term "social business," and the creation of legal structures to enable profit-making companies to prioritize public rather than shareholder interest, have to do with entities that may offer shares of equity and receive equity investment in order to

grow, while retaining and being held accountable for social and/or environmental impact. For more on social–business hybrids, see Chapter 5, "Social Enterprises: Fulfilling the promise of social enterprise," by Jon Huggett, and Chapter 18, "Social Finance: Financing change, changing finance," by Jed Emerson. More details: UK Government's Community Interest Company, www.cicregulator.gov.uk; US's Low-Profit Limited Liability Company (L3C), www.leg.state.vt.us/docs/legdoc.cfm?URL=/docs/2008/acts/ACT106.HTM; and Benefit Corporation (B Corp), www.bcorporation.net/index.cfm/fuseaction/content .page/nodeID/be2fd378-d039-4d35-90a7-48b824bcac78/externalURL.

8   Bridgespan, www.bridgespan.org; CompassPoint, www.compasspoint.org.

9   www.salesforce.com/company/foundation.

10 www.computertroubleshooters.org.

11 Paul Connolly and Peter York, "Building the Capacity of Capacity Builders: A study of management support and field-building organizations in the nonprofit sector," prepared by The Conservation Company, supported by funding from the David and Lucile Packard Foundation, with additional assistance by The Alliance for Nonprofit Management and Grantmakers for Effective Organizations, June 2003.

12 MAPLight.org, www.maplight.org; NGOWatch is a sibling website of Global Governance Watch, a project of conservative think tanks in the US, www.globalgovernancewatch .org/ngo_watch.

13 Charity Navigator, www.charitynavigator.org/; Charity Watch by American Institute of Philanthropy, www.charitywatch.org; GuideStar, www.guidestar.org.uk/Default.aspx; Standard and Poor's, www.standardandpoors.com/home/en/us.

14 www.philanthropycapital.org.

15 The subject of grantmakers and foundations is covered more fully in Chapter 8, "Philanthropy: Powering philanthropic passions," by Thomas Menkhoff.

16 The subject of venture philanthropy is covered more fully in Chapter 9, "Venture Philanthropy: Venturing into entrepreneurial philanthropy," by Rob John.

17 www.ideorg.org/OurMethod/Prism.aspx.

18 The subject of social enterprises is covered in Chapter 5, "Social Enterprises: Fulfilling the promise of social enterprise," by Jon Huggett.

19 www.sasix.co.za.

20 "How Can I Track My Investment," SASIX, www.sasix.co.za/about_us/faqs/how_can_ i_track_my_investment.

21 Social Markets, www.socialmarkets.org/; "Impact Metrics," Social Markets, www .socialmarkets.org/impact-metrics.

22 www.microplace.com.

23 www.oikocredit.org.

24 www.wokai.org. In 2009, 14 percent of Wokai's contributors were from China while the rest came from other countries.

25 Mobile Metrix describes its services as follows: "Using handheld computers, Mobile Metrix collects data on a variety of issues including employment, job skills, health

conditions, education levels, finances, land, and housing. Mobile Metrix selects outstanding young adults (averaging 16–24 years) to be data collectors in their own communities. We extensively train these youth (our MobileAgents™) in survey techniques, technology, and professionalism to ensure the utmost data quality," www .mobilemetrix.org/the-solution/business-model.html.

26   MeaningMine describes its services as follows: "MeaningMine has . . . near-real-time, round-the-clock monitoring of 500,000 news articles daily . . . [and] captures 4 million posts a day from all the major social media sources including: blogging/podcast platforms (eg WordPress); social video (eg YouTube); photo sharing sites (eg Flickr); microblogs (eg Twitter); wikis (eg Wikimedia Foundation Sites); reviews (eg Amazon); and forums (eg DigitalSpy). Using a combination of data mining and text analytics, MeaningMine automatically maps the information landscape that surrounds your organisation—looking for statistical and linguistic patterns, dominant trends, emerging issues, regional differences, key influencers, and insights," http://polecatting.com.

27   www.grasp.org.

28   www.geofunders.org/currentmembers.aspx.

29   *Grantmakers for Effective Organizations 2008 Annual Report*, www.geofunders.org/ annuralreports.aspx.

30   www.lgt.com/en/private_kunden/philanthropie.

Chapter 8

Philanthropy

Powering
Philanthropic Passions

THOMAS MENKHOFF

Practice Associate Professor, Singapore Management University

Philanthropy has often been associated with mega-giving and mega-givers. The fact is that it covers a multitude of donors, modes of giving, and beneficiaries. That said, all forms of philanthropy are experiencing unusual changes.

Four major trends can be observed. The first is borderless philanthropy, with rising charitable giving beyond the US and increasing cross-border philanthropic flows. The second is e-philanthropy and the spread of giving, enabled by technology, in innovative ways. The third is philanthrocapitalism, with the engagement of business entrepreneurs and their many ideas, ambitions, and resources for increasing social impact. The fourth is collaborative philanthropy, as givers and even governments seek to collectively create greater social impact.

All these trends are motivating the rich and not-so-rich to give more and in new ways, and thus powering philanthropy, leading it toward an exciting and, sometimes, surprising future.

$\mathbf{P}$hilanthropy conjures up images of the mega-rich giving away their wealth to the poor of the world.

Technically, though, the term "philanthropy" covers a multitude of donors, modes of giving, and beneficiaries. Philanthropic givers can range from the widow with two mites[1] and the man in the street dropping spare change into a tin can thrust at him, to multibillionaires like George Soros and Bill Gates. Not unexpectedly, it is the mega-givers who capture the public imagination, not just with the size of their gifts but also with their unusual methods and ambitions.[2] In many cases, these mega-philanthropists are making a big difference in changing society and in transforming our social ecosystem.

That said, philanthropy, in all its myriad forms, has become more diverse and interesting in its sources, approaches, and goals.

Philanthropy as Usual

Modern-day philanthropy is widely accepted as having its genesis in Andrew Carnegie and his *Gospel of Wealth*.[3]

It was during the industrial boom years of the 20th century that Carnegie and John D. Rockefeller[4] began giving away their massive wealth through foundations with corporate-like structures. Since then, foundations have been the vehicles by which many of the wealthy channel their giving. Their numbers and the value of their assets across the world have grown steadily, particularly so in the US. There, the number of grantmaking foundations increased from 505 in 1944 to more than 75,000 in 2008 and is projected to reach 100,000 by 2020.[5] Similarly, foundation assets correspondingly grew from US$1.8 billion to US$583 billion in the same period. In fact, annual foundation grants amount to nearly US$43 billion, representing about 13 percent of the total philanthropic giving in the US in 2008.

The foundations of the last century changed the paradigm of giving, from almsgiving to organized and professionally managed grantmaking. The approach of most is a structured and disciplined process to giving grants. While there is no standard approach given the diverse forms of foundations, the grantmaking process typically includes the following elements: identification of potential nonprofit organizations (NPOs), evaluation of grant applications, disbursement to successful grantees of the grants usually in tranches, and the subsequent monitoring of progress through regular reports from the NPOs.

Over the years, the world has moved faster than the world of traditional grantmaking. While social organizations have grown in diversity, and social problems have grown more complex, traditional foundations have stayed stuck with the *modus operandi* of the past: Their target of funding remains the NPOs; their focus of giving and performance measures remain program-specific; their length of investment is typically between one and three years; and their partnering roles remain limited.[6]

To put this in perspective, despite the widespread publicity accorded to amounts given to, and by, foundations, foundation giving, as indicated above for the US, represents only a small fraction of total philanthropic giving. In turn, philanthropic giving represents only about 12 percent of the total sources of NPO revenue across the world.[7]

However, with the emergence of new types of philanthropists who seek to be more responsive to a changing and more complex world, significant change in the philanthropy space has been afoot for the last decade or so.

Philanthropy Unusual

The time does seem opportune for philanthropy unusual. The increasing transfer of wealth to private hands, the enhanced connection through technology, and the diversification of players in the philanthropy world all mean that philanthropy is scaling up, as is its impact.[8] In short, a reigniting of philanthropic passions is taking place.

Much is already happening and this can be encapsulated in four major trends of modern-day philanthropy:

- Borderless philanthropy, with rising charitable giving beyond the US and increasing cross-border philanthropic flows
- E-Philanthropy and the spread of giving, enabled by technology, in new and innovative ways
- Philanthrocapitalism, with the engagement of business entrepreneurs and their many ideas, ambitions, and resources for increasing social impact
- Collaborative philanthropy, as givers and even governments seek to collectively create greater social impact.

Borderless Philanthropy

In an increasingly globalized world, philanthropy has gone borderless in several respects.

First, led by the US, the interest in high-end philanthropy is rippling across the globe. For example, Philanthropy UK reports that there is a growing class of rich people in the UK, and that the "more wealthy individuals are becoming philanthropists, with the most noticeable change seen at the higher end of the wealth spectrum."[9]

However, it is not just the developed world where mega-philanthropy is taking hold. Even in the emerging economies, many philanthropists are making headlines for their generous giving. A sampling:

- In Mexico, Carlos Slim, who made his fortune in telecommunications, pledged US$6 billion to his three charitable foundations.[10]
- In India, software czar Azim Premji gave US$101 million to start a foundation that is now planning a university to train teachers.[11]
- In the Middle East, Saudi billionaire Prince Alwaleed bin Talal, who has donated more than US$2.4 billion over the last 30 years, has started a foundation to consolidate his efforts.[12]
- In Hong Kong, tycoon Li Ka-shing has pledged one-third of his estimated US$18.8 billion fortune to his foundation.[13]
- In China, property tycoon Yu Pengnian has donated his entire fortune to his foundation, bringing the total he has given to US$1.2 billion.[14]

The cultural diversity of these donors should not come as a surprise. With globalization, more millionaires are being minted more quickly outside than within the US. A Cap Gemini and Merrill Lynch World Wealth Report estimates that, in 2009, Asia-Pacific had 2.4 million millionaires and the region was fast catching up with North America's 2.7 million. The prediction is that, by 2013, the wealth of high net-worth individuals in Asia-Pacific will surpass that of those in North America.

Despite these numbers, the generosity levels outside the US need to increase. In a study by management consultancy Bain & Co., charitable giving in India, Brazil, and China, for example, is equivalent to about 0.6, 0.3, and 0.1 percent, respectively, of the country's GDP in 2009. This compares with 2.2 percent in the US.[15] This means that the levels of giving in these countries range from 5 to 27 percent of the US level.

China, an emerging economic superpower, has huge potential. In 2009, the top 50 Chinese philanthropists donated US$572 million, a four-fold increase from six years ago.[16] While in absolute dollars, this may be just 14 percent of the US$4.1 billion given by the top 50 US philanthropists that same year,[17] the ratio is 63 percent when measured in purchasing power parity (PPP) terms.[18] With the increasing level of giving by mainland Chinese and their growing wealth, the level of philanthropic giving in China could one day rival that in the US in absolute, and not just PPP, terms.

The overseas Chinese have, in fact, led the way for the mainland Chinese in philanthropic giving. For example, as the ethnic Chinese population in Southeast Asia continues to become more engaged in mainstream civil society, more of the affluent Chinese have given back to their societies. Unlike the first-generation Chinese immigrants who were unable or unwilling to write wills, donate money for social causes, or leave bequests to charities due to their socio-economic insecurity, the second- or third-generation Chinese enjoy much better material conditions, are more exposed to community work, and are setting up foundations as well as practicing strategic corporate social responsibility through their corporate vehicles.[19] An example is Indonesian-Chinese philanthropist Mochtar Riady (Chinese name: Lie Mo Tie), the founder of the Lippo Group. Through their conglomerate, the Riady family sponsors an education foundation that operates schools, universities, and a recently inaugurated nanotechnology research institute, among other philanthropic activities.[20]

Secondly, many of these philanthropic flows are taking place across borders. The Hudson Institute, an international think tank, found that total private financial flows (consisting of investment, philanthropy, and remittances) from all donor countries to developing countries have been steadily increasing over the last few years. In fact, private financial flows were three-and-a-half times the public flows (consisting of official development assistance and other government loans) in 2006.[21] In the US, the largest donor country, private philanthropy and remittances to developing countries constitute four-and-a-half times the official aid abroad.

Part of this financial flow consists of funds sent by emigrants who are working and living in the developed countries to their poorer home countries. According to the World Bank, remittances by these diaspora communities reached an all-time high of US$297 billion in 2006, double the amount remitted in 2000.[22] Indeed, there has been an increasing interest in diaspora philanthropy because of the growing participation of diasporas in the community and national development of their homelands. Having made good in host countries, these people want to give back to their country of origin, not just in monetary terms, but also in terms of their talent and goodwill in multiple ways. Recognizing that the diasporas are major sources of foreign direct investments, commercial contacts, political connections and advocacy, and technology transfer, many governments have begun actively courting them.[23]

Finally, some of the cross-border philanthropic flows are in reverse. Traditionally, philanthropy has been stereotyped as white Anglo-Saxons helping their backward, colored brethren in the developing world. The opposite is beginning to happen.

One way this is occurring is through donations to their alma mater by those from the East who are educated in the West. For example, Hong Kong tycoon Gordon Wu donated a total of US$118 million to Princeton University.[24] In 2010, Zhang Lei, the founder of Beijing-based Hillhouse Capital Management, donated an auspicious US$8,888,888 to Yale. He explained, "Yale has been helping China for more than 100 years. Many Chinese leaders were educated at Yale. But the relationship has been one-way for too long and I want to help change that."[25]

Even when there are no personal connections, those from the emerging economies are giving based on causes and needs. For example, One Foundation—a Chinese foundation set up by movie star Jet Li and the Red Cross Society of China that focuses on disaster relief—donated US$100,000 to the victims of the Haiti earthquake.[26]

E-Philanthropy

Philanthropy has often been associated with the big-time givers, even though the ordinary man has done his part when asked. NPOs and fundraisers, however, have tended to focus on big-time donors because of the relative returns from resources invested in fundraising.

However, infocomm technology is enabling the reach and mobilization of the masses to give in ways and at costs not previously possible.[27] Small contributions made through the web or the mobile phone can be easily and efficiently aggregated into million-dollar sums.

The effectiveness of these tools is evident when natural disasters strike. For example, one week after Hurricane Katrina struck New Orleans in 2005, the Salvation Army had received US$22.7 million from online giving; Habitat for Humanity received US$2.7 million, four times the amount it received in other forms of gift during the same time frame.[28] Similarly, in January 2010, Network for Good, an online charity portal, received US$5 million for victims of the Haiti earthquake within two weeks of the calamity.[29]

The experience of fundraising for disaster relief shows how online giving, appropriately utilized, can tap the initial groundswell of giving quickly and efficiently before public interest ebbs. More remarkably, online giving can level the fundraising pattern in favor of smaller charities. In the analysis of the donations made through the Network for Good online portal, smaller charities appeared alongside larger well-known relief organizations on the top 10 list.[30]

Apart from the reach and the time responsiveness of online giving, the big attraction to donors is the direct connection to the beneficiaries. NPOs such as Kiva and DonorsChoose are successfully providing an efficient instant matching service for donors and beneficiaries.

Kiva allows people to lend money via the internet to microfinance institutions around the world, which in turn lend the money to small businesses.[31] Founded in 2005, Kiva has already distributed over US$110 million in loans from over 630,000 lenders and donors.

DonorsChoose allows people to donate directly to specific projects at public schools.[32] Since it started in 2000, it has helped 88,000 teachers obtain over US$30 million in books, art supplies, technology, and other resources to benefit eight million students in the US.

Despite all its advantages, e-philanthropy is still not a significant part of total philanthropic giving. In the US, this was estimated at US$15.4 billion, or around 5 percent of total charitable giving, in 2008.[33] In the same year, a total of 203 bigger charities reported an overall collection of US$1.4 billion from online giving.[34]

Three hurdles stand in the way of e-philanthropy becoming more mainstream: legitimacy, transparency, and donor fatigue.

Legitimacy of websites is a perennial problem of the internet, whether for fundraising or otherwise. In the immediate aftermath of the Haiti disaster, malware programs were redirecting users wanting to make charitable donations to scam fundraising sites for disaster relief.[35] Yet, to require donors to validate that each and every appeal is legitimate would be time-consuming and off-putting for them.

Transparency of the process behind the screen can also be an issue. Take the *modus operandi* of Kiva. From the lender's standpoint, kiva.org posts profiles of needy entrepreneurs in developing countries. Individuals then choose and lend money to the specific entrepreneur they wish to help. Kiva aggregates the loan capital and transfers it to an appropriate microfinance institution to disburse to the chosen entrepreneur. However, in practice, the entrepreneurs have received their loans from the microfinance institution long before their photos and profile were posted. It was a matter of how it was presented in one sense, but Kiva, which states that transparency is one of its three key values, faced accusations that the "direct person-to-person connection Kiva offered was, in fact, an illusion."[36]

Finally, there is the question of donor fatigue. It is not easy for any NPO to reach out to the masses and maintain its appeal, day in and day out. Disasters always provoke an immediate outpouring of aid, and the plight of a person profiled on the web pulls at the heartstrings, but ennui can creep in.

For individual NPOs, these obstacles are not insurmountable. An organization needs to implement measures to specifically deal with these issues. For example, DonorsChoose, which funds teachers' needs, sends equipment requested, not cash, to the school to avoid misappropriation of funds. Kiva sought to resolve the transparency issue by apologizing for the miscommunication and provided greater clarity on how the process actually works.[37] Creative marketing should always be ready to work up new angles. It is putting it all together so that one has a killer application, rather than evolving the solution piecemeal, which will probably be the bigger challenge for democratizing philanthropy.

Philanthrocapitalism

Many of the new mega-givers are successful business entrepreneurs who have brought their business background and thinking into the social world. Such donors believe that many social problems may, in fact, be more effectively solved by dealing with them as business problems and by applying business approaches. Since they are now redirecting the money they have made in their business to the social sector, they are able to define the agendas and approaches by which the money is to be used.

Their agendas can be very ambitious. For some, it is nothing less than solving the problems of the world. Bill Gates, for example, has said that he wishes to redress "the awful inequities in the world—the appalling disparities of health, and wealth, and opportunity that condemn millions of people to lives of despair."[38] Of course, he has backed up that ambition with massive sums of money from his foundation.[39] The approaches of these businesspeople are, well, business-like. They seek to apply the regular corporate concepts of good management discipline and focus on delivering outcomes, but they also blend edge-of-the-envelope approaches derived from venture capitalists with new-fangled financial instruments only understood in the high world of complex finance.

The line between what is business and social gets blurred in the process. For example, Google.org, the philanthropic arm of search engine behemoth, Google, invested in eSolar, a commercial start-up for developing low-cost solar thermal plants. This move is consistent with one of Google.org's overall objectives, which is to develop renewable energy cheaper than coal.[40]

Similarly, the Omidyar Network, a social investment firm established by Pierre Omidyar, the founder of eBay, invests in both for-profit businesses with a strong socially oriented angle, and nonprofits. Since its inception in 2004, it has committed US$325 million, of which US$144 million has gone to for-profit ventures. The Omidyar Network believes that market-based solutions from for-profit companies can help to catalyze broad, positive social impact; hence, its investment approach transcends the typical boundaries that separate for-profit investing and traditional philanthropy.[41]

This phenomenon has led to the coining of the term "philanthro-capitalism," which has evolved to cover the plethora of business- and market-based approaches to dealing with social issues.[42] Within this umbrella of philanthrocapitalism are social enterprises (social–business hybrids funded with a mix of commercial and philanthropic capital), venture philanthropy (social venture funds that apply venture capital techniques and tools to civil society organizations), and the employment of new forms of social finance. These topics are covered separately elsewhere in this book.[43]

Collaborative Philanthropy

Traditional foundations have usually taken a stand alone and direct donor-to-recipient approach to giving. Increasingly, they are collaborating with other institutions to fund projects. Even The Bill & Melinda Gates Foundation, one of the world's largest foundations with total assets of US$30 billion,[44] has worked actively with other foundations, such as with The Rockefeller Foundation in the Alliance for a Green Revolution.[45] Although there is more money than ever before, foundations are recognizing that the scale of the problems and their ambitions require the power of partnerships and diversity of talents that only an alliance with other organizations can bring.

Indeed, the importance of collaboration has led to the emergence of brokers and aggregators such as the Clinton Global Initiative and the Global Impact Investing Network.

The former leverages on the political influence of its founder, former US President Bill Clinton, to convene meetings of prominent political leaders, businesses, and foundations so as to make resources, knowledge, and ideas meet. Founded in 2005, the Initiative has, in its first five years, drummed up 1,700 commitments valued at US$57 billion to improve the lives of 220 million people around the world.[46]

The Global Impact Investing Network, initiated by The Rockefeller Foundation, focuses on the common base of impact investing and rallies like-minded foundations and businesses to facilitate for-profit investing that addresses social and environmental challenges. Among its founding members are the Acumen Fund, Annie E. Casey Foundation, The Bill & Melinda Gates Foundation, Calvert Foundation, Capricorn Investment Group, and Citigroup.[47]

Perhaps there may be no better brokers and collaborators than the philanthropists themselves encouraging their peers to give. This was what Ted Turner, founder of CNN, attempted to do in 1997 when he gave US$1 billion to the UN with an open challenge to his fellow wealthy "skinflints" to "open their purse strings."[48] While this started the ball of "competitive philanthropy" rolling, less than 5 percent of the mega-rich in the US have been deemed generous donors in 2010.[49] Thus, in June 2010, Bill Gates and Warren Buffett, already two of the world's largest givers, launched a campaign to ask every billionaire in the US to pledge to give away 50 percent of their wealth. If they succeed, this will change the face of philanthropy—beyond the mega-rich and beyond the US.[50]

These collaborations also draw in government bodies and support. Public–private sector partnerships have been found to be effective in marrying the power of the government's authority and infrastructure with private philanthropy's financing and grassroots reach. Rather than one that is constrained by long-term goals, this collaborative paradigm cultivates a spontaneous approach by developing local initiatives, encouraging co-financing, and mobilizing peer-to-peer relationships through professional associations and volunteers.[51]

An example of a public–private partnership is the Mexican government's co-funding of collective remittances from Mexican hometown associations in the US back to Mexico. To encourage such flow back, the Mexican government has a "3-for-1 program," whereby the federal, state, and municipal governments each contribute one dollar for every dollar raised by the associations. This not only encourages and increases the flow of funds—more than US$24 billion from 2,000 associations—but has also improved governance in recipient Mexican communities by providing a channel for negotiations between migrants, communities, and the government of Mexico.[52]

Philanthropy Decoded

Although new types of philanthropists and methods are emerging, the reasons that people give have not changed that much. The factors that influence the giving decision range from the traditional (moral) values of doing good, altruism, and leaving a legacy, to personal interests arising from business, reciprocity, or a passion for specific causes, to even negative drivers such as face or guilt. However, the emphasis of certain factors may vary across countries and cultures.

Many studies on motivations for giving have focused on the wealthy and the US, where modern philanthropy first made its mark and is still most prevalent today. Francie Ostrower argues that philanthropy is a defining element of elite culture in the US.[53] She sees the display of wealth through giving as indicating the philanthropist's success, which should not be interpreted as buying face or showing off wealth, but as an act of giving that extends beyond merely the monetary. Elite philanthropy is to be seen as a sort of calculated investment that opens doors for the wealthy to identify with and participate in prestigious nonprofit organizations and the elite networks with which these organizations are associated.

Another study by Prince and File identifies seven different kinds of philanthropists, based on their motivations:

- The communitarians, who think that doing good simply makes sense (they usually help their own community to prosper)
- The devout, who believe that doing good is God's will (they mostly give to religious institutions)
- The investors, who treat doing good as a business (they give in order to achieve tax and estate interests)
- The socialites, who do good because it is fun (they intend to help to make the world a better place)
- The altruists, who do good because it feels right (they are the selfless donors with generosity and empathy)
- The repayers, who do good to repay the kindness they personally benefited from—for example, from a school or a medical center

– The dynasts, who believe that doing good is part of their family tradition.

Certainly, US philanthropy strongly influences philanthropy outside the US. Many of the instances of mega-giving by billionaires in Europe and Asia occurred soon after examples were set by US billionaires such as Ted Turner and Bill Gates. In Hoon Chang Yau's analysis of several US-educated Indonesian-Chinese founders of philanthropic foundations such as James Riady, Putera Sampoerna, and Cherie Nursalim, he concludes that American-styled philanthropy is a platform for these magnates to enter into global elite networks.[54] While mutual help and giving are ingrained in many Asian cultures, establishing foundations also brings these tycoons the prestige of being in the leagues of other renowned philanthropists such as Bill Gates.

In their study of Chinese philanthropy, Hoon and Menkhoff found that, unlike the first-generation Chinese migrants who prefer to donate to their hometowns or home provinces, second- and third-generation immigrants are less parochial in their giving and more inclined to respond to national needs in their country of residence. Their philanthropic acts increasingly transcend ethnic and communal boundaries.[55]

With the spread of international mutual aid networks such as The Family Business Network,[56] which promotes multi-generational thinking of family businesses including in philanthropic giving, there will be cross-fertilization of thinking and approaches across borders. And, as philanthropy becomes more globalized and transcends national, ethnic, and cultural differences, so have the reasons and style of giving become more alike.

Philanthropy Futures

In the last decade, the philanthropy scene has been an exciting one. The powering of philanthropic passions in new and unusual ways has been variously labeled as "Philanthropy 3.0," "The Golden Age of Philanthropy," and "The Second Philanthropic Revolution" to describe parts of, or the collection of changes taking place in, the giving world.[57]

What will philanthropy be like going forward in the coming decades? To be sure, the four major trends highlighted in this chapter will continue to play out. In an increasingly globalized world, cross-border philanthropic

Philanthropy 2020

Global Philanthropy and Needs will Expand
- A new generation of Asian and non-US philanthropists will emerge to rival the Americans.
- International giving flourishes, as younger donors see themselves as citizens of the world.
- Nations will sign a "global compact on philanthropy" wherein countries will agree to meet minimum standards for oversight of their charities.
- Climate change work will be more about humanitarian issues (the impact on people and communities) than about the environment.

Demographic Changes will Impact Needs
- An ageing population in the developed countries means a potential surge of talented volunteers and new philanthropic wealth.
- There will be an increase in demands for health care and other social services.
- There will be more emphasis by charities on multi-generation issues.
- As cross-border migration increases, philanthropy will be more inclusive and localized.

Technology Gets More Interactive and Indispensable
- New tools will lead to greater sharing of information.
- Recipients of charity will offer more detailed feedback to organizations and donors.
- Donors can more easily track results of their gifts.
- There will be better data available on all aspects of the nonprofit world.
- There will be increased public scrutiny of charities.

An Increase in Charitable Business
- There will be more of a blended business–nonprofit approach to charity.
- Large companies will more thoroughly integrate giving into their operations.
- There will be increased scrutiny by lawmakers and the public, resulting in growing disclosures about how nonprofit groups operate.

Other Trends
- The lingering effects of financial crisis and continuing economic woes will play out.
- An obesity epidemic could spur an increase in charitable efforts in healthy living.
- Wealth inequality is expected to grow and increase international aid efforts.
- There will be greater government–charity partnerships.
- The shifting religious landscape will affect how people give and the causes they support.

Source: "Philanthropy in 2020: Challenges for the nonprofit world in the next decade," *The Chronicle of Philanthropy*, January 14, 2010.

flows will not only increase but may become more unpredictable as new relationships are forged across the globe. Technology will continue to enable giving in new, innovative, and surprising ways. Business and charity will influence each other; they will continue to mix until perhaps neither will be recognizable in the blend. Indeed, collaboration with the large diversity of participants and needs around the world may make for strange and interesting bedfellows.

Recently, some nonprofit leaders and futurists took a peek into their crystal balls to ponder what the charity world and philanthropy might look like in a decade's time. The box "Philanthropy 2020" captures some of their thinking.

Some of the trends and forecasts made by the experts are already happening and transforming the nonprofit space. How philanthropy and its players will respond and harness the full potential of the new wave of enthusiasm and challenges will determine its effectiveness as a major force of change. Being 10 years ahead would be a good start.

Endnotes

1   In the Bible, Jesus speaks of a poor widow who donated only two mites, the least valuable coin of that era, but she was giving everything she had, while the wealthy contributed only a small portion of their abundance. See Gospel of Mark, Chapter 12, Verses 38–44.

2   Examples of these are contained in the later sections of this chapter: "Borderless Philanthropy" and "Philanthrocapitalism."

3   Andrew Carnegie, "Wealth," *North American Review*, No. CCCXCI, June 1889. Later republished in England as "The Gospel of Wealth," a title Carnegie subsequently adopted as his own. Andrew Carnegie reference at the Carnegie Corporation of New York, www.carnegie.org.

4   John D. Rockefeller reference at The Rockefeller Foundation, www.rockfound.org.

5   The giving statistics in this paragraph are extracted from: (1) *Philanthropy in the 21st Century: The Foundation Center's 50th Anniversary Interviews* (New York: The Foundation Center, 2007); (2) *Giving USA 2009: The Annual Report on Philanthropy for the Year 2008* (Glenview, IL: Giving USA Foundation, researched and written by the Center on Philanthropy at Indiana University, 2009); (3) Katherine Fulton and Andrew Blau, *Looking out for the Future: An orientation for twenty-first century philanthropists* (Cambridge, MA: Monitor Company Group, 2005); and (4) Steve Lawrence and Reina Mukai, *Foundation Growth and Giving Estimates: Current outlook* (New York: Foundation Center, 2010).

6   These comments were made of traditional foundations and are contrasted with the methods of the venture philanthropy funds. Leslie R. Crutchfield, "Guerilla Philanthropy: The Robin Hood Foundation," *Who Cares*, September/October 1997; Lucy Bernholz,

"Foundations for the Future: Emerging trends in foundation philanthropy," The Center on Philanthropy and Public Policy, Research 1, January 2000; Christine W. Letts, William Ryan, and Allen Grossman, "Virtuous Capital: What foundations can learn from venture capitalists," *Harvard Business Review*, March 1997.

7   Lester M. Salamon, S. Wojciech Sokolowski and Associates, *Global Civil Society: Dimensions of the nonprofit sector, Volume Two* (Bloomfield, CT: Kumarian Press, 2004). The statistic is based on a study across 34 countries.

8   Katherine Fulton and Andrew Blau, *Looking out for the Future: An orientation for twenty-first century philanthropists* (Cambridge, MA: Monitor Group, 2005).

9   "Wealth and Philanthropy: The views of those who advise the rich," *Philanthropy UK*, September 2007, www.philanthropyuk.org/Resources/WealthandPhilanthropy newresearch.

10 "Profile: Carlos Slim," *BBC News*, March 10, 2010, www.news.bbc.co.uk/2/hi/business/8560812.stm. Interestingly, despite the sizable pledge by Carlos Slim, he is known to be a philanthropy skeptic. His conviction is that "poverty is not fought with donations, charity, or even public spending, but that you fight it with health, education, and jobs."

11 "Azim Premji is India's Bill Gates: Forbes," *Hindustan Times*, May 1, 2010, www.hindustantimes.com/Azim-Premji-is-India-s-Bill-Gates-Forbes/H1-Article1-537893.aspx.

12 "Prince Alwaleed Bin Talal Foundation Donates $60,000 to Minaret of Freedom Institute," *Saudi Gazette*, April 12, 2010, www.saudigazette.com.sa/index.cfm?method=home.regcon&contentID=2010041269107.

13 Parmy Olson, "Li Ka Shing Can't Take It With Him," *Forbes*, August 25, 2006.

14 "Tycoon donates $645m," *The Straits Times*, April 22, 2010. www.straitstimes.com/BreakingNews/Asia/Story/STIStory_517792.html.

15 "India's Rich not so Charitable," *The Straits Times*, March 23, 2010. www.straitstimes.com/BreakingNews/Money/Story/STIStory_505505.html.

16 "2009 Single Yearly Donation List," Hurun Report: Luxury Business Portal, www.hurun.net/listen154.aspx.

17 "The Philanthropy 50: Americans who gave the most in 2009," *The Chronicle of Philanthropy*, February 7, 2010, www.philanthropy.com/article/The-Philanthropy-50-Americans/64019/.

18 The PPP is a method of computing the value of a currency by taking into account the living standards in each country. The Chinese donation of 3.9 billion yuan translates to US$572 million at current exchange rates. Using the 2003 (most recently available) ratio of PPP conversion factor to the official exchange rate of 0.217, the PPP value of the Chinese donation is US$2.6 billion. See www.devdata.worldbank.org/wdi2005/Table5_7.htm for PPP rates.

19 Thomas Menkhoff, "Chinese Philanthropy in Southeast Asia: Between continuity and change," *Social Space*, 2009.

20 Empire builder Mochtar Riady and his son James (current chairman of the Lippo Group) are both philanthropists. See: Hoon Chang Yau, "Face, Faith, and Forgiveness: Elite

Chinese philanthropy in Indonesia," in *Chinese Philanthropy in Asia: Between continuity and change, special issue of Journal of Asian Business*, ed. Thomas Menkhoff and Hoon Chang Yau (2010); "48 Heroes of Philanthropy," *Forbes Magazine*, February 26, 2009, www.forbes.com/global/2009/0316/054_philanthropy.html.

21 *The Index of Global Philanthropy 2008* (Washington, DC: The Hudson Institute, 2008), www.hudson.org/files/documents/2008%20Index%20-%20Low%20Res.pdf. In 2006, private investment and philanthropy was US$209.4 billion, remittances were US$122.4 billion, and total official flows were US$94.6 billion.

22 Ibid. It is always hard to distinguish between how much of remittances from migrants to their homeland is for family members and how much for (other) philanthropic purposes. One argument is that all such remittances are philanthropic because it is for the betterment of the lives of those in developing nations, whether or not the recipients are family members of the givers.

23 Paula Doherty Johnson, *Diaspora Philanthropy: Influences, initiatives, and issues* (Boston: The Philanthropic Institute Inc. and The Global Equity Initiative, Harvard University, May 2007).

24 "Princeton Celebrates Sir Gordon Wu's Extraordinary Support," Princeton University, May, 2007, www.giving.princeton.edu/news/archive/wu.xml.

25 Ai Yang, "Donation to Yale Sparks Debate," *China Daily*, January 11, 2010, www.chinadaily.com.cn/china/2010-01/11/content_9295651.htm.

26 "One Foundation donated USD100,000 to Victims in Haiti Earthquake," One Foundation, March 8, 2010, www.onefoundation.cn/html/79/n-1079.html.

27 The subject of e-philanthropy is also covered in Chapter 10, "Donor Management: Closing the funding gap," by Paulette Maehara; and Chapter 17, "Technology: Rebooting technology for society," by Robert Chew.

28 "Donors clicking to give dollars to relief efforts," *The NonProfit Times*, October 1, 2005.

29 "Donations to Help Haiti Exceed $528 million, Chronicle Tally Finds," *The Chronicle of Philanthropy*, January 27, 2010, www.philanthropy.com/article/Donations-to-Aid-Haiti-Exce/63756/.

30 "Haiti Relief Trends Observed on $4 Million in Network for Good Donations," Network for Good, January 22, 2010, www1.networkforgood.org/haiti-trends-4m-donations.

31 www.kiva.org.

32 www.donorschoose.org.

33 Based on analysis by Blackbaud, a leading technology company serving nonprofits. Its analysis is based on *Giving USA* 2008 data along with other metrics and surveys. The figures represent a 44 percent increase over the previous year. See www.forums.blackbaud.com/blogs/connections/archive/2009/06/10/giving-usa-report-for-2008-and-online-fundraising-estimates.aspx.

34 Noelle Barton, "How the Chronicle Compiled its Online-Giving Survey," *The Chronicle of Philanthropy*, May 7, 2009. Probably the most comprehensive survey conducted on

online giving, the data is based on responses from the top 400 charities and represents a 22 percent increase from the previous year.

35 Bruce Watson, "Haiti Earthquake Brings Charity Scams Out of the Woodwork," *DailyFinance*, January 20, 2010, www.dailyfinance.com/story/haiti-earthquake-brings-charity-scams-out-of-the-woodwork/19324648.

36 David Roodman, "Kiva is not quite what it seems," Center for Global Development, October 2, 2009, www.blogs.cgdev.org/open_book/2009/10/kiva-is-not-quite-what-it-seems.php; Stephanie Strom, "Confusion on Where Money Lent via Kiva Goes," *The New York Times*, November 8, 2009, www.nytimes.com/2009/11/09/business/global/09kiva.html?_r=1&scp=1&sq=kiva&st=cse; Zev Lowe, "Kiva, Transparency and P2P Microlending,"The Lemonade Stand, November 10, 2009, www.zevlowe.com/?p=53.

37 "Matt Flannery, Kiva CEO and Co-founder, Replies,"Center for Global Development, October 12, 2009, www.blogs.cgdev.org/open_book/2009/10/matt-flannery-kiva-ceo-and-co-founder-replies.php.

38 "Remarks of Bill Gates, Harvard Commencement,"*Harvard University Gazette Online*, June 7, 2007, www.news.harvard.edu/gazette/2007/06.14/99-gates.html.

39 To date, US$10 billion has been given out in grants by The Bill & Melinda Gates Foundation. Bill Gates made a pledge in January 2010 for a total of another US$10 billion over the next 10 years for vaccines."Gates Foundation Gives $10 billion for Vaccines," *CNNMoney*, January 29, 2010, www.money.cnn.com/2010/01/29/news/economy/Gates_Foundation_grant_vaccines/index.htm.

40 "Google.org announces core initiatives to combat climate change, poverty, and emerging threats—Google Press Release," January 17, 2008, www.google.com/intl/en/press/pressrel/20080117_googleorg.html.

41 Reflected to FY2008, www.omidyar.net/about_us/financials.

42 The term "philanthrocapitalism" was first coined by Matthew Bishop in an article in *The Economist*. He has since written a book on the subject. See Matthew Bishop and Michael Green, *Philanthrocapitalism* (New York: Bloomsbury Press, 2008), www.philanthrocapitalism.net.

43 See Chapter 5, "Social Enterprises: Fulfilling the promise of social enterprise," by Jon Hugget; Chapter 9, "Venture Philanthropy: Venturing into entrepreneurial philanthropy," by Rob John; and Chapter 18, "Social Finance: Financing change, changing finance," by Jed Emerson.

44 The Bill & Melinda Gates Foundation 2008 Combined Statements of Financial Position, www.gatesfoundation.org/annualreport/2008/Pages/combined-statements-financial-position.aspx.

45 www.agra-alliance.org.

46 www.clintonglobalinitiative.org/default.asp.

47 "Press Release: Global Impact Investing Network launched," The Rockefeller Foundation, September 25, 2009, www.rockefellerfoundation.org/news/press-releases/global-impact-investing-network-launched; www.globalimpactinvestingnetwork.org. More information on the organizations available at Acumen Fund, www.acumenfund.org;

Annie E. Casey Foundation, www.aecf.org; Calvert Foundation, www.calvertfoundation .org; Capricorn Investment Group, www.capricornllc.com; Citigroup, www.citigroup .com/citi/homepage.

48 Maureen Dowd, "Ted Turner Urges 'Ol' Skinflints' to Open Their Purse Strings Wider," *The New York Times*, August 23, 1996.

49 Donna Gordon Blankinship, "Gates, Buffett Lobby the Rich for Donation Pledges," *The Huffington Post*, June 24, 2010. Specifically, the article pointed out that "only 17 people on the Forbes list of the 400 wealthiest people in America are also on the Chronicle's list of the most generous American donors."

50 Carol J. Loomis, "The $600 Billion Challenge," *Fortune*, June 16, 2010.

51 *The Index of Global Philanthropy 2008* (Washington, DC: The Hudson Institute, 2008).

52 Dovelyn Rannveig Agunias, *Remittances and Development: Trends, impacts, and policy options* (Washington, DC: Migration Policy Institute, 2006).

53 Francie Ostrower, *Why the Wealthy Give: The culture of elite philanthropy* (Princeton, NJ: Princeton University Press, 1997).

54 Hoon Chang Yau, "Face, Faith, and Forgiveness: Elite Chinese philanthropy in Indonesia," in *Chinese Philanthropy in Asia: Between Continuity and Change, Special Issue of Journal of Asian Business*, ed. Thomas Menkhoff and Hoon Chang Yau (2010).

55 Chan Kwok Bun, "Doing Good as Exchange," in *Chinese Philanthropy in Asia: Between Continuity and Change, Special Issue of Journal of Asian Business*, ed. Thomas Menkhoff and Hoon Chang Yau (2010).

56 The Family Business Network was set up in 1990 and is now represented in more than 50 countries with a membership of more than 3,200 family business leaders with 25 chapters in America, Asia, and Europe. www.fbn-i.org.

57 Philanthropy 3.0: Shelly Banjo, "Not Your Parents' Philanthropy," WSJ Blogs, March 8, 2010, www.blogs.wsj.com/financial-adviser/2010/03/08/not-your-parents-philanthropy; New Golden Age of Philanthropy: "A New Golden Age of Philanthropy?" Philanthropy News Digest, The Foundation Center, January 4, 2007, www.foundationcenter.org/pnd/ specialissues/content.jhtml?id=165400065; The Second Philanthropic Revolution: Willie Cheng, *Doing Good Well* (Singapore: John Wiley & Sons, 2009).

Chapter 9

Venture Philanthropy

Venturing into Entrepreneurial Philanthropy

ROB JOHN
Advisor, Asia Venture Philanthropy Network

From its springboard in Silicon Valley a decade ago, venture philanthropy has grown into a global movement.

At its heart is a highly engaged partnership that offers development finance coupled with nonfinancial advice that social purpose organizations need in order to grow sustainably.

The landscape of venture philanthropy contains a diverse mix of players, including neo-philanthropists, traditional foundations, the private equity community, and even governments, working with social entrepreneurs, social enterprises, and other investees.

These venture philanthropists are creating new forms of social finance, and new ways to increase and measure the impact of their investees' work.

Social entrepreneurs and social purpose organizations need access to capital as well as business acumen to drive innovation and reach an adequate scale of social impact. Venture philanthropy is a growing global movement that offers these resources by adapting existing tools of venture capital for social benefit.

The term "venture philanthropy" may have been first coined in 1969 by American philanthropist John D. Rockefeller III to describe, before a US Congressional committee, an adventurous approach for funding unpopular social causes.[1] However, it was not until the late 1990s that the term and its meaning as used today became popular.

Christine Letts and William Ryan's 1997 paper in the *Harvard Business Review*[2] has been credited in many quarters with the initial thought leadership for this movement. They urged foundations to employ venture capital tools to invest in the capacity building, rather than the programmatic needs, of social purpose organizations. Porter and Kramer[3] further challenged foundations to create value and not simply be a passive conduit for transferring finance from private sources to grantees.

In the late 1990s, Silicon Valley's newly wealthy dot-com entrepreneurs-turned-philanthropists took up the challenge and became associated with a form of high-engagement philanthropy; though, in many ways, it is not surprising that the intrusion into the social sector world by these neo-philanthropists was not always warmly embraced by incumbent grantmakers.[4]

In the midst of this nascent growth, a number of business entrepreneurs keen to apply commercial skills to their grantmaking launched new US-based funds. Paul Brainerd (founder of Aldus and Pagemaker) set up Social Venture Partners; Mario Marino (technology entrepreneur) established Venture Philanthropy Partners; and George Roberts (private equity firm KKR) experimented with supporting social enterprises through the Roberts Enterprise Development Fund.[5]

This growing attention has also prompted established foundations to re-look at their approaches to grantmaking. Through these developments, venture philanthropy has firmly taken hold in the social space and rapidly evolved in form and function.

Venture Philanthropy Baseline

Several terms have been used interchangeably to describe venture philanthropy: strategic philanthropy, high-engagement philanthropy, effective philanthropy, or engaged philanthropy. Indeed, the multiplicity of terms is a reflection of the ever-evolving and innovative approaches applied to this new form of social finance.

The defining feature of venture philanthropy is not the kind of finance offered or return on investment sought. In fact, venture philanthropy is more like a broad spectrum of practices, with different practitioners emphasizing various aspects more than others do. However, we can draw out some of these common principles and processes from the present practitioners.

Principles

Generally speaking, there are five core principles of venture philanthropy practice that, when combined, distinguish it from other forms of social finance:[6]

1. *Funding as Investment:* Venture philanthropists view their funding as helping organizations improve their operations. They will commit to funding during the transitional period that typically lasts three to five years. Importantly, they view their funding as "investments" in the organization, rather than as purchasing their services on behalf of beneficiaries. While many traditional social sector funders do provide long-term funding, they seldom have the characteristics of a typical investment in organizational development. Viewing funding as an investment creates an investor–investee relationship where there is better alignment of common goals, greater shared accountability, and a deeper sense of true partnership.

2. *Building Capacity and Infrastructure:* Most social purpose organizations operate below capacity, with underdeveloped systems, and few resources for developing people. Venture philanthropists focus on helping build stronger, more sustainable organizations. They expect their funds to be deployed on salaries, systems, and infrastructure, rather than direct project costs. Increased capacity allows an organization to reach more people with better services. This investment in capacity is motivated by a mutually agreed plan that the organization will deliver greater social value as a result of greater organizational robustness.

3. *Focus on Outcomes:* Venture philanthropists are concerned that the organizations they support create real social impact resulting from the organizational change they are funding. They assist these organizations to effectively communicate social impact to all stakeholders. They seek to pick "winners"—organizations with the credible potential to scale up and deliver more benefits to society. To do this, they remain focused on outcomes. Through an

agreed strategic plan, systematic reporting, and milestone-based funding, they hold the organization to account for its operational performance and social impact generated.

4. *An Engaged and Focused Relationship:* Venture philanthropists generally work with a small number of organizations at any one time, preferring a deeper engagement than might otherwise be possible with a large portfolio of grantees. This feature lies at the heart of venture philanthropy and it is, perhaps, what distinguishes it most from traditional funding models. Venture philanthropists are also committed to adding as much value as possible beyond finance. It is not unusual for a venture philanthropy fund to accept one or more places on the board of the organization or to attend board meetings as an observer, to add value in both governance and strategy.[7] This is not the normal practice of social sector funders.

5. *Investing in People and Leaders:* Capable leadership is essential for robust organizations going through a period of growth. Yet, many traditional funders prefer to offer funding based on the merits of a project proposal and the reputation of the organization. Just as a venture capital or private equity firm places considerable weight on the capabilities of a business entrepreneur and management team, so venture philanthropists tend to weigh up a potential investment by the qualities of the social entrepreneur, the nonprofit leader, and the team. Trustees or directors are expected to exercise their statutory duty and hold management teams to account. Unlike private equity firms, however, venture philanthropists do not have financial equity ownership powers to interfere dramatically with the board or replace it extensively. Instead, they will provide the resources to help nurture strong executives and boards.

These five principles are among the characteristics of good grantmaking or social investment. In venture philanthropy, they converge to an intense relationship with a focus on sustainable building of capacity to deliver growth in mission and impact. It is viewed as an active, hands-on investment in an organization and its people.

Investment Process

Not unlike the venture capital investment process, how a venture philanthropist decides to invest in a charitable organization also follows similar fundamental principles:[8]

1. *Deal Flow:* Generating a constant flow of potential high-quality investments through proactive searching is considered one of the most challenging aspects of managing a successful venture philanthropy fund. Potential investment targets can be identified through existing portfolio organizations, networking with other funders, and business plan competitions.

2. *Investment Appraisal:* There is a clear and transparent process for appraising and selecting organizations for investment. The venture philanthropist would judge the investee's leadership capabilities and potential. This includes a screening of focus, geography, and social relevance, and getting an overall picture of the organization's activities, projects, and partners. Further due diligence follows with analysis of the business plan and interviews with staff and managers, covering key aspects of the organization and its mission.

3. *Portfolio Management:* The plan for the investment phase would be mutually agreed upon and set out in the investment contract. The fund will ensure the portfolio is, overall, well managed, with linkages and opportunities for cross-investee learning where possible. A typical venture philanthropy fund may have 5 to 10 portfolio investees, enabling the venture philanthropist to develop a relatively hands-on relationship with an investee. When problems arise with the investee, the venture philanthropist is well positioned to offer advice and support, as well as to leverage its networks and expertise.

4. *Adding Value through Nonfinancial Services:*[9] The blend of nonfinancial services and financial capital is a defining feature of the venture philanthropy approach. Nonfinancial services offered may focus on people (e.g. mentoring, recruitment, and board strengthening) or address operational issues (e.g. strategic planning, marketing, branding, and finance). Some advice is long-term and sustained during the investment, or it may address short-term, one-off needs. Inputs can come from the venture philanthropists or via strategic partnerships with external consultants.

5. *Performance Measurement:* The intensive, time-bound nature of a venture philanthropic investment is often tied to ambitious growth plans and calls for tight performance metrics. This is a complex and evolving area that cannot be simply reduced to measuring financial viability or return. Although the investment contract will set out clear deliverables and milestones, funders and investees

will need to agree to a performance measurement framework that gathers, analyzes, and communicates relevant data. The Balanced Scorecard[10] methodology has been used by some funds for this purpose.

6. *Exit:* Although venture philanthropy investments are not viewed as being open-ended, they may, as mentioned, last as long as two to five years. The concept of an "exit" would be discussed openly with the organization's leadership team before an investment decision is approved; this helps to manage expectations and bring a sense of discipline to the relationship, with metrics in place to measure success that will, in turn, trigger the exit. Well-developed capacity for fundraising and a healthy balance sheet are some examples.

The Venture Philanthropy Landscape

Official statistics on the size and classification of the venture philanthropy sector do not exist. This is an emerging field for which information on funds and activities is neither mandated nor widely known. This is compounded by the lack of a generally accepted definition of what constitutes a venture philanthropy operation. Alternatively branded as a model, or a philanthropic approach, some existing and new organizations have adopted the term, while others have not.

However, we can make some broad estimates based on the known players and the participation at venture philanthropy industry associations and forums. The number of "purist" funds which have largely embraced the venture philanthropic model would likely number 150 globally.[11] Most of these would be characterized as managing a small portfolio, providing capital for growth, and a mechanism for delivering nonfinancial services. We may add to this list of purist funds another 100 or so organizations, such as traditional foundations and other capacity builders who are incorporating elements of the venture philanthropy approach into their grantmaking and support activities.

By their very nature, these venture philanthropy organizations and funds evade an easy taxonomy. However, we can perhaps better understand the landscape of venture philanthropy by looking at the following dimensions of these organizations:

- Size of funding
- Founders' origins
- Investment and operating approach.

Size of Funding

While many funds are legally constituted as charitable foundations, not all jurisdictions require public disclosure of assets and expenditure. This can lead to a rather opaque view of the financial size of the growing global venture philanthropy movement. It is perhaps an irony that some venture philanthropy funds do not disclose their investment and financial details while criticizing the nonprofit sector for a lack of transparency.[12]

In the UK and the US, where there is a high level of statutory public disclosure of venture philanthropy funds, we can see that there is a wide spread of fund asset sizes, ranging from less than US$1 million (e.g. the Venture Partnership Foundation) to those with more than US$1 billion (e.g. the Children's Investment Fund Foundation).[13]

However, measuring funds by the size of their assets as in the venture capital industry may not be fully meaningful. Venture capital funds are closed, and all funds are meant to be deployed for investments to maximize financial returns. Venture philanthropy funds, on the other hand, are a mix of endowments (some in perpetuity and some to be spent down over a period of time) and those that continually raise new money.[14] In addition, a large part of the venture philanthropic investments tends to be in the form of grants where the money does not return, let alone grow.

Thus, the annual (grantmaking) expenditure of these funds is more representative of the scale of the fund's operations than the asset size of the funds. Table 9.1 provides a sample listing of venture philanthropy funds based on annual expenditure of the funds across the three major regions of the US, Europe, and Asia.

Founders' Origins

In recognizing venture philanthropy as a new field that is in the process of expanding its reach globally, one useful classification is by origin of the founder(s).

Owing to similarities to the venture capital business model, many private equity and hedge fund professionals have initiated venture philanthropy organizations.

Table 9.1 A Selection of Worldwide Venture Philanthropy Funds by Annual Fund Expenditure

	US	Europe	Asia
Known number of funds[15]	45	48 in 17 countries	26 in 8 countries
Funds with up to US$5 million in annual expenditure	REDF Blue Ridge Foundation New York Full Circle Fund Great Bay Foundation for Social Entrepreneurship Echoing Green Foundation	Venture Partnership Foundation (UK) BonVenture (Germany) Good Deed Foundation (Estonia) Fondazione Oltre (Italy) Voxtra (Norway) Impetus Trust (UK) Breakthrough (UK) UnLtd Ventures (UK)	Edelgive Foundation (India) SVP (Singapore & Tokyo) apVentures (Singapore) Dasra (India) ADM Capital Foundation (Hong Kong) Flow Inc. (Taiwan) ETIC (Japan) Social Ventures Australia
Funds with between US$5 million and US$20 million in annual expenditure	New Profit Inc. NewSchools Venture Fund Venture Philanthropy Partners Social Venture Partners (SVP)[16]	Private Equity Foundation (UK) Media Development Loan Fund (Czech Republic) LGT Venture Philanthropy Foundation (Switzerland) The One Foundation (Ireland)	Aavishkaar (India) Jet Li One Foundation (China)
Funds with more than US$20 million in annual expenditure	The Robin Hood Foundation James Irvine Foundation The Edna McConnell Clark Foundation Acumen Fund	Children's Investment Fund Foundation (UK)	

Successful business entrepreneurs in search of a philanthropy legacy are attracted by the business-like approach of venture philanthropy. Social entrepreneurs who recognize the power of harnessing businesspeople and their business-like approach to giving have also set up such funds.

Some established, professionally managed grantmaking foundations have reengineered their operations along venture philanthropy lines— either embracing or avoiding the label. Family offices with a philanthropic inclination could also embrace the venture philanthropy approach.

Even governments have taken the plunge to experiment with this new approach to giving and growing the sector.

Table 9.2 provides a sample list of venture philanthropic organizations that are based on their founders' origins.

Table 9.2 Examples of Worldwide Venture Philanthropy Funds by Founders' Origins

FOUNDER'S ORIGINS	US	Europe	Asia
Private equity related	REDF	Fondazione Oltre (Italy)	Social Ventures Australia
Hedge fund related	Robin Hood Foundation	Children's Investment Fund Foundation (UK)	ADM Capital Foundation (Hong Kong)
Business entrepreneur	Venture Philanthropy Partners	The One Foundation (Ireland)	Sopoong (South Korea)
Social entrepreneur	New Profit Inc.	Good Deed Foundation (Estonia)	UnLtd India
Professional grantmaking foundation	Edna McConnell Clark Foundation	King Baudouin Foundation (Belgium)	Jet Li One Foundation (China)
Government (as initiator or major partner)	Social Innovation Fund (a "fund of funds" in pilot stage)	Inspiring Scotland (UK)	
Family office	Webber Family Foundation	Bonventure (Germany)	Legacy Advisors (Hong Kong)

Investment and Operating Approach

Venture philanthropy organizations adopt a range of different approaches and techniques to target and support their investee organizations.

Some venture philanthropy funds are targeted solely at social enterprises, others at charities. In terms of the stage of these investee organizations, most funds will take on existing organizations with a track record, history of operations, and ambitions for credible growth. Only a small number of funds focus on the much riskier early stage investee.

Venture philanthropy organizations use a range of financial instruments to help their investees. For more traditional venture philanthropy funds, grants are commonly used. Increasingly, venture philanthropists are experimenting with other forms of finance which allow recycling of funds (e.g. patient capital structured as debt), or the ownership of equity (or forms of "quasi-equity"). The more innovative venture philanthropy funds will look for a blended return on investment—that is, a quantifiable social and financial return on capital.

With regards to their own corporate structure, most funds are created as independent entities. Depending on their mission and operations, some may be legally incorporated as nonprofit charitable foundations or regulated investment funds. We are beginning to see some funds emerge from preexisting organizations—for example, a specialist venture philanthropy department as part of a larger grantmaking foundation.

Table 9.3 provides examples of venture philanthropy funds using these different investments and operating approaches across the three regions.

The Venture Philanthropy Adventure

The rush of the last decade has seen a diverse group of players exploring, and experimenting with, a myriad of approaches to venture philanthropy. For those who have embarked on this adventure, they are likely to encounter:

- A growing global movement
- Traditional foundations changing their grantmaking approaches

Table 9.3 Examples of Worldwide Venture Philanthropy Funds by Investment and Operating Approach

APPROACH	US	Europe	Asia
Investee Type			
• Charity/nonprofit	Full Circle Fund	Invest for Children (Spain)	Non Profit Incubator (China)
• Social enterprise	REDF	Breakthrough (UK)	Flow Inc. (Taiwan)
Investee Stage			
• Early stage	Echoing Green	Andrews Charitable Trust (UK)	UnLtd India
• Growth	New Schools Venture Fund	Impetus Trust (UK)	Dasra (India)
Financial Instrument			
• Grant	Social Venture Partners	ARK (UK)	Jet Li One Foundation (China)
• Loans	Acumen Fund	Venturesome (UK)	Foresters Community Investment Fund (Australia)
• Equity	Adena Ventures	Canopus Foundation (Germany)	Aavishkar (India)
Corporate Structure			
• Stand alone	New Profit Inc.	Voxtra (Norway)	Social Ventures Australia
• Departmental		King Baudouin Foundation (Belgium)	
Geography			
• Domestic	Robin Hood Foundation	UnLtd (UK)	Social Ventures Australia
• International	Acumen Fund	Rianta Capital (UK/India)	ADM Capital Foundation (Hong Kong)

- An engaged private equity community
- Emerging governmental participation
- Social entrepreneurs and social enterprises as desirable investees
- New forms of social finance
- Need for marketplace intelligence.

A Global Movement

The pioneers of venture philanthropy certainly were American; most of them from Silicon Valley who generously applied their newfound wealth and insights from their technology ventures.

By the early 21st century, interest in what was perceived as a controversial American movement arrived in Europe, landing first in the UK. The first British fund to describe itself as a venture philanthropy organization was Impetus Trust which was launched in 2002 by individuals with venture capital and consulting backgrounds.[17]

Subsequently, numerous isolated initiatives across Europe gave focus to this movement. It resulted in the founding of the European Venture Philanthropy Association (EVPA)[18] in 2003 by five executives from the European private equity industry. EVPA's popularity was further cemented by its endorsement from the European Private Equity and Venture Capital Association (EVCA), sponsorship by several leading private equity firms, and support from European grantmaking foundations and their influential network, the European Foundation Centre. It is today headquartered in Brussels and has a membership of some 120 organizations across 20 countries.

In a landmark work on European foundations, Luc Tayart de Borms, while applauding the energy and innovation found in US philanthropy, emphasized that the strengths of European philanthropy lie in a European social model "based on social cohesion: full employment, open democracy, and transparency in governance."[19] European practitioners have since not just adapted, but also innovated, the classical US venture philanthropy models. The particular features of European venture philanthropy include a highly networked group of venture philanthropy funds, influential European foundations, and private equity firms across 30 countries pushing the envelope on more adventurous funding instruments.[20]

With venture philanthropy firmly established in the US and Europe, the movement has begun to take root in Asia in recent years. The initial mapping exercises by the Asia Venture Philanthropy Network, which was established in 2010,[21] revealed growing venture philanthropy activity in the region. The Social Venture Partners model, first founded in Seattle, Washington, is being replicated in Singapore and Tokyo and adapted in Hong Kong. ADM Capital, a Hong Kong-based investment advisor, launched its own venture philanthropy foundation to invest in regional organizations. Indian venture philanthropy funds are actively investing in a wide spectrum of social investees. European and American venture philanthropy funds such as ARK, LGT Venture Philanthropy, and Rianta Capital have also made investments in Asia. There are also signs of interest in social entrepreneurship and innovation in philanthropy in China. Over the last five years, over 800 private foundations have registered in China, some employing the language of venture philanthropy. In July 2010, the China Foundation Center was launched.[22]

A number of transitional economies in the world have benefited from cross-border venture philanthropy investments. For example, since 1996, the Media Development Loan Fund has provided US$55 million in low-cost financing to 69 independent media companies in 23 countries. For the past 10 years, the Nonprofit Enterprise and Self-sustainability Team has been helping social enterprises grow sustainably throughout Central Europe and Latin America.[23]

These domestic and international initiatives continue to sow the seeds of a venture philanthropy movement that has impacted the world in immeasurable ways.

Traditional Foundations

The legacy of venture philanthropy will, arguably, be most visible in its ability to influence traditional philanthropy.

In his masterly book on the American Foundation, Joel Fleishman argues that today's venture philanthropists are "merely conducting themselves as great figures like Andrew Carnegie did and as he urged other wealthy donors to do in his *Gospel of Wealth*."[24] He suggests that "venture philanthropy and social entrepreneurship will increasingly shape not only the way philanthropy is organized in the US and other wealthy countries, but also the ways that foundations carry out their grantmaking." He goes on to argue that long-standing foundations will evolve venture philanthropy characteristics to better serve the organizations they support with methods that "significantly overachieve in impact, the dollars spent the old-fashioned way."

In the US and Europe, we are seeing established foundations engage in the venture philanthropy movement:

- The Edna McConnell Clark Foundation now operates a model that contains venture philanthropy principles after reviewing the effectiveness of its 30-year old grants program.[25]

- The King Baudouin Foundation in Belgium launched its own internal venture philanthropy fund in November 2009 with a budget of €1 million (US$1.2 million).[26]
- Fondazione CRT, one of the largest banking foundations in Italy, actively promotes venture philanthropy through conferences and provides co-funding for an Italian venture philanthropy fund, Fondazione Sviluppo e Crescita CRT (Foundation and Growth CRT), with commitments of US$170 million.[27]

The Private Equity Community

First seen in the UK and now an emerging trend worldwide, the participation of the private equity community in venture philanthropy continues to be a much sought after resource. In recent years, private equity firms have been under government and media scrutiny over their business practices and profiteering. While many individual private equity professionals may be generous philanthropists, the industry as a whole had been reluctant to commit to a strategic and open approach to social responsibility. Arguably, this is now changing, in part due to the new opportunities afforded by the growth of venture philanthropy models.

The basic operational elements of venture philanthropy—an approach that views high-potential nonprofits as entities to be invested in—appeals to those whose day job is selecting commercial companies with unrealized growth potential, investing in them with growth finance, and adding value through a range of nonfinancial services. In other words, individual private equity professionals and firms find that these more meaningful forms of philanthropy and corporate social responsibility are well aligned with their core business practices and skills.

Even as private equity firms and individuals invest in venture philanthropy, they bring with them the ecosphere of firms and individuals that provide services to private equity. Thus strategy consultants, lawyers, accountants, and other professionals serving private equity industry also end up offering free consultation to venture philanthropy funds and their portfolio organizations.

The EVPA had been proactive in encouraging greater engagement with private equity. It sought and obtained the endorsement of the industry body EVCA.

The Private Equity Foundation (PEF)[28] is another prime example of the private equity sector coming together in support of venture philanthropy. PEF was launched in 2006 in the UK by 28 global private equity and related firms. By aiming to harness the skills capital in the private equity industry as well as its financial capital, PEF signals a deepening and increasingly visible commitment by the private equity industry to its social responsibilities.

Governments

With the increasing visibility of venture philanthropy's support of organizations that are resolving social issues, it is unavoidable that governments worldwide are taking a second look at the efficacy of their involvement in the social sector and jumping into the fray to provide funds in support of the industry.

Although examples are currently few and far between, the Obama Administration's Social Innovation Fund[29] appears to be strongly supportive of the venture philanthropy approach. Established in 2010, the US$50 million fund is available for re-granting to intermediaries engaged in social innovation. The *Chronicle of Philanthropy* notes that although the seed funds appear limited, "foundations and nonprofit groups [are required to] match the federal money." As a result, the fund will generate US$200 million in support on an annual basis. Over five years, this adds up to a potential US$1 billion investment in the social sector.[30]

Other departments in the US government are also gearing up to support venture philanthropy, as evidenced by the US Department of Education's announcement of its US$650 million Investing in Innovation Fund in October 2009.[31]

Social Entrepreneurs and Social Enterprises

The rise of social entrepreneurs in the last decade has created more investment opportunities for venture philanthropy funds. With their natural predisposition toward entrepreneurship, trading models, and business acumen, venture philanthropy organizations are well positioned to support the rapidly growing, global social enterprise movement.[32]

The pioneering venture capitalist Sir Ronald Cohen paints a compelling picture of the relationship between hi-tech entrepreneurship and venture capital.[33] He describes this as resembling the two strands of the Double Helix—an intimately wound mutuality where one strand supports the advance of the other. This analogy recognizes that business entrepreneurs need access to the specialist finance of venture capital to develop their ideas and to start up and grow the enterprises. Similarly, the evolving movement of social entrepreneurship and social enterprises needs an equivalent source of financing—and this, venture philanthropy can provide.

Social Finance

Venture philanthropy organizations stretch their creativity to provide a range of financing options from non-returnable grants, debt and equity, to new-fangled hybrid instruments that combine them.[34]

An example is Venturesome, a £16 million (US$23 million) UK-based fund that aims to increase the range of financing available to charities and social enterprises.[35] Since 2002, it has offered a range of financial services to over 200 organizations. It manages four funds targeted at different kinds of investees. During the screening process, Venturesome's team seeks to understand the organization's social mission and business model, reviews its funding structure, and assesses its need for risk finance. Venturesome aims to "recycle" its investments while accepting a much higher risk than traditional lenders. To date, its historic loss rate across all three funds is 3 percent, although it expects this to rise to 10 percent across its entire portfolio over the coming years.[36]

Intelligence in the Marketplace

Conventional investment wisdom holds that where information is lacking, opportunities do not materialize as investors make poor decisions or face risks that are deemed too high. The social sector is even more information-opaque, and potential funders are sometimes frustrated by the lack of transparency and absence of high-quality, independent information. This has led to initiatives that try to bring "market intelligence" to the social sector and provide funders with information about social organizations and their progress at addressing social issues.

GuideStar International is a web-based platform that provides data on social organizations. It is currently fully operational in the US and UK and is expanding to Latin America, Africa, and Asia. It recently announced a merger with the global civil society organization database, TechSoup Global.[37]

New Philanthropy Capital was set up in 2002 to provide in-depth sector and specific intelligence on charities through its open reports that are styled like investment analyst research notes and customized reports for individual funders.[38] This approach encourages investment decisions that are based on an understanding of quality information from the sector of interest.

Venturing into the Future

In the last decade, venture philanthropy has mobilized new resources, formed new networks, created new financial instruments, and pioneered new approaches to grantmaking in growing the social sector.

Whither the future of venture philanthropy? The short answer would be more of the same "new." However, these will likely be more ambitious, more creative, and more diverse.

It will be more ambitious because many of these venture philanthropists are not content with addressing the localized social issues they started with, but are seeking to solve the world's social problems. They come from a background of thinking big and making it big. They will apply that same mindset to resolving social issues.

It will be more creative in grantmaking approaches and in the development of new financial instruments that blend the values of the commercial and social worlds. Already, hybrid debt-equity financing and secondary markets for these financial instruments are emerging.

It will be more diverse. Beyond funding the traditional nonprofits and emerging social enterprises, venture philanthropists are increasingly looking toward funding and catalyzing social innovation. The methods they use are also becoming more diverse, from direct funding and services, to the use of competition, campaigns, and cross-sector collaboration.

It will be an exciting future.

Endnotes

1   Rockefeller used the term "venture philanthropy" in a 1969 congressional committee hearing leading to the *Tax Reform Act*. The term was also used in 1984 in the annual report of the Peninsula Community Foundation to describe a new breed of philanthropists.

2   Christine Letts and William Ryan, "Virtuous Capital: What foundations can learn from venture capital," *Harvard Business Review*, March/April 1997.

3   Michel Porter and Mark Kramer, "Philanthropy's New Agenda: Creating value," *Harvard Business Review*, November/December 1999.

4   Bruce Sievers, *If Pigs Had Wings: The appeal and limits of venture philanthropy* (Washington, DC: Center for Public & Nonprofit Leadership, 2001), www.cpnl.georgetown.edu/doc_pool/Nielsen0103Sievers.pdf.

5   Social Venture Partners, www.svpi.org; Venture Philanthropy Partners, www .venturephilanthropypartners.org; REDF, www.redf.org.

6   These five principles are adapted from the work of leading US venture philanthropist Paul Shoemaker of Social Venture Partners. See "Social Venture Philanthropy at 10: Problems, promises, prospects," transcript of a conference given at the Bradley Center for Philanthropy and Civic Renewal, Hudson Institute, Washington, DC, on November 27, 2007.

7   Rob John, *Beyond the Cheque: How venture philanthropists add value*, Skoll Centre for Social Entrepreneurship Working Paper (Oxford: Saïd Business School, 2007).

8   The investment process is described in further detail in the publication by Luciano Balbo, Deirdre Mortell, and Pieter Oostlander, *Establishing a Venture Philanthropy Fund in Europe: A practical guide* (Brussels: European Venture Philanthropy Association, 2008).

9   The EVPA recommends a best practice code for the provision of nonfinancial services to its investees. It can be summarized as: (1) Do no harm; (2) Help—not do it for—the organization; (3) Evaluate attitudes, not just skills, of third party providers; and (4) *Pro bono* work should be treated like paid work. See Rob John, *Beyond the Cheque: How venture philanthropists add value*, Skoll Centre for Social Entrepreneurship Working Paper (Oxford: Saïd Business School, 2007).

10   The first adaptation of the Balanced Scorecard for use by a venture philanthropy fund is documented by the tool's creator, Robert Kaplan, in a Harvard Business School case study: "New Profit Inc.: Governing the Nonprofit Enterprise," *Harvard Business School Case Study*, July 2001.

11   As shown in Table 9.1, the number of known venture philanthropy funds is 128 (Europe: 48; Asia 26; US 45; plus another 9 outside of these 3 regions). The actual number would be higher than this and we have estimated this at about 150, including models on the periphery of venture philanthropy and funds known to be starting up.

12   This is one area where venture philanthropy networks and associations can encourage minimum standards of public disclosure of their assets and grants.

13   Venture Partnership Foundation, www.vpf.org.uk; Children's Investment Fund Foundation, www.ciff.org.

14   Also, some funds may have large endowments but only spend a fraction on venture philanthropy-type investments. For example, the Robin Hood Foundation spends more than US$130 million annually, but most of this is actually general grantmaking, not venture philanthropy. See www.robinhood.org/home.aspx.

15   The sources of the estimates are: (1) US: From the last-known survey of US venture philanthropy funds—*Venture Philanthropy 2002: Advancing non-profit performance through high-engagement grantmaking* (Washington, DC: Community Wealth Ventures Inc., 2002). (2) Europe: The figure of 48 is based on all of EVPA's "full" members as of April 2010, plus a number of "associate" members that are starting up and do not yet have mature operational models. There will be active and starting-up venture philanthropy funds in Europe that are not members of EVPA, so the overall figure is likely to be higher. (3) Asia: This is based on initial mapping exercises by AVPN in eight Asian nations in early 2010.

16   The 18 listed Social Venture Partner franchises in the US are treated as separate funds. See www.svpi.org/our-members.

17 www.impetus.org.uk.

18 www.evpa.eu.com.

19 Luc Tayart de Borms, *Foundations: Creating impact in a globalised world* (London: John Wiley & Sons, 2005).

20 Rob John, "Venture Philanthropy Takes Off in Europe," *Die Stiftung*, September 2008.

21 The Asia Venture Philanthropy Network is established by Doug Miller and Rob John, both of whom were involved with the start up of the EVPA. See www.avpn.asia.

22 SVP Tokyo, www.sv-tokyo.org; SVPI, www.svpi.org; ADM Capital, www.admcap.com & ADM Capital Foundation, www.admcf.org; ARK, www.arkonline.org; LGT Venture Philanthropy, www.lgt.com/en/private_kunden/philanthropie/index.html; and China Foundation Center, www.foundationcenter.org.cn.

23 Media Development Loan Fund, www.mdlf.org; Nonprofit Enterprise and Self-sustainability Team (NESsT), www.nesst.org. MDLF and its founder, Sasa Vucinic is further covered in Chapter 6, "Social Entrepreneurship: Of pattern changers and changemakers," by Chris Cusano.

24 Joel Fleishman, *The Foundation: The great American secret* (Cambridge, MA: PublicAffairs, 2007).

25 Philanthropy News Digest, "Interview with Michael Bailin, President of The Edna McConnell Clark Foundation," September 27, 2002, www.foundationcenter.org/pnd/newsmakers/nwsmkr.jhtml?id=4700076.

26 www.kbs-frb.be/domain_search.aspx?theme=243340&LangType=1033.

27 "The Foundation's Development and Growth—CRT," FondazioneSviluppo e Crescita-CR, presentation on October 15, 2008, www.fondazionecrt.it/index/eventiNews/news/Fond_sril_cresc.html. Translation available on the website. CRT Foundation also convened a conference on venture philanthropy in June 2008, as reported in the news release "Venture Philanthropy: Un modello per l'Italia?" at www.fondazionecrt.it/index/eventiNews/eventi/venture_phil.html.

28 www.privateequityfoundation.org.

29 www.nationalservice.gov/about/serveamerica/innovation.asp.

30 Cheryl Dorsey and Paul Schmitz, "Social Innovation Fund Sends Important Signal to Grant Makers," *The Chronicle of Philanthropy*, 22(5), 2009, www.nonprofitfinancefund.org/docs/2010/1-14-10ChronOfPhil.pdf.

31 Ibid.

32 Social entrepreneurs and social entrepreneurship is covered in Chapter 6, "Social Entrepreneurship: Of pattern changers and changemakers," by Chris Cusano. Social enterprise is covered in Chapter 5, "Social Enterprises: Fulfilling the promise of social enterprise," by Jon Huggett.

33 Ronald Cohen, *The Second Bounce of the Ball* (London: Weidenfeld & Nicolson, 2007).

34 These new forms of finance are covered in Chapter 18, "Social Finance: Financing change, changing finance," by Jed Emerson.

35 www.cafonline.org/default.aspx?page=6903.

36   Venturesome's model is highly innovative, which makes comparison of its recycling loss rate difficult to compare to other funders in the social or commercial markets. What is important to note, however, is that Venturesome is introducing a new "mindset" to both donors and charities. Donors can now view their donations as being beyond one-off grants. But instead of having the potential to finance social change in multiples through recycling, charities are more confident in accepting that their financing need not be wholly dependent on non-returnable grants.

37   GuideStar International, www.guidestarinternational.org (details can be found in the *Alliance Magazine*, www.alliancemagazine.org/node/3272); Techsoup Global, www .techsoupglobal.org/.

38   www.philanthropycapital.org.

Community

Chapter 10

Donor Management

Closing the Funding Gap

PAULETTE MAEHARA
President and CEO, Association of Fundraising Professionals

Many nonprofit organizations struggle for funds. Yet, going by current levels of giving relative to the capacity of givers, the potential for more funds is huge.

Professional fundraisers and a fundraising industry have emerged to help with the important function of fundraising. The key to good donor management is understanding what donors want and what stewardship of the donor relationship involves.

In this new environment of giving, there is much that nonprofit organizations can harness from new possibilities presented by the new rich and by online giving, while heeding the issues presented by third-party fundraisers and concerns over donor privacy.

$\mathbf{M}$uch of the resources needed by nonprofit organizations (NPOs) are contributed by the community: time (volunteers) and money (donations).

Financial resources are critical to every NPO, and most NPOs today recognize the importance of fundraising. However, many lack the expertise or are looking for alternative sources of funding; social enterprises and new forms of social finance are coming into vogue in this regard.[1]

Yet, the potential for a higher level of donations to meet the funding gaps of NPOs is out there, ripe for the picking.

The Funding Potential

It may be a surprise to many donors that, in fact, NPOs across the world receive very little by way of donations to fund their operations. In relative terms, donations only account, on average, for about 12 percent of an NPO's revenue, the rest coming from fees and services (53 percent) and government grants (34 percent).[2] Among countries, though, private giving, on average, ranges from 2 to 43 percent of total NPO revenue. This shows the potential that could be reached in countries with low percentages.

The greater question is what the capacities of givers are and how much they have given relative to those capacities.

In a comparative study of giving across major countries, Charities Aid Foundation (CAF) found a wide range in the proportion of what individuals give relative to their country's GDP (see Figure 10.1).[3] The levels range from a low of 0.14 percent for France to a high of 1.7 percent for the US, which is 12 times more. There are, of course, many reasons for the country differences, such as culture, religious beliefs, wealth distribution, social insurance schemes, and tax incentives. The US, for instance, has a tax regime that encourages private giving. Nevertheless, with the US setting the benchmark, the potential for the other countries is a multiple of their current giving levels.

But is the US level of giving a good standard to aspire to? The CAF's study notes that "there is no direct relationship between high average incomes and a high proportion of national expenditure given to charity." Several other studies have shown that while the wealthy give more, they actually give less as a proportion of their income than those less well off.[4]

Figure 10.1 Countries Ranked by Giving as a Percentage of GDP

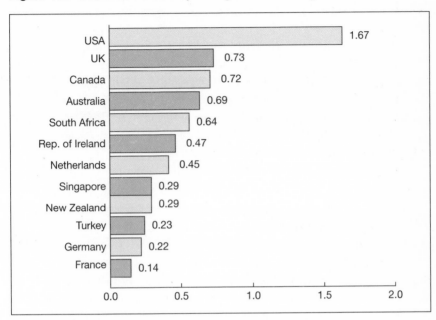

Source: *CAF Briefing Paper: International comparisons of charitable giving*
(West Malling, UK: Charities Aid Foundation, 2006).

Analyzing this "generosity gap" in the US using 2003 tax data, Claude Rosenberg and Tim Stone estimated that if the affluent donated the same proportion of their income as did those less well-off, there would be at least US$25 billion more in donations; and if the affluent gave as much as they could reasonably afford (in the view of the authors), that amount would increase to US$100 billion a year.[5]

No matter how the numbers are cut, it would appear that the potential is huge for greater giving to help close the funding gap for NPOs. The challenge is how NPOs can harness this funding potential.

Most NPOs have staff and volunteers who focus on fundraising. Many of the larger and more mature NPOs have dedicated fundraising staff, sometimes entire fundraising departments with 50 or more staff.[6]

Over time, a fundraising industry has emerged and grown, with fundraising professionals who work in NPOs and are supported by a plethora of consultancies, training organizations, educational institutions, research groups, conventions, and specialty vendors. Where appropriate, they have also developed their own networks for sharing their experiences and learning. With over 30,000 members in 212 chapters across the world, the Association of Fundraising Professionals is the largest industry association of its kind.[7]

Indeed, the professional approaches to fundraising and donor management are manifold and often sophisticated. But fundamentally, most professional fundraisers will provide three broad pieces of advice on harnessing the potential of donors:

- Understand the donor—in particular, what he or she wants.
- Steward the relationship with the donory
- Heed emerging donor issues and fundraising opportunities.

What Donors Want

What each donor wants may vary from individual to individual and, depending on the maturity of the nonprofit sector, these wants may have different levels of sophistication. While all donors are unique, there is a baseline of donor expectations that NPOs should endeavor to meet. These can be divided into five key requirements:

- Ethical behavior
- Meaningful and impactful programs
- Efficient and effective management
- Donor communications
- Donor appreciation.

Ethical Behavior

Ethical behavior is a basic expectation of all NPOs. Fundraising is based on trust. If donors do not trust an NPO to behave ethically, why would they give to it? In recent surveys, ethics ranks at, or near, the top in terms of donor concerns and expectations.[8] Each NPO should be guided by its own code of conduct—principles that guide it to act appropriately and ethically in all matters. Organizations may also seek guidance from the International Statement of Ethical Principles in Fundraising.[9]

Above all, NPOs should be cognizant of the Donor Bill of Rights (see the box, "The Donor Bill of Rights"), which lists explicitly the "rights" and expectations a donor should have when making a contribution.[10]

The Donor Bill of Rights

Philanthropy is based on voluntary action for the common good. It is a tradition of giving and sharing that is primary to the quality of life. To ensure that philanthropy merits the respect and trust of the general public, and that donors and prospective donors can have full confidence in the nonprofit organizations and causes they are asked to support, we declare that all donors have these rights:

1. To be informed of the organization's mission, of the way the organization intends to use donated resources, and of its capacity to use donations effectively for their intended purposes.

2. To be informed of the identity of those serving on the organization's governing board, and to expect the board to exercise prudent judgment in its stewardship responsibilities.

3. To have access to the organization's most recent financial statements.

4. To be assured their gifts will be used for the purposes for which they were given.

5. To receive appropriate acknowledgment and recognition.

6. To be assured that information about their donation is handled with respect and with confidentiality to the extent provided by law.

7. To expect that all relationships with individuals representing organizations of interest to the donor will be professional in nature.

8. To be informed whether those seeking donations are volunteers, employees of the organization, or hired solicitors.

9. To have the opportunity for their names to be deleted from mailing lists that an organization may intend to share.

10. To feel free to ask questions when making a donation and to receive prompt, truthful, and forthright answers.

The Donor Bill of Rights was developed by the Association of Fundraising Professionals, the Association for Healthcare Philanthropy, the Council for Advancement and Support of Education, and the Giving Institute: Leading Consultants to NonProfits.

It has been endorsed (in formation) by Independent Sector, National Catholic Development Conference, National Committee on Planned Giving, Council for Resource Development, and United Way of America.

Meaningful and Impactful Programs

It goes without saying that donors want to support NPOs that are making a difference. They want to know the impact that the NPO has on its beneficiaries, the value it generates, and the benefits it brings to the furtherance of its social cause.

It is not uncommon for NPOs to present their accomplishments purely as a bunch of numbers and statistics. While numerical accomplishments can be inspiring to some, to the vast majority, they can be overwhelming or even alienating. NPOs are in the people business and should not lose sight of the fact that people give to people; people give to their communities, and are inspired by others' actions. Numbers are important, but for most donors, numbers alone do not suffice.

Using metrics to demonstrate impact has become a growing trend in response to the perceived demands of a new wave of "venture philanthropists" who have started to "invest" in NPOs. These new donors bring strong business perspectives to their giving.[11] As a result, more NPOs have begun focusing on expenditures and quantifiable results, and developing all sorts of metrics and benchmarks to chart their progress. However, other analysts note that relatively few donors are interested in metrics, and a few are actually opposed to the idea.[12] Some donors feel that performance metrics are a poor use of NPOs' scarce resources.

The answer lies somewhere in the middle. Finding new ways to incorporate qualitative depictions of organizational impact, rather than simply capturing financial ratios or other statistics, can only be beneficial. Some of these alternative depictions include expert evaluations, peer reviews, board reviews, client satisfaction surveys, testimonials, media coverage, notable supporters, and partnerships with sector bodies. In the final analysis, anything that presents an organization's impact in a new and refreshing way can be very inspiring to donors.

Efficient and Effective Management

Donors have long been interested in supporting NPOs that show efficient and effective management. Lately, the emphasis on efficiency and, in particular, fundraising and administrative costs, has become of paramount importance due a number of high-profile cases of misappropriation of funds.

Every organization has fundraising and administrative costs, and these are important and necessary because they allow an organization to implement its mission. New research[13] shows that organizations with higher fundraising and administrative costs may actually be more effective in providing programs because they have the appropriate infrastructure and funding support.

Unfortunately, many organizations are defensive and almost apologetic about their fundraising and administrative costs. Alternately, they find ways to lower these costs at the expense of their operational infrastructure—or worse, they simply fudge their numbers to make their books look better. None of these solutions is acceptable.

Another aspect of efficiency is being able to demonstrate it. In a 2006 study on the philanthropic beliefs and behaviors of the wealthy, donors were asked what they wanted from NPOs when they were considering making a contribution. A few key items and disclosures were identified as important: the financial statements of the nonprofit, independent audits, and disclosure of staff compensation and perks.[14] Whether donors actually look at these documents or understand them is less important than the fact that the NPO has them and makes them accessible. Donors are looking to get a sense of the philosophy and transparency of an organization by validating the kind of information that is readily available and easily obtained.

Donor Communications

Communication is one of the most important aspects of donor engagement and is probably the one least fulfilled. It is not that NPOs do not communicate with donors—on the contrary, most do. But many do not communicate as well as they could or as often as they should, leaving numerous opportunities unexplored.

There are three words that are generally absent but that should guide communication efforts: meaningful, relevant, and personal. The most powerful kinds of communications have meaning for the organization, are relevant to the cause, and are personal to the donor. News-letters and annual reports serve an important purpose in communicating accomplishments and activities, but they do not carry the attachment and power that a personal handwritten letter, a phone call, or even an email will carry. The message will be all the more impactful if it comes from the nonprofit leaders themselves. People give to people, and it is this active involvement that makes communications that much more personal.

Donor Appreciation

Donor appreciation is the most basic and straightforward of all expectations. Yet, it is often not done well, or sometimes not at all. There are donors who decide which organizations they will support—or continue to support—by looking at previous gifts and identifying which organization sent thank-you acknowledgments.

Three simple practices stand out. First, an organization can never thank a donor enough. This does not mean that this appreciation needs to be direct and constant. While donors do not need more than one official thank-you letter and phone call, referencing their gifts in other communications and when an NPO representative meets them in person is always a good idea.

Secondly, thank-you letters and other types of recognition are not means to another end. That is, NPOs should not give recognition so they can ask for another gift. They give recognition to donors because they are sincerely thankful for their support.

Thirdly, an NPO's effort at recognition needs to be meaningful, relevant, and personal. This includes giving unique gifts tailored to each donor's background and interests, and—where appropriate—containing information about the organization or the impact of the donor's gift. It is precisely this type of detail that makes the recognition more meaningful and personal.

Donor Stewardship

Donor stewardship can be defined as "the process whereby an organization seeks to be worthy of continued philanthropic support, by the acknowledgment of gifts, donor recognition, honoring of donor intent, prudent investment of gifts, and the effective and efficient use of funds to further the mission of the organization."[15]

Importantly, donor stewardship encompasses building the relationship between NPOs and donors to facilitate sustained giving. NPOs achieve this by delivering on their promises and by the worthiness of the cause being supported.

Developing the relationship is key in fundraising. It is not just about trying to create donors, but friends—people who will serve as advocates, confidantes, advisors, and champions, and who not only give, but also volunteer and cumulatively contribute to the NPO's development. Thus, the essence of fundraising is not about receiving a one-time gift, since one round of solicitation is rarely enough to sustain a cause.

Stewardship is also about fulfilling created promises and expectations. The promises and expectations may be different for each NPO and its donors, but they relate to issues covered earlier in this chapter: ethical behavior, program effectiveness and impact, efficiency, communications, and donor recognition. Fulfilling these promises and meeting the donor's expectations will strengthen the relationship between the donor and the organization.

Fundraising Trends

Beyond the foundational aspects of donor management, NPOs are well advised to heed market trends and developments and be aware of donor issues and new opportunities for raising funds. While some may ebb and flow as fundraising evolves, some of the key trends in the current giving environment are:

- The new rich
- Online giving
- Third-party fundraisers
- Donor information and privacy.

The New Rich

Private wealth is increasing, and with it, a new type of donor and giving scene is emerging.[16] According to Philanthropy UK,[17] 75 percent of the *Sunday Times* Rich List in 1995 had inherited their wealth and 25 percent were self-made; today the figure is reversed. Couple this with a report[18] on giving by the rich in the UK where it was found that the new philanthropists, being more self-assured with their earned success, would like to be more involved in their giving. This includes providing the necessary support and expertise for NPOs to test innovative ideas.

A similar rise and enthusiasm can also be found in Asia. A 2007 Asia-Pacific wealth report[19] of individuals with net assets worth US$1 million or more showed that the fastest expansion in the number of millionaires in 2007 came not from the traditional clubs up north in Asia, but from Southeast Asia. As a regional group, Asians devoted a good 12 percent of their wealth—higher than their counterparts in North America, the Middle East, and Europe—to nonprofit causes.

Of late, the work of many fundraisers has focused on higher-end donors. In the UK, close to half of total donations in 2009 came from the 2 million donors who gave more than £100 (US$145) per month, compared to the 11.3 million (or 42 percent of donors) who gave under £10 (US$15) per month.[20] In the US, the most wealthy 10 percent account for about half of individual giving in America.[21] Clearly, the successful and informed individual is a critical partner that the NPO fundraiser cannot ignore.

Online Giving

In any discussion on the impact of modern lifestyles, technology, especially the internet and mobile phones, will always be a subject—and deservingly so. Infocomm technology is changing dramatically how NPOs operate, how NPOs can interact with their donors and vice versa, and, indeed, how donors want to engage.[22]

According to a 2006 research report on donor loyalty in the US, online donors typically are the most engaged and loyal of nonprofit organizations' supporters. More than 50 percent of those surveyed stated that they are "pretty familiar" with the groups they support, and almost 60 percent reported that they have asked someone else to make a contribution to a specific NPO. Even more importantly, one of the report's conclusions is that "online engagement—starting with volunteering an email address—is the most significant indication available to an organization that an individual is open to a relationship."[23]

Thus, if an NPO wants to develop a relationship with a donor, a website that invites donors to register is important. Of course, many organizations have gone beyond a simple website. They have sought to make it interesting and interactive to engage the donors with the NPO and its beneficiaries. World Vision, for example, allows donors to specify the country, age, and gender of the child(ren) they wish to sponsor.[24] DonorsChoose goes further to allow netizens to donate directly to specific projects at public schools.[25]

However, NPOs also need to be cautious about how they use technology. In the aftermath of natural disasters, online fundraising through the internet and mobile phones has proven to be popular and effective, because they are so easy and quick to use. These characteristics are perfect for disaster relief fundraising, but not necessarily for building donor relationships. While texting can offer new communication channels in terms of informational updates, no great relationships can be formed over mobile phone texting. While technology may help make giving faster and more convenient, it can also make philanthropy more impersonal, which means NPOs have to double their efforts to create the connection.

Third-Party Fundraisers

The use of third-party fundraisers is popular with some NPOs. It is convenient to let a third party do the tedious work of fundraising. The charges by the third-party fundraiser, if used, would be deemed acceptable to the NPO; many NPOs rationalize that it would have cost them the same or more to do it themselves.

However, there are two main issues that require attention.

First, NPOs should realize that donors and the public see no difference between the NPO and the third-party fundraiser during a solicitation. Hence, the third-party fundraiser's behavior will color the donor's perceptions of the NPO. It is critical, therefore, that any third-party fundraiser be required not only to operate within the legal limitations, but also to abide by the same high ethical principles and practices as the NPO. When problems arise, rarely is an NPO able to distance itself from the controversy. Donors and the public simply do not view the two as separate—even if they know the third party was hired by the NPO. NPOs must think of the third-party fundraisers as extensions of their own staff and demand the appropriate checks, processes, and conduct. The same would, of course, apply to volunteers fundraising on behalf of the NPO.

Secondly, compensation is usually a big issue. Most fundraising codes of ethics prohibit the use of commissions or percentage-based compensation, whereby a fundraiser is paid a percentage of the funds successfully raised. There are numerous reasons for this prohibition: Charitable missions can become secondary to self-gain; donor trust can be unalterably damaged; and there is incentive for self-dealing to prevail over donors' best interests. In addition, percentage-based compensation, however administered, can produce "reward without merit."[26]

Donors usually have a problem with compensation for fundraisers. In the US, for example, annual state reports about the percentage of monies that third-party fundraisers receive always make for big headlines and cause public uproars.[27] Donors just do not want fundraisers to get a percentage, no matter how small, out of every gift they make. They give gifts to support the overall mission of an NPO, and that can include salaries, overheads, and other administrative costs. But when the costs are explicitly spelled out as going to a third party, they react negatively. Most donors expect that fundraisers, if they are not employed directly by the NPO, should be volunteers doing it out of the goodness of their hearts.

Donor Information and Privacy

In order to build strong relationships with donors, NPOs need to get to know their supporters—their interests, likes and dislikes, job, family, etc. The rapid growth of infocomm technology has made it increasingly easy for NPOs to harvest such information about existing and potential donors, store it, and mine it for follow-up fundraising purposes.

This has raised concerns about donor privacy. Donors are concerned about what kind of information is collected, how it is being stored, who has access to it, and how it is being used. Many countries now have laws regarding how and what sort of donor data can be collected, with or without the permission of the donor.

However, beyond these legal restrictions, donor data should be governed by the NPO's ethical obligations to the donor. Many fundraising codes have specific standards related to donor privacy.[28]

The golden rule is to ensure transparency by limiting the information asked for, and then collected, to what a donor would be happy to read if he came across his file.

Closing the Gap

In summary, the future is promising for NPOs and fundraisers seeking to close the funding gap.

Through the decades of development of the fundraising industry, best practices on donor management and donor stewardship have evolved to ensure loyal supporters in the donor base. In addition, enabling technology and changing demographics provide new opportunities for the alert and the creative.

In following up with all these elements, NPOs and fundraisers should always heed the cardinal rule of good donor stewardship: The interests of donors come first and among them, ethical conduct is paramount.

Endnotes

1 See Chapter 5, "Social Enterprises: Fulfilling the promise of social enterprise," by Jon Huggett, and Chapter 18, "Social Finance: Financing change, changing finance," by Jed Emerson.

2 Lester M. Salamon, S. Wojciech Sokolowski and Associates, *Global Civil Society: Dimensions of the nonprofit sector, Volume Two* (Bloomfield, CT: Kumarian Press, 2004). The data of relative revenue sources for NPOs is for 38 countries.

3 *CAF Briefing Paper: International Comparisons of Charitable Giving* (West Malling, UK: Charities Aid Foundation, November 2006), www.cafonline.org/pdf/International%20 %20Giving%20highlights.pdf. The study was the result of surveys on individual giving in a number of countries whose wealth covers over half of the total global economy.

4 The Charities Aid Foundation study made this point: "there is evidence in the UK that poorer people give away higher proportions of their income than the rich." Other reports that support this include: Claude Rosenberg and Tim Stone, "A New Take on Tithing," *Stanford Social Innovation Review*, Fall 2006; *Individual Giving Survey 2006* (National Volunteer & Philanthropy Centre, 2006); Joe Saxton, Michele Madden, Chris Greenwood, and Brian Garvey, *The 21st Century Donor* (London: nfpSynergy, September 2007).

5 Claude Rosenberg and Tim Stone, "A New Take on Tithing, " *Stanford Social Innovation Review*, Fall 2006.

6 For example, ActionAid UK has 60 staff in its Fundraising Department, www.actionaid .org.uk/_content/documents/Information%20Pack%20for%20Project%20Information% 20and%20Support%20Officer.doc.

7 www.afpnet.org.

8 *Talking About Charities 2008* (Edmonton: The Muttart Foundation, 2008), www.muttart .org/sites/default/files/downloads/TAC2008-03-CompleteReport.pdf; *Philanthropic Beliefs and Behaviors of the Wealthy* (New York: The Luxury Institute and PhilanthropyNow, October 2006); "Ignore Donor Intent at Your Peril," Association of Fundraising Professionals, January 9, 2006, www.afpnet.org/Audiences/ReportsResearchDetail. cfm?itemnumber=3576.

9 "International Statement of Ethical Principles in Fundraising," Association of Fundraising Professionals, December 7, 2006, www.afpnet.org/Ethics/IntlArticleDetail .cfm?ItemNumber=3681.

10 "Donor Bill of Rights," Association of Fundraising Professionals, the Association for Healthcare Philanthropy, the Council for the Advancement and Support of Education, The Giving Institute: Leading Consultants to Non-Profits, 1993, www.afpnet.org/Ethics/ EnforcementDetail.cfm?ItemNumber=3359.

11 "An Investor Approach to Charitable Giving," *TD Economics Topic Paper*, October 18, 2005, www.td.com/economics/topic/ca1005_NPO.pdf; Jackie Boice, "Fundraising and the New Wealth: A reality check," *Advancing Philanthropy*, March/April 2001, www.afpnet .org/Publications/ArticleDetail.cfm?ItemNumber=809. See also Chapter 9, "Venture Philanthropy: Venturing into entrepreneurial philanthropy," by Rob John.

12 Katie Cunningham and Mark Ricks, "Why Measure?" *Stanford Social Innovation Review*, Summer 2004.

13 Mark Hager, Thomas Pollak, Kennard Wing, and Patrick Rooney, "Getting What We Pay For: Low overhead limits nonprofit effectiveness,"*Nonprofit Overhead Cost Project,* Brief 3, 2004, www.coststudy.org, www.urban.org/UploadedPDF/311044_NOCP_3.pdf.

14 *Philanthropic Beliefs and Behaviors of the Wealthy* (New York: Luxury Institute and Philanthropy Now, 2006).

15 Barbara R. Levy and R. L. Cherry (eds), *AFP Fundraising Dictionary Online,* Association of Fundraising Professionals, 1996, www.afpnet.org/files/ContentDocuments/AFP_ Dictionary_A-Z_final_6-9-03.pdf.

16 Chapter 8, "Philanthropy: Powering philanthropic passions," by Thomas Menkhoff, explores further the opportunities represented by the new rich and the globalization of philanthropy.

17 Philanthropy UK, "Top 10 Trends in British Philanthropy," www.philanthropyuk.org/ Resources/Top10trends.

18 Therese Lyod, "Why Rich People Give—Summary," Philanthropy UK, www .philanthropyuk.org/Resources/WealthandPhilanthropynewresearch.

19 Extracted from Shu-Ching Jean Chen, "When Asia's Millionaires Splurge, They Go Big," *Forbes,* October 19, 2007, www.forbes.com/2007/10/19/asia-rich-report-face-markets-cx_jc_1019autofacescan01.html.

20 *UK Giving 2009: An overview of charitable giving in the UK, 2008/09* (London: National Council for Voluntary Organisations, 2009).

21 "Charitable Giving in the UK and USA," Philanthropy UK, www.philanthropyuk .org/Resources/USphilanthropy.

22 The impact of technology, including infocomm technology, on NPOs, including fundraising, is explored in Chapter 17, "Technology: Rebooting technology for society," by Robert Chew. E-Philanthropy, or technology-enabled giving, is covered in Chapter 8, "Philanthropy: Powering philanthropic passions," by Thomas Menkhoff.

23 *Donor Loyalty: The holy grail of fundraising* (Arlington, VA: Craver, Matthews, Smith, and Company, and The Prime Group, 2006).

24 www.worldvision.org.

25 www.donorschoose.org.

26 "Position paper: Percentage-based compensation," Association of Fundraising Professionals, October 2001, www.afpnet.org/Ethics/EthicsArticleDetail.cfm?itemnumber=734.

27 Kevin Donovan, "Charities Admit Fundraising Mess—Sick Kids, World Vision both vow to stop commission-based canvassing via third party,"*The Star.Com,* July 15, 2007, www.thestar.com/news/canada/article/236046; Marion Scott, "Return of the Vulture Exclusive: Charity bosses probe fundraiser," *Sunday Mail Scotland,* June 4, 2006.

28 "Code of Ethical Principles and Standards," Association of Fundraising Professionals, 1964, www.afpnet.org/Ethics/EnforcementDetail.cfm?ItemNumber=3261.

Chapter 11

Volunteerism

Matching the Supply and Demand of Volunteers

LAURENCE LIEN
CEO, National Volunteer & Philanthropy Centre

For many individuals, the act of volunteering lies at the core of being human. For volunteer host organizations (VHOs), volunteers provide the much-needed manpower and community engagement to fulfill their missions effectively.

However, there is a mismatch in the volunteer labor market. Volunteers struggle to be placed, and VHOs struggle to find enough of the right volunteers. This mismatch has to be solved at two levels. At the market level, there needs to be more and better market information, brokering, and clearing mechanisms for the supply and demand of volunteers. At the participant level, VHOs must recognize the volunteer market realities, and develop and implement strategies to raise, manage, and retain volunteers.

V olunteering lies at the core of being human. If all of our relationships were merely transactional—defined by what we get back in monetary or other tangible benefits for what we put in—the world would be unlivable. When it comes to helping our families and friends, giving tends to come naturally, even if these relationships are also breaking down. But it is in the outreach to those who are the least like us that giving is most needed and valued.

Volunteers are at the core of the nonprofit sector. They provide the much-needed manpower, energy, and spirit to drive the work and outcomes of nonprofit organizations (NPOs). In economic terms, the value of volunteers in 2008 for 36 countries aggregated US$378 billion, more than twice that of charitable giving. In manpower terms, volunteer time would have equated to 20 million (unpaid) NPO workers, or 44 percent of the total workforce (paid and unpaid) of the nonprofit sectors in these 36 countries.[1]

It seems rather straightforward: NPOs need resources and can benefit immensely from people who can give free help—people with good hearts who want to "pay it forward" and volunteer their time and expertise. What we have, then, should be a "match made in heaven" or a "win-win proposition."

In practice, it is not so simple. Many NPOs find it difficult to get volunteers to help out with their work. Trend studies in volunteering suggest that there are deeper, more complex issues, and new paradigms for balancing the supply and demand of volunteers are needed.

Volunteerism Trends

Volunteerism levels seem to be relatively stable in most countries. Cross-country comparison, however, is not easy due to limited availability of data and measurement issues. Based on available data, Figure 11.1 provides a chart showing volunteer participation rates (as a percentage of population) for the US, the UK, Australia, and Singapore.[2]

Two observations can be made.

First, volunteerism levels in different countries can be markedly different, from the mid-teens in Singapore to the forties in the UK. Part of this may be due to measuring methodologies, and part of it due to cultural factors. In Anglo-Saxon countries, for example, volunteerism is

Figure 11.1 Countries' Volunteer Rates

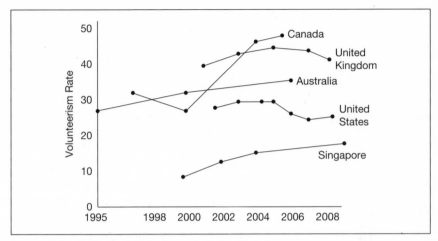

Source: National Volunteer & Philanthropy Centre's analysis.[3]

more deep-rooted; whereas in Asian societies, much of the focus and help rendered tends to revolve around the extended family and clans (which is typically not considered volunteering).

Secondly, participation levels have generally been steady across the years in most countries. However, when the total number of volunteer hours (or volunteer hours per capita) is analyzed, the participation levels have generally stabilized or decreased slightly. In Singapore, for example, total volunteer hours dropped from 74 million in 2002 to 45 million in 2008. In the US, total volunteer hours has held steady at around 8 billion each year. In the UK, average volunteer hours for four weeks has hovered around eight. Only Australia has shown good improvement, from a total of 704 million hours in 2000 to 730 million in 2006.[4]

With the size of the nonprofit sectors growing and with a ready latent supply of volunteers in most countries, the question then is why many organizations that need volunteers (often called "volunteer host organizations," or "VHOs") are struggling to find the volunteers they need. It is also not just a matter of numbers, but also of the kind of volunteers, as most VHOs have their particular manpower needs.

To meet their requirements, VHOs and the nonprofit sector need a better understanding of the supply and demand factors of the volunteering equation.

Supply (Volunteers)

The nature of volunteering and the profile of volunteers have changed significantly over the years.

Volunteers are drawn from society at large. Thus, trends impacting society can have a knock-on effect on volunteering.

Societal Trends

Four key societal trends impact the supply and nature of volunteers.

The first trend is an aging population. In many countries, the elderly have traditionally formed the largest group of volunteers because they have the time and economic freedom to engage in voluntary work. In the wake of a growing global aging population, this segment may represent an even larger pool of volunteers. On the other hand, "new age" seniors now have alternative fulfilling demands on their time, such as grandparenting and senior leisure activities. Also, many are expected to continue working, due to underfunded pensions and insufficient personal savings. They may also avoid volunteering altogether if they face ageist attitudes or perceive a loss in status.

The second trend is Generation Y (GenYers). They are often better educated and net savvy. They interact differently from older generations, often in social groups online, openly expressing their views, their wants, and their needs. Although they are more confident and assertive of what they want, they are also more concerned about social justice issues. Many have had more opportunities to experience community service from a young age, so they are no stranger to volunteerism. Increasingly, they value work that has meaning and improves the lives of others. As active global citizens, they are interested in cross-border volunteering opportunities. While there is no significant population demographic increase for the GenYers, their awareness of social issues and their propensity to want to get involved increases the pool of available volunteers.

The third trend is the perceived scarcity of time.[5] In the rat race of today, the time-compressed individual will say, "I'm too busy. I don't have time to volunteer." To some extent, the time crunch is about values and individual priorities. With increasing wealth, there is also competing use of time as leisure, travel, and entertainment options expand. At the same time, with globalization, it is the better-educated individuals—who also have a greater propensity to volunteer—who are pressured to work harder and travel more for work.

The fourth trend is the blurring of sector boundaries. Increasingly, the public, private, and nonprofit sectors are working in partnership to solve society's complex problems and, in a way, they are growing the pool of volunteers. Thus, we now see the growth of corporate social responsibility (CSR) efforts. Many employees prefer to work at companies that give back to society. They welcome employee volunteer opportunities and the ability to participate in *pro bono* projects. Another growth area is the rise of social enterprises. Businesspeople, while not strictly volunteers, give up the promise of profits to build sustainable businesses that promote the social good. Government agencies, like NPOs, also actively mobilize volunteers, often in large numbers—for example, to work on projects in government schools, public libraries, hospitals, and emergency services. With widening government deficits in many developed countries, governments' interest in promoting volunteerism is likely to increase.

The 21st Century Volunteer

As a result of such societal trends, the kinds of volunteers that come forward has changed significantly in the new century. While there are obviously differences across countries, volunteers in urban settings tend to have an observed profile that can be characterized as being less committed, more demanding, and more cause-driven.

They are less committed to working long-term on specific projects, preferring short-term opportunities with flexible schedules. This does not mean that they are less committed *per se*, just that they may not be willing to commit up front to being a regular volunteer. Many, in fact, become repeat volunteers when managed properly, resulting in the trend of serial episodic volunteering.

They are more demanding of the value they give and receive. These volunteers increasingly want projects to be valuable to society, to the VHO, and to themselves. While not necessarily volunteering just for their personal gain, volunteers today have less tolerance for volunteer projects that "waste" their time because they are badly led, or because their skills and experience are grossly underutilized.

They are more cause-driven, more conscious of the value and impact they can bring to the social cause they support. They are not just time-givers, for they look beyond volunteering for its own sake to a higher-order goal and purpose.[6] They want to make a difference in a field of focus for which they personally have a passion.

Some observers have called this the rise of the selfish volunteer who constantly asks, "What's in it for me?" This is an unfair charge. Volunteers have always had a mix of motivations—some extrinsic and some intrinsic. What is certain is that the motivators and expectations of volunteers have changed, and they are irreversible. And rather than hang on to paradigms or programs that are outdated, it is incumbent on VHOs to understand these motivations and to design and package the volunteering opportunities accordingly.

Demand (VHOs)

VHOs should have a clear view as to why they demand volunteers and what value they derive from them.

Faced with this question, many VHOs will likely point to their manpower needs and how they could not afford to pay fully for all of it; hence the need for volunteers—or, rather, unpaid labor. Indeed, if they can afford it; many VHOs will prefer to hire paid labor—after all, paid staff would likely be more readily available, more easily deployable, and more compliant.

Yet, VHOs who regard volunteers merely as "free labor" and staff augmentation miss seeing the wood for the trees. They fail to appreciate the real value of volunteerism—which is engagement with the community.

Community Engagement

A volunteer comes from the community. A committed volunteer can generate substantial multiplier effects within the community, through either public activism or private word of mouth. In fact, friend-raising often leads to better fundraising.

A case in point is Room to Read, which started out building schools and establishing libraries in Nepal's rural communities in 2000.[7] It has since grown into a global organization with more than 760 schools and 10,000 libraries reaching more than four million children in developing countries. It is able to do this through 40 volunteer chapters on four continents where, collectively, over 3,000 volunteers help the organization network, plan events, collect books, and raise awareness of the organization. In 2008, the chapters raised over US$6.4 million—more than 28 percent of Room to Read's operating budget for the year.

When volunteerism is viewed as community engagement, the demand for and supply of volunteers is constantly renewed. A longitudinal study of AmeriCorps service members found that its programs have significant positive impacts on the members' connection to community, knowledge about problems facing their community, participation in community-based activities, and personal growth through service.[8]

Indeed, there are instances where the VHO can only function if the community is involved. Because they aim to empower residents, not take over service provision, community development initiatives in the neighborhood would not take off if there were no resident volunteer support and effort. An example is the Dudley Street Neighborhood Initiative in Boston, in the US. It is an innovative, high-performing, and holistic community change effort that continues to thrive. Its residents have a shared goal of creating a vibrant, high-quality, diverse urban village. To date, more than half of the 1,300 abandoned parcels of land in the neighborhood have been permanently transformed into over 400 new high-quality affordable houses, community centers, schools, a community greenhouse, and other public spaces.[9]

The engagement of volunteers can be with overseas communities. Since its inception in 1961, the US Peace Corps has activated more than 200,000 volunteers to serve in 139 host countries, working on issues ranging from AIDS education to information technology and environmental preservation.[10] The UK's equivalent, Voluntary Service Overseas, has similarly placed over 42,000 volunteers in over 140 developing countries, including Africa, Asia, the Pacific, the Caribbean, Eastern Europe, and Latin America.[11]

Community Raising

Indeed, the engagement of volunteers on a mass scale can lead to the raising of entire communities.

A VHO that is doing just this, one community at a time, is Gawad Kalinga, a Philippines-based poverty reduction NPO that was founded by Tony Meloto. Gawad Kalinga (meaning "to give care") revamps slums into viable neighborhoods as volunteers and beneficiaries work together to build homes and, in the process, a revitalized community. The movement has drawn people from all over the world to adopt villages and give their time and money to help build them. Since its launch in 1995, Gawad Kalinga has transformed more than 1,700 poverty-ridden and crime-laden communities throughout the Philippines. Meloto's vision is to reach five million families by 2024 and help make the Philippines a first world nation by then.[12]

The Olympics, including the Winter Olympics and Special Olympics, are events that require the raising of the nation for the event to function and be successful. The 2000 Olympics in Sydney mobilized 47,000 volunteers; the 2004 Olympics in Athens mobilized 160,000 volunteers; and the 2008 Olympics in China mobilized 1.7 million volunteers (including 74,000 volunteers for main events, 400,000 city volunteers, and more than a million "social volunteers").[13] All those who volunteered were clearly patriotic and proud to be part of what could be a once-in-a-lifetime hosting of the historic games in their country.

Matching Supply and Demand

For VHOs to successfully recruit and use volunteers from the community, their demand for such volunteers must be adequately matched by the supply of those volunteers.

In order for this match to occur, the value to each party (the volunteer and the VHO) must exceed their individual costs. Figure 11.2 provides a summary of the respective value and costs of the volunteering exercise.

Figure 11.2 The Value and Costs of VHOs versus Volunteers

	Demand (The VHO)	Supply (The Volunteer)
Value	Manpower replacement cost Community engagement	Private value Public value Positive experience
Costs	Volunteer coordination	Search and exit costs Opportunity costs Personal expenses

For VHOs, a clear cost is involved in coordinating volunteers: the cost of recruiting, training, managing, and retaining these volunteers. For each VHO, the value they receive from using volunteers should exceed these costs. This would likely be the case especially if the VHO properly factors in the community engagement value, in addition to the direct value of the manpower.

For individual volunteers, they have their reasons for volunteering: It is a mixture of private value (e.g. a personal connection to someone in the VHO) and public value (e.g. giving back). In addition, their volunteering is likely to be maintained if they have an overall positive experience and self-fulfillment. The overall value of volunteering must exceed their costs of volunteering: the search and exit costs of finding the volunteer job, the opportunity costs they have to forgo with the alternative use of their time, and any personal expenses (e.g. transportation costs) that are not reimbursed by the VHO.

Volunteer Labor Market Mismatch

Yet, despite everyone's best intentions, there is often a mismatch in the volunteer/VHO demand and supply equation. While many VHOs complain that they cannot find enough volunteers, at the same time, many people say they cannot find volunteer opportunities, or rather the right type of volunteer opportunities.

There are several possible reasons for this mismatch. There could be imperfect information and lack of an adequate market-clearing mechanism for the supply of and demand for volunteers. Or, volunteers and VHOs are looking for different levels of commitment: Many VHOs look for a volunteer who can come on the same day, at the same time, every week for a few years; whereas time-scarce volunteers may only be able to do episodic volunteering. Another reason might be that VHOs are not developing enough meaningful opportunities that best utilize the skill sets of the educated populace.

In the regular human resource marketplace, market forces will ensure that any market failure is not prolonged. Wage levels and labor mobility will adjust so that, eventually, companies (the demand side) will get the employees (the supply side) they need and can afford.

However, in the volunteer labor market, the mismatch can continue for a long time because there is no market-clearing mechanism of wage levels. Some VHOs seek to shortcut or correct this, at least in their mind, by providing allowances and tangible incentives that sometimes can be so generous they look more like employment benefits than volunteering. Such incentives will backfire in the long term as they can, in fact, lower volunteer satisfaction by reducing the intrinsic value of the volunteering experience.

Solutions

Solutions to the volunteer labor market mismatch lie at two levels.

At the market level, mechanisms are needed for more market information, brokering, and clearing of the supply of and demand for volunteers. This has happened in many countries with the creation of national volunteer centers, such as the National Volunteer & Philanthropy Centre in Singapore, the Points of Light Institute in the US, and Volunteering England; and with established online portals such as VolunteerMatch and idealist.org.[14] In addition, there are networks and organizations that deal with narrower bands of volunteers. For example, Boardmatch Ireland targets volunteers taking on board roles at NPOs, and the Kind Exchange in Singapore matches volunteer professionals with VHOs who require professional services.[15] Most of these organizations have an online volunteer registration and matching service.

At the participant level, VHOs must recognize volunteering market realities and tailor their demands to fit the population from which they are drawing their volunteers. Simply put, they need to develop and implement new strategies to raise and retain volunteers.

Volunteer Raising and Retention Strategies

To raise and keep volunteers in a virtuous cycle and clear the market, so to speak, VHOs should invest in the following key strategies in the context of their specific local and sector environments:

- Appreciate volunteerism
- Enhance volunteer engagement
- Provide professional volunteer resource management.

Appreciating Volunteerism

At the outset, it is important that VHOs give more importance to volunteerism.

Much has been said about the value of volunteerism to the VHO. It is not just about replacing staff, but also about community engagement. This means viewing the VHO's mission and objectives more broadly and seeing it as part of its mission to source opportunities and engage citizens and residents as volunteers for a greater public good.

Too many NPOs cast their mission too narrowly and miss out on many potential volunteer opportunities. This is sometimes the result of over-professionalization of the services they provide—be it in the areas of health-care provision, arts management, or social work. Numerous human services would not be as effective if they were merely professionally provided, as the compassion provided by the volunteers can be an integral part of making that service effective.

An example of a professional service that can be as, if not more, effectively delivered by community volunteers as by full-time paid professionals is Befrienders Worldwide.[16] Their volunteers are trained to provide a crucial function: listening to and supporting those in distress with suicidal thoughts and intentions, and discouraging them from suicides. Since 1953, their 31,000 Good Samaritans[17] in over 400 volunteer centers in nearly 40 countries have played a mission-critical role in helping to reduce suicides all around the world.

Just as VHOs should appreciate volunteerism, they should also appreciate their volunteers. Apart from the usual thank-you gestures, the best appreciation that VHOs can give their volunteers is to provide them the kind of volunteering experience that fulfills each of them. A volunteer with a positive experience is more likely to continue to volunteer, to advocate for the cause, to graduate to higher-value volunteering, and to be a more generous donor.

Enhancing Volunteer Engagement

To provide volunteers with that positive experience, there must be a sufficient understanding of volunteers and engagement at a deeper level beyond the work itself.

VHOs should take a volunteer-centric approach toward involving volunteers. A frequent mistake made by VHOs is to craft volunteering needs solely from the "demand-side" or the beneficiaries' perspective. Whether it is a for-profit business or a nonprofit organization, labor supply—its quantity, quality, and expectations—profoundly influences a business plan. There is, thus, a need to understand volunteers and how they are motivated, and to engage them accordingly. A VHO's volunteer engagement plan should consider the skills, knowledge, and capabilities of its readily available pool of volunteers, and the VHO should be flexible enough to adjust opportunistically to any changes. A VHO should create the need for the volunteer in areas that are beneficial to their cause, but without instigating mission drift and dilution.

Despite the perceived shortage of volunteers, there are many potential volunteers who can be brought into the fray if new, flexible models are created. Younger volunteers belong to the "taste and see" generation who want to try out different opportunities before settling on committing to them for the long term. In today's time-starved world, many would like to volunteer without being necessarily saddled with a fixed volunteering schedule. The episodic volunteering model is one that many VHOs have introduced to cater to such volunteers.

HandsOn Network, the largest volunteer network in the US and with more than 250 HandsOn Action Centers in 16 countries, develops episodic volunteer opportunities with VHOs and matches volunteers to these opportunities through an online portal with real-time updates on available slots.[18] These programs break the mindsets of many VHOs' *ad hoc* programs only for *ad hoc* volunteers, and regular projects only for regular volunteers. Instead, VHOs, under HandsOn, structure regular projects using "episodic" volunteers and trained volunteer leaders.

The HandsOn programs are structured with quality control. While episodic volunteering can be resource-intensive to manage, it can be a means to an important end—to allow new volunteers to try out a diverse range of projects to find their niche. Their goal is to convert as many of these volunteers as possible into repeat volunteers and lifelong supporters for the VHOs. To facilitate the transition of episodic volunteers into longer-term volunteers, better volunteer management is required. To mitigate the cost of episodic volunteering, the projects can be structured such that they are also managed by volunteers; this is part of empowering volunteers for higher value-added activities. Volunteer leaders can also take charge of designing and planning for new projects.

Integrating volunteering with other aspects of the life of the volunteers—work, family life, and hobbies—is another successful way of engaging volunteers. For instance, corporate volunteering is a major growth area as companies look to increase their community involvement by improving their engagement with the communities in which they operate. For employees, they find the integrated experience of engagement with their companies as well as the community to be much more fulfilling.

Professional Volunteer Resource Management

A VHO must invest in good, professional volunteer management; this is akin to good human resource management for their paid staff. Trained professionals would understand the motivations of volunteers better, structure the volunteer job to maximize both public and private value, and have proper volunteer appreciation and motivation programs. All these require dedicated resources to nurture and sustain the volunteers within the organization.

Too often, volunteers are treated as cheap, unskilled labor. VHOs do not invest in them the same way that they would invest in staff. This is unwise, as it can trigger a vicious cycle of neglect and diminishing supply.

Good volunteer management requires the entire process of recruitment, induction, development, communication, and appreciation. Although this may appear similar to regular human resource management, the two are distinctly different. In recruiting volunteers, the sources would typically be much wider than for paid staff. Paid staff also usually have much more clearly defined roles and job fit; finding a fit for a volunteer and the work that he or she can do is a much more fluid and dynamic process. Staff have contractual, ongoing relationships with the organization, whereas volunteers are there by choice and only at certain times. There is, thus, a need to build an ongoing relationship with volunteers.

An example of a VHO with structured volunteer management practices is the National Court Appointed Special Advocate Association (National CASA) in the US which supports and promotes court-appointed volunteer advocacy for abused and neglected children.[19] Its network of over 1,000 local community program offices recruit, train, and support volunteers in their work, while offering critical leadership and support through national campaigns, comprehensive online resources, and in-person support to state and local programs. In 2009, its 68,000 guardians advocated for 240,000 children.[20]

Some organizations have done so well with volunteers that their supporters have set up volunteer support organizations dedicated to helping them recruit and manage volunteers. An example is the John F. Kennedy Center for the Performing Arts (also known as the Kennedy Center), which has a membership and volunteer organization called Friends of the Kennedy Center. It has 500 regular volunteers who come weekly, and 450 *ad hoc* volunteers who help out at special events and festivals of the Kennedy Center. In total, the volunteers clock about 100,000 hours per year, more than 100 hours per person, amounting to a value of US$2 million to the Kennedy Center. Yet, Friends of the Kennedy Center is managed by only two paid staff from the Kennedy Center; the rest of the organization, including committees, volunteer recruitment, and management, is being done by the volunteers themselves.[21]

In managing volunteers, the volunteer jobs need to be tailored to the particularities of the volunteers to get the best fit. Conceptually, there are three kinds of "volun-tiers":

- *Level 1, Generalist Volunteers:* This represents the mass base of volunteers who can undertake work that does not need specialized skills. This also includes volunteers who can pick up any needed skills on-the-spot, on-site.
- *Level 2, Specialist Volunteers:* This smaller base of volunteers takes on skilled jobs, utilizing their talents and proficiencies to serve in areas that lack the supply of such skills. This includes corporations and individuals who provide *pro bono* professional services such as legal advice, IT services, or even plumbing services.
- *Level 3, Leadership Volunteers:* These are the even fewer, usually senior-level, volunteers who take on leadership positions on the VHO governing boards, advisory councils, and committees.

Not all volunteers fall neatly into a single category. It does not mean that Level 1 volunteers are unskilled or do not pick up any skills while volunteering. If a volunteer has become regular, it would be ideal to develop them and put them in leadership positions, though the progress may not be always linear. The emphasis should be on utilizing volunteers in work that most meaningfully engages their expertise, experience, and interest. VHOs should also not assume that a volunteer would naturally want to use their specialist skills. Some volunteers want their volunteer project to have nothing to do with their day job. Managing expectations of the volunteers is very important in such cases.

However, the focus on expertise must have an important overlay—the need to ignite a volunteer's passion and compassion. This is critical to spurring long-term volunteer commitment. The engagement with a VHO's beneficiaries can bring out compassion in volunteers; it may even transform their outlook and behaviors. Hopefully, it will fuel sustained participation.

Raising Volunteers, Raising Communities

Volunteering for the right VHO can indeed be a match made in heaven for both parties. For the volunteer, it is food for his soul. For the VHO, a good volunteer relieves its manpower needs and fuels better community engagement.

However, for the match to work sustainably, VHOs need to wake up to the realities of the volunteer marketplace and put in place strategies to more effectively raise, manage, and retain volunteers. Our society will become that much richer in every sense of the word not just when sufficient volunteers are raised to meet the needs of VHOs, but when entire communities are raised because the volunteers are properly stewarded.

Endnotes

1   The data cited in this paragraph is taken from a 2008 presentation made by Lester Salamon based on the Johns Hopkins Comparative Nonprofit Sector Project, a study of nonprofit activity across some 46 countries. The figures cited in this paragraph are as of 2008 and are the aggregate for 36 countries. The total paid and unpaid workforce would be 45.5 million full-time equivalent workers. Current information and data on the Johns Hopkins study is available online at www.ccss.jhu.edu/index .php?section=content&view=9&sub=3. The latest book summarizing the results of the study is: Lester M. Salamon, S. Wojciech Sokolowski and Associates, *Global Civil Society: Dimensions of the nonprofit sector, Volume Two* (Bloomfield, CT: Kumarian Press, 2004). Volumes One and Two of the publication encompass separate countries covered in the ongoing study.

2   Data is not available for every year in every country. Not all countries conduct national surveys of volunteerism annually. The trend line is drawn by joining the data points in those years when data is available.

3   The table is created from data compiled by the National Volunteer & Philanthropy Centre. Sources of volunteerism rates are as follows:

(1)   Singapore: *Survey on Individual Giving 2004: Volunteerism findings* (Singapore: National Volunteer & Philanthropy Centre, 2004), www.nvpc.org.sg/Library/ Documents/ResearchReports/survey2004.pdf; *Individual Giving Survey 2008* (Singapore: National Volunteer & Philanthropy Centre, September 18, 2008), www.nvpc.org.sg/Library/Documents/ResearchReports/08IGS_SURVEY% 20FINDINGS.pdf.

(2)   UK: *2008–09 Citizenship Survey: Volunteering and charitable giving topic report* (London: Department for Communities and Local Government, April 2010), www .communities.gov.uk/documents/statistics/pdf/1547056.pdf.

(3)   US: National Data, Volunteering in America, Corporation for National & Community Service, www.volunteeringinamerica.gov/national.

(4)   Australia: *Voluntary Work, Australia* (Australian Bureau of Statistics, July 9, 2007), www.ausstats.abs.gov.au/Ausstats/subscriber.nsf/0/C52862862C082577 CA25731000198615/$File/44410_2006.pdf.

4   Sources of data are similar to in endnote 3 above. Data is as follows:

(1)   Singapore: Total volunteer hours (in millions): 2002: 74; 2004: 35; 2006: 49; 2008: 45.

(2)   UK: Average hours spent on volunteer activity in last four weeks: 2001: 8.1; 2003: 8.1; 2005: 8.3; 2007: 7.6; 2008: 8.6.

(3)   US: Total volunteer hours (in billions): 2002: 8.0; 2004: 8.5; 2006: 8.1; 2008: 8.0.

(4)   Australia: Total volunteer hours (in millions): 1995: 512; 2000: 704; 2006: 730.

5   In NVPC's Individual Giving Survey 2008, the top reason for a volunteer stopping to volunteer was lack of time. National Volunteer & Philanthropy Centre, "Volunteerism," in *Individual Giving Survey 2008*, September 18, 2008, www.nvpc.org.sg/Library/Documents/ResearchReports/08IGS_SURVEY%20FINDINGS.pdf.

6   Elisha Evans and Joe Saxton, "The 21st Century Volunteer," *nfpSynergy*, www.nfpsynergy.net/includes/documents/cm_docs/2010/2/21st_century_volunteer.pdf.

7   www.roomtoread.org.

8   *Serving Country and Community: A longitudinal study of service in AmeriCorps (early findings)* (New York: Corporation for National & Community Service, updated April 2007), www.nationalservice.gov/pdf/06_1223_longstudy_executive.pdf.

9   www.dsni.org.

10   www.peacecorps.gov.

11   www.vso.org.uk.

12   "Tony Meloto and Gawad Kalinga: No more slums!" Mighty Rasing, www.mightyrasing.com/a-leaders-life/tony-meloto-gawad-kalinga/; "Gawad Kalinga Founder, Antonio P. Meloto—Builder of Dreams," *Asian Journal*, January 5, 2010, www.asianjournal.com/aj-magazine/midweek-mgzn/4121-gawad-kalinga-founder-antonio-p-meloto-builder-of-dreams.html; Gawad Kalinga site: www.gk1world.net and www.gk1world.com.

13   Sydney Olympics: Jill Haynes, *Socio-economic Impact of the Sydney 2000 Olympic Games* (Barcelona: Centre d'Estudis Olímpics i de l'Esport (UAB)—International Chair in Olympism, 2001). Athens Olympics: www.athensguide.org/athens2004.html. China Olympics: Carol Huang, "For Beijing's Olympic Volunteers, the Rules are Many," *The Christian Science Monitor*, July 17, 2008, www.csmonitor.com/World/Asia-Pacific/2008/0717/p04s01-woap.html; site at http://en.beijing2008.cn/83/67/column211716783.shtml.

14   National Volunteer & Philanthropy Centre, www.nvpc.org.sg; Points of Light Institute, www.pointsoflight.org; Volunteering England, www.volunteering.org.uk; VolunteerMatch, www.volunteermatch.org; idealist.org, www.idealist.org. VolunteerMatch is the top search engine for volunteering in the US. While idealist.org is based in the US, it is positioned as a global clearing house for volunteers.

15   Boardmatch Ireland, www.boardmatchireland.ie; The Kind Exchange, www.thekindexchange.com.

16   www.befrienders.org.

17   "The Good Samaritan" is the Biblical story of the Samaritan who helps a complete stranger in distress notwithstanding that the stranger is a Jew, a tribe unfriendly to the Samaritans. The colloquial phrase, "Good Samaritan" has come to mean someone who helps a stranger, and the "Samaritan" label has been incorporated into some organizations' names when they do works of a charitable nature, including counseling for suicide.

18   HandsOn Network is the volunteer-focused arm of Points of Light Institute. See www.handsonnetwork.org.

19   www.casaforchildren.org.

20   www.casaforchildren.org. Examples of its volunteer management programs: offering of web-based recruitment resources and ideas for recruitment of volunteers; provision of a screening toolkit for screening of volunteers; and a National Court Appointed Special Advocate (National CASA) Volunteer Training Curriculum that was developed for training volunteers, and provides information on supervising, firing, and recognizing volunteers under retention of volunteers. "Working with Volunteers", CASA, www.casaforchildren.org/site/c.mtJSJ7MPIsE/b.5466253/k.7C7C/Working_with_Volunteers.htm.

21   www.kennedy-center.org/support/volunteers.

Chapter 12

Corporate Social Responsibility

Toward Moral Capitalism

STEPHEN YOUNG
Global Executive Director, Caux Round Table

Corporate social responsibility (CSR) plays a vital role in ensuring that corporate interests align with the broader social and environmental interests of the community in which businesses operate.

However, the basis for CSR and what it entails is not well agreed among the players in the economy. A fundamental question is: Is CSR about good business or necessary ethics?

There are different approaches to ensuring the take-up of CSR: from encouraging moral capitalism (such as celebrating corporate heroes) and discouraging brute capitalism (such as identifying and shaming corporate abuse), to mandating it through rules and regulations. Two new approaches—reporting companies' CSR practices to investors, and potentially quantifying nonfinancial CSR variables—show great promise.

Consider these figures: In 2000, the total value of the world's liquid capital stocks was estimated at US$79 trillion. Divide that amount into the planet's six billion human population and you get US$27,000 per person. But where was this US$79 trillion? It predominantly sat in four jurisdictions: the US, countries in the Euro zone, the UK, and Japan.[1]

Now, juxtapose this wealth against the vast social disparity and environmental issues that generating it causes, especially in the less developed countries of the world.

This is where corporate social responsibility (CSR) comes in.

CSR is fast becoming an appealing response to the brute competition of the marketplace where self-interest triumphs over virtue. In effect, CSR is about seeking a return to the originally intended good of commerce as defined by Adam Smith—which is to achieve a just society through the prudence of business investors who, with the benefit of experience, would respect the discipline of the market. Capitalism as conceived by Adam Smith, who also wrote a treatise on moral sentiments, is compassionate and could be called "moral capitalism."

CSR efforts are gaining momentum. Various players are coming together to advocate, set benchmarks, and regulate the social responsibility of companies. Each has its own definition of CSR, what the practice emphasizes, and how it should be approached. Companies, too, are becoming more vigilant about CSR reporting, in part driven by the threat of negative publicity and financial damage arising from bad corporate practices.

Clarifying Corporate Citizenship

The multitude of diverse forces and actors that are shaping CSR has contributed to the fuzziness about what being a good corporate citizen involves. Despite the extensive literature on the topic, there exists little common agreement about what CSR actually entails or even why it is needed from a corporation's standpoint.

Defining CSR

The first widely accepted definition of CSR was Archie B. Carroll's concept of economic, legal, ethical, and philanthropic responsibility that first became known in the 1970s. The CSR firm, he said, "should strive to make a profit, obey the law, be ethical, and be a good corporate citizen."[2]

Over the last two decades, different CSR guidelines, codes, and standards of industry best practices and principles have been proposed by various institutions. Among these, the UN, the Caux Round Table, and the International Organization for Standardization (commonly known as ISO) have three of the most comprehensive CSR models.

The UN's Global Compact for CSR establishes a set of guidelines for voluntary ratification by private firms, unions, and nongovernment organizations (NGOs) (see Figure 12.1).[3] First announced in 1999, the Compact has become the world's largest corporate citizenship and sustainable initiative with over 7,700 corporate participants and stakeholders from 130 countries.

The ISO, which comprises representatives from various national standards organizations, has developed standards—such as the ISO 14000 series for environmental management systems—that apply to any business or organization regardless of size, location, and revenue.[4] The most recent standard, ISO 26000 (or simply ISO SR),[5] was released in 2010 and covers a wide range of subjects including organizational governance, human rights, labor practices, environment, fair operating practices, consumer issues, and community involvement and development. Unlike other ISO management systems standards, ISO 26000 does not contain requirements and is not certifiable.

Some guidelines emerge from within the business sector itself. An example is the Caux Round Table (CRT), an international organization of senior business executives that aims to promote ethical business practices.[6] CRT's approach to responsible business consists of the seven CRT Core Principles, which are summarized in Figure 12.2. The principles recognize that laws and market forces, while necessary, are inadequate guides for responsible business conduct.

The CRT Core Principles are supported by more detailed Stakeholder Management Guidelines that cover each key dimension of business success: customers, employees, shareholders, suppliers, competitors, and communities.

Rationale for CSR

One of the real issues confronting business executives is why they should fully embrace CSR. Underlying this debate is the rationale for the very existence of the corporation. Fundamentally, there are two very distinct philosophical approaches: Milton Friedman's focus on the moral obligation

Figure 12.1 The UN Global Compact's Ten Principles

The UN Global Compact's ten principles in the areas of human rights, labor, the environment, and anti-corruption enjoy universal consensus and are derived from:

- The Universal Declaration of Human Rights
- The International Labour Organization's Declaration on Fundamental Principles and Rights at Work
- The Rio Declaration on Environment and Development
- The United Nations Convention Against Corruption

The Global Compact asks companies to embrace, support, and enact, within their sphere of influence, a set of core values in the areas of human rights, labor standards, the environment, and anti-corruption:

Human Rights

Principle 1: Businesses should support and respect the protection of international proclaimed human rights; [and]
Principle 2: make sure that they are not complicit in human rights abuses.

Labor Standards

Principle 3: Businesses should uphold the freedom of association and the effective recognition of the right to collective bargaining;
Principle 4: the elimination of all forms of forced and compulsory labor;
Principle 5: the effective abolition of child labor; and
Principle 6: the elimination of discrimination in respect of employment and occupation.

Environment

Principle 7: Businesses should support a precautionary approach to environmental challenges;
Principle 8: undertake initiatives to promote greater environmental responsibility; and
Principle 9: encourage the development and diffusion of environmentally friendly technologies.

Anti-Corruption

Principle 10: Businesses should work against corruption in all its forms, including extortion and bribery.

Figure 12.2 The Caux Round Table's Seven Core Principles for Responsible Business

Principle 1: Respect stakeholders beyond shareholders.

Principle 2: Contribute to economic, social, and environmental development.

Principle 3: Respect the letter and the spirit of the law.

Principle 4: Respect rules and conventions.

Principle 5: Support responsible globalization.

Principle 6: Respect the environment.

Principle 7: Avoid illicit activities.

of business to make money;[7] and Aristotle's ethical theory of responsibility to others, a stakeholder theory of enterprise.[8]

In a famous response to the initial demand for business ethics, Milton Friedman and his University of Chicago colleagues argued that the only moral obligation of a business was to make a profit.[9] Concern for management of externalities was the business of government. If certain lines of business activity were found objectionable, then the proper remedy was to regulate against them.

The Friedman approach was to seal off the business sector as much as possible from penetration by civil society and government. Such a position minimizes CSR engagement while maximizing private sector autonomy: The corollary is that market pricing mechanisms will produce optimal social outcomes.

The Aristotelian approach, on the other hand, revises the concept of the firm into a more complex system. Here, the enterprise is not regarded as a legal entity closed to outsiders under its own economic sovereignty. Nor does it rest on its own financial capital, with command and control of its employees and adversarial relationships with customers, suppliers, and investors.

The Aristotelian stakeholder theory of the firm proposes that any large firm is really a *de facto* partnership of investors, customers, employees, managers, and suppliers, with more junior partners in the community and a circle of dependents that includes the environment and competitors. The firm is only one participant in the "polis," or community, of collaborating individuals seeking happiness through virtuous conduct.

In short, the Friedman CSR theory is about business creating social outcomes, if there is one, through pure economic effort. The Aristotelian alternative is that business should be ethical, not only in the outcome, but also in the process.

Ensuring CSR

Whether CSR is about good business or necessary ethics is an ongoing debate. Meanwhile, advocates on both sides do recognize the long-term value of implementing CSR in the corporate world.

The different approaches taken to incorporating CSR into an organizational culture can be grouped into those that:

- – Encourage CSR
- – Discourage corporate social irresponsibility
- – Mandate CSR.

Encouraging CSR

The approaches to encouraging CSR range from spreading the message of good CSR practices to forming networks to facilitate it.

The message that is sent differs slightly depending upon which CSR theory one subscribes to.

Those from the Friedman school of thought will argue that CSR can be—or probably most often is—good for business and should be practiced when it makes business sense. They will quote studies by the likes of The Institute of Business Ethics where it was shown that UK companies with corporate codes of ethical conduct achieved profit-turnover ratios which were 18 percent higher than comparable companies without similar explicit commitments to ethical business conduct.[10] In another longitudinal study by Harvard Business School, it was found that companies with embedded cultures of respect for customers and employees as well as stockholders outperformed companies without such a culture by a huge margin during an 11-year period.[11]

Those from the Aristotelian school of thought will take the view that CSR is necessary for the long-term good of the community in which the corporation operates. In its messaging, Aristotelians will highlight the social and environmental ills that befall poor corporate practices and ask what good there is to a wealthy and powerful enterprise if it thrives only within a crumbling environment and society.

Along the way, advocates of CSR have formed coalitions and networks to gather support, spread the message, celebrate CSR paragons, and provide tools and guidelines to foster CSR. The CRT and the UN Global Compact are examples of such platforms.

Several research and monitoring bodies also survey the CSR landscape to celebrate companies that practice good CSR. The New York-based Reputation Institute, for instance, identifies best practices of CSR from around the world and, through a carefully thought-out survey methodology, ranks companies based on their leadership, performance, product, citizenship, and workplace.[12]

Most business schools include the study and promotion of CSR in their curricula. Some of these initiatives go beyond individual institutions. The MBA Oath, a voluntary pledge to "create value responsibly and ethically," is driven by a coalition of MBA students and graduates from over 500 MBA programs worldwide.[13] Beyond Grey Pinstripes provides an alternative ranking of business schools through a survey that features innovative full-time MBA programs that incorporate issues of social and environmental stewardship into curricula and research.[14]

Discouraging Corporate Social Irresponsibility

The opposite of persuasion is dissuasion. Supporters of this approach seek to blame and shame the practitioners of brute capitalism—those who seek maximum profits regardless of the adverse consequences on the environment and the community.

Hence, when corporations go astray in their unfettered pursuit of profits—as in the 1980 *Exxon Valdez* incident, the Enron saga, and most recently the global financial crisis—the press and the public can be relentless in pointing out what should not be. In some cases, activists will organize boycotts of offending companies; prominent examples being McDonald's (notably with "McLibel"), Shell (for Brent Spar and Ken Saro-Wiwa), and Nestlé (use of breast milk substitutes in developing economies).[15]

Some NGOs seek to discourage brute capitalism by proactively ferreting out and naming culprits of corporate excesses. CorpWatch, for example, is a nonprofit that monitors, investigates, and exposes corporate violations of human rights, environmental crimes, fraud, and corruption around the world.[16] It blew the whistle on working conditions in Nike's operations in Vietnam in 1997, and highlighted the war and disaster profiteering by the likes of Bechtel, DynCorp, and Halliburton in recent years in Afghanistan, Iraq, and Florida (Hurricane Katrina).

Most NGOs monitor and report on corporate violations in their specific areas of interest. For example, Greenpeace focuses on corporate environmental mismanagement, and Bank Track highlights social and environmental impacts of financial investments.[17]

Yet, there are other NGOs which may go to the extreme of seeking justice through the courts. The Center for Biological Diversity has used legal suits to bring to light the effects of corporate activity on the biodiversity of the US. Its innovation was to "systematically and ambitiously use biological data, legal expertise, and the citizen petition provision of the powerful *Endangered Species Act* to obtain sweeping, legally binding new protections for animals, plants, and their habitats."[18]

Mandating CSR

There are those who believe that voluntary CSR will not prevail because of the nature of the corporate beast. This fits in with Friedman's view of capitalism: That the corporation's first, and perhaps only, priority is its own economic interests; and that if there are any social responsibilities, they should be spelled out in regulations as a parameter for businesses. It can also fit in with the Aristotelian view of capitalism, where social responsibility—whether volunteered or mandated—is necessary.

A prominent example of mandating CSR is Indonesia. Announced in late 2007, Article 74 of the revised Indonesian company law stipulates that firms must allocate budgets for CSR programs, and the programs must be run according to government regulations. This unique piece of legislation made Indonesia the first country to mandate CSR across the board.[19]

However, much of mandated CSR occurs in specific areas, through labor laws, codes of governance and ethical conduct, and environmental regulations. The regulations will come from government, but in the early stages, it is usually NGOs that lobby for them.

An example of the latter is Friends of the Earth International, the largest grassroots environmental network in the world.[20] It has called for a legally binding international framework for corporate accountability. The key elements of its proposed framework include duties on corporations, directors' liability for breach of environmental and social laws, rights of redress for citizens, communities' rights to resources, consistently high standards of behavior, sanctions, the role of the international criminal court, monopoly controls, and implementation mechanisms.

New Approaches

There are, of course, limitations to these various CSR approaches. Voluntary CSR through moral suasion or dissuasion will remain, well, at best, voluntary. Mandatory CSR (with the brave exception of Indonesia) is difficult to prescribe and put into law other than on a narrow basis.

Two recent approaches that combine elements of the above three but which focus on two new areas may have more promise: CSR disclosures to the investment community, and financial analysis.

Disclosures to Investors

The previously mentioned approaches focus primarily on governments, NGOs, and corporations impressing upon the corporate world the importance of socially responsible behavior. Since shareholders are the primary stakeholders (or the only relevant stakeholder, according to Friedman), involving them in CSR efforts can be more effective.

Investors have clout when they actively champion CSR. They may even be able to negotiate with a company's management for changes to policies and practices. For example, after negotiations with activist investors, PepsiCo agreed to increase its global recycling efforts, while Procter & Gamble agreed to begin marketing fair trade coffee.[21] Most investors are, of course, not the activist sort; but turning them into socially responsible investors can help pressure their investee companies to be more socially responsible.

Socially responsible investing (SRI) has been around for some time now. Traditionally, it involves the creation of funds that screen companies for their social purpose and approaches before including them in the funds' portfolios. Companies can be screened for positive purposes, especially those involved in clean technology, microfinance, global health, and job creation; or they can be screened for negative purposes to avoid "sin industries" (e.g. tobacco or armaments) or unwholesome activities (e.g. apartheid-related business in South Africa and complicity in human rights violations).[22] Examples of SRI funds include the Domini Funds, DWS Global Climate Change Fund, Caspian Advisors' Bellwether Microfinance Fund, and most Islamic funds.[23]

Historically, SRI has suffered from two sets of limitations: making a (one-off) binary "yes" or "no" decision to include or exclude a stock from a portfolio, when CSR is really a spectrum of choices; and the limited information available about what companies are doing from a CSR standpoint.

The current movement to get companies to disclose their CSR efforts to all their current and potential investors will help to broaden the base of companies that recognize the importance of CSR. The reporting of environmental, social, and governance (ESG) policies and implementation by corporations is being supported by various governments, international organizations, and institutional investors.[24]

The UN, in conjunction with the UN Environmental Programme Finance Initiative and UN Global Compact, has developed the Principles for Responsible Investment (PRI), a set of aspirational and voluntary guidelines for investors who wish to address ESG issues.[25] This is becoming the benchmark that European and American institutional investors and fund managers are relying upon to evaluate the CSR of portfolio companies.

PRI and other forms of ESG reporting are currently mainly voluntary in nature. In time, as the guidelines become more refined, it is hoped that ESG reporting may be mandated. Bursa Malaysia, the Malaysian stock exchange, has gone down this route in a rudimentary way to require all its public listed companies to disclose their CSR practices (and that of their subsidiaries) using the Bursa Malaysia CSR Framework as a set of guidelines.[26] If a company has no such CSR practices, a statement to that effect is also required.

A sterling example of CSR commitment and reporting can be found in Marks & Spencer's Plan A. Launched in January 2007, this ambitious corporate plan outlines 100 commitments that the company intends to achieve over five years, including working with customers and suppliers to combat climate change, reduce waste, use sustainable raw materials, and trade ethically. Although its sustainability plan requires an investment of £200 million (US$294 million) over five years, the initiative has already proven cash positive. Marks & Spencer was ranked as the most reputable company in the eyes of British consumers in the Global Reputation Pulse Study 2009.[27]

Financial Analysis

Reporting on ESG factors, whether mandated or voluntary, is very much a matter of qualitative reporting on nonfinancial factors. At the end of the day, if such ESG reporting does not embrace financial drivers, it will not rest easily with the business sector.

The next wave of CSR must therefore work on getting disclosure that converts environmental and social costs into financial costs. Valuation analysis from investment theory can be adopted for such CSR purposes. In this way, CSR variables, which are primarily nonfinancial, can be integrated into mainstream approaches for doing business.

In almost every corporation, the components of risk are the intangible relationships of the firm with its stakeholders: future customer loyalty, future brand equity, future access to capital, future productivity, loyalty of employees, and future conditions of government regulation, among others. These risk components can be averted by investing in five types of firm capital: reputation capital, social capital, financial capital, human capital, and physical capital.

To focus solely on financial capital would lead a company to sell short on social and reputation capital. This was precisely the situation with Bear Stearns and Lehman Brothers in the recent global financial crisis. A culture of excessive risk taking, short-term borrowings, high leverage to cover trading speculation, and large bonuses for senior managers led to illusions of profitability and a degraded social capital. This, in turn, led to a loss of reputational capital when potential creditors lost confidence in the business model. This lack of attention to stakeholder relationships ultimately led to an inability to raise capital and function on a sustainable basis, thus contributing to the 2008 collapse of financial markets.

Understandably, quantifying nonfinancial capital is a challenge. Given the success that accountants have in assigning costs to stock options which had distorted corporate management and investors' behaviors, this raises the question of just when we will be able to accurately quantify and internalize the external social costs of corporate actions.

Moving Forward

In his vision of "CSR 2.0," Wayne Visser pointed out that there must first be "a clarification and reorientation of the purpose of business [which is] to serve society . . . without eroding our ecological and community life-support systems."[28]

CSR therefore mediates between the three sectors of the economy: the business sector, which creates the wealth of nations; government, which provides for public goods; and civil society, which fosters and sustains social capital.

CSR is the zone in which interactions between business and government, business and civil society, and government and civil society, exist and unfold in social reality. It aligns business decisions and actions with the well-being of the community, the key stakeholder for government and civil society. CSR thus keeps business within the zone of responsible fiduciary stewardship and ensures that businesses are a responsible part of the overall ecosystem in which they operate.

The challenge has been getting corporations to accept and incorporate this message of alignment. The debate will continue, but much progress has been made. For continued progress, all parties—governments, civil society, corporations, consumers, and investors—must be an active part of the CSR movement.

Endnotes

1   "SMU Students Forum Explores Why Poverty Persists in Asia and How Individuals Can Make a Difference: Part 1," *Knowledge@SMU*, March 3, 2008, http://knowledge .smu.edu.sg/article.cfm?articleid=1122.

2   Archie B. Carroll, "The Pyramid of Corporate Social Responsibility: Toward the moral management of organizational stakeholders," *Business Horizons*, July–August 1991.

3   www.unglobalcompact.org/AboutTheGC/TheTenPrinciples/index.html.

4   www.iso.org/iso/iso_14000_essentials.

5   The draft document of the ISO26000 is available at http://isotc.iso.org.

6   The Caux Round Table has an annual meeting in Caux, Switzerland and publishes best practice guides for various types of organizations. See www.cauxroundtable.org.

7   Milton Friedman, "The Social Responsibility of Business is to Increase Profits," *New York Times Magazine*, September 13, 1970, http://doc.cat-v.org/economics/milton_friedman/ business_social_responsibility.

8   Aristotle, *Nichomean Ethics* (written around 350 B.C.), http://classics.mit.edu/Aristotle/ nicomachaen.mb.txt; Aristotle, *The Eudamian Ethics*, www.perseus.tufts.edu/hopper/ text?doc=Perseus:text:1999.01.0050; see also Norman E. Bowie,"A Kantian Approach to Business Ethics," in *A Companion to Business Ethics*, ed. Robert E. Frederick (Oxford: Wiley-Blackwell, 2002).

9   Milton Friedman,"The Social Responsibility of Business is to Increase Profits," *New York Times Magazine*, September 13, 1970.

10   Simon Webley and Elise More, *Does Business Ethics Pay? Ethics and financial performance* (London: The Institute of Business Ethics, 2003).

11   John P. Kotter and James L. Heskett, *Corporate Culture and Performance* (New York: The Free Press, 1992). The authors conducted four studies between 1987 and 1991, from which the conclusions were formed.

12   www.reputationinstitute.com.

13   www.mbaoath.org.

14   www.beyondgreypinstripes.org.

15   "The McLibel Trial," *McSpotlight,* www.mcspotlight.org/case/index.html; Lynn Sharp Paine, *Value Shift: Why companies must merge social and financial imperatives to achieve superior performance* (New York: McGraw-Hill, 2003); The Nestlé Boycott: Baby Milk Action website, www.babymilkaction.org/pages/boycott.html.

16   www.corpwatch.org.

17   Greenpeace, www.greenpeace.org/international/l; Bank Track, www.banktrack.org.

18   "Our Story," Center for Biological Diversity, www.biologicaldiversity.org/about/story/index.html.

19   Erin Lyon, "Indonesia's Controversial CSR Law Remains Mandatory," *CSR Asia,* April 16, 2009, www.csr-asia.com/index.php?id=13245.

20   www.foei.org.

21   Tucker Gilmman, "Socially Responsible Investments," *People Trends Magazine,* June–August 2009.

22   Jessica Freireich and Katherine Fulton, "Investing for Social and Environmental Impact," *The Monitor Institute,* 2009, www.monitorinstitute.com/impactinvesting/documents/InvestingforSocialandEnvImpact_FullReport_005.pdf.

23   Domini Funds, www.domini.com; DWS Global Climate Change Fund, www.dws.com.sg/EN/facts/FactSheetOverview.aspx?fundID=4062; Caspian's Bellwether Microfinance Fund, www.caspian.in/bellwether.aspx.

24   A global survey of examples of ESG policies and programs is compiled by Michael J. Kane at www.unpri.org/files/MKane-GlobalESGSurvey-July2009.pdf.

25   www.unpri.org.

26   www.bursamalaysia.com/website/bm/about_us/the_organisation/csr/approach.html.

27   When it was launched in 2007, Marks & Spencer's Plan A involved 100 commitments on "doing the right thing." This has since been expanded to 180 commitments to be achieved by 2015. See http://plana.marksandspencer.com/about; "M&S Says Sustainability 'Plan A' Cash Positive," *Environmental Leader,* June 5, 2009, www.environmentalleader.com/2009/06/05/ms-says-sustainability-plan-a-cash-positive/; "British Consumers Rank Top 50 Companies By Reputation," *Marketing Magazine,* June 4, 2009, www.marketingmagazine.co.uk/news/911066/British-consumers-rank-top-50-companies-reputation.

28   Wayne Visser, "CSR 2.0: The evolution and revolution of corporate social responsibility," in *Responsible Business: How to manage a CSR strategy successfully,* ed. Manfred Pohl and Nick Tolhurst (London: John Wiley & Sons, 2010).

Chapter 13

Media

Amplifying the Social Beat

ALAN WEBBER
Co-founder, Fast Company

The media has long been known as a gatekeeper of information with a disproportionate influence over its audience. It therefore needs to be responsible in its role of news communicator, advocate, watcher, and participant.

The major trend in the changes taking place within the media industry is the emergence of alternative media (online news, blogs, and social media) that are competing with traditional media forms (print, radio, and television). Alternative media can be a challenge and a boon to nonprofit organizations as a result of the increase in delivery channels, brevity of content, user-created content, and new leveraged opportunities.

Neither the mainstream nor alternative media has done justice to the phenomenon of social entrepreneurship, social enterprises, and social innovation. The time is ripe for the media cultivation of a turnaround society, starting with the creation of an online integrated platform that can energize the community of these transformative movements.

T hat old chestnut, "the influence of the media," gets a good roasting every now and then. Much discussion tends to revolve around how media sensationalizes the negative aspects of society and unduly influences our impressionable youth. The prevailing view is that the media has an inordinate ability to directly impact the world views of its audience.[1]

Along with this power to influence, the media is asked to be cognizant of the responsibilities it bears in relation to the various roles it plays.

At the same time, it is wise for the nonprofit sector and nonprofit organizations (NPOs) to understand the sources of power of the media and the individual media forms, and to determine how these can best be harnessed for positive social change.

The Power of the Media

The power of the media lies in its ability to amplify—and ignore—news. It has the unique ability to take a small event happening in a small corner of our world and carry it halfway across the globe and then back again. Some stories, circumnavigating the world several times over, will have more cachet with readers and viewers.

A prime example of the media's power is found in the coverage of disasters. The old TV adage, "if it bleeds, it leads," found its fullest expression in the extensive live coverage of disasters such as the Asian tsunami of December 2004 and, more recently, the Haiti earthquake of January 2010. The impact on viewers is no less impressive. Within a month of the heart-rending images of the Asian tsunami and its victims appearing on front pages of newspapers and being flashed on TV screens across the world, an estimated US$7 billion had been pledged.[2] For the Haiti earthquake, nearly US$1.8 billion was pledged in the first month after the disaster.[3]

Conversely, other humanitarian disasters that are "slower" and devoid of scenes of mass graves and crying survivors often do not receive the same level of coverage by the media. For example, Reuters AlertNet puts the war in the inaccessible Democratic Republic of Congo, which ended in 2003, at the top of a list of "forgotten emergencies."[4] In that conflict, known as "Africa's World War," 3.8 million people died, mostly due to disease and malnutrition—a number which was several multiples of the 300,000 people killed in the Asian tsunami. Such is the disproportionate attention to issues based on editorial judgments of newsworthiness.

NPOs are not immune to the vagaries of today's media. While many NPOs perform acts of sheer heroism on a daily basis, the fact that it gets done on a daily basis also means that it is less newsworthy. Instead, what tends to get (disproportionately) covered is the occasional charity scandal.

A pertinent example is the saga of the National Kidney Foundation (NKF), Singapore's biggest charity.[5] The NKF had brought a defamation suit in 2005 against Singapore Press Holdings (SPH) over the latter's article highlighting NKF's lack of transparency and public accountability. The court revelations had all the key elements of a newsworthy storyline for an NPO: a five-figure monthly executive compensation, a gold tap in the CEO's washroom, and first-class travel. The backlash that followed led to fallout of donors with the charity, the immediate resignation of the CEO and the board, and, eventually, stricter regulatory reforms implemented across the charity sector.

Recognizing the power of the media, some NPOs have dedicated staff whose role is to manage media relations.

In some cases, NPOs create their own media channels. The Natural Resources Defense Council is an example of an NPO which has its own online TV channel, podcasts, and blog to connect with its 1.2 million strong membership and online activist audience.[6] Its success in engaging its stakeholders has been due, in part, to its effective use of media by becoming a media outlet itself.

The Roles of the Media

Indeed, given the multiple roles that media can play, it is useful to understand how it exercises its influence in the social space. Four of the most commonly understood roles of the media are:

- News communicator
- Advocate
- Watcher
- Participant.

News Communicator

This is the least controversial role of the media—everyone expects the mass media to report on the news. However, even though news reporting is a fairly straightforward role, the selection of what is newsworthy does reflect prejudices and positions, intentional or subconscious.

Each media outlet, led by its editor, has its own priorities to reflect, whether they be those of the government (for state-controlled media), big business (for those media owned by multinational conglomerates), or simply its readership (which most would claim).

Decision makers in the media are not elected by the general public but they are subject to "vote at the checkout counter" by readers. Unfortunately, consumers can often make their purchases based on what is on the cover of the publication.

Editors can get their priorities mixed up, too. The front page of the *San Francisco Chronicle* once featured a very small NPO. The budget was tiny and the NPO had little significance, but the story was too good to pass up: its head had run off to an exotic location with the organization's funds and with a woman who was not his wife. Meanwhile, buried inside the same paper was a story about a medical organization that was taking compounds abandoned by for-profit pharmaceutical companies and using them to treat diseases of poor people in third world countries. On the front page is the scandal, while buried inside is news of a positive social enterprise.

Apparently, news is not just merely communicating happenings for some journalists. For their stories to sell, they try to bring life to it, at times using allegories and references that can mislead the readers. For instance, in the reporting of the crisis in Darfur, several established print media referred to the state of affairs as genocide. This was despite Médecins Sans Frontières—a nongovernment organization better known as Doctors Without Borders that was on the ground—insisting that it was not, and that describing the massacres as genocide masked the political opportunism that underscored these events and did not help in the real work of conflict resolution in the area.[7]

Advocate

As an advocate, mass media can promote the work of the nonprofit sector. Quite apart from sensational reports that amplify charity scandals, the media often does share on the positive aspects of the sector as well.

The wide-ranging reach of nonprofit sector work has opened up new segments in the media industry. No longer confined to just the local news sections of the newspapers, there are magazines, such as *Good* and *Ode* to tell the stories of individuals, teams, and organizations that seek to do good in this world. There are also publications and websites that focus entirely on a growing nonprofit audience. Examples include *The Chronicle of Philanthropy*, *Stanford Social Innovation Review*, and *Beyond Profit*.[8]

The traditional media does advocate for the nonprofit sector. Often, this is in a seasonal manner, when it uses its publicity might to market and raise money for charitable causes. For example, the BBC runs fundraising campaigns such as the Radio 4 Appeal, Comic Relief, and Emergency Appeals for selected charities. The impact of these campaigns is impressive. Its 2009 Comic Relief TV extravaganza, for instance, saw a strong line-up of celebrities raising a total of £57.8 million (US$83.4 million).[9]

However, these campaigns do not come about without risk and ethical considerations. The BBC has noted that it puts its brand name on the line whenever it urges its audience to donate to a particular charity. There are also concerns about whether the use of humor or drama to raise funds for the suffering and underprivileged across the UK and Africa is appropriate; yet, if appeal messages are too didactic and somber, it may not make the impact that the campaign is looking for.[10]

Watcher

The mass media is also known as the Fourth Estate, a reference to the press in its watchdog role. In this role, the media is counted upon to expose wrongdoings by businesses, governments, and even NPOs. The Watergate political scandal of the 1970s which led to the resignation of US President Richard Nixon is often enshrined as a classic example of the necessity of the media's watchdog role.[11]

The nonprofit sector is no less immune to scrutiny by the media. The seven-year sentence of United Way's then-CEO William Aramony in 1992 for misuse of donor funds is emblematic of the media's role as a watcher. After receiving persistent media queries on Aramony's rumored lavish lifestyle, the United Way of America's board engaged external investigators to check its accounts. Even though they could not find concrete evidence to show that Aramony had personally enriched himself, the loose record keeping and lumped accounting of his personal and business expenses were enough to cause donors to withdraw their support and led, eventually, to Aramony's resignation and conviction.[12]

Several years later, after reforms to the way American charities were run had been implemented, the effect of media reports on such charity scandals lingered. In 2006, Kevin McCarthy, the CEO of the United Way chapter in Inland Valley, California, lamented the perception that financial shenanigans in the charity sector were widespread, due to skewed media coverage and selective memory. He noted that the 1992 scandal happened in the organization headquarters, and that the 2,100 chapters around the nation had little to do with it except in paying their dues. Yet, McCarthy said that he was regularly reminded of the scandal by people remarking to him, "Oh, you guys couldn't keep your own house clean."[13]

Such is the value attached to the media's watcher role and the power of negative news. While the media plays a useful role in keeping the charities in check, it can also get carried away in its coverage, leading to a partisan effect that may outlast the actual damage done.

Participant

While the media outlets are often nonpartisan bystanders in the nonprofit sector, they are also entities in their own right, sometimes with specific agendas to push and sometimes acting as a direct participant in the creation of news stories. When the NKF took legal action against SPH for the latter's allegedly defamatory article, it claimed that SPH may have had an agenda due to the fact that the NKF was a strong supporter of Mediacorp, a major competitor to SPH.[14]

Some media organizations are created to be participants in a specific cause on a sustained basis. One example is WITNESS, an organization that uses video to advance human rights.[15] It has provided video cameras and training to over 150 groups in 50 countries around the world. The videos are used as evidence before courts, regional commissions, and the United Nations, as tools for public education, and as a deterrent to further abuse. WITNESS videos have been broadcasted by the BBC, CNN, ABC, and satellite and cable stations worldwide. Such coverage, for example, has forced Mexico to reform its psychiatric facilities, and the Philippines to investigate the murders of numerous indigenous activists. It has also catalyzed the passage of the *Trafficking Victims Protection Act* in the US.

Another example of media participation is the aptly named Participant Media. Founded by philanthropist Jeff Skoll, Participant Media is a film and television production company that finances, produces, and distributes socially relevant films and documentaries. Perhaps, its most well-known effort is *An Inconvenient Truth*, which has, arguably, fostered the current movement on climate change. Other notable efforts include *The End of the Line*, which addresses the issue of overfishing; and *Food, Inc.*, which examines large-scale agricultural food production in the US.[16]

The most common criticism that comes up for media companies that are focused on specific issues is their objectivity. Can a documentary really be objective if it already knows what kind of message it wants to impress upon its viewers, especially when it finds evidence to the contrary? *An Inconvenient Truth* came under such criticism when a British High Court judge ruled that nine statements in the film were not supported by mainstream scientific consensus.[17]

Media Trends and Social Impact

The media is not spared from the forces of change that it reports on. Changes in technology and its audience have significantly impacted the media industry and its players, but it has been the forces of change in the business environment that have most significantly impacted traditional media.

Mass media used to be the province of a dozen or so multinational conglomerates that controlled interests in a variety of traditional media outlets (print, radio, and television). The vertical and horizontal integration among media companies of the past decade has changed the shape and nature of these players. A question that has arisen is whether the domination of media by entertainment conglomerates is corroding the quality of journalism.[18]

Even as traditional media compete among themselves and seek mergers and acquisitions, technology is introducing a new set of powerful players, popularly known as alternative or online media, into the arena.

Without a doubt, the rise of the web and alternative media, together with a new generation of readers, is transforming the media landscape in ways that are still being understood. For the social sector, the relevant implications of this media transformation are:

- The multiplicity of delivery channels
- The increasing brevity of content
- The advent of user-created content
- Unlimited new opportunities to leverage the new media.

Multiple Delivery Channels

News and other content used to be available only through print or the airwaves at predetermined times. The web and related technologies have increased dramatically the number and kinds of channels (computers, mobile phones, personal digital assistants, etc.) for pushing and pulling content on demand. As readers increasingly migrate from hardcopy newspapers to advertisement-supported online papers, tech-savvy adopters are customizing the news feeds to choose what, when, and how they want to read the news content.

This development means there are more opportunities for NPOs to be heard.

However, the increasing fragmentation of media power also means that NPOs have not just to engage the mainstream newspapers and television, but also have to ensure that they maintain a presence on the relevant social networking platforms, especially the ones where their particular "tribe" is congregating.[19]

In addition, the role of a communications manager is becoming an increasingly vital one for the NPO seeking to navigate the multiple media channels.

Content Brevity

The proliferation of data worldwide is increasing at an exponential rate. The average American is said to be bombarded with about 34 gigabytes of information per day.[20] A consequence of information overload and our finite time is that today's news and articles are getting shorter.

At the same time, as newspapers and magazines are financially undercut by the web, they will be increasingly pressured to get the ratings and succumb to the simple formula of shock and awe. So the stories will get shorter and shorter, and perhaps more attention seeking. That does not, of course, mean that more stories will be reported.

The shortened attention spans of readers mean that long, citation-heavy essays may no longer be read in their entirety, if at all. Thus, NPOs should tailor their content to be more bite-sized (or perhaps, more blog-sized).

Twitter, with its 140-character limit on any message, represents the extreme end of this move toward content brevity. Twitter-inspired events such as Twestival, which organized 202 off-line events around the world for charity, have become the *de facto* online tool for organizing and taking action.[21]

User-Created Content

The rise of online media has not only seen traditional media loosen its grip on the audience; it has led to a reversal of roles. With the rise of blogs and social networking sites, the population at large is no longer just the consumer of information; it is the producer as well. Content creation and presentation is no longer the domain of professional journalists and their editors. Everyone can create content, and people do.

There are now participatory news sites such as Korea's OhmyNews, Ground Report, and NowPublic that feature news reports from people who have no training in journalism.[22] News articles produced by "traditional" journalists may not necessarily be accepted as gospel truth, as they have been in the past. Now, they are scrutinized, analyzed, and countered in blogs; while alternative and independent news[23] can be easily accessed on websites such as the Consumer Report and the Drudge Report.[24]

In the online world, communication with stakeholders is therefore no longer a one-way street. NPOs have to make their platforms interactive so that their community can have a stake in content creation. An example is Social Edge, a program of the Skoll Foundation that has consistently initiated discussions on various issues related to the social sector.

However, the multiplicity of social networking platforms such as Facebook, MySpace, and Twitter, and the consequent avalanche of user-generated sharing across multiple social networking sites, does make it hard to track the extent to which the organization's affairs are being discussed or dissected in the blogosphere. That is a new reality which NPOs and other organizations will have to contend with in this brave new world. For a change, the jury is out on who the gatekeeper of information is and who is influencing the other.

New Opportunities

For an NPO, the new media landscape provides opportunities that are limited only by its imagination and creativity.[25]

Who could have imagined, for example, that a combination of computer tools, social networking platforms, and a documentary about random street buskers from across the world could generate nearly 20 million views on YouTube and raise funds for the Playing for Change Foundation?[26] But this is exactly what its founder Mark Johnson achieved.

Opportunities for NPOs that have proven to work successfully with the new media include viral marketing, crowd sourcing, and new ways of fundraising.

Viral marketing is the use of social networks to create brand awareness through self-replicating viral processes. An example is CarrotMob, a form of activism that leverages consumer power to incentivize socially responsible business practices.[27] Businesses compete with one another to see who can do the most good, and then a mob of consumers buys products to reward the business that made the strongest commitment to improve the world. All actions are documented and spread through a combination of Twitter, Vimeo, and blogs to reach a worldwide audience.

Crowd sourcing is the outsourcing of tasks to a large group by an open call often via social networks. InnoCentive, for example, leverages social networks to connect companies, academic institutions, the public sector, and NPOs with more than 200,000 scientists and other creative thinkers to solve some of the world's toughest challenges.[28] Organizations post their challenges on the InnoCentive website, and offer significant financial awards to the people who find the best solutions. InnoCentive manages the entire process.

Fundraising may appear to be a simple question of connecting donors with causes. The web, however, provides not just the means to connect high numbers of donors and NPOs in many-to-many relationships (e.g. ammado and Facebook's App Causes); it facilitates the connection with a high level of granularity (e.g. Kiva enables microloans) and creativity (e.g. the American Cancer Society raised US$200,000 by hosting its Second Life version of "Relay for Life" fundraiser).[29]

The Turnaround Society

Our discussion thus far has been about how the social sector can harness the power of the media. What more can the media do for the social sector than it already has?

Consider that mainstream media has traditionally focused on human interest stories. It used to be about scandals, but now there is interest in the good things that are done by social organizations. However, there is still generally not much coverage on capacity building and the more esoteric aspects of the social sector, such as the growth trends of social entrepreneurs, social enterprises, and social innovation. Perhaps the reason is that such phenomena are harder to explain, harder to report, harder to categorize, and harder to narrate. What's more, these challenges are often complicated by other diverse players that are competing and shouting for their own definitions to be heard above the rest.

Yet, when we consider the social movements that are taking place around the world, the rise of social entrepreneurs, social enterprises, and social innovation has the most potential to truly transform the social sector and the world at large. It is thus surprising that for all that is happening in these three related areas—the youthful energy that is coming out of colleges and universities; the money and investment that companies, philanthropists, and institutes are putting into these causes; and all the start-ups and entrepreneurial ventures that are taking shape all over the world on a daily basis—the media is still taking relatively little notice. To be sure, a few heroes—such as Grameen's Muhammad Yunus—have been highlighted, but much of what is going on seems to have gone undetected.

Indeed, this general lack of media coverage has meant that these socially transformative movements have been forced to mount what is, in essence, a tacit conspiracy to turn society around for the better. It is time to make this "turnaround society" more explicit than tacit, and perhaps to help accelerate these movements.

Alternative media, as we have seen, can provide many of the answers. There is already some exposure of social entrepreneurship, social enterprises, and social innovation on the web, particularly through the blogs, social media, and websites built around specific narrow communities.

Much more, however, needs to be done to push the turnaround society to the forefront.

Perhaps, one approach that seems almost self-evident is a full-fledged, web-based magazine or platform, one devoted entirely to the subject of social transformation and including the fields of social entrepreneurship, social enterprises, and social innovation. This should be targeted at building up a community comprising not only the "do-ers" but also the full range of participants who make up the larger ecology of the field— the academicians, thought leaders, capacity builders, philanthropists, beneficiaries, governments, and yes, the media.

Such an online platform will also provide the critical services of advocating change; connecting people and ideas; stimulating and hosting conversations; and creating the community. By facilitating the communication flow between the players in the social ecosystem, the online platform creates a neutral space for ideas exchange and cultivates a common language of positive social change.

This dedicated one-stop online platform will take advantage of the economics and technology of the web, while providing the critical functions needed. In the process, it gives greater energy, shape, and direction to a movement that is already taking off, and now only needs a media-assisted boost to become the next big thing.

Endnotes

1   Discussion of the influence of the media can be found in: Elihu Katz and Paul Felix Lazarsfeld, *Personal Influence: The part played by people in the flow of mass communications* (Piscataway, NJ: Transaction Publishers, 2006); Elisabeth Noelle-Neumann, "The Spiral of Silence: A theory of public opinion," *Journal of Communication*, 1974; Edward Herman and Noam Chomsky, *Manufacturing Consent: The political economy of the mass media* (New York: Pantheon, 1988).

2   "Tsunami aid: Who's giving what," *BBC News*, January 27, 2005, www.news.bbc .co.uk/2/hi/asia-pacific/4145259.stm.

3   "Haiti aid effort one month after earthquake," *BBC News*, February 12, 2010, www .news.bbc.co.uk/2/hi/8509333.stm.

4   "AlertNet Top 10 'Forgotten' Emergencies," AlertNet, www.alertnet.org/top10crises .htm.

5   Willie Cheng, "NKF: The saga and its paradigms," in *Doing Good Well: What does (and does not) make sense in the nonprofit world* (Singapore: John Wiley & Sons, 2009).

6   www.nrdc.org. Its TV channel is NRDC.tv.

7   David Hoile, "The Media and Darfur: Sensationalism and responsibility," The European Sudanese Public Affairs Council, www.espac.org/darfur/the-media-and-darfur .asp#73.

8   *Chronicle of Philanthropy*, www.philanthropy.com/section/Home/172; *Stanford Social Innovation Review*, www.ssireview.org; *Beyond Profit*, www.beyondprofitmag.com; *Good Magazine*, www.good.is/; *Ode Magazine*, www.odemagazine.com/#.

9   "Comic Relief Reaches Record £57 million," *BBC News*, March 14, 2009, www.news .bbc.co.uk/2/hi/7939425.stm.

10 For a more comprehensive discussion, see Fergal Keane, "Please Give Generously," *BBC Radio 4*, February 20, 2010, www.bbc.co.uk/programmes/b00p7h3y.

11 The scandal began with the arrest of five men for breaking into the Democratic National Committee headquarters in Washington, DC. Subsequent investigations connected the men to the 1972 Committee to Re-elect the President. It was also revealed that President Richard Nixon had a tape-recording system in his office which implicated him in covering up the break-in. See William B. Dickinson, Mercer Cross, and Barry Polsky, "Watergate: Chronology of a crisis," *Congressional Quarterly Inc.*, 1973.

12 Charles E. Shepard, "United Way Head Resigns Over Spending Habits," *The Washington Post*, February 28, 1992, www.tech.mit.edu/V112/N9/united-way.09w.html; "Former United Way Chief Convicted in Fraud Trial," *McCook Daily Gazette*, April 4, 1995, www .news.google.com/newspapers?nid=1933&dat=19950403&id=JtggAAAAIBAJ&sjid=Fm sFAAAAIBAJ&pg=1459,3197093.

13 Sharon Hoffman, "For U.S. Charities, a Crisis of Trust: Scandals, accountability problems combine to undermine public support," *msnbc.com*, November 21, 2006, www.msnbc .msn.com/id/15753760/ns/us_news-giving.

14 Sharon Loh and Selina Lum, "SPH Had an Agenda?: NKF chief withdraws claims," *The Straits Times*, July 12, 2005. Later in the court case, NKF withdrew the claim that SPH may have had that agenda.

15   WITNESS was founded by Peter Gabriel, the leader of the now-defunct band Genesis, in 1992. See www.witness.org and www.petergabriel.com.

16   Participant Media, www.participantmedia.com/films.php; *An Inconvenient Truth*, www .climatecrisis.net/; *End of the Line*, www.endoftheline.com/; *Food, Inc.*, www.foodincmovie .com/. See also Lewis Solomon, *Tech Billionaires: Reshaping philanthropy in a quest for a better world* (Piscataway, NJ: Transaction Publishers, 2008).

17   "Gore Climate Film's Nine 'Errors'," *BBC News*, October 11, 2007, www.news.bbc .co.uk/2/hi/uk_news/education/7037671.stm.

18   See "The Big Ten," *The Nation*, January 7/14, 2002, www.thenation.com/special/bigten .html.

19   Relevant social networking platforms could include Facebook's The Causes application, ammado and specialized communities for social enterprises, humanitarian relief, etc. See also Seth Godin, *Tribes: We need you to lead us* (London: Penguin Group, 2008).

20   Roger E. Bohn and James E. Short, *How Much Information? 2009 Report on American Consumers* (San Diego, CA: Global Information Industry Center, University of California, 2009), www.hmi.ucsd.edu/pdf/HMI_2009_ConsumerReport_Dec9_2009.pdf.

21   Twitter, www.twitter.com; Max Gladwell, "10 Ways to Change the World through Social Media," *Mashable the Social Media Guide*, June 2009, www.mashable.com/2009/05/12/ social-media-change-the-world.

22   OhmyNews, www.english.ohmynews.com/; Ground Report, www.groundreport.com/; NowPublic, www.nowpublic.com.

23   There have, of course, been concerns about the standard of reporting by these alternative forms of journalism; plagiarism has been cited as one of the gravest misconducts.

24   Consumer Report, www.consumerreports.org/cro/index.htm; Drudge Report, www .drudgereport.com.

25   Examples of how social media can be used by nonprofits can also be found in Chapter 17, "Technology: Rebooting technology for society," by Robert Chew.

26   YouTube—Stand By Me, www.youtube.com/watch?v=Us-TVg40ExM; www .playingforchange.com.

27   www.carrotmob.org/about.

28   www.innocentive.com/about-us-open-innovation.php.

29   Ammado, www.ammado.com; Kiva, www.kiva.org; Relay for Life, Sandra W. Bettger, "Nonprofits and Second Life: Promoting causes Second Life for real-world impact," Giving Circles Network, October 16, 2008.

Government

Chapter 14

Government

Affirmative Government for Social Good

PETER SHERGOLD

Macquarie Group Foundation Professor, Centre for Social Impact

Government seeks to maximize the well-being of its citizens. The social sector has the same ultimate objective but it, and the multifarious stakeholders who seek to give it voice, may not always be seen by government to have the same agenda.

The attitude of government toward nonprofit organizations affects how it calibrates the conduct of its key functions of funder, promoter, regulator, and player. Government may view nonprofits alternately as "friend," "filler," or "foe," depending on the time, circumstances, and organizations involved.

While government wields power and authority, it can seek to harness the power of the nonprofit sector through an affirmative approach that recognizes the mutuality of objectives. Such an affirmative government is marked by a whole-of-government and citizen-centric approach to decisions and interactions, recognition of the public good that nonprofit organizations provide, an agenda of social inclusion for citizen empowerment, and collaborative governance of the community and its constituents.

D emocratic governance is based upon an implied contract between the institutions of the state and the people who are subject to their authority. The state provides national security and economic and social protection. The citizenry, in return, offers loyalty. The role of elected governments, and the public services that work for them, is to seek to maximize the well-being of its citizens. How governments can, should, and have (or have not) done so is the subject of much ongoing discussion.

For government, the community-based, nonprofit organizations (NPOs) that comprise the social sector represent a major constituency that needs to be served. More significantly, the sector can help or impede government agendas. How governments act and react to it can differ greatly. They can work with the social sector as partners or view it as an unwelcome source of political opposition. They can seek to counter NPO advocacy, treat NPOs as independent "charities," subsidize their community efforts, or engage them in the delivery of government programs and services.

History is checkered with examples of mighty governments that have sought to discipline civil movements: the Tiananmen Square incident in China; the suppression of the human rights protest in Iran; and the Burmese military junta's crackdown on dissidents, including monks. At the other end of the spectrum, we have seen enlightened governments that have sought to promote the growth and influence of civil society: the Obama administration's initiatives such as the Office of Social Innovation and Civic Participation, and the UK's Office of the Third Sector.[1]

To understand how a government can best work with the social sector to achieve the objective of meeting its citizens' needs, we need first to examine the various functions performed by government and the kinds of relationships it has with the social sector.

Governmental Functions *vis-à-vis* the Social Sector

Government is a complex machine. Its bureaucratic structures are often demarcated, cumbersome, and slow moving. There are numerous governmental organizations in a complicated structure, carrying out a myriad of functions for its citizens. In general, there are four major functions of government relative to the social sector:

- Funder
- Promoter
- Regulator
- Player.

Government as Funder

In most countries, the government is a significant funder of the social sector. On average, this works out to about 35 percent of the sector's revenue.[2] In some countries—in particular, the European welfare states where the proportion tends to be the highest—the funding level can go up to 77 percent.[3]

Funding generally comes in two forms: grants and contracts.

Government grants in support of the NPOs' programs are not unlike the grants given out by foundations. Essentially, they are subsidies to NPOs to engage in activities—often supported by volunteering, philanthropic donations, and corporate investments—that deliver beneficial social impact. To ensure accountability of public funds, they are usually awarded on the basis of defined expectations of performance. Funding has to be acquitted. The main penalty for poor performance takes the form of adjustments to, or denial of, the next grant request.

Contracts are essentially commercial purchase-for-service arrangements to deliver government programs. A form of outsourced purchaser–provider relationship, they usually define quite clearly the deliverables and payment terms in a service agreement. They thus give the government relatively more control over the selection of suppliers and the framework of service delivery than grants.

Whichever funding method it adopts, government faces the challenge of achieving the social goals it has set, while ensuring that the greater share of funds goes to deserving high-performing organizations that consistently deliver "value for money." Unfortunately, this appropriate emphasis on performance too often manifests itself as a stringent focus on compliance, in which government funds come with an unnecessarily large burden of regulatory intrusion. The NPOs that take funds from governments can find that they end up "supping with the devil."[4] This problem is compounded when funding comes from multiple levels (international, national, state, or local) of government. Bureaucratic inertia, partisanship, and miscommunication can result at each of these levels.[5]

For NPOs, the challenge of governmental support is public service micromanagement and a weakening of the NPO's advocacy voice. Often funding is inadequate and only partially covers program or project costs. Part of this is due to overhead caps that government may stipulate that do not reflect the organization's real costs.[6]

A significant danger in accepting governmental funding is its potential to unduly influence or distort a program's social purpose. When organizations rely too heavily on governmental funding, they can end up taking on the bureaucratic traits of the funders, succumbing to mission creep, and sometimes appearing to their clients to be little different from for-profit contractors-for-hire.[7] It is sometimes argued that the welfare reform advocacy groups in the US that accepted governmental funding in the form of outsourced services progressively mutated from their advocacy role to become government service providers.[8] In effect, NPOs often find themselves starting to be viewed as agents of government.

Government as Promoter

The government's influence extends beyond just the financial. It can also act to enhance and support the viability and capacity of the social sector, so that the impact of social organizations is amplified.

Government can promote the viability of the social sector through measures that ensure social organizations are appropriately recognized and given the opportunity not only to deliver services but also to influence the making of government policy. This can take the form of providing a public platform for "third sector"visibility, legitimizing the role of nonprofit activities or organizations in service delivery, or even changing its policy or administrative environment to boost the efficacy of the work done by NPOs.

The UK has taken a strong lead in this role by forming the Office of the Third Sector, a direct part of the Cabinet Office, which "enabl(es) the sector to campaign for change, deliver public services, promote social enterprise, and strengthen communities."[9] In the US, the Obama administration regularly delegates officeholders to participate in social sector events, allowing them to be champions for what the sector needs.[10] In Australia, the Labor government has recently committed to a National Compact to base the relationship between the Australian government and NPOs on principles of advocacy, consultation, and collaboration.[11]

Government can also promote the capacity building of the social sector by supporting the growth and development of organizations, leaders, and staff to improve their abilities. This form of promotion focuses on the improvement of the external and internal factors that influence the efficacy of social organizations. One possible step is to build platforms that make social sector resources and supporters visible and available.

At a time of economic downturn, government funding can often help to provide financial stability to NPOs. A recent Australian survey suggests that when NPO investments were diminishing in value, corporate support was decreasing, and donations were falling, government funding provided an increasingly important source of financial support.[12] In the US, the Strengthening Communities Fund created by the Department of Health and Human Services seeks to help communities severely affected by the economic downturn. One part of the fund is a Nonprofit Capacity Building Program that provides grants to nonprofits and faith-based organizations to assist families in economic distress.[13]

Government as Regulator

The regulator role is a natural one for government.[14] It is expected of it. Its function is to provide an enabling legal environment which allows social organizations to thrive, while protecting the trust placed in them by the public.

Salomon and Toepler theorize that an enabling legal framework can be constructed by "minimizing transaction costs" in the social sector.[15] Laws can affect the transaction costs incurred both directly and indirectly in creating, funding, and operating social organizations. An enabling legal environment should seek to reduce transaction costs associated both with the provision of social services (supply) and the utilization of such services by beneficiaries (demand).

Legal factors that affect the supply costs (providing social services) include the framework of regulatory authority, the processes of NPO association, the fiduciary duties of board members, and the financial treatment of charitable activities. The regulation of incorporation, taxation, and reporting requirements for NPOs should be freed of unnecessary prescription and duplication.

Conversely, demand costs (utilizing social services) can be affected by transparency levels of NPOs, the governance of their organizations, their ability to fundraise and harness volunteer support, and their scale and capacity.

Salamon and Toepler conclude that countries that have favorable regulatory frameworks often contain these common characteristics:

- People have a fundamental legal right to associate with each other into groups, albeit with clear formation eligibility conditions and process.
- Citizens can legally and easily be aware of, and have access to, social organizations that meet a variety of needs.
- Citizens can legally and easily express their confidence in social organizations.
- The legal system allows for financial viability of social organizations, typically through tax exemptions on revenue, or special tax treatment of contributions.

Based on their framework, Salamon and Toepler found that of the 13 countries included in its preliminary study, Israel, the Netherlands, and the US were ranked as the most enabling countries with favorable legal regimes for nonprofit activity. Brazil and Japan ranked the lowest. The ranking broadly correlates to the level of nonprofit activity in the countries; that is, the more favorable the legal regime for nonprofit action, the more highly developed is the nonprofit sector in that country.

Government as Player

Government has a vested interest in ensuring that the social needs of its citizens are provided for. It can do so indirectly by subsidizing the operations of social service organizations, or directly by funding and delivering the services. Where the line is drawn between government and the social sector providing the social service will vary among countries. Indeed, it is often the subject of intense debate between the public and social sectors.

Governments in welfare states have taken on active roles in the provision of social services across the board. In the Nordic states, for example, an estimated 90 percent of all personnel in the social and educational services are public employees.[16] Many governments are, selectively, players in specific social service programs. In Australia, for instance, Centrelink is a one-stop statutory agency set up to help people become self-sufficient and to support those in need.[17] It disburses social security payments and is a conduit for the delivery of many human services on behalf of a range of government departments.

Health care is a good example of a sector where the level of government involvement differs significantly from country to country. This can range from the government playing an extensive role through financing and health-care provision, to a situation in which health-care provision is left solely to market forces.[18]

Extensive government involvement in health care can be found in the UK, Spain, most Scandinavian countries, New Zealand, and Hong Kong. In these countries, many hospitals and clinics are owned by the government, while medical professions and fees are largely regulated.

An alternative is the national health insurance model, where health-care providers are private but the means of financing these services come from a government-run insurance program to which every citizen contributes. Examples of countries employing this model include Canada, Taiwan, and South Korea.

There are, however, areas where the activity should logically be the domain of the civil sector but, in fact, government is the player. Watchdogs, civic action bodies, religious institutions, and other such bodies should, arguably, be independent of the government. However, in some countries, they are controlled by the state. For instance, state-run religious and welfare institutions are commonly found in centrally controlled countries such as China and Myanmar.

Government's Relationship with the Social Sector

How government carries out its respective functions influences—and is very much influenced by—its interactions with the social sector.

Academics have sought to explain the complex relationships between the public and social sectors. Lester Salamon identifies four patterns of government–nonprofit relations: authoritarian, government-dominant (social democratic), third-sector dominant (liberal), and partnership (corporate).[19] Adil Najam has postulated a Four-Cs relationship: cooperation, confrontation, complementarity, and co-optation.[20] Dennis Young has identified three models: supplementary, complementary, and adversarial.[21]

Young's model has been widely referenced. It argues that governments can take three attitudes toward the social sector:

- Social sector as friend, where NPOs are partners in solving social issues and delivering public goods

- Social sector as filler, where NPOs fulfill social demands that government chooses not be involved in
- Social sector as foe, where NPOs push government to change its policies and approach, and to be accountable to the public.

Social Sector as Friend

Government as friend will actively help build the capacity of the social sector and treat NPOs as partners in providing social services.

The UK government is one that has been demonstrably proactive in the capacity building of the social sector. It has collaborated with the third sector in many sector reviews and initiatives. One such program, ChangeUp, initiated in 2004, has done much to build the capacity and infrastructure of the voluntary and community sector and resulted in the creation of the Capacitybuilders agency.[22]

In the provision of social services, government works in partnership with the social sector largely by funding NPOs to deliver social services. The rationale is that this approach plays to the strengths of the two sectors. The government has the comparative advantage in tax collections and authoritative influence. However, if the social services are directly undertaken by the government, there is a concern that overhead costs and transactional work add layers of bureaucracy that, in turn, lowers the returns on investment. The social sector is seen to be well placed to play this role because it has a better sense of society's needs and has the expertise to provide direct services more efficiently. It empathizes with those to whom it delivers support. It can have greater social impact at lower cost.

The school system in the Netherlands, for example, is government-funded but it is operated independently by social organizations along secular or religious lines. In Germany, "free welfare associations" (community-formed and government-funded) account for the majority of social and welfare services, operating over 68,000 institutions in health care and services for youth, families, the elderly, and the disadvantaged.[23]

Social Sector as Filler

In this model, government takes the lead and exercises its prerogative over which services it wishes to provide, leaving the social sector to fill the gaps.

This is premised on the belief that state resources should be minimized when it comes to providing for individual community (as opposed to national) good. The government needs to balance the diversity of needs and make sure that the taxpayers' contribution does not pay for too many services that are not required by the average citizen. Consequently, it limits its involvement and where the government is unwilling or unable to provide for a specific segment of society, social organizations step in to deliver these services. In general, where the government invests less in social services, the social sector will inversely need to fill the gap. NPOs, functioning on the principles of cooperation and mutualism, shoulder greater responsibility. Government may choose to subsidize their efforts.

This filler or supplementary relationship is evidenced in many developing countries such as the Philippines, Mexico, and Pakistan, where government resources are stretched and fail to deliver services to all their citizens, and the social sector becomes an indispensable provider of community services.[24] This is not new. Indeed, the role of innovative community organizations in providing social support, health care, education, and housing was a key part of the social fabric of countries such as the UK, New Zealand, Australia, and Canada before the era of the welfare state.

Another interesting demonstration of the filler approach is Japan's social sector in the 1990s, which was largely guided or controlled by the government and functioned almost as an extension of the public sector. NPOs were classified in a way that aligned with the areas of government. They were expected to provide services that would otherwise be too costly for the government. The NPOs also served as a retirement opportunity for senior civil servants, allowing younger personnel in the government to be promoted.[25]

Social Sector as Foe

In an adversarial relationship, government can sometimes see its function as a watchdog over the social sector, and vice versa. This kind of relationship is premised on the dictum that government and the social sector provide checks and balances on each other. In many developing countries, it is NPOs operating as civil society organizations that provide effective political opposition. And in many developed countries, it is NPOs that come together as social movements to pursue racial or gender equality, social justice, or environmental sustainability.

Although the terms "foe" and "adversary" may give rise to an impression of confrontation, in fact the relationship can be manifested in constructive ways. Viewed positively, it is a form of healthy rivalry, as both government and the social sector publicly argue their respective visions of the public good. The social sector, by virtue of its connection to the grassroots, portrays itself as more in tune with society's needs and prods the government to address them. The government, by virtue of its authoritative position, argues that public resources are finite and that it is expected to keep potential abuses in the social sector in check.

There are obviously negative instances of adversarial relationships. This is often the case in centrally controlled nations where the government dominates most aspects of political and social life, and views dissenting opinions as provocative. In Russia, for example, "many civil servants view the activities of the non-commercial and non-governmental organizations as a threat to their single-handed rule."[26] Indeed, in 2006, when a series of non-violent demonstrations were held against corruption in government, the Russian government introduced new laws that imposed excessive documentation, restrictive registration, and unwieldy operational procedures for NPOs.[27]

Mixed Feelings

Neither government nor the social sector is monolithic. The relationships that each has with the other differ depending upon the circumstances, issues, and players involved.

Take Singapore as an illustration. Over the last decade, the government has implemented initiatives such as the creation of the National Volunteer & Philanthropy Centre to promote greater volunteerism and giving. It has supported social enterprises through the establishment of the Social Enterprise Committee, the ComCare Enterprise Fund, and the Social Enterprise Association. It has taken a lead role in promoting corporate social responsibility. These examples of the government's promotion of social harmony are the mark of a friend of the sector, albeit bearing the hallmarks of a corporatist state.[28]

The Singaporean government is also renowned for its "many helping hands" approach to social services by funding voluntary welfare organizations.[29] Not surprisingly, governmental funding accounts for the majority of the expenditures of NPOs in Singapore. However, this is seen by some in civil society as a filler approach where "the state dictates a supplementary role for civil society—a role of 'many helping hands' to take over welfare functions that it chooses to withdraw from."[30]

In other instances, particularly for advocacy groups, the Singaporean government sometimes takes an attitude toward such civil society players in which they are portrayed as foe. Some of its laws and practices toward civil discourse are seen to create a "disabling environment of fear and uncertainty."[31] Such views were reinforced during the annual meetings of the International Monetary Fund and the World Bank, which were hosted in Singapore in 2006. At this event, the Singaporean government banned and deported several activists and restricted the protest activities of international civil society organizations (CSOs) at the conferences despite the World Bank actively supporting the attendance of the CSOs and the activists.[32]

Relationship Impact on Functions

The attitude that government takes toward the social sector influences not just the extent to which it carries out its respective functions relative to the sector, but also how it does so. Figure 14.1 depicts the relative impact of the government's relationship with the social sector on its core functions.

Figure 14.1 Impact of Social Sector Relationship on Government Functions

Relationship / Function	Friend	Filler	Foe
Funder	●	◑	○
Promoter	●	◑	○
Regulator	○	◑	●
Player	○	◑	●

Where the relationship is that of a friend or partner of the sector, the government's focus is to promote the growth and capacity building of the social sector. It will fund social sector organizations while restraining itself from being a direct provider of social services. Its regulations are the most enabling for the growth of the sector.

Where the relationship is that of a foe, the opposite occurs. The government tends to be the major provider of social services and seeks to rein in the sector through heavy regulation. It pays scant attention to promoting the sector, and provides funding only to the extent that NPOs are subservient to it.

Midway between these two extremes is where the government treats the social sector as filler. The government decides what it wants to provide by way of social services, generally restricting itself to programs that will be accessed by the majority of citizens, and leaves the social sector to provide for those excluded, subsidizing these organizations where necessary. It will also seek to promote the social sector but in a more restricted manner and mainly toward its agenda of having the social sector fill the gaps.

Toward an Affirmative Government

The manner in which different governments have evolved their approaches to working with the social sector has reflected historical circumstance, economic development, and the ideological premises of the players involved. There are times when "filler" and even "foe" relationships are appropriate, although "friend" would be what many enlightened governments seek most of the time.

At its core, government and the social sector really have the same broad objective—the well-being of society and its citizens. Ideally, government should meet its objective through a positive approach that transcends the questions of functions and relationships with the social sector, to recognize this mutuality of objectives. It can be postulated that an "affirmative government" is marked by at least three key features:

- A whole-of-government approach to decision making which seeks to be "citizen-centric" in its interactions with the public
- An agenda of social inclusion for citizen empowerment, recognizing the requirement for government and the social sector to work together to support those most in need
- Collaborative governance of the community and its citizenry.

Whole-of-Government

Most of the problems of public policy do not respect organizational boundaries; nor do most citizens who are the subject of public policy. Yet, both the effective development of policy, and its goal of efficient delivery of social services, are often hindered by the territorial administration of different government departments.

This is a truth that many public services now accept. In the UK, there is commitment to the notion of "joined-up" government and the "seamless" delivery of programs. In Canada, there is a strong emphasis on "horizontalism" in the delivery of services. In New Zealand, the focus is on departments integrating their policy analysis early before it can be "owned" by a single department. In Singapore, the Public Service for the 21st Century initiative seeks to encourage a mindset of continuous improvement and a citizen-centric approach among its public servants.[33]

The need for a whole-of-government perspective to decision making and dealing with citizens and the citizen sector is obvious. The means of achievement are not.

Mainstreaming a whole-of-government mindset and approach will require:

- *Coordination:* All governmental agencies need to work together in a coordinated manner. There should be a framework of cooperative structures that stretches from top to bottom, with taskforces that cross governmental ministries and departments, and a single shop-front for citizens and organizations to deal with the government. Citizens need to be able to transact business with government—in person, by telephone, or online—as easily as possible. Services need to be built around the needs of the citizen, rather than be structured for the administrative convenience of bureaucracy.
- *Flexibility:* Program guidelines should no longer be treated as rigid rules that serve to constrain administrative innovation. Departmental allocations of budgets should be able to move between agencies, and between programs, in pursuit of whole-of-government objectives.
- *Accountability:* There should be regular reporting on programs against a range of socio-economic indicators designed to test the effectiveness of the delivery of beneficial social impact. Outside expertise should be harnessed to give credibility to program evaluation.
- *Collegiate Leadership:* There should be joint leadership by senior civil servants to achieve a whole-of-government approach. Sometimes, this may be achieved informally by establishing a harmonious leadership group. Sometimes, on particular issues, it may require the establishment of a cross-agency task force. Accountability for results should go all the way to the top, with top-ranking civil servants being assessed on their collaborative behaviors.

Social Inclusion

The goal of social inclusion is to provide equal opportunities for all citizens—regardless of income, creed, race, ethnicity, gender, or beliefs—to meet their potential.

It is widely accepted that barriers to social and economic advancement impose costs not just on those who lose out but on society as a whole. An inadequate supply of skilled workers, high levels of welfare dependence, and low levels of civic engagement, for instance, impose significant costs. Both workforce participation and workplace productivity are lowered and the costs of social welfare and community order increased.

The adverse impact is not just economic. People who feel politically disempowered fuel the growing lack of trust in the institutions of democratic governance. Those who are marginalized are less likely to subscribe to the values of civil respect, tolerance, and orderliness that underpin legal authority and ethical conduct. Society fragments.

The problem with trying to understand the nature of social inclusion is the tendency to define it by reference to specific "excluded groups," the particularities of their disadvantaged circumstance, and how the obstacles they face might be overcome. Most commonly, the response to exclusion comes in the form of individual support payments (such as unemployment benefits, rent assistance, or aged pensions) and social programs (such as increased access to job training, social housing, or home care).

While there is nothing inherently wrong with such government transfer programs, two common mistakes of implementation stand out.

First, the governments which fund the programs and the public services, and the NPOs who often deliver them, too frequently treat those they help as beneficiaries. Perceived as dependents, it is scarcely surprising that those who receive support see themselves as dependent. The very act of public provision reinforces the unequal relationship between government bureaucracy and the welfare recipient. The recipient learns helplessness and passivity. The system creates stigma and perpetuates isolation.

Secondly, the complex plethora of financial support provided by different tiers of government, particularly in welfare states—including payments, subsidies, concessions, and rebates—often means that the individual is better off doing nothing (and keeping the benefits) than doing something (and seeing the benefits reduced). Effort goes unrewarded. The desire to return to education, access training, or find a part-time job is often eroded if success brings little (if any) immediate financial reward.

Social inclusion, at its most fundamental level, will require citizens to be actively engaged in the way in which governments provide them with support. NPOs, who are closer to those who require assistance and often advocate their interests, can play an important role in ensuring that those who receive services are able to wield effective choice in how those services are tailored to their particular circumstances.

However, there is also the opportunity for governments to engage citizens directly through what, in the UK, are called "in control" programs. Citizens, given the opportunity to self-direct their publicly funded services, will be empowered to articulate their own destiny. Communities, given the chance to exert greater influence over their child-care facilities, schools, training providers, neighborhood centers, and public housing, will be able to govern their own institutions. By enabling people to participate in the design of their own public support, by allowing them to become "co-producers" of the services they need, an inclusive society can be built. Its fundamental premise is that individuals, acting separately or in concert, can be given the opportunity to be placed in control of their own future.

An example would be people with a disability in Western Australia. For more than two decades, they have been given greater opportunity to decide on how best the state government can respond to their needs. Through a network of local area coordinators, the Disability Services Commission works with persons with a disability to organize their own budgets.[34] The operating ethos, based on self-advocacy, is that people with disabilities are in the best position to determine their own needs and goals. The role of NPOs remains important but, rather than being deliverers or brokers of services, they increasingly work with families to inform, facilitate, and support individual decision making.

In an inclusive society, the ambition both of public services and of community organizations should be to move from being funders and deliverers to becoming brokers, facilitators, and coaches. They should seek to work with—not for—the individuals that they support, helping the disadvantaged to make informed decisions on their own. The social capital created by individuals as they work with others to tailor programs and manage budgets to their own needs, builds community engagement.

Co-production gives citizens greater authority to participate in the design and delivery of government policies and, by doing so, encourages participatory democracy. Civil society is energized. The citizen becomes the center of attention. In a recent study in Australia on the effectiveness of the individual funding approach, all the respondents said that "individual funding had improved their control, choice, independence, and self-determination."[35]

Collaborative Governance

One of the trends of modern governments is the increasing outsourcing of public services to private sector and community institutions. This is a healthy trend reflecting the increasingly symbiotic relationship between public and nonprofit sectors. Many public services can be implemented more cost-effectively and to higher standards by organizations that care about those to whom they deliver.

However, NPOs can be burdened by a level of bureaucratic red tape far greater than is necessary for public accountability purposes—micromanagement by public servants that stifles social innovation—and are tempted to self-censor their advocacy voice in order to win business. To avoid these constraints, the contractual relationship based initially on compliance has to be transformed into a partnership for performance in which public and private goals and values are aligned.

Collaboration between the public and social sectors goes beyond the spirit of partnership in outsourced contracts. Government can, for example, fund small-scale bottom up social initiatives that are community based. Instead of trying to fit the proposals into government-constructed agenda, or to fund them from within the existing range of prescribed government programs, people can be given the opportunity to identify and resolve local problems.

Collaborative governance starts with an understanding of stakeholder needs and agreement on shared responsibilities. A stakeholder charter that seeks to inform expectations and address the extent to which they are met is an important vehicle for building and maintaining levels of trust across the network of those who engage with government.[36] Shared responsibility agreements should reflect the negotiation of responsibilities between the government and the community to achieve mutual goals.

A culture of collaboration between government and the social sector is crucial to the creation of a shared-power world. A potential outcome is a "center-less society" in which public policy is made and delivered by an interdependent mix of government, markets, and networks. Many players get to play a part, including NPO advocacy groups and lobbyists.

However, it is important to recognize that public service is likely to remain at the political heart of governance networks. Government retains extensive powers. There are many reasons for this: its resource capability; its collective experience and knowledge; its legislative and regulatory authority; the financial control it wields through grants, loans, and contracts; its access to influence; and its exercise of soft power.

The processes of government–social sector collaborations will continue to reflect a hierarchical relationship between the actors. The government often externally imposes the structure of the collaborations and decides on representation. Structures will tend to maintain public service dominance. While the deliberative processes of networks result in agreements, conclusions, or recommendations, most major policy decisions would be taken outside of the collaborative group.

Genuine collaboration in governance will involve recognition of interdependence within the network of institutional structures. It will depend upon accepting mutuality of interests. It should not unthinkingly assume consensus. Parties will come to the table with competing interests. Their different perspectives will only be resolved—indeed, they will only properly be understood—by honest interaction and genuine negotiation. The entire process of seeking solutions needs to be iterative.

Through a process of integration, collaboration can bring a network of interested parties to mutually beneficial outcomes, sometimes even in unexpected ways. When collaboration works, the whole can be greater than the sum of its parts. Success in collaboration will require new forms of leadership behaviors, particularly on the part of public servants who remain central to most discussions on public policy and administration. Instead of imposing agendas, they need to negotiate them. Collaboration can be enhanced by a clear indication that public servants will champion the collective decisions of the group—using their disproportionate power on behalf of the collaborative venture.

Government for the People?

The relationship between the state (represented by governments and their public services) and the social sector (represented by an extraordinary diversity of NPOs) is characterized by asymmetric power. It is not yet, and perhaps cannot ever be, a partnership of equals.

However, there are many examples in history of governments overcoming bureaucratic inertia to push through changes in collaboration with social sector players to tackle long-standing social issues such as poverty, abuse, and discrimination. Recent trends suggest more democratic governments taking up the challenge of fostering a closer relationship with the social sector, embracing ideas emanating from the sector, and working with social sector organizations to effect social change. Couple the political will with the vast resources and authority vested in government, and the outcomes could create much greater social impact—not just better services but, through the creation of social capital, a more civil, engaged, and participatory citizenry.

That is the challenge for the future. The government that succeeds will be affirmed to be one that is truly a government for the people.

Endnotes

1　Tiananmen Incident, www.news.bbc.co.uk/onthisday/hi/dates/stories/june/4/newsid_ 2496000/2496277.stm; Iran government suppression, www.reuters.com/article/ idUSTRE60N1AO20100124; Burmese military crackdown, www.news.bbc.co.uk/2/ hi/7016608.stm; Obama Office of Social Innovation and Civic Participation, www .whitehouse.gov/administration/eop/sicp; UK Office of the Third Sector: Emily Fennell, Karin Gavelin, and Richard Wilson, *Better Together: Improving consultation with the third sector* (London: Office of the Third Sector, Cabinet Office, 2008), www.cabinetoffice .gov.uk/media/99612/better%20together.pdf.

2　The data cited in this paragraph is taken from the Johns Hopkins Comparative Nonprofit Sector Project, a study of nonprofit activity across 46 countries of the world. The data provided is the latest update available from the website and presentations by the institute. Figures cited are as of 2008. See www.ccss.jhu.edu/index.php?section=conte nt&view=9&sub=3. For publications, see Lester M. Salamon, "Government-Nonprofit Relations from an International Perspective," *Nonprofits & Government: Collaboration & conflict* (2nd edition) (Washington, DC: The Urban Institute, 2006); and Lester M. Salamon, S. Wojciech Sokolowski and Associates, *Global Civil Society: Dimensions of the nonprofit sector, Volume Two* (Bloomfield, CT: Kumarian Press, in association with the Johns Hopkins Comparative Nonprofit Sector Project, 2004).

3　Ibid.

4　Peter Saunders and Martin Stewart-Weeks, *Supping with the Devil: Government contracts and the nonprofit sector* (St Leonards, NSW: The Centre for Independent Studies, 2009).

5　Ann Goggins Gregory and Daniel Stid, "How Governments Can Spur High Charity Performance," *The Chronicle of Philanthropy*, December 2009.

6　Ibid.

7　Ibid.

8　Steven Rathgeb Smith, "Governments and Nonprofits in the Modern Age," *Society*, May/ June 2003.

9　Available at the National Archives, www.webarchive.nationalarchives.gov.uk/+/http:// www.cabinetoffice.gov.uk/third_sector/about_us.aspx.

10　Melody Barnes, head of the White House Domestic Policy Council, was a speaker at the Independent Sector Annual Conference 2009, and regularly maintains communication with representatives from the social sector to incorporate their priorities into the US government's agenda. See "Interview with Diana Aviv, Head of Independent Sector," National Council of Voluntary Organisations, 2010, www.ncvo-vol.org.uk/engage/ features/state-of-the-nation.

11　www.nationalcompact.gov.au.

12　*Managing in a Downturn: A comprehensive survey of the impact of the economic downturn on not-for-profit organizations* (Kensington, NSW: PricewaterhouseCoopers, Fundraising Institute Australia and Centre for Social Impact, July 2009).

13　www.hhs.gov/recovery/programs/scf/index.html.

14　The subject of the regulator, primarily in the context of charities, is covered more fully in Chapter 15, "Regulator: Love, law, and the regulator," by Stephen Lloyd.

15   Lester M. Salamon and Stefan Toepler, "The Influence of the Legal Environment on the Development of the Nonprofit Sector," Working Paper Series Number 17, Center for Civil Society Studies, The Johns Hopkins University Institute for Policy Studies, 2000.

16   Stein Kuhnle, "The Nordic Approach to General Welfare," *Nordic News Network*, March 1998, www.nnn.se/intro/approach.htm.

17   www.centrelink.gov.au.

18   T. R. Reid, *The Healing of America: A global quest for better, cheaper and fairer healthcare* (New York: The Penguin Press, 2009).

19   Lester M. Salamon, "Government–Nonprofit Relations from an International Perspective," in *Nonprofits & Government: Collaboration & conflict* (2nd edition), ed. Elizabeth T. Boris and C. Eugene Steurle (Washington, DC: The Urban Institute, 2006).

20   Adil Najam, "The Four-C's of Third Sector–Government Relations: Co-operation, confrontation, complementarity and co-optation," *Nonprofit Management & Leadership*, 10(4), Summer 2000.

21   Dennis R. Young, "Alternative Models of Government–Nonprofit Sector Relations: Theoretical and international perspectives," *Nonprofit and Voluntary Sector Quarterly*, 29(149), 2000.

22   Capacitybuilders, www.capacitybuilders.org.uk.

23   Lester M. Salamon, "Government–Nonprofit Relations from an International Perspective," in *Nonprofits & Government: Collaboration & Conflict* (2nd edition), ed. Elizabeth T. Boris and C. Eugene Steurle (Washington, DC: The Urban Institute, 2006).

24   The level of fee-based funding relative to government funding for these countries is significantly above average in these countries. Data from Johns Hopkins Comparative Nonprofit Sector Project per endnote 2.

25   Takayoshi Amenomori, "Japan," in *Defining the Nonprofit Sector* (New York: Manchester University Press, 1997).

26   "Work of NGOs Frequently Restricted in Russia Without Reason—Medvedev," *Interfax*, April 15, 2009; Johnson's Russia List, www.cdi.org/russia/johnson/2009-70-12.cfm.

27   "Choking on Bureaucracy," Human Rights Watch, February 19, 2008, www.hrw.org/en/reports/2008/02/19/choking-bureaucracy; "Analysis of Law #18-FZ: On Introducing Amendments to Certain Legislative Acts of the Russian Federation," *The International Centre for Not-for-Profit Law*, February 17, 2006, www.icnl.org/knowledge/news/2006/01-19_Russia_NGO_Law_Analysis.pdf.

28   National Volunteer & Philanthropy Centre, www.nvpc.org.sg; Social Enterprise Committee report, www.mcys.gov.sg/web/SocialEnterpriseCommitteeReport.html; Comcare Enterprise Fund, www.mcys.gov.sg/web/serv_E_CEF.html; Singapore Social Enterprise Association, www.seassociation.sg.

29   The "many helping hands" approach positions the government as the planner and regulator of the many sources of social help. Family is the first line of defense, failing which, the various community bodies, social services, and private organizations can be leveraged to help the individual uplift himself. The government provides much of the funding to these community and other providers to support the intervention. See Yap Mui Teng, "Many Helping Hands" presentation at "Tackling Poverty in Hong Kong, What

Next?" Public Policy Roundtable Series, jointly organized by Governance in Asia Research Centre, City University of Hong Kong & SynergyNet, February 23, 2008, www.cityu .edu.hk/garc/ARC/ARCfile/PF/Roundtable/23Feb2008_Presentation_Yap_Mui_Teng.pdf; and Minister Abdullah Tarmuggi's speech to World Summit for Social Development, Copenhagen, on Singapore's approach to social development, March 10, 1995, www .un.org/documents/ga/conf166/gov/950310074254.htm.

30   Constance Singam and Tan Chong Kee, "Available Spaces, Today, and Tomorrow," in *Building Social Space in Singapore*, ed. Constance Singam, Tan Chong Kee, Tisa Ng, and Leon Perera (Singapore: Select Publishing, 2002).

31   Ibid.

32   References on Singapore 2006: Chua Mui Hoong, "Tough Singapore Can Show Softer Side," *The Straits Times*, September 15, 2006; David Boey, Li Xueying, and Peh Shing Huei, "Singapore: We will honor obligations as host," *The Straits Times*, September 15, 2006; "Update: Civil society groups announce boycott of WB-IMF annual meetings in Singapore," *Bank Information Centre Update*, September 15, 2006, www.bicusa.org/ en/Article.2948.aspx; "CSO Access in Singapore," *Civil Society Newsletter of the IMF*, November 2006, www.imf.org/External/NP/EXR/cs/eng/2006/111706.htm#access.

33   UK, www.news.bbc.co.uk/2/hi/special_report/1998/11/98/e-cyclopedia/211553.stm; Canada, www.oag-bvg.gc.ca/internet/English/parl_oag_200511_04_e_14942.html; New Zealand, www.goodpracticeparticipate.govt.nz/building-government-capability/whole-of-govt.html; Singapore, http://app.psd.gov.sg/data/Corporatebook/psfor21stcentury .html and www.ps21.gov.sg/home.html.

34   www.disability.wa.gov.au/index.html?s=1190165648.

35   Karen R. Fisher et al., *Effectiveness of Individual Funding Approaches for Disability Support*, Department of Families, Housing, Community Service and Indigenous Affairs, Occasional Paper No. 29 (Canberra, ACT: Commonwealth of Australia, 2010).

36   *Ahead of the Game: Blueprint for the Reform of Australian Government Administration* (Commonwealth of Australia, March 2010). In Australia the recent blueprint for the reform of government administration, which focused on creating more open government, recommended that a citizen survey be conducted to collect feedback on public satisfaction with government service delivery.

Chapter 15

Regulator

Love, Law, and the Regulator

STEPHEN LLOYD
Senior Partner, Bates Wells & Braithwaite

In the past decade, charity laws in many jurisdictions around the world have been subject to review.

In the ensuing debate, fundamental questions have been raised about the role and workings of the regulator. The adjustments being made, and major charity law reforms in several jurisdictions, are resulting in regulators and regulations that are more in tune with the happenings in the charity world.

However, the law will always, by necessity, struggle to keep pace with modern-day challenges such as increasing public service delivery by charities, new forms of social financing vehicles, the need to prevent charities from being a conduit for terrorism financing, and cross-border philanthropy.

Ⅰn the past decade, major reforms to charity laws have taken place in many jurisdictions around the world. In between these major reforms, there have been ongoing refinements to charity legislation as the law attempts to keep pace with the realities of the charity world.

Reforms often occur in the immediate aftermath of charity scandals. The Scottish reform of 2005 was hurried along by the investigations into Moonbeam and 56 other charities.[1] The Singapore reform of 2006 came hot on the heels of the explosive National Kidney Foundation saga.[2] The *Boston Globe*'s investigative articles on foundation abuse in 2004 led to proposed reforms by the US Senate Finance Committee.[3]

Other types of crisis, such as the terrorist attacks of September 11, 2001 in New York and Washington, DC, have also resulted in tighter regulations on foreign donations.

In some cases, charity reform could be a more proactive response by the government of the day to the broader changes in society that is based on a vision of where it should go. Such an example is the British government's *Charities Act 2006*, which was a collaborative effort between government and charities.[4]

In the course of these charity law reforms, there is often debate about the role and workings of the regulator, sometimes questioning the fundamentals of even why a regulator should exist. In this chapter, we shall examine the following core questions that relate to the charity regulator:

- Why should there be a regulator?
- Who should be the regulator?
- What are the functions of the regulator?
- What should the regulator regulate?
- How should the regulator regulate?
- What are the modern-day challenges that regulators face?

Why Regulate?

This may seem like a rhetorical question to some. The question that politicians and the public tend to ask, especially in the wake of charity scandals, is not"Why is there a regulator or regulations?"but, rather, " Where is the regulator?"This, in turn, leads to calls for more regulation.

Normally, however, the question is raised in cooler circumstances, in the context of the greater value of self-regulation by the charities and the sector. After all, many professions such as law, accountancy, and real estate rely on self-regulation by their practitioners (although the extent depends on the jurisdiction). And some industries such as the computer industry—which is pervasive and can have a massive financial impact on companies and the economy in the event of wrongdoing—are largely unregulated.

The major reason that is normally given for calls for regulation in the charity field is public interest. Charities exist for the public good, and much of their funding comes from the public.[5]

In today's legal construct, charities are often set up as entities with legal controllers who are individuals, organizations, or sometimes government bodies. Yet, they exist for the good of the community. The regulator thus ensures that charities are about "private action, public good."[6] In his analysis of charity governance, Willie Cheng holds that regulation is a much-needed second level of governance in order to ensure that a charity is properly accountable to its moral owners—that is, the community.[7] The first level of governance is the corporate governance performed by the board of directors, which is typically directed at accountability to the legal controllers.

At other times, the question of "Why regulate?" is raised in the context of concerns that regulation can lead all too easily to bureaucracy and control which distract charities from their core missions. The issue, then, is really about how much regulation there needs to be in order to retain trust and confidence in the sector.

Who Regulates?

Apart from the matter of self-regulation, it would seem the obvious answer is that it is the government that regulates. However, the government is not a monolithic entity and so, the more specific question should be, "Which government or (quasi-government) body should regulate?"

Though the answer to this last question can have as many variations as there are government departments, we can draw out several common characteristics.

Single or Multiple Regulators

In most countries, charities are, in fact, subject to multiple regulators.

A major reason for this is that charities are often not legal entities in their own right. In the case of most Commonwealth countries, a charity has first to be constituted as a company limited by guarantee (under a Companies Act or equivalent); a society (under a Societies Act or equivalent); or a trust (under a Trustees Act or equivalent). It then applies for registered charity status (under a Charities Act or equivalent). Charities are thus regulated in respect of the legal structure for generic governance and also in respect of their charity status for charity governance. They are also sometimes regulated separately for their tax status (which will be discussed further below).

One regulator may carry out one or more functions, or may share all or part of a function with other regulators. For example, the Charity Commission in England and Wales has a concurrent jurisdiction with the Attorney General and with the courts for some of its powers, and both the Charity Commission and Her Majesty's Revenue and Customs (HMRC) are concerned with the recognition of charitable status for different classes of charity.

Multiple regulation brings with it added bureaucratic red tape for charities with multiple reporting requirements. The burden of compliance has become a major concern for many charities. A move to reduce this multiple regulation in the UK is the introduction of the charitable incorporated organization under recent charities legislation.[8] This legislation introduces a one-stop approach so registration will bring with it incorporation of the legal structure and recognition of charitable status, thus reducing not only registration formalities but also ongoing reporting requirements.

Federal versus State Regulators

Another reason for multiple regulators is the distinction between federal and state governments.

Federal countries such as the US, Canada, and Australia divide up charity regulations between the two. Historically, matters such as governance, breach of trust, and *cy-près*[9] applications are reserved to the states or provinces, whereas charity registration and regulation for compliance with the tax statutes are matters for the federal level.

In Canada, the jurisdictional issue has always been cited as an obstacle to the introduction of a federal charity regulator independent of government. However, a recent study has proposed reform of the system through the creation of a federal–provincial Canadian Charities Council which would assume a wider role of charity regulation.

Single or Multiple Registers

An important issue is whether there should be a single register for all charities of whatever description or size throughout the country. Multiple registers mean different regulators have oversight over different segments of the charity sector.

In some countries, charities are regulated according to their type of activity. For example, in Sri Lanka, voluntary welfare organizations are regulated under the *Voluntary Social Service Organizations Act,*[10] in addition to regulation in accordance with their legal structure. In civil law countries, there are usually separate laws and regulations for foundations and associations. In England, certain types of charities known as excepted or exempt charities are not registered with the Charity Commission but have been recognized as charities by HMRC and are also regulated by other bodies.

Some countries have separate registers for domestic and foreign charities.

A single public register for all charities has the merit of greater transparency and accountability. This was acknowledged in the new Scottish charity legislation,[11] which introduced compulsory registration for all Scottish charities and many foreign charities (including English charities) operating in Scotland, with no exceptions. In England, the *Charities Act 2006* took a step toward a single register by requiring some of the larger exempt and excepted charities to register.

Regulation by the Tax Authorities

Regulation of charities by the tax authorities is a common model in both common law and civil jurisdictions. This is often in addition to regulation of some aspects by government agencies or the courts.

Traditionally, the role of the Revenue was usually restricted to compliance with the tax legislation. However, in several countries, the concept of regulation has been enlarged so that the support role can be seen as a form of proactive regulation and a policy function has been introduced. The Canada Revenue Agency and the US Internal Revenue Service are two examples that have opened up to charities in recent years.

Regulation by Government Authorities

In the majority of countries, all or part of the regulation of charities is carried out by government authorities (other than the Revenue). This may be by a single department for all charities or different departments related to the legal structure or activities of the organizations.

Even where a commission or the Revenue is the primary charity regulator, government offices may also have a role. For example, in many common law countries, the Attorney General or Public Trustee retains its historic role as the protector of trusts and charities. The enforcement role will often be carried out by the courts rather than the government office. Disadvantages of regulation by a government office are the lack of independence and the potential failure to recognize the distinctive role of charities as part of civil society.

Charity Commissions

Some countries have a commission as regulator. The Charity Commission of England and Wales is a leading example of this model.

A feature of the commission model is independence from the government. In England and Wales, both the Commission and the sector regard this independence as crucial. Following extensive debate on how the independence of the Commission could best be secured, the *Charities Act 2006* specifically requires that "in the exercise of its functions, the Commission shall not be subject to the direction or control of any Minister of the Crown or other government departments."[12] In addition, the chairperson of the Commission and board members come from a range of backgrounds, including the charity sector. What's more, they are appointed following a process of open competition.

Independence, however, is not absolute, as board members are appointed by the Minister and all the funding comes from the Treasury. The Commission is accountable directly to Parliament, while its decisions are subject to the Charity Tribunal and the courts. It is also subject to audit by the National Audit Office. Its accountability to charities and the public is ensured through an Independent Complaints Reviewer, and the board meetings are held in public with opportunity for direct questioning.

A current priority for the Commission is the development of the application of the public benefit requirement for charities.[13] The new requirement for charities charging high fees in order to benefit those who cannot afford to pay has proved to be highly controversial in the context of independent schools; it has brought the Commission under the spotlight of the national media. The tax breaks arising from the charitable status of independent schools have long been a controversial political issue, but under the *Charities Act 2006* it was an issue left to the Charity Commission to address, without clear legal underpinning. This ambiguity has reignited the debate about the independence of the Commission and illustrates the difficulties of its position.

Notwithstanding these issues, the charity commission model is now being adopted in other common law countries. New Zealand, Scotland, and Northern Ireland now have commissions, and Ireland is soon to follow.[14] Their functions and features vary, however. For example, Scotland does not have the same powers of enforcement as in England and Wales; this function is retained by the courts. Ireland will not have the power to develop new charitable purposes. In general, they all are largely independent of government with functions of registration, support, and supervision. A full comparative study of the four charity regulators of England and Wales, Scotland, Ireland, and Northern Ireland was included in a paper by Kerry O'Halloran.[15]

Hybrid Models

A hybrid model has been developed in East Africa where the regulator in Kenya and Tanzania is a government office with a board which has representatives from the sector. This approach is linked to an element of self-regulation, with a sector body established by statute with wide powers to enforce a code of conduct.

An innovative model is found in the Philippines where a charity umbrella body, the Philippine Council for NGO Certification, has both the delegated power to certify special tax status for NGOs and a role in setting standards for the sector. The Philippines model has gone the furthest in self-regulation.

In other countries, self-regulation has been confined to setting standards and codes of conduct; this is often backed by sanctions, including expulsion from a sector body.

Experiments in self-regulation have often run into difficulties. They have either lacked teeth or been plagued with internal disputes.

What Functions?

In their book, *Charity Law and Social Policy*,[16] Kerry O'Halloran, Myles McGregor-Lowndes, and Karla W. Simon describe the four functions of charity regulation as protection, policing, mediation/adjustment, and support.

The Charity Commission of England and Wales is perhaps the only charity regulator that performs all these four functions. We will therefore refer to examples from this body when examining these four functions.

Protection

The original intent of the protection function was to ensure that the purpose of a donor's gift was respected in perpetuity, for the sake of the sacred nature of the trust.

However, in recent times, the focus has moved toward extending the nature of charitable status to a much broader spectrum of needs and activities. Thus, the Commission has stated that "it takes a constructive approach in adapting the concept of charity to meeting the constantly evolving needs of society."[17] In recent years, this positive approach has led to the recognition of a number of new charitable purposes, including the promotion of sustainable development, the advancement of human rights, and the promotion of equality and diversity.

Policing

Policing is probably the regulator's most prominent role. Many see it as a necessary function to prevent the abuse or misuse of funds in charities. Regulators do this by overseeing the activities of charities, by ensuring appropriate charitable practice, and by promoting standards for transparency and accountability.

The policing role can conflict with the support role. There has long been debate in the charity sector about how far it is possible for one body to be both friend and policeman. Will a charity in difficulties be less likely to approach the Commission for fear of wider repercussions? Should advice and guidance be a role for the sector itself, rather than the regulator? These matters were raised in the debates on England and Wales' Charities Bill but were settled in the *Charities Act 2006*, which confirmed the very wide-ranging powers of the Commission to give advice.

Mediation and Adjustment

The mediation and adjustment function calibrates the law to fit current social circumstances.

A key part of this function is ensuring that the definition of charitable status and public benefit relates to the immediate social context. In many countries, there is no legislative definition of charitable status and hence the regulator has to rely on the "spirit and intendment" rule[18] while providing access to an appropriate forum to resolve differences.

Appeal forums vary in England and Wales. An appeal against Commission decisions, including refusal of registration, has always gone to the high court. In recent years, however, there have been very few appeals. A Charity Tribunal was introduced by the *Charities Act 2006* with the aim of providing a quicker, cheaper route that should lead to clarification of some areas of charity law.[19] Similar tribunals are being introduced in Ireland and Northern Ireland.

Support

The support or enabling function seeks to balance the coercive or rule-enforcing effect of the policing and protection functions.

Thus, one of the principles in the Charity Commission's strategic plan—"working together across the sector"[20]—has been realized through a greater partnership between the charity umbrella bodies in the delivery of the support function.

Another part of the support role is through the use of its quasi-judicial powers to make *cy-près* schemes to update a charity's purposes. This is a concurrent jurisdiction with the High Court. The potential to facilitate the more effective use of charitable funds has been increased by the *Charities Act 2006*, as the *cy-près* occasions have been broadened and the procedures streamlined.

What Activities?

The overriding objective of the regulator will determine the areas of activity being regulated. In general, charity regulation has tended to focus on three key activity areas: registration, governance, and fundraising.

Registration

A key objective of regulation is to ensure that only the right organizations are called charities. Registration (and deregistration) is the process by which charities are allowed entry and exit. The latter can be sometimes forced. In some jurisdictions, the power to register and deregister may be the only effective sanction that a regulator has to ensure the proper behavior of charities.

Registration requires the existence of a register and criteria for registration. Effective regulation requires the regulator to rigorously apply the "public benefit" test, and the "exclusively charitable" and "spirit and intendment" rules.[21]

Governance

The rationale for a regulator's focus on governance is captured in a paper by the US Advisory Committee on Tax Exempt and Government Entities which noted that "a well governed charity is more likely to obey the tax laws [and] safeguard charitable assets and charitable interests than one with poor governance."[22]

In most countries, self-regulation plays an increasingly important role in governance through the development of standards and codes of conduct by umbrella bodies and intermediaries. In England and Wales, the voluntary and community sector has developed its own Code of Good Governance which has been widely adopted but has no formal accreditation or enforcement procedures.[23] In Singapore, the Charity Council, an advisory body to the regulator, operates under a Code of Governance based on the "comply or explain" approach.[24]

Fundraising

Fundraising can be a hot issue for the public and, thus, the regulator. Potential regulatory concerns include:

- The proportion of charity assets devoted to fundraising, rather than the direct furtherance of the charitable purposes
- Reputational issues affecting public trust and confidence in charity arising from misleading, deceptive, or predatory fundraising
- Arrangements involving undue private benefit to individuals or businesses, such as the employment of commission-based professional third-party fundraisers
- The conduct of lotteries and gaming
- Data protection arising from direct mail
- Donor confidentiality issues.

The regulation of fundraising activities will usually be divided among a number of regulators involving disclosure backed by sanctions, licensing, or self-regulation linked to standards.

New methods of fundraising bring new challenges for regulation. Many jurisdictions have laws that regulate public fundraising through physical canvassing door-to-door and on the streets. However, the increasing use of online mechanisms via email and the web has largely escaped regulation.

How It Regulates?

The aim of regulation is to promote compliance with charity laws and instill public confidence. This aim can be achieved through varying means, depending on the underlying philosophy of the regulator which, in turn, will determine the sanctions and resources needed to do the job.

Philosophy

How a regulator should regulate depends largely on its philosophy toward its responsibility and risk management.

Cheng identifies two contrasting approaches to regulation: a "black box" model, where the charities are positioned as trusted institutions with the government's seal of approval; and a "glass house" model, where donors make decisions on specific charities in a *caveat emptor* (donor beware) environment.[25] The implications of a black box approach are more comprehensive and prescriptive rules, extensive regulatory powers, and significant resources for the regulator to enforce compliance. The glass house approach favors minimal regulation while emphasizing public transparency and disclosure by charities.

Most regulators lie along the spectrum between the two approaches. The Charity Commission of England and Wales leans toward the glass house model, while the US Internal Revenue Service and Canadian Revenue lean toward the black box model.

The Charity Commission has identified its approach as one of proportionate risk-based regulation. It has produced guidance on how the risk-based approach to regulation works in both its compliance and services to charities.[26] This approach has led to a greater emphasis on larger charities and also on "zero tolerance issues" such as allegations of links to terrorist organizations, fraud, and abuse of children and vulnerable adults. Risks may be not only to charitable assets, but also to the beneficiaries and the reputation of the individual charity and the sector.

In contrast, the US Internal Revenue Service and the Canada Revenue Agency have traditionally approached regulation with the objective of preventing abuse of the tax-exempt status. However, the focus of regulation in these two countries is now widening to look beyond the immediate fiscal regulatory concerns and include aspects of support. The element of proportionality is also being introduced.

The returns required by regulators in the different jurisdictions illustrate the different approaches. In the US, larger charities are required to complete a very lengthy return[27] and provide details such as the compensation of senior staff, political campaigning and lobbying, and activities outside the US. In contrast, in England, only a short return is required of all charities, with the main requirement being to report serious incidents. For larger charities, an additional return is required but here the emphasis is on the impact of the charity's activities. The Commission is increasingly concerned with the issue of the impact and effectiveness of charities and the role of trustees in this respect. A recent initiative in the UK on progressive governance has gone further and suggested that improving performance, rather than compliance, should be the major focus of all charity regulation.[28]

In both the US and the UK, the reporting requirements are linked to the turnover of the charity. The US has aptly named the form, "900—EZ" for charities up to US$1 million and "99-N the postcard" for the smallest charities with annual income up to US$25,000. In England, there are graduated reporting requirements, with the smallest charities (up to £25,000, or US$36,000) exempted from the need to file accounts and reports, although all charities must provide copies of their accounts and reports to members of the public on request.

Sanctions

The rationale for regulation also determines the sanctions for noncompliance.

Where the tax authority is the regulator, as in the US and Canada, the primary sanction is revocation of charity registration.

In contrast, where the regulator is a body set up to protect charitable assets, as is the case with the Charity Commission, the assets must be kept within the charitable sector and any regulatory action will normally be taken against the trustees, with the ultimate sanction being the transfer of assets to another charity with similar purposes.

Some intermediate sanctions have now been introduced in the US and Canada. In Canada, failure to keep proper books and accounts can result in the suspension of tax receipting privileges. Carrying on unrelated business can incur a 5 percent penalty on the gross revenue from the unrelated business. Other sanctions include education letters and compliance agreements.

The Charity Commission has very extensive powers to take regulatory action against trustees, although these are exercised with circumspection. They include the suspension or removal of trustees or employees, freezing of bank accounts, and the appointment of an interim manager to take over the management of the charity under the supervision of the Commission. An appeal from all these decisions goes to the new Charity Tribunal.[29]

By contrast, the Office of the Scottish Charity Regulator only has limited powers and enforcement remains a matter for the courts.

Regulatory Challenges

Beyond the fundamentals of the role and workings of the regulator, the law and the regulator need continually to adjust to new trends and innovations by the charity world. Several of the challenges faced by regulators in this increasingly complex world are summarized below.

Public Service Delivery by Charities

A major development in the last few years has been the blurring of boundaries between the public sector and the charity sector over public service delivery.

Increasingly, governments are outsourcing public services such as aspects of health care and education to charities and the private sector. However, concerns over the impact that this may have on the independence of charities have led the Commission to publish detailed guidance on the issues to be addressed when charities engage in public service.

Nevertheless, the question of how charities can retain their independence while receiving all, or substantially all, of their funding from government remains.

Social Finance

The boundaries between the private sector and the charity sector are also blurring. Over the last few years, the huge growth of social enterprises and other forms of creative financing vehicles for the charity sector has created hybrid social–business organizations that are in a category of their own.

Regulators have responded by creating new legal forms for such hybrid organizations—for example, the Community Interest Company in the UK and the Low-profit Limited Liability Company in the US.[30]

Counter-Terrorism

In the aftermath of 9/11, there was increased concern about how charities may be used as conduits for terrorism financing.[31] Governments quickly introduced new guidance on how charities in their respective jurisdictions should manage their operations, especially at the international level.[32] All the guidelines generally include rigorous financial oversight, high levels of disclosure and transparency, and significant new due diligence practices. These guidelines have evoked a strong negative response from the charity sector.

In his award-winning article on counter-terrorism laws and the impact of terrorism on civil society, Mark Sidel compares the approaches of the US, the UK, and Australia.[33] He contrasts the British approach, which relies significantly on the charity regulator as the "first responder" and a key partner in the battle against terrorism, with the American approach, which concentrates on direct action by prosecutors, rather than working with charity regulators. He concludes that, based on current information, the broad-based counter-terrorism legislation in Australia has not been used against charities.

Cross-Border Philanthropy

The growth of global philanthropy has raised new issues of charity law and regulation as donors call for streamlined cross-border giving.

Emphasizing that "in a global economy, we must also have global philanthropy," Steve Gunderson of the Council on Foundations has called on countries to "make their regulatory systems compatible with those that exist in other countries, and countries should also consider whether there are ways to streamline and reduce registration requirements for foreign philanthropic institutions."[34]

However, there are many barriers to achieving this goal: different models of regulation, different tax treatments of charities, and different definitions of charity. And even as countries revise legislation with new definitions of charity, there appears to be more divergence, rather than convergence, between countries.

The good news is that there are moves toward greater cooperation. The Charity Commission of England and Wales has established an international program to work with regulators in Singapore, Pakistan, Kenya, and other countries.[35] In 2006, the UK and Ireland Charity Regulators Forum was set up and meets on a quarterly basis to discuss common issues.

In addition, charity law regulators in the UK, the US, Canada, Australia, and New Zealand now meet every two years to discuss matters of common concern, including cross-border issues.

Catching Up

In today's dynamic world of new possibilities, reality can lag vision by several years, even decades; and the law, in particular, has tended to lag reality by at least several more years.

While this is generally true for charity law around the world, some of the models put in place by recent charity reforms, such as that of The Charity Commission for England and Wales, have led to a more responsive regulatory framework that can allow for the creativity of the market while achieving the overall objective of ensuring the public interest.

Endnotes

1 "Charity Reform 'Long Overdue'," *BBC News*, October 19, 2003.

2 Sharifah Mohamed, "Tracing Singapore's Social Sector," *Social Space*, 2008.

3 See www.acreform.com/who/history.html.

4 The charities came together as a federation of leading charities and charitable organizations called the Coalition for a Charities Act. It was convened by the National Council for Voluntary Organizations (the umbrella body for the voluntary sector in England, with sister councils in the rest of the UK). See www.ncvo-vol.org.uk/press/releases/?id=3564&terms=charity%20reform.

5 Donations from the public as a primary source of funding are changing for many charities. In jurisdictions such as the UK, charities are increasingly relying on earned income, often from contracts with government.

6 This phrase headlined the publication, *Private Action, Public Benefit: Review of charities and the wider not-for-profit sector* (London: Strategy Unit, Cabinet Office, September 2002) which describes the proposals for charity reform in the UK.

7 Willie Cheng, "Nonprofit Governance: Who governs a nonprofit, really?" in *Doing Good Well: What does (and does not) make sense in the nonprofit world* (Singapore: John Wiley & Sons, 2009).

8 See Charitable Incorporated Organization (CIO) (March 2009) at www.charity-commission .gov.uk/registration/charcio.asp.

9 The *cy-près* doctrine, in the context of charity law, allows a court to amend the terms of a charitable trust as closely as possible to the original intention of the testator or settlor to prevent the trust from failing.

10 *Voluntary Social Organizations Act,* No. 31 of 1980.

11 *Charities and Trustee Investment (Scotland) Act 2005* (2005 asp10).

12 *Charities Act 2006,* section 6(1).

13 *Charities and Public Benefit: The Charity Commission's general guidance on public benefit* (Liverpool, UK: Charity Commission, January 2008), www.charitycommission.gov.uk.

14 Some countries with commissions are not listed here because the defining characteristic of a commission is its independence from government. Thus, although Singapore has a Commissioner of Charities, the function sits within the Charities Unit, a government department in the Ministry of Community, Youth and Sports without any governing board (but with an advisory Charity Council). See www.charities.gov.sg.

15 Kerry O'Halloran, "Regulatory Reforms in England and Wales, Ireland, Northern Ireland and Scotland," a paper delivered at the MCL Conference at Queensland University of Technology, April 2009, https://wiki.qut.edu.au/display/CPNS/Modernising+Charity+ Law+Conference+Papers.

16 Kerry O'Halloran, Myles McGregor-Lowndes, and Karla W. Simon, *Charity Law and Social Policy: National and international perspectives and functions of law relating to charities* (Dordrecht: Springer, 2008).

17 *RR1—Recognising New Charitable Purposes* (London: Charity Commission, October 2001), www.charity-commission.gov.uk.

18 A full explanation of the "spirit and intendment rule" can be found on page 43 of Kerry O'Halloran, Myles McGregor-Lowndes, and Karla W. Simon, *Charity Law and Social Policy: National and international perspectives and functions of law relating to charities* (Dordrecht: Springer, 2008).

19 See www.charity.tribunals.gov.uk for reports of the first cases.

20 *Charity Commission Annual Report 2006–2007.*

21 The criteria for charities vary by jurisdiction. To pass the "public benefit" test, the organization must show that it provides a tangible benefit to the public, that its beneficiaries are not a restricted private group, and that the group's activities are not contrary to public policy. The "exclusively charitable" rule requires that the organization's purposes are all, not just partially or mainly, charitable. In the UK, the "spirit and intendment" rule provides" a line of retreat based on the equity of the Statute in case

[the regulator or Courts] are faced with a purpose (e.g. a political purpose) that could not have been within the contemplation of the Statute [defining charitable use]." (See Charities Definition Inquiry at www.cdi.gov.au.)

22 Bonnie S. Brier, Ana Thomson, Betsy Buchalter, Sean Delany, Fred Goldberg, and Mary Rauschenberg, "The Appropriate Role of IRS with respect to Tax Exempt Organisation Good Governance Issues," Advisory Committee on Tax Exempt and Government Entities, June 11, 2008.

23 *Good Governance: A code for the voluntary and community sector* (London: The National Hub of Expertise in Governance, June 2005), www.ncvo-vol.org.uk.

24 *Code of Governance for Charities & Institutions of a Public Character* (Singapore: The Charity Council, November 2007), www.charities.gov.sg.

25 Willie Cheng, "Regulation: Black box or glass house?" in *Doing Good Well: What does (and does not) make sense in the nonprofit world* (Singapore: John Wiley & Sons, 2009).

26 *Risk and Proportionality: Framework for the Commission's compliance work* (Liverpool, UK: Charity Commission, July 2008); *A Risk and Proportionality Framework for the Commission's Services to Charities* (Liverpool, UK: Charity Commission, March 2009). Available at www.charity-commission.gov.uk.

27 Form 990, www.irs.gov/charities.

28 Paul Jump, "Acevo Sets Up Governance Reform Meeting," *Third Sector,* November 17, 2009, www.thirdsector.co.uk/Channels/Governance/Article/967166/Acevo-sets-governance-reform-meeting. The article refers to a speech by RNIB's chief Kevin Carey.

29 The first tribunal case, *Nagendram Seevaratnam v CC and AG 2009*, CA/2008/0001, was an appeal against the removal of a trustee.

30 More information on CIC, L3C, and other hybrid organizations is contained in Chapter 18, "Social Finance: Financing change, changing finance," by Jed Emerson.

31 *UN Security Council Resolution 1373*, United Nations, September 28, 2001. NGOs, including charities, were vulnerable to exploitation by proscribed groups for financing for terrorist purposes.

32 See *OG 96: Operational Guidance—Charities and Terrorism Charity* (Liverpool, UK: Commission for England and Wales, last update August 29, 2007); "Charities in the International Context," Canada Revenue Agency, last updated October 16, 2008, www.blumbergs.ca/images/uploads/Charities_in_the_International_Context.pdf; "U.S. Department of the Treasury Anti-Terrorist Financing Guidelines: Voluntary best practices for U.S.-based charities," first issued November 2002, updated September 29, 2006, available at www.ustreas.gov/press/releases/hp122.htm.

33 Mark Sidel, "Counter-Terrorism and the Enabling Legal and Political Environment for Civil Society: A comparative analysis of 'war on terror' states," *The International Journal of Not-for Profit Law*, 10(3), June 2008. This paper won the 2008 ICNL-Cordaid Civil Liberties Award.

34 Lindsay Driscoll and Peter Grant, "Philanthropy in the 21st Century," a discussion paper prepared for the Honorary Treasurers Forum (London: Cass Business School, City University, 2009).

35 The International Programme of the Charity Commission, www.ngoregnet.org.

Change Enablers

Chapter 16

Culture and Leadership

Transformative Leaders Wanted

MAXIMILIAN MARTIN
Senior Partner, IJ Partners

Growing social needs and other factors are creating a leadership deficit in the nonprofit sector. Many solutions are being worked on to increase the quantity and quality of nonprofit leaders.

However, the world needs, above all, leaders who can lead transformational change in their organizations and the social sector. Many social issues of the day require transformative change, rather than mere social remedies.

Transformative leaders need to be able to address the challenges of the new environment and cultural change with appropriate leadership strategies. Two new sources of such leaders hold promise: business leaders who are crossing over into truly problem-solving philanthropy, and social entrepreneurs engaged in pattern change.

In the past decade, the social sector has entered an impressive phase of innovation and growth. New people, new models, and new organizations are all changing the game, transforming the social ecosystem.

The growth of the sector requires resources—money and people. While some money is available, it has always been a constraint that the sector lives with while still making things happen. The spirit of the people involved in the social sector makes all the difference—volunteers and (poorly) paid workers who overcome the odds of their situation.

With the transformative growth of the sector, leadership is all the more critical. For among the human resources, it is the social leaders who drive the initiatives and change. But is the sector up to the task in producing and delivering these leaders?

The Nonprofit Leadership Deficit

Studies of recent years point to a shortfall in the current and future availability of nonprofit leaders.[1] Part of this is due to the war for talent that is taking place across the public, private, and social sectors.[2]

Chief among these studies is an extensive survey by The Bridgespan Group in 2006 on the leadership requirements of US nonprofit organizations (NPOs).[3] It projected that, by 2016, US NPOs with revenues of more than US$250,000 would need to attract and develop some 640,000 new senior managers, a figure that was nearly two and a half times the number then employed. To put the challenge in context, Bridgespan stated that this was "equivalent to recruiting over 50 percent of every MBA graduating class at every college and university across the country, every year for the next ten years." Further, the study noted that the deficit could even swell to double that, from 640,000 to 1.25 million senior executives, based on historic trends.

The study attracted significant coverage and response from the sector, with most commentators being in broad agreement with the analysis. Many suggested solutions.[4] The study, some noted, is indicative of the larger leadership deficit facing the global NPO sector.[5]

A host of factors has been cited for the leadership shortfall. Part of it is the relative unattractiveness of a nonprofit job: a lack of administrative and management support, compensation levels that fail to match the demands of stressful leadership jobs, and frustrations with boards of directors and donors. All of these factors have contributed to a high turnover rate.[6] Another part of it is demographics: With an aging population, the number of potential leaders in the prime age bracket of 34–54 will shrink.

Catch-Up

As the debate continues, many solutions have been offered to address the gap and some have been adopted.

To start, there are suggestions on how the numbers can be increased by looking at new sources for these nonprofit leaders. One would be to attract idealistic outstanding young people keen on serving others. Another would be to mine the increasing number of sector shifters, those mid-career professionals who are looking for greater meaning in their lives.[7]

We have been facing a generational shift, from an aging Baby Boom generation to the successive Generations X and Y. Studies are being conducted to understand the needs of the next generations (what it will take to attract and develop them) as well as the Baby Boomers (what it will take to extend their professional lives and pass on their wealth of knowledge and expertise).[8]

Meanwhile, there are many educational and development opportunities for nonprofit leaders. For more than a decade, tertiary institutions have been offering courses on public and nonprofit leadership; philanthropic bodies have financed leadership development programs for mid-career staff members of charities; a variety of institutions offer conferences, seminars, and training workshops to harness leadership; and articles, books, and even manuals on excellent nonprofit leadership have been published.[9]

Leaders for Transformational Change

Yet, beyond the obvious lack of nonprofit leaders, the sector needs, more critically, certain kinds of leaders—those that can lead the transformation of NPOs and the sector. Many social issues of today require transformative change, rather than mere social remedies.

We need to find transformative leaders who can address the challenges of the new environment and the need for cultural change with appropriate leadership strategies.

New Environment

Evidence of the urgency and opportunity for change and transformation is all around us.

Uneven population growth and environmental degradation are forcing society to face the perennial problem of shortages of food, water, and other resources. Yet, at the same time, technological possibilities are enabling us to transcend our human limitations.[10]

Social leaders find that they are inheriting a punitive social world while at the same time being heir to a whole new set of opportunities to make a difference.[11] However, runaway technological innovation, environmental uncertainty, and discontinuous change all reduce our ability to intervene even when we are armed with comprehensive and reliable data. Indeed, with the explosion and fluidity of knowledge, many are paralyzed by information overload. As a result, intervention on social issues is a constant experiment and the leader needs to be deft in managing the different stakeholder expectations.

Culture Change

A key aspect of the new environment is the underlying change in culture that is slowly creeping in.

Values and culture can be elusive and interpreted differently. What may appear sluggish, soft, and foolish to the increasing number of corporate executives getting involved in the sector, for instance, can be interpreted as patient, kind, and compassionate by those who have been in the social sector for a long time. There is no clear right or wrong to the interpretation; what matters is the mandate given by community members.

But increasingly, these binaries in values are becoming less stark and relevant. We are witnessing the professionalization of philanthropy and the nonprofit sector.

Some foundations have now moved on from the "theory of hope" to the "theory of change" in grantmaking.

Business discipline such as greater accountability and higher performance is creeping into the social sector as much as social responsibility is now the new buzzword for corporations in the post-financial crisis. In the same way that business organizations are increasingly seeing their life-span shortened, NPOs are also facing pressures to shape up or ship out; indeed, to demonstrate their performance and for grant money to be tied to these indicators.

The greater interactions between the actors have aided this process. The state of flux, asymmetric interdependence, and obsolescence of established models create opportunities for leadership.

The challenge for nonprofit leaders is not just to embrace the cultural change, but to move the sections of the social sector that are resistant to the change. Such resistance is to be expected given that complexity and change can induce a reflex reaction that seeks to protect the institution and *status quo*, even though this infrastructure might be proving to be outmoded.

Take, for example, the Norse community that moved to Greenland more than a thousand years ago. Their community life was enviable: economically viable, culturally rich, and well integrated. Yet, this was also a community that ended in a sad state, dying of starvation and leaving behind barren what used to be rich grasslands. In-depth analysis of this phenomenon revealed that the members of the community had refused to adapt their social values and lifestyles, out of pride in their cultural identity.[12]

The lesson is simple: Be relevant or be gone. But idealism, which is the very strength of the social sector, can also be its Achilles heel. The Norse community possessed assuredness in its cultural vision but was unfortunately disconnected from the ground realities and, so, ceased to exist.

This is thus another lesson for the nonprofit leader: Realistic expectations of how human beings function and how they create social change are a leader's best bet for long-term success.

Leadership Strategies

Exercising leadership means influencing highly complex, interactive, interdependent, and often intangible processes where individuals and groups build social realities.[13] Getting this right is a real challenge. The leader needs to understand the leadership challenges, be cognizant of the values and culture of the community he or she is in, and plan leadership strategies accordingly.

Social leadership strategies intervene from different angles, improving the odds in the leadership field. They provide direction from the top, tap into the creative potential of change agents at the grassroots and intermediate management levels, and supply structural design features that allow for efficient transaction costs that maximize flows of information and resources.

There are three fundamental leadership strategies: epic, engineering, and enlightenment leadership.

Driven mainly by the leader's charisma, epic leadership refers to the ability to move people to do amazing things. In this "great man" view that runs through so much of history, leaders are larger-than-life individuals. They are the great modelers and pattern creators who make all the difference. Traditionally, political figures, especially the revolutionaries, represent this form of leadership. Increasingly, social entrepreneurs such as Bunker Roy of Barefoot College in India, or Paul Farmer of Partners in Health in the US, and, by proxy, celebrities such as Bono of U2, are joining this group.[14]

Engineering leadership refers to the ability to design incentive systems that reward aligned behavior throughout an organizational pyramid, and to set boundaries on what not to do. This leadership approach lies at the other end of the continuum from epic leadership, and focuses on structures and design systems. While important in managing the downside of charity abuse, the more subtle strength of the engineering strategy lies in the discipline that it imports from the scientific and corporate world, thus working on the socio-institutional landscape that produces outcomes for the beneficiaries. Examples are business leaders such as Bill Drayton (Ashoka), Bill Gates, Jeff Skoll, and, three generations earlier, J. W. McConnell—all of whom crossed over into the social sector, bringing their wealth of management experience and tools to systemize nonprofit work.[15]

Enlightenment leadership refers to the ability to catalyze leadership actions across all levels of an organization or social movement, thus galvanizing true commitment and effective self-organization. In times where sets of knowledge and expertise diverge and people are not blindly respectful of authority, it is especially crucial to acknowledge that leadership does not just emanate from the top. The enlightenment strategy in leadership recognizes that leadership emerges at every level of an organization, regardless of an individual's position of formal authority in a given organizational pyramid. The emerging social innovation field best exemplifies this approach. *The Big Issue* in Britain and Un Techo Para Chile ("A Roof for Chile") are examples of how grassroots mobilization can generate impact when the followers are given space to create value.[16]

Given the global context of increasing technological sophistication, interaction over long distances, "fixed" human nature, and the diversity of people, the best strategy would be to combine the three leadership approaches—epic, engineering, and enlightened leadership—to fit the situation. Such a smart combination is most likely to influence the organization and motivate its people to deliver the intended outcomes.

Finding Leaders

If we look through *TIME* magazine's list of 100 influential leaders in 2009, we will notice the large number of celebrities, sports personalities, and entrepreneurs who made it to the 20 "Heroes and Icons" category. Only five of the 20 names are associated with a nonprofit.[17]

Consider also the fact that more than half of those who made it to the 2009 *NonProfit Times* (NPT) "Power and Influence Top 50" list deal with capacity-building issues of the nonprofit sector in the areas of management and funding.[18]

We can make two observations of the *TIME* and NPT lists which seek to identify those individuals who are perceived to "most affect our world" and influence the nonprofit sector, respectively.

First, much social impact or presence is seen to be coming from cross-over business leaders and the institutions they have created, infusing the nonprofit sector with impact management. These are leaders in problem-solving philanthropy.[19] The 2009 NPT list, for example, includes the heads of the Rockefeller Brothers Fund, The William and Flora Hewlett Foundation, and The Bill & Melinda Gates Foundation.

All three foundations are focused on achieving social impact at scale. The Bill & Melinda Gates Foundation, for instance, has taken on the issue of public health in sub-Saharan Africa. In only a few years, it has raised the level of intervention efforts while mobilizing resources to create results that far outweigh the traditional sources of aid to these countries.

The second observation is that the transformational social leader does not appear to need to serve end-beneficiaries, and may not even work directly in the social sector to create impact. Alas, visibility is often what counts. However, there is, indeed, a group of social leaders directly involved with end-beneficiaries that is transforming the sector. These are the social entrepreneurs who are deploying scalable market-type mechanisms for social change, such as microfinance.[20] In many ways, the work of people such as Bill Drayton of Ashoka typifies a new type of citizen leadership that is transforming the sector and the world.[21]

These two groups of newcomers—the global problem-solving philanthropists and the pattern-changing social entrepreneurs—add considerably to the pool of transformative leaders that the sector badly needs.

Leading into Tomorrow

The number and quality of our individual and collective leadership will likely make the critical difference on a planet inhabited by over nine billion people in the foreseeable future. Consider the implications of three factors: the rising complexity of human civilization resulting from adaptation to environmental stress and advances in technology and genetics; asymmetric interdependence where a small group of people can inflict major damage and trigger policy change on a massive scale, as happened in the aftermath of September 11; and the obsolescence of established models for doing business or addressing social problems through government transfer payments. They will all create formidable opportunities for leadership in all fields—politics and government, business, and civil society.

In the social sector, imaginative newcomers with their problem-solving philanthropy and social entrepreneurial solutions are making a big impact. Together with the incumbent social leaders, the leadership work to be done has not diminished—on a crowded planet that is facing serious sustainability challenges, the time available to deliver is simply limited.

A lot can be done to improve the odds. But a degree of humility is nevertheless required. Success cannot be fully pre-seeded, and in the very long run, outcomes are a function of the vagaries of history as much as of leadership intent. In transforming the sector, the leaders should themselves be prepared to be transformed.

Endnotes

1   Thomas J. Tierney, "The Nonprofit Sector's Leadership Deficit," White Paper by The Bridgespan Group, March 2006; Pablo Eisenberg, "Challenges for Nonprofits and Philanthropy,"*Challenges for Nonprofits and Philanthropy: The courage to change* (Medford, MA: Tufts University Press, 2005).

2   Elizabeth Chambers, Mark Foulon, Helen Handfield-Jones, Steven Hankin, and Edward Michaels III,"The War for Talent," *The McKinsey Quarterly*, August 1998.

3   Thomas J. Tierney, "The Leadership Deficit," *Stanford Social Innovation Review*, Summer 2006. Only US nonprofits with annual revenues of more than US$250,000, excluding hospitals and institutions of higher education, were considered in the survey.

4   "The Nonprofit Sector's Leadership Deficit: Commentaries,"The Bridgespan Group, March 2006.

5   Observations of the global leadership deficit come from many quarters, one of which is the UN Secretary General Ban Ki-Moon who called for a "special brand of leadership," one that should focus on"delivering global goods: freedom from hunger, health and education and security from terror or the threat of Armageddon.""World Needs a Global Leadership: Ban Ki-Moon,"*rediff Business*, May 22, 2009, www.business.rediff .com/report/2009/may/22/world-needs-global-leadership-ban-ki-moon.htm.

6   Jennifer C. Berkshire, "Charity CEO's Tales of Woe," *The Chronicle of Philanthropy*, March 9, 2006.

7   Michelle Bonoan and Naree Viner, "Execs Find Fulfillment in Nonprofit Leadership," *Wall Street Journal Sunday*, May 18, 2008.

8   *What's Next: Baby Boom-age leaders in social change nonprofits* (New York: Building Movement Project, 2007); *Next Shift: Beyond the nonprofit leadership crisis* (New York: Building Movement Project, 2007); *Ready to Lead? Next generation leaders speak out* (San Francisco: CompassPoint Nonprofit Services, 2008).

9   Pablo Eisenberg, "How to Stem the Nonprofit Leadership Deficit," *The Chronicle of Philanthropy*, September 28, 2006.

10   For example, see Ray Kurzweil, *The Singularity is Near* (New York: Penguin, 2005).

11   Maximilian Martin, "Leadership in a Globalizing World: Addressing the challenges," Social Science Research Network, April 23, 2002, www.ssrn.com/abstract=1322244.

12   Malcolm Gladwell, "The Vanishing: Review of Jared Diamond's 'Collapse'," *New Yorker*, January 3, 2005, www.newyorker.com/archive/2005/01/03/050103crbo_books.

13   Maximilian Martin and Michael Jung, "Organizational Leadership Fields: Aiming for impact at the next level," *Viewpoint*, Social Science Research Network, March 15, 2009, www.ssrn.com/abstract=1366291; Maximilian Martin, "Philanthropy's Leadership Challenge," *Viewpoint*, Social Science Research Network, March 1, 2006, www.ssrn .com/abstract=1322271; Maximilian Martin, "Between Entrepreneurship and Surveillance: An interpretive political economy perspective on the globalizing organization," *Entwicklungsethnologie*, 11(1), Social Science Research Network, June 1, 2002, www .ssrn.com/abstract=1322262.

14   Bunker Roy of Barefoot College, www.barefootcollege.org; Paul Farmer of Partners in Health, www.pih.org.

15   Bill Drayton of Ashoka, www.ashoka.org; J. W. McConnell Foundation, www .mcconnellfoundation.ca/en/news/staff-at-the-2009-philanthropic-foundations-canada-conference; Skoll Foundation, www.skollfoundation.org; Bill & Melinda Gates Foundation, www.gatesfoundation.org/Pages/home.aspx.

16   *The Big Issue*, www.bigissue.com; Un Techo Para Chile, www.untechoparachile.cl.

17   "The 2009 TIME 100," *TIME*, 2009, www.time.com/time/specials/packages/completelist/ 0,29569,1894410,00.html.

18   "The 2009 NPT Power and Influence Top 50," *The NonProfit Times*, 23(15), August 15, 2009.

19   The subject of philanthropy is covered more fully in Chapter 8, "Philanthropy: Powering philanthropic passions," by Thomas Menkhoff, and in Chapter 9, "Venture Philanthropy: Venturing into entrepreneurial philanthropy," by Rob John.

20   The subject of social entrepreneurship is covered more fully in Chapter 6, "Social Entrepreneurship: Of pattern changers and changemakers," by Chris Cusano.

21   Bill Drayton is the founder of Ashoka, which seeks to identify and develop social entrepreneurs. Profile of Bill Drayton at www.ashoka.org/team/drayton, and of Ashoka at www.ashoka.org.

Chapter 17

Technology

Rebooting Technology for Society

ROBERT CHEW

Chairman, Information Technology Standards Committee

Technology is constantly changing the way our world works. Historically, its uptake has been most evident in the nonsocial sectors. However, the social sector is increasingly recognizing the power of technology to foster innovation and solve society's more difficult problems.

This applies in particular to four clusters of technologies with high potential and relevance for social transformation: environmental technologies (wind power, solar power, hydro power, and clean water), health technologies (accessible and affordable health-care solutions), robotics (rehabilitation and socially assistive robotics), and info-communications (from back office applications to social media).

However, technology is a tool that can also be abused. To harness the full value of technology, its use should be properly planned and integrated with the processes and the people upon whom it impacts.

At 21:53 UTC on Tuesday, January 13, 2010, an earthquake of magnitude 7.0 M_w[1] struck the Caribbean nation of Haiti. It was the most violent earthquake to strike the impoverished nation in a century. More than 220,000 people died, and an estimated 1.3 million people were made homeless.[2]

The world's response was immediate and extensive. Governments, corporations, nonprofit organizations (NPOs), and individuals raced to help in a "global emphatic response."[3] Within two hours, the US had mobilized the USS *Carl Vinson* (one of the world's biggest warships), the USNS *Comfort* (a state-of-the-art hospital ship), and thousands of troops. Within days, NPOs such as the Red Cross, Médecins Sans Frontières (Doctors Without Borders), and Action Against Hunger arrived with medical and emergency aid. All over the world, people provided donations and support.

Images of the destruction and messages of help were flashed out to the rest of the world. Within 24 hours of the first quake, Haitian Prime Minister Jean-Max Bellerive appeared on CNN appealing for help. Within 48 hours, the American Red Cross had received nearly US$35 million in donations, more than half of which came from online contributions. Its mobile phone fundraiser brought in US$3 million within 36 hours.[4] Within a month of the earthquake, American charities had raised over US$709 million[5] and by April 2010, international donors had pledged nearly US$10 billion.[6] Volunteers also came to help. Many were mobilized through online and social media. Within a few hours, a social media campaign by Julie Collazo of MatadorNetwork.com recruited 150 volunteers to fly to the Dominican Republic to assist with the relief efforts.[7]

Hundreds of technology volunteers gathered in person and online to develop new tools and adapt existing ones to support the relief workers in Haiti. One such tool, Person Finder: Haiti Earthquake, was created by incorporating existing Google technology to help find missing persons.[8] Yet another open source portal, called Ushahidi, allowed for the "crowd sourcing" of crisis information from SMS, email, and the web, and then mapped it for crisis response and recovery.[9]

Meanwhile, on the ground, workers using transport, housing, and medical technology cleared the way and directly helped the victims of the disaster. The US warships brought with them the capability to generate 400,000 gallons of fresh water a day. Their spy drones created maps of the hardest-hit areas to help retrieve those who were trapped or lost. Icology Group deployed its low-cost, interlocking I-Wood housing system to provide emergency and transitional shelters.[10]

The scale and speed of this humanitarian response would not have been possible without technology. Had the same kind of technology been available and mobilized for the Shaanxi earthquake in China in 1556, the deadliest earthquake on record, the outcome would probably have been very different. Some of the 830,000 people—about 60 percent of the region's population—who died might have survived. Certainly, the reconstruction and rehabilitation of the survivors would have been far faster and more thorough with outside support. Instead, the Chinese in Shaanxi soldiered on, isolated from the rest of the world.

Promising Technology

Technology has not just enabled humanitarian efforts; it has had a pervasive impact on all areas of our lives. In fact, technology has literally changed, many times over, the face of the world and how its people work and live. The industrial revolution was made possible by the steam engine and mass production; the new agricultural revolution was brought about by agricultural mechanization; and the information revolution had its roots in the advent of computers.

Technology has touched our lives, organizations, and society in such a ubiquitous manner that we quickly assimilate and often take for granted new technological innovations.

But the uptake of technology varies for different sectors; it is more rapid and pervasive in the private and even the public sector than in the social sector. This is due, in part, to the social sector's financial constraints. Another reason is the social sector's inclination for authenticity and, thus, a preference for natural tools rather than artificial, man-made gadgets.

Nevertheless, the social sector has gradually found that embracing technology can create the social innovations that solve otherwise intractable social problems. There are now networks and forums such as AshokaTech[11] for NPOs and social entrepreneurs who are focused on technology-based solutions for the social space; the Nonprofit Technology Network,[12] which facilitates information sharing and knowledge exchange among nonprofit technology professionals; TechSoup,[13] which helps NPOs obtain and use technology to heighten their impact; and Information and Communication Technologies for Development,[14] which carries out information and communications technology research and makes the results freely available to poor and marginalized communities.

In this section, we will examine four clusters of technologies that have particular relevance and high potential for the social sector:

- Environmental
- Health
- Robotics
- Info-communications (or "infocomm" for short).

Environmental Technologies

The 20th century saw explosive industrial and economic growth powered by technology. However, this was achieved without much consideration for the impact on the environment and sustainability. The 21st century, on the other hand, will be the century of sustainable industrial and economic growth.[15]

This is a huge opportunity for the social sector to take the lead. By their very nature, NPOs are more attuned to sustainability issues than commercial organizations. Today, the technology to deliver green and clean energy as well as clean water to the more remote places of the world is becoming more affordable and accessible.

The three main clean energy sources are wind (wind power), sun (solar power), and water (hydropower).

Wind turbines in wind farms are used to convert wind energy into electricity. Of interest to the social sector are the smaller wind farms which could be easily installed to supply electricity to isolated locations. For example, the US NPO, Green Empowerment, installed 20 small wind turbines to convert wind energy to electricity in the small Peruvian village of Alumbre in 2008. This paved the way to help address the wider issue of electrification in a country where 70 percent of the rural communities lack electricity.[16] The bigger 500 watt wind turbine at the top of the hill charges batteries that supply light to the school classrooms, while the smaller turbines deliver electricity directly to homes.

Solar power is the generation of electricity from sunlight. The sun emanates more than sufficient energy to fulfill the world's needs. Solar energy does not give out carbon emissions. It will not run out (or at least not for a very, very long time) and, like wind and hydro power, it is free. Today, there are small-scale solar energy generators that are suitable for remote and emergency use. For example, soon after the Haiti earthquake, Sun Ovens, partnering with Friends of Haiti Organization, delivered cardboard solar cookers and ovens as well as food supplies to the thousands of homeless living in makeshift camps, thus helping to alleviate their hunger.[17]

Hydropower has been in use for hundreds of years. A hydroelectric plant produces hardly any direct waste and has a considerably smaller carbon footprint per unit of electricity produced compared to fossil fuel powered electricity plants. Small-scale hydroelectric plants can deliver an energy range of a few kilowatts up to 10 megawatts of micro hydropower. An Indonesian NPO, IBEKA (People Centered Economic and Business Institute), strives to bring light and energy to the rural populations of Indonesia where, even today, about half of its population continues to live without electricity. It has introduced micro hydropower plants to over 50 villages in Indonesia.[18] Hydropower from the open sea is also being tested with wave farms in Portugal.[19]

Clean water is a critical need in a world where over a billion people lack access to safe drinking water.[20] To help address this, NPOs are also deploying small-scale versions of water treatment technology in developing countries. An example is the Agua Pura Project that provides clean water to rural Guatemala. The project developed a practical, low-cost, solar-powered system that purifies water while also storing it.[21]

Clean energy and clean water should be our planet's future. Indeed, Professors Mark Jacobson of Stanford University and Mark Delucchi of the University of California have proposed a radical plan for 100 percent of the world's energy to be supplied by wind, water, and solar resources by 2030.[22] Their vision calls for 3.8 million large wind turbines, 90,000 solar plants, and numerous geothermal, tidal, and rooftop photovoltaic installations worldwide. They estimate that this will cost less than the projected cost per kilowatt-hour for fossil-fuel and nuclear power, but the challenges will be the shortage of specialty materials and the lack of political will.

Whether that larger vision can be realized is unclear; for the moment, the use of smaller and portable versions of energy and water technologies can help address the needs of rural and poor communities. In the near future, we should see a massive rollout of small-scale green energy and water systems delivered by NPOs that will complement larger green facilities set up by governments and corporations.

Health Technologies

In 1900, the average life expectancy in the US was 47 years. In 2009, it was 78.[23] While this remarkable increase of over 60 percent is the result of a number of factors, including the increased availability of a clean and safe water supply, a significant factor is the advancements in medicine and health care.

So pervasive are the health-care technologies today that we may not always realize that only a century ago, these were not available. Some of the most significant health-related technologies of the last 100 years or so are shown in Figure 17.1.

Figure 17.1 Health Innovations and Discoveries of the 20th Century

Electrocardiograph machine (1903)

Respirator (1927)

Artificial pacemaker (1930s)

Kidney dialysis machine (1945)

Contact lens (1946)

Artificial hip replacement (1950s)

Artificial heart valve (1951)

Open heart by-pass surgery (1953)

Kidney transplant (1954)

Totally internal pacemaker (1960)

Laser treatment for the eyes (1963)

Soft contact lens (1971)

Computerised axial tomography, or CAT scan (1972)

Arthroscope (late 1970s)

Controlled drug delivery (1980s)

Magnetic resonance imaging, or MRI scan (1981)

Permanent artificial heart implant (1982)

Implantable cardioverter defibrillator, or ICD (1985)

Deep brain electrical simulation system (1987)

Laser surgery on human cornea (1987)

The human genome project (1990)

Source: *Greatest Engineering Achievements of the 20th Century*, National Academy of Engineering, www.greatachievements.org.

Many of these technologies and medical treatments are too expensive and inaccessible to the poor and needy in developing countries. In addition, the diseases and health-care conditions prevalent among the poor are often ignored by modern health technology and pharmaceutical research companies because they are not commercially attractive.

It is heartening to see that new forms of philanthropy are directing research dollars toward meeting these needs. The best-known example is The Bill & Melinda Gates Foundation's Global Health Program.[24] Its mission—to help ensure that technology-based health solutions are created and delivered to those who need them most—focuses on health problems in the developing world that cause great harm but get too little attention. To date, the Foundation has committed US$10 billion to global health grants addressing malaria, HIV/AIDS, tuberculosis, vaccine-preventable diseases, polio, pneumonia and flu, and diarrhea.

Increasingly, NPOs leverage entrepreneurship and technology to bring practical health-care solutions to the underserved. For example, California-based VillageReach implemented a health-care distribution network to bridge the "last mile" of villages in remote areas of Mozambique. To do this, it adopted practices and systems from the logistics and supply chain industries. This has greatly eased the bottleneck in the delivery of life-saving drugs to the people who need them. According to an independent study, VillageReach's work has improved the standard childhood vaccination rate in Mozambique from 68 percent to 95 percent.[25]

NPOs are also developing low-cost, easily deployable health-care solutions, similar to what is happening with environmental technologies. One such organization, Diagnostics For All (DFA), uses biotechnology and microfluidics to create low-cost, easy-to-use, point-of-care diagnostics designed specifically for the 60 percent of the developing world that lives beyond the reach of urban hospitals and medical infrastructures.[26] In 2008, DFA developed 3D microPAD, an inexpensive diagnostic device which uses paper and adhesive tape to analyze bodily fluids to detect levels of sugar and protein—markers for diabetes and kidney failure. These small, portable, and low-cost devices will provide tremendous benefits to public health in poor nations with little or no access to complex laboratory diagnostic equipment.

With research funding directed at addressing less commercially attractive but harmful health conditions and diseases, with low-cost, point-of-care products such as 3D microPAD, and with distribution solutions like those from VillageReach, global health care for one and all may, one day, finally be achievable.

Robotics

"I, Robot" is not just the name of Isaac Asimov's book or the movie; iRobot is a household name—the brand of a range of robots for cleaning, communication, learning, and play.[27]

Robotics is the science and technology of designing, developing, and manufacturing robots. The term "robot" was first coined by Czech dramatist Karel, derived from "robota," which means slave-like labor. Robots can be deployed to do unpleasant manual tasks, such as household chores that humans do not want to do. They can be programmed to do repetitive tasks, such as assembling automobiles. They can perform dangerous procedures, such as clearing explosives. They can also assist people who are ill, disabled, or elderly in their daily lives.

From the social sector standpoint, important contributions are emerging in the areas of rehabilitation and assistive robotics. Both help restore the disabled and the aged to an optimal level of physical, mental, and social well-being.

Rehabilitation robotics applies robotics to therapeutic procedures to achieve the best possible motor or cognitive functional recovery for persons with impairments caused by strokes, orthopedic traumas, and diseases.[28] Assistive robotics develops robotic aids to support the independent living of persons such as the severely disabled and the elderly who have chronic limitations in motor or cognitive abilities.[29] Often, these two types of robotics are referred to interchangeably. For our purposes, we shall use the term "rehabilitation robotics" to include both types.

One of the first rehabilitation manipulators, the CASE manipulator, was built in the early 1960s.[30] This was a powered orthosis with four degrees of freedom that could move a user's paralyzed arm. Another early project was the work carried out at the Veterans Administration Prosthetics Center in New York in the 1970s which introduced the first use of a robotic arm mounted to a wheelchair.

Another active area of rehabilitation robotics research and application is influenced by the commercial developments in "automatic guided vehicles."[31] This has led to the development of a number of "smart" wheelchairs that incorporate features to avoid obstacles, negotiate difficult situations such as doorways, and follow a track laid on the floor. The CALL (Communication Aids for Language and Learning) Center's latest Smart Wheelchair has various movement controls, bump collision detection, a line follower, and a speech synthesizer to communicate commands and report events.[32]

There are NPOs that focus on the use of rehabilitation robotics. For instance, Neil Squire Society aims to help create an environment where every person with a physical disability can make the most of his or her ability and contribute to society.[33] One of its projects, the Neil Squire Robotic Assistive Appliance, is a robot that allows users who have severe mobility impairment to move and position objects of up to two kilograms in mass and to perform manual tasks such as turning the pages of a book.

As difficult as it is to design and build robots that can assist with physical mobility, it is harder to make robots that interact with people socially. The Center for Robotics and Embedded Systems at the University of Southern California designs machines that can be therapeutically useful through social interaction—coaching, motivating, and monitoring people with cognitive and physical disabilities.[34]

CosmoBot is one such socially assistive robot.[35] CosmoBot is used at the Mayo Clinic in Rochester, Minnesota, for physical therapy of children with disabilities such as autism, Down Syndrome, cerebral palsy, and muscular dystrophy.[36]

Another project, KASPAR (Kinesics and Synchronisation in Personal Assistant Robotics) aims to develop robots to help autistic children improve their social skills and overcome their learning disabilities.[37]

The applications of robotics technologies are many, and they have had significant impact. However, many of these technologies can be inaccessible to those who may benefit from them. They first have to be brought out of the labs. Those already commercially available have to be made affordable. In addition, there is the challenge of gaining acceptance of using robots among those most in need. These challenges, especially the cost of the technologies, are likely to remain for some time.

Infocomm Technologies

The last, but arguably most far-reaching, of the technologies is infocomm— a convenient label for the cluster of computing, information technology, and communication technologies.

We take so much of what we have for granted that we may not realize how rapidly infocomm has transformed our lives. The video *Did You Know?*,[38] on globalization and the information age, is a sobering reminder that we are truly living in exponential times.

The social world can benefit by leveraging off much of what is already out there. A good place for NPOs to start is in the automation of their back office. Commercial companies are inundated with choices of software solutions for general and specialized application areas. Nonprofit-specific applications such as regulatory compliance, donor management, and volunteer management have been more limited because of the nonprofit sector's general lack of attention to office infrastructure. However, with the availability of shared services, SaaS (Software as a Service), and cloud computing, there is now an opportunity for NPOs to obtain back office automation at more affordable costs to increase their productivity.[39]

The internet and social media (Facebook, Twitter, etc.) are already being used by many nonprofits to reach out and engage their respective stakeholders. A key value of the new media is that it is simple, instantaneous, and viral. The first images of the Haiti earthquake did not come from television networks or traditional media; they were "Tweeted."[40] Indeed, many mainstream media journalists were receiving updates through Twitter and other social media.

The uses of the internet and social media are virtually limitless. NPOs can, and have, used the internet to fundraise, counsel,[41] market, transact, connect, match, and collaborate. SocialVibe is a social networking site with over a million members that rewards publishers of media content through mechanisms such as donations to their charity of choice.[42] Ammado seeks to be the Facebook of the social world by connecting nonprofits, socially responsible companies, and givers.[43] Second Life, a virtual world populated by avatars of users who create a parallel life for themselves, enables NPOs to educate real people (in their avatar form) about their causes, or even to hold virtual fundraisers to raise real money.[44]

Another value of the web is the ability to "micro" anything—to transact at a granularity not possible in the off-line world. Thus, Kiva and TrickleUp allow their users to make micro-loans to beneficiaries in developing countries.[45] Micro-volunteering company The Extraordinaries allows anyone to use their spare time to benefit their favorite cause using a mobile phone or personal computer.[46]

The humble mobile phone has been a boon to the rural poor.[47] It provides them with communication and web connectivity previously unavailable because telecommunication companies would not invest in expensive landlines to these remote areas.[48] DataDyne replaces cumbersome and costly paper-based methods with the mobile phone to collect data for nonprofits in international development and global health care.[49] An Indian entrepreneur, Anurag Gupta, has used a smartphone to create what is, in effect, a US$200 bank branch.[50]

Interestingly, the social sector has benefited significantly, if quite indirectly, from the infocomm boom. Perhaps the best example is the contributions by successful infocomm entrepreneurs and organizations. Jeff Skolls of eBay, Bill Gates of Microsoft, and Larry Page and Sergey Brin of Google are examples of the new philanthrocapitalists who give massive amounts of money, time, and ideas to social causes. Several infocomm companies have also sought to make available free or cheap hardware and software solutions to the developing world through such programs as One Laptop Per Child and Microsoft's Unlimited Potential initiative.[51]

What does the future hold for infocomm? More than any other technological field, computing has been the forerunner and prime example of the "smaller, cheaper, faster" mantra. Advances in wireless and miniaturized chips already allow embedded smart computers to interact with each other in almost any conceivable equipment. Sense and response[52] networks will become pervasive. Information flows will be dynamic and give rise to new capabilities for analysis, automation, and control.

It is incumbent on those of us in the social sector to understand and leverage these capabilities, for they are a key enabler to accelerating social change.

The Other Side of Technology

We have thus far examined the positive aspects of technology. However, while technology is a tremendous tool, it can also be abused and it needs to be properly harnessed.

The Dark Side

Following the Haiti earthquake, we saw that the Red Cross was wildly effective in using mobile communications to raise funds very quickly. Unfortunately, a number of fraudulent imitators of the Red Cross's text-to-donate programs quickly sprung up and donors had to be asked to verify the authenticity of fundraisers.[53] Criminal gangs were also swindling donors by setting up bogus charities and seeking contributions online.[54]

The same technologies we have observed delivering positive changes to our livelihoods can be used to deliver much harm.

It is well known that the communications and social networking technologies are used by terrorist groups. Anwar Awlaki, a radical Muslim cleric, has been using the internet and blog sites to proclaim violence as a religious duty.[55] Terrorist organizations are using social networking sites such as Facebook to recruit new members.[56] Terrorists are using the techniques of credit card fraudsters, such as phishing, to falsely obtain credit card information and to launder money to finance terrorist operations.[57]

While health-care advances are designing and developing new drugs to cure diseases, the same technologies can be used to conduct bioterrorism. Unmanned aerial vehicles can be used by terrorists to project their attacks at locations more difficult to reach and to launch previously.[58]

Thus, the same reach enabled by technology for humanitarian access could well be exploited for darker purposes.

Exploiting Technology

In the case of the Haiti earthquake, word of the tragedy spread very quickly and people from all over the world responded just as quickly.

Within a week of the earthquake, food and medicines were bottlenecked at the airport. Yet, they could not be distributed to the needy because the planning and logistics were not in place.[59] There was confusion over who was coordinating the relief effort: the US, which controlled the main airport; or the UN, which stated that it was overseeing distribution; or the Haitian president, who declared that he was in charge. Médecins Sans Frontières stated that the confusion probably led to hundreds of avoidable deaths because it was not able to get essential supplies into the country.[60]

The chaos in a situation like the Haitian earthquake may be understandable, but it also highlights that technology on its own is usually not sufficient to solve the problem in many situations.

Rather, for technology to be properly leveraged, it needs to be properly thought through and implemented. The technological aspects of a solution need to be integrated with the processes and the people who are impacted by it.

A good example of this is Aravind Eye Care System, a nonprofit eye-care group in India.[61] Its hospitals have examined over 1.7 million patients, at a rate of over 250,000 patients yearly. To achieve this scaled impact, Aravind relies on advanced infocomm technologies (e.g. telemedicine and electronic medical records) and eye-care technologies (e.g. intra-ocular lens and ophthalmic needles). Beyond these technologies, Aravind is well known for its innovation in redesigning the processes of eye operations to be both efficient and of top quality. Thus, while a typical Western eye operation takes 30 minutes, one at Aravind takes less than 10 minutes. In addition, Aravind invests in staff training and development that are aligned with its processes and technologies. Aravind is named after Sri Aurobindo,[62] an Indian spiritual leader who taught that mankind could transcend to a heightened state through service and working fully with nature. Aravind Eye Care System is thus inspired to integrate technology with processes and people to deliver a superior level of service.

Nonprofits: The New Leader in Technology Use?

As we enter the second decade of the 21st century, the nonprofit and technology sectors are no longer considered alien to each other. The nonprofit sector has increasingly demonstrated that it is able to embrace the power of technology to solve social issues.

That power is increasing exponentially in the case of infocomm technologies. Technology will provide us with a greener environment, healthier lives, livelier communities, and, overall, a richer world. It is, in short, a critical enabler for transforming the social ecosystem.

It is thus time for the nonprofit sector to move from being behind among the public and the private sectors, to not just embrace technology, but possibly to be a leader in its harnessing and exploitation.

Endnotes

1   Seismologists measure the size of earthquakes in terms of energy released on the moment magnitude scale (MMS), denoted as M_w where w indicates work accomplished. (Previously, earthquakes were measured on the Richter scale.) For comparison, the following earthquakes registered these M_w: Sichuan, 2008—7.9; Sumatra, 2007—8.5; Asian tsunami (Sumatra, Indian Ocean), 2004—9.3; Shaanxi, 1556—8.0.

2   "World Raises $14b Aid for Haiti," *The Straits Times*, April 1, 2010.

3   Jeremy Rifkin, "The Earthquake that Triggered a Global Emphatic Response: What the Haitian crisis tells us about human nature," *The Huffington Post*, February 12, 2010.

4   The online phone campaign asking donors to send a US$10 donation by texting "Haiti" to 90999 was started at 8 p.m., January 12. By 9 a.m., January 14, more than US$3 million had been raised. In total, more than US$22 million has been raised. Thomas Heath, "U.S. Cellphone Users Donate $22 million to Haiti Earthquake Relief via Text," *The Washington Post*, January 19, 2010, www.washingtonpost.com/wp-dyn/content/article/2010/01/18/AR2010011803792.html.

5   Caroline Preston, Nicole Wallace, and Ian Wilhelm compiled a list of charities and their donations for the Haiti earthquake, as reported in www.philanthropy.com/article/American-Charities-Raise/64193.

6   "World Raises $14b Aid for Haiti," *The Straits Times*, April 1, 2010.

7   Laura Bly, "Haiti Relief Groups Need Money, Not Volunteers," *USA Today*, January 14, 2010, www.usatoday.com/travel/news/2010-01-14-haiti-relief-groups_N.htm.

8   www.haiticrisis.appspot.com.

9   www.ushahidi.com.

10   "Easy to Build, Low Cost, Secure Transitional Shelters for Haiti," Press Release by Icology Group, March 26, 2010, www.icologygroup.com/assets/icology_press_release.pdf.

11   AshokaTech is a blog for the Ashoka community on technology and inventions. It is part of a partnership of Ashoka and the Lemelson Foundation to align technology and social entrepreneurship to improve the world. It organized a major Tech4Society forum in February 2010. See www.tech.ashoka.org.

12   Nonprofit Technology Network, nten, www.nten.org.

13   www.techsoupglobal.org.

14   www.ict4d.org.uk.

15   Charles Fishman, "Sustainable Growth—Interface, Inc.,"*Fast Company*, March 31, 1998, www.fastcompany.com/magazine/14/sustaing.html.

16   Levi Novey, "Wind Power Blows into Peru and Brightens Future,"*In the Americas*, June 17, 2008, www.ecolocalizer.com/2008/06/17/wind-power-blows-into-peru-and-brightens-future; Annagarwood,"The Winds of Change,"Green Empowerment: The Blog, March 13, 2008, www.greenempowerment.wordpress.com/2008/03/13/the-winds-of-change.

17   Doug Hoover, "Sun Ovens for Haiti," *Amazines*, January 28, 2010, www.amazines .com/article_detail.cfm/1367082?articleid=1367082.

18   IBEKA (People Centered Economic and Business Institute) is founded by Ashoka Fellow, Tri Mumpini. See "Lighting up Rural Indonesia through Community-owned Hydropower Projects,"Knowledge@SMU, October 4, 2008, www.knowledge.smu.edu .sg/article.cfm?articleid=1167. Mumpini's profile is at www.ashoka.org/node/3870.

19   "Portugal to Host World's First Wave Farm,"RenewableEnergyWorld.com, May 19, 2005, www.renewableenergyworld.com/rea/news/article/2005/05/portugal-to-host-worlds-first-wave-farm-30275.

20   Larry West, "World Water Day: A billion people worldwide lack safe drinking water," About.com, www.environment.about.com/od/environmentalevents/a/waterdayqa.htm.

21   This is a joint project by Caltech, Art Center College of Design and the Landivar University. See "Agua Pura: Providing access to clean water in rural Guatemala," Designmatters at Art Center, Summer 2009, www.designmatters.artcenter.edu/index .php/projects/agua-pura-providing-access-to-clean-water-in-rura/agua-pura-providing-access-to-clean-water-in-rural-guatemala.html.

22   Mark Z. Jacobson and Mark A. Delucchi, "A Path to Sustainable Energy," *Scientific American*, November 2009, www.eec1.ucdavis.edu/publications/PathtoSustainableEnergy-Nov2009.pdf.

23   This information is from *CIA World Factbook* at www.cia.gov/library/publications/the-world-factbook/rankorder/2102rank.html.

24   www.gatesfoundation.org/global-health/Pages/overview.aspx.

25   "Ensuring that Health Care Reaches 'The Last Mile'," College of Arts & Sciences, University of Washington, December 2009, www.artsci.washington.edu/newsletter/ Dec09/VillageReach.asp; James Daily, Leah Hassleback, David Lubinski, and Sophie Newland, *Last Mile Informatics for Immunization Programs: A HealthTech report* (Washington, DC: Village Reach, US Aid, and Path, July 2009). Also see VillageReach at www.villagereach.net.

26   www.dfa.org/about/approach.html.

27   *I, Robot* was a book of short stories about robots by Isaac Asimov. The 2004 science fiction film of the same name diverges from the book. The iRobot corporation is at www.irobot.com.

28   www.tab.ieee-ras.org/committeeinfo.php?tcid=18.

29   Ibid.

30   Y. Kim and A. M. Cook, "Manipulation and Mobility Aids," in *Electronic Devices for Rehabilitation,* ed. John G. Webster (New York: John Wiley & Sons, 1989).

31 An automated (or automatic) guided vehicle is a mobile robot that follows markers or wires in the floor, or uses vision or lasers.

32 The CALL Centre in Edinburgh, UK has over 25 years of experience in this area of providing communication and assistive technologies for people with disabilities, www .callscotland.org.uk/About-Us/What-We-Do.

33 www.neilsquire.ca.

34 http://cres.usc.edu/Research/labs.php.

35 CosmoBot was developed by AnthroTronix, an engineering company in Silver Spring, Maryland, US, www.anthrotronix.com.

36 www.atkidsystems.com/parent_testimonials.aspx.

37 Kaspar is led by Dr. Robins from the University of Hertfordshire, UK. The project is funded by the European Union and, besides the UK, has participating organizations in The Netherlands, Italy, Spain, and France. See www.kaspar.feis.herts.ac.uk and John Blau, "'Kaspar' the Robot Helps Autistic Kids Play," *Computerworld*, June 19, 2007, www .computerworld.com/s/article/9025258/_Kaspar_the_robot_helps_autistic_kids_play.

38 There are several versions of the five-minute video *Did You Know?* on www.youtube .com. It highlights how infocomm has progressed exponentially.

39 A white paper prepared by the Lien Centre, *Promoting Nonprofit IT Enablement in Singapore* (Singapore: Lien Centre for Social Innovation, November 24, 2009), discusses the various application areas and technology approaches in which NPOs can leverage IT for their front and back offices.

40 "Haiti 'Biggest Disaster of the Twitter Era'," *The Sydney Morning Herald*, January 14, 2010, www.smh.com.au/technology/technology-news/haiti-biggest-disaster-of-the-twitter-era-20100114-m8wb.html.

41 For example, the Marine Parade Family Service Centre in Singapore has a cyber-counseling program that uses the web to reach out and counsel youths online. It has found this medium attractive for young people who are used to online activity and may prefer the anonymity of the web in discussing their problems. See www.metoyou.org.sg.

42 www.socialvibe.com.

43 www.ammado.com.

44 www.secondlife.com.

45 See www.kiva.org and www.trickleup.org.

46 www.beextra.org.

47 The value of the mobile phone, of course, extends beyond the rural poor. With its ability to pinpoint where the user is, location-based mobile phone services are expected to take off. Today, even our physical locations can be shared on a social network using location apps such as Foursquare and Gozilla.

48 "Upwardly Mobile in Africa," *BusinessWeek*, September 24, 2007, www.businessweek .com/magazine/content/07_39/b4051054.htm.

49 www.datadyne.org.

50 A bank representative goes to the village with a smartphone and a fingerprint scanner. Savers line up, give their identification number, scan their fingerprints, and then deposit or withdraw small amounts of rupees. The story is found in Eric Bellman, "Indian Firms Shift Focus to the Poor," *The Wall Street Journal*, October 20, 2009.

51 See www.laptop.org and www.microsoft.com/unlimitedpotential/default.mspx.

52 Sense and response refers to an event-driven IT infrastructure for forming fast and well-informed decisions and putting them into action.

53 Bruce Watson, "Haiti Earthquake Brings Charity Scams out of the Woodwork," *DailyFinance*, January 20, 2010, www.dailyfinance.com/story/haiti-earthquake-brings-charity-scams-out-of-the-woodwork/19324648/.

54 "Gangs Use Online Scams to Target Haiti Cash," *TODAY*, February 18, 2010.

55 "Profile: Anwar al-Awlaki," *BBC News*, January 3, 2010, www.news.bbc.co.uk/2/hi/middle_east/8438635.stm.

56 Miles Johnson, "Terrorists Recruiting on Net via Facebook," *scotsman*, February 17, 2008, www.news.scotsman.com/latestnews/Terrorists-recruiting-on-net-via.3786178.jp.

57 Jeremy Simon, "The Credit Card–Terrorism Connection," Credit Cards.com, www.creditcards.com/credit-card-news/credit-cards-terrorism-1282.php.

58 Eugene Miasnikov, "Threat of Terrorism Using Unmanned Aerial Vehicles: Technical aspects," Center for Arms Control, Energy, and Environmental Studies at MIPT, www.armscontrol.ru/uav/report.htm.

59 "Haiti Earthquake Relief is Stifled by Chaos in Port-au-Prince," *The Washington Post*, January 19, 2010.

60 Liz Robbins, "Aid Workers Scramble Amid Haiti's Chaos," *The New York Times*, January 13, 2010, www.nytimes.com/2010/01/14/world/americas/14aid.html; Chris McGreal, "Haiti Aid Agencies Warn: Chaotic and confusing relief effort is costing lives," *The Guardian*, January 18, 2010, www.guardian.co.uk/world/2010/jan/18/haiti-aid-distribution-confusion-warning.

61 www.aravind.org.

62 www.aravind.org/aboutus/genesis.asp.

Chapter 18

Social Finance

Financing Change, Changing Finance

JED EMERSON
Founder, Blended Value Group

It has long been accepted that financial capital is critical to social change efforts. Yet, it is only recently that social finance has been viewed as a defined and important marketplace.

Today, a myriad of financial instruments, ranging from the traditional grant to complex debt/equity hybrids, is available to nonprofits and social enterprises. These instruments come from a variety of sources, from the traditional grantmakers to new social investors.

At the start of a new decade and after a turbulent economic stress period, social finance offers unprecedented opportunities to innovate within capital markets for impactful investment and sustainable change.

S ecuring appropriate capital is a constant concern to all those engaged in advancing social change, be they for profit or otherwise.

For most nonprofit organizations (NPOs), identifying adequate and aligned funding seems to be a challenge of the plenty. Among the thicket of grants, individual donations, investment funds, government support, and earned income strategies, it is clear that capital seekers are facing unprecedented variety and creativity in funding sources.

Yet, problems of common definition arise for those who seek to integrate market-based approaches with the creation of social impact. The increasing number of potential investment tools creates a challenge for mission-driven for-profits and nonprofits interested in leveraging financial performance, as many funders feel they are neither "fish nor fowl"—falling into a dark hole between philanthropy and commercial investments. '

Despite these challenges, it is clear an evolution of capital markets, financial instruments, and funding strategies is well underway.

The Social Finance Landscape

Defining this landscape is important as it provides us with a set of frameworks and definitions to better understand how the efforts of one set of players fits with those of others, and allows us to advance measures of social return, impact, and relative performance. Perhaps more importantly, embracing a common framework for defining capital and enterprise is critical to making both cooperation and joint action possible.[1]

In exploring available financial instruments, it is useful to think in terms of two key aspects of financing:

- *Forms of Financing:* These include "free" money (donations), revenue (earned income from activities), debt, and equity.
- *Sources of Financing:* These include donors, traditional grantmakers, the new philanthropists, social investors, and commercial third parties.

Figure 18.1 maps out the range of financing options against these two dimensions of financing.

The chart also seeks to reflect a third dimension—the range of financial returns sought by asset owners and how such financial returns may intersect with social impact.[2] In this respect, Tim Freundlich has described social capital as spanning three broad categories:[3]

Figure 18.1 The Social Finance Landscape

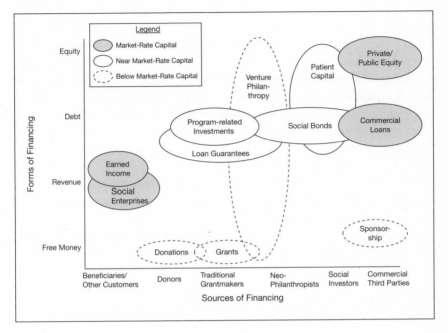

- *Market-Rate Capital:* This would be financing that is offered on terms similar to what would be available in the commercial market. Examples are socially screened funds such as Calvert Group or the Domini Index, or sustainable investment funds that integrate social and environmental factors into their analysis of publicly traded companies.
- *Near-Market-Rate Capital:* Some community development institutions offer investors a return on capital with a small interest premium.
- *Below-Market-Rate Capital:* This is capital that may return principal but does not yield a risk-adjusted financial return or interest rate fees in line with the true level of risk assumed by the lender. As we define a capital continuum, we can view donations as the extreme end of below-market-rate capital.

Donations and Grants

Traditionally, many NPOs have focused on donations and grants, or what is often considered as "free" money to fund their activities.

However, that is not to say that donations and grants do not incur any cost. For a start, many NPOs spend significant hours and financial resources on fundraising activities and the grant application process. After the donation or grant is awarded, nonprofits must account to these donors or grantmakers in line with the expectations and conditions of the gift.

Donations are often solicited from individuals and organizations. Grants are often awarded by foundations or governmental funding bodies. Individuals, however, may also award a grant through a donor-advised fund or other aggregation vehicle.

Broadly speaking, there are three types of grants:

- *Program grant*, which is awarded to support the operation of a certain program or service (e.g. counseling for homeless individuals or an after-school program).
- *Project grant*, which is awarded for a specific finite activity, often within a larger program (e.g. a project to build a certain number of homes for a displaced community after a natural disaster).
- *General operating grant*, which is awarded to an NPO to support its overall program or management needs.

Within the nonprofit sector, there continues to be debate regarding which type of grant is most effective in advancing the work of the sector. Many philanthropic leaders and sector representatives are calling for more foundations and individuals to award unrestricted general operating grants as a core part of their grantmaking practice.[4]

Sponsorship

Sponsorship provides an organization with the opportunity to be associated with a specific charitable event (such as a charity golf tournament) or the NPO itself. The conditions for sponsorship would typically be due acknowledgment in the respective event or the organization's collaterals. Most companies tend to provide sponsorship as a show of support for the NPO, rather than with any expectation of full benefit from the value of its sponsorship. However, cause-related marketing can also bring real value to the sponsoring for-profit corporation—value that can add to its financial bottom line in a variety of ways.

For NPOs, the out-of-pocket cost of sponsorship may initially be viewed as less than that for traditional fundraising options, consisting primarily of the cost of solicitation. However, NPOs may incur significant costs in managing the sponsor relationship and, when combined with the possible negative implications of being affiliated with a for-profit, this approach should not be taken lightly. The experience of the nonprofit sector with cause-related marketing and corporate sponsorship has been both positive and negative, so care should be taken when exploring options of partnership between nonprofit and for-profit ventures.

Earned Income and Social Enterprises

One traditional method of funding operations is to charge for any products or services provided by the NPO, whether this be at a discounted rate relative to the market or not. Earned income represents about 53 percent of the nonprofit sector's revenue across the world.[5]

The fees could be charged to beneficiaries of the organization (e.g. the cost of kidney dialysis to patients) or to third-party customers (e.g. retail customers that purchase handicrafts made by the rural poor). Where the fees are charged to beneficiaries, they would be discounted from market rates. Where the fees are charged to third parties, they often are products made, or services provided, by the beneficiaries of the organization.

The desire to be financially sustainable for the long term has led many nonprofits to create separate social enterprises[6] to generate revenue from the market. Social enterprises may be linked in some form with the operations of the nonprofit (e.g. the use of beneficiaries of the organization in performing the service or manufacturing the product) or be an entirely standalone venture, having no relationship to the mission of the nonprofit (e.g. a café set up by an advocacy group for the environment).

Loans and Loan Guarantees

NPOs, as with commercial organizations, may make use of commercially available debt as a standard tool for managing their finances. Such debt, whether it is commercial loans or lines of credit, would typically be secured at competitive, market-level rates.

Commercial loans may also require guarantees; these can help reduce the cost of the loan. Donors and philanthropic institutions seeking to mobilize their assets in greater support of their social organization partners may also offer such loan guarantees.[7]

Although a nonprofit may actually be a better credit risk to lenders than for-profit counterparts of similar size, mainstream lenders often perceive them as carrying greater credit risk since they are "nonprofit" and often have few assets (such as a building) to secure the loan. Loan guarantees are therefore a useful tool for nonprofits and other social organizations wishing to obtain loans to fund the expansion of their operations and impact. Recent innovations in this category of social finance include the pooling of loan guarantees to create significant, multimillion-dollar sources of capital, such as that offered by Micro-Credit Enterprises.[8]

Program-Related Investments

In recognition of the burden of commercial debt instruments, foundations make soft loans called Program-Related Investments (PRIs) to NPOs or, less frequently, to the for-profit ventures. Unlike commercial loans, the interest rates charged for PRIs are low, or the loans may even be interest-free. Although PRIs have historically been associated with community development and housing, the Foundation Center has observed that their use has spread to "nearly all fields . . . especially education, the environment, arts, and culture, human services, health, and church support."[9]

The use of PRIs has several advantages for foundations. First, since the funds expended will return to the foundation at some future point in time, foundations are able to "recycle" limited grant funds. Secondly, foundations are able to support larger capital projects that grants alone may not have allowed them to finance. Thirdly, foundations can innovatively use PRIs as a form of senior debt within the capital structure of an organization, which allows the funder to "leverage" its assets to reduce the risk to other social investors that may fund the organization, possibly leading to more funds, lower interest rates, or both.

That said, PRIs are not without their downside. While a simple grant award is made and done with, there is some risk with a PRI that the funds may not be repaid.

For recipient organizations, PRIs enable the development of long-term relationships with funders. They also assist growing organizations in building institutional credit rating and managerial capacity through effective debt management.[10]

However, recipient organizations also face market risk when making use of PRIs to fund capital projects. In affordable housing or community development ventures, for example, downturns in the real estate market will affect the value of the properties being developed and thus affect the payback schedule and capacity.[11] Furthermore, various covenants or performance requirements may be placed on the PRI, which may add pressure on the organization to perform. Finally, NPOs may not have the resources to develop staff expertise to successfully manage the loan process and track loan performance.

Social Bonds

Bonds are debt instruments where loans are offered against an organization's assets or prospects of future cash flows that will be used to pay back the loan, and provide investors with both principal and interest payments. Bonds typically last over a year and are used for longer-term financing, not to meet short-term cash flow needs.

Bonds have been used to finance social activities for many years. In the US, this has been traditionally targeted at affordable housing development. Another example is the issuance of Tax Exempt Bonds by hospitals and educational institutions in the US to finance new buildings or other expansion. Ratings agencies will assign a risk rating to each of the bonds.

In recent years, there have been a number of innovations in bond financing worth noting: the microfinance bond, the cause bond, the social impact bond, and the global development bond.

Issued by microfinance institutions, microfinance bonds are used to increase lending to micro-entrepreneurs. For example, in 2004, BlueOrchard Finance and Developing World Markets offered a US$40 million bond as the first cross-border bond capital to microfinance institutions.[12]

Cause bonds[13] are structured on the basis of commitments to utilize future pledges of support for a given cause to fund bond payments. For example, the International Finance Facility for Immunisation (IFFI) launched the Vaccine Bond in 2006 to fund vaccination programs. This bond allows GAVI Alliance (formerly the Global Alliance for Vaccines and Immunisation) to borrow against donor nation pledges of future aid. The IFFI is managed through the World Bank, which coordinates donor relations and oversees the 10- and 20-year binding commitments and payments. Under this structure, GAVI has successfully raised more than US$2 billion. A critical aspect to the success of this offering is that "donors commit money to guarantee the price of vaccines once they have been developed, thus creating the potential for a viable future market."[14]

Social Finance, a UK consultancy, has devised social impact bonds (SIBs), a variation of the cause bond. SIBs aim to "drive significant nongovernment investment into addressing the causes of deep-rooted social problems."[15] Assuming interventions to address social problems will result in improved social outcomes that, in turn, lead to taxpayer and government savings, the proposed SIBs will be issued based on a commitment from government to use a proportion of such savings to reward nongovernment investors that fund the early intervention activities. SIBs will need to enunciate clear definitions of success and impact. Innovatively, they are structured so that the future value of the bond is a function of the impact generated by the entity receiving bond financing for its work.

A more recent innovation is the new asset class known as global development bonds (GDBs). These bonds allow institutional investors to buy risk-rated debt instruments that finance sustainable development and other economic activity with social and environmental impacts.[16] Initial discussions have focused upon GDBs for infrastructure and health services. For example, Michael Eckhart of the American Council on Renewable Energy has presented a vision of GDBs linked to financing solar development in developing nations.[17]

Private/Public Equity

Equity allows investors to be part owners of an organization and hence to participate in the organization's financial success through dividend payouts or increased valuation which may be sold to other investors. Equity may be public (meaning that the company is listed on a public stock exchange) or private (all other companies).

The option to secure true equity investments (whether on a private or public equity basis) is not available to NPOs. Although legally "owned," such ownership is of little transferable value since NPOs will not make any returns for its holders. The exception would be some for-profit social enterprises established with part of the profits going to shareholders.

Nevertheless, there needs to be a basic understanding of the various stages of investing by social entrepreneurs and nonprofit managers. This lack of understanding has contributed to the undercapitalization of social organizations and the general fragmentation in social capital markets. To make matters worse, there is no perceived logical progression in capital or defined "exits" for those providing one form of capital to those providing another.

Generally speaking, the flow of capital controlled by for-profit, equity investors moves along the continuum shown in the following box, "The Equity Investment Life Cycle." Naturally, this is an extremely simplistic outline of the process. In reality, it is a very complex process with many moving parts and different types of investors playing various roles with a variety of capital investment structures.

The Equity Investment Life Cycle

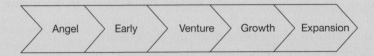

Angel 〉 Early 〉 Venture 〉 Growth 〉 Expansion 〉

- *Angel Stage:* An entrepreneur has an idea for a new business venture. With funds out of his or her own pocket and from "friends, families, and fools," he or she uses this money to test and develop the idea. Assuming the idea proves worthy, the entrepreneur then seeks small amounts of additional capital from other angel investors. These angels would become actively involved in working with the entrepreneur as a mentor, sounding board, and facilitator, making use of their personal networks to open doors for the entrepreneur.

- *Early Stage:* The entrepreneur begins to seek venture capital investors whose private equity investment funds from a host of outside investors are interested in generating a high financial return in exchange for the high risk of investing in a start-up. The venture capitalist is usually someone with deep expertise and often hands-on experience in a given area of business development. In exchange for their capital, they frequently require the entrepreneur to surrender a significant percentage of ownership of the firm, something many entrepreneurs are loath to do. Venture capital is often invested on a four- to seven-year basis at the end of which the investor will expect to see a financial return on the investment through new investors or accumulated profits.

- *Venture Stage:* As the company progresses, further capital may be needed. The valuation is higher, but so is the price for the equity. The venture capitalist may increase its investments or bring in other investors.

- *Growth Stage:* Over the course of its development, the enterprise moves to the growth stage, wherein it grows its core operations. Depending upon the investors and company, the investors and managers of the firm may decide to pursue capital from the public markets through an initial public offering, after which ownership shares in the firm are traded in public equity capital markets.

- *Expansion Stage:* From growth, the enterprise moves to expansion wherein the company replicates its core operations and goes to scale. Some companies wait until this stage before tapping the public capital markets.

Patient Capital

From a financial perspective, NPOs do not technically have equity to offer investors in return for their capital. Financial equity speaks to issues of both ownership and financial returns/profit for the investor. For social enterprises, however, there is the potential to generate revenues and returns, and hence the ability to pay back the investor—if this is desired.

What is needed then, for NPOs and social enterprises, is a type of "patient capital" that not only may be offered as loans or quasi-equity on longer time frames than what is traditionally available, but also fits the growth needs and social objectives of social ventures.

Patient capital can be debt or equity based, but it is structured on terms that may suit social ventures better than traditional commercial investments. In the case of patient equity capital, financial returns for investors may be in the form of annual cash distributions together with the potential increasing value of the underlying organization. In the case of patient debt capital, the return may come in the form of principal payback over an extended time horizon together with a regular interest payment that is often below market rate.

Patient debt capital is being explored by an increasing number of social entrepreneurs operating enterprises that are nonprofit. One form gaining increasing attention is equity-like or quasi-equity capital.[18] Quasi-equity capital is debt, but it is structured on terms that include longer maturity periods and with greater risk exposure than a traditional loan might assume. When debt is positioned in this way, it takes on many of the characteristics of equity (longer investment terms of five or more years, and high risk exposure) and yet it retains the commitment to pay back principal with a fixed rate of return for the investor. The returns, while positive, would be below market rate, but can be structured to rise as revenue rises. Exit strategies include repayment, revenue royalties, warrants (convertible to equity at a predetermined future time), or "alternative public offerings."

This type of capital is typically provided by social investors such as foundations, governmental funding entities, or individual donors with a strong social motivation. They are willing to accept unconventional terms for their capital in exchange for the promise of scaling up the potential social impact of a social enterprise or NPO.

Venture Philanthropy

The last decade has seen the emergence of successful entrepreneurs who are applying venture capital-like approaches to their giving. Broadly classified under the umbrella of venture philanthropy, they are highly engaged with their investee organizations, providing development finance and extra-financial advice. Their financial support ranges from outright grants to loans and the new creative forms of quasi-equity covered above.[19]

Hybrid Social–Business Organizations

As an increasing number of organizations pursue their social mission through both for-profit and nonprofit structures, traditional legal structures have proven to be a challenge for the mobilization and issuance of capital to fund these organizations. Traditional structures do not reflect the reality that nonprofit ventures generate economic value for society, and that for-profit ventures can create social and environmental value.

As such, many social enterprises and their parent NPOs are generally created under multiple legal structures with the accompanying administrative burden and sometimes confusion over tax exemption status, unrelated business income tax issues, and ownership control.

There have been many calls to rectify this by creating legally recognized hybrid organizations that offer the promise of overcoming the limitations of an "either/or nonprofit/for-profit" legal structure. To their credit, the authorities in the US and UK have taken up the challenge to define new legal structures known variously as CIC, L3C, and Flexible Purpose Corporations, all of which are described in the box on "Hybrid Social–Business Organizations."[20]

While these innovations in corporate form and structure have been well received in some quarters of the social enterprise movement, others have raised questions regarding whether they divert attention from the central challenge of bringing new capital into social enterprises.[26] Some feel that the real issue is less one of legal restrictions than investor motivation and reticence to invest in social enterprises, regardless of form. No doubt, this debate will continue and only time will tell if the new structures do indeed attract new capital.

Hybrid Social–Business Organizations

Community Interest Company (CIC)[21]   The CIC was established by the UK government in 2005. The aim is to create an organization with the flexibility of a traditional for-profit, yet with the social mission of a nonprofit. CICs are "designed for social enterprises that want to use their profits and assets for the public good."

CICs have some special features to ensure they are working for the benefit of the community. The assets they own are secured to applications for the good use of the community, and there are limitations to dividend and interest payments made to shareholders and financiers.

Currently, over 3,400 firms in the UK have opted to register themselves under this new corporate form.

Low-profit Limited Liability Company (L3C)[22]   The CIC's American cousin, the L3C, is defined as "a form of limited liability company (LLC) and possesses many characteristics of a typical LLC." However, the primary purpose of the L3C is not to earn a profit, but to achieve a socially beneficial objective, with profit as a secondary goal. It is limited to a financial return on investment of 5 percent or less.

An L3C must be organized and operated at all times to "significantly further the accomplishment of one or more charitable or educational purposes," to not pursue the "production of income or the appreciation of property" as its significant purpose, and not be organized "to accomplish any political or legislative purposes."

Flexible Purpose Corporation[23]   The Flexible Purpose Corporation (formerly called the "H-Corp") is proposed by the California Working Group for New Corporate Forms as a modification to the General Corporation Law for the State of California.

The Flexible Purpose Corporation allows for the creation of for-profit companies created with the purpose of pursuing not only financial value for the firm, but also additional purposes. Such purposes could be "one or more charitable, or public purpose activities that could be carried out by a California nonprofit public benefit corporation." It should also promote positive effects or minimize adverse effects of the corporation's activities on its stakeholders, the community and society, or the environment.

It allows directors and managers to pursue "both/and" strategies of value creation within markets and communities. Investors in an H-Corp would know right up front that this is the intent and could project possible financial returns on their investments accordingly.

B-Corp[24]   While technically not a new legal or hybrid form of company, the B-Corp (the "B" standing for "For-Benefit") company is a for-profit company that integrates stakeholder accountability into its corporate charter. The name "B-Corp" is a trademarked brand which is awarded to companies that meet threshold requirements with regard to social and environmental practices.

B-Corp companies "meet comprehensive and transparent social and environmental performance standards, institutionalize stakeholder interests, [and] build collective voice through the power of a unifying brand."[25] Companies become certified as B-Corp (which they may then use on labels and in promotional activities) by completing a performance survey regarding social and environmental practices targeted to their industry or type of business.

Financial Innovations on the Horizon

As we assess how far social finance has evolved in recent years, outlining important trends and future innovations is a real challenge. Although it may seem the rhetoric still outpaces the actual creation of multibillion-dollar social capital markets, it is clear that new expectations and investment options will continue to drive meaningful financial innovation that leads to expanded impact. Specific areas of continuing innovation are moving faster than the printed word may document, yet there are domains in which transformations are taking place that deserve mention.

Capital Aggregation and Intermediation

Recent years have seen a pioneering movement of foundations and donors coming together behind high-impact organizations to structure and aggregate long-term philanthropic capital. This aggregated capital aims to fuel their continued growth and expansion, and can be invested into more than one organization.

In the US, groups such as The Edna McConnell Clark Foundation, New Profit Inc., SeaChange Management, The Nonprofit Finance Fund, and Growth Philanthropy Network have raised rounds of "growth capital" to support social enterprises in youth development, education, and other areas. For example, The Edna McConnell Clark Foundation led an effort to raise expansion capital through philanthropic investment by bringing together a pool of US$120 million in philanthropic funds to invest in three portfolio philanthropic investees.[27]

Such efforts to aggregate long-term growth capital for social organizations promise not only to offer the possibility of meaningful "exits" for early-stage donors, but also to help advance the creation of better-functioning capital markets for social entrepreneurs.

Mainstreaming of Integrated Investing Practices

The idea—much less the actual practice—of institutional investors integrating social and environmental factors into their investing practices had once seemed far-fetched. Yet today, numerous institutional investors are exploring the implications of global climate change, employment practices, corporate governance, sourcing practices, and other factors, in order to manage their financial assets more profitably. Increasingly, these considerations are not viewed as "nice to have" or an "add on," but rather as central to any sound execution of fiduciary responsibility.

These integrated approaches to mainstream investment continue to transform traditional capital markets, as they lay the seeds for greater receptivity by institutional investors to the notion of socially motivated capital. In the future, it will become increasingly possible for financially responsible and compelling social enterprises to identify and secure capital from new investment partners that was unavailable in previous decades.[28]

Mainstreaming of Impact Investing Products

Concurrently, a growing number of socially motivated capital providers are investing in an ever increasing pool of impact investing products and instruments—that is, the types of bonds, investment funds, and other capital vehicles described earlier in this chapter.

These early adapters create a track record of both learning and emerging successes upon which others may build, creating stepping stones upon which other investors begin to journey further into the realm of social finance. The efforts of these investors to design and allocate capital to microfinance bonds and sustainably managed timber funds, for example, have begun to cement the links between investing and philanthropy.

In the near future, several Impact Fund of Fund[29] ventures are expected to be launched in the US and Europe. These ventures will offer investors an array of options for allocating portfolio assets to impact investing. This trend will only continue to gain momentum and attract capital, to the benefit of both investors and social ventures.

Social Investment Exchanges and Secondary Markets

While the vision for creating a social stock exchange has certainly been with us for at least a decade,[30] it has only recently been that technology—combined with advancements in metrics, general reporting, and valuation—has enabled that vision to be realized.

The pioneers have been Brazil's Social and Environmental Stock Exchange in 2003, South Africa's Social Investment Exchange in 2006, and the Portuguese Social Stock Exchange in 2009. Similar exchanges will be created in the UK, Canada, and Kenya in 2010.[31] While the concept sounds exciting, there are challenges regarding attaining scale, maintaining viability, and accommodating the mindset of investors. The pioneering exchanges have been able to raise only very limited capital in their first few years of operation.

Other platforms, such as Mission Markets and Socential, will also offer commercial and social investors the opportunity to invest in social enterprises. In addition to these initiatives, sites such as MIX Market enable investors to identify and analyze microfinance institutions, while GlobalGiving and Kiva expand their efforts to link peer-to-peer donations to individual organizations seeking philanthropic investments.[32]

These initiatives are just the beginning of a wave of innovations taking place in direct impact investing and the development of secondary social markets. In essence, the participants in the social capital marketplace could exchange "social equity" through their social investment activities. It is too early to say what the results of these innovations will be; their promise is yet to be fully attained. However, it is clear there are rapidly changing approaches to facilitate the movement of funds from those seeking to invest wisely in the direction of those who are managing ventures that change the world.

The New Fiduciary Generation

The definition of what it means to be a responsible fiduciary is evolving both in the real-world marketplace and in business school classes on finance and capital markets. While it is easy to assume that the concept of fiduciary responsibility has been set in law for generations on end, the concept, and actual legal responsibilities, of fiduciaries have changed significantly with time.[33] Today's generation of fiduciaries oversee investment in bonds, stocks, real estate, even hedge funds, and private equity funds that were barely known 30 years ago.

While these changes have come with changes in market dynamics, investment strategies, and capital opportunities, there is also an evident generational difference in the approach to social investment and philanthropy. When compared to previous generations, today's Millennium Generation operates within a more integrated worldview rather than "making money now and giving it away later."

The majority of the youth live in the emerging markets or the developing world, where the implications of cultural and generational shifts are pronounced. British firm Barclays' wealth survey of donors under the age of 45 in the UK and the US found that they prefer giving through smaller, more nimble vehicles that will not outlast them. This new generation of giving is based on a model of "contract," rather than "donation," with a clear expectation of funds usage.[34]

This new "fiduciary generation" will continue to evolve in its understanding of fiduciary duties, bringing yet more opportunities for the allocation of capital with strategies that seek to link financial performance with social and environmental impacts.

Performance Metrics

A lack of standardized metrics continues to inhibit the capacity of investors to effectively manage their capital investments and define returns (whether social or financial). There are difficulties in shifting the frame of reference from a highly fragmented (commercial vs. social market) to one that is transparent and fully liquid. And a host of language, terminology, and practice issues will need to be explored—and resolved—if we are to advance beyond the present fragmentation of today's various market actors.

Generally speaking, small individual donations are often made without an expectation of formal reporting or documentation of impact; whereas at the institutional, grant level, most foundations require a more formal approach to reporting. George Overholser, who has written extensively on this issue, makes the point that "building an enterprise is fundamentally different than buying from an enterprise. And yet, standard nonprofit accounting sheds no light on the building versus buying distinction."[35]

A growing number of social organizations understand that documented performance and impact are critical to differentiating their work from other ventures in an increasingly complex ecosystem of organizations competing for limited resources.

This challenge of accountability for impact is not limited to those receiving charitable support, as funders and donors themselves are finding the public spotlight more frequently focused on them as well. The Center for Effective Philanthropy, Keystone Accountability for Social Change, and other organizations are applying a variety of stakeholder assessment tools to assist foundations and funders of various types in documenting their own impact and quality of effective charitable funding.[36]

Capitalizing on the New Markets

The capital market crisis of 2009 remains a central concern for all; yet, the global financial crisis and recession also offer an opportunity to reflect on the developments that affect the social capital markets.

While it is difficult to compare across asset classes and investment approaches, during the recent capital crisis period, many social investors saw their mission-related investments hold to a steady performance—often in the range of 4–7 percent. At the same time, many commercial market investments declined by 20–40 percent. Of course, all investors were affected in some way by the turmoil in the capital markets. However, when the actual performance of impact investments is considered together with returns from sustainable investment funds, the implications for traditional asset management and investing practices are clear. When considered together with innovations in venture philanthropy and the continued interest in bringing new financial instruments to market, it is realistic to assume that capital availability for social enterprises will continue to expand over the coming years.

Confronted with such developments and a new understanding of risk, return, and fiduciary duties, growing numbers of investors and asset owners will continue the drive to move capital into investments which deliver varying levels of financial return with social and environmental impacts. Sustainable investing within commercial markets, impact investing, and the growth of tactical philanthropy will continue to respond to the diverse needs of entrepreneurs for capital.

The future of social capital markets is uncertain and difficult to predict—but it is highly promising. For us to deliver on this promise, significant evolution among capital investors, citizen organizations, and social entrepreneurs must continue to take place. We should seek to rise above the orthodoxies of the past, look for the common elements of our work that link us, one to the other, and define both the uniqueness of each contributor and the common concepts that bind our future possibilities for success and advancement.

This is not the first time this call for collaborative action has been made,[37] but today we have a set of linked initiatives and capital that for the first time makes what was possible now probable. That is, if we have the vision to take the steps necessary to capture that possibility and truly become the change we seek.

Endnotes

1 Shari Berenbach, Laura Callanan, and Kevin Jones, "Defining a Common Language," a paper presented at SOCAP08 Conference, 2008.

2 Jed Emerson, "A Capital Idea: Total foundation asset management and the unified investment strategy," Research Paper Number 1786, Stanford Business School, January 2002, www.blendedvalue.org/media/pdf-capital-idea.pdf.

3　Presentation by Tim Freundlich of the Calvert Foundation for Social Investment at a forum on "Creating Social Capital Markets for Fourth Sector Organizations: Opportunities and challenges," sponsored by The Aspen Institute and the Fourth Sector Network, held on June 14, 2007 in New York City, www.fourthsector.net/attachments/13/original/Capital_Markets_June_2007_summary.pdf?1229660398.

4　For information on the Independent Sector's call for more general operating support grants, see www.independentsector.org/media/opsupportPR.html. For Grantmakers for Effective Organizations' report on the topic, see www.geofunders.org/generaloperatingsupport.aspx.

5　Lester Salamon, Wojciech Sokolowski and Associates, *Global Civil Society: Dimensions of the nonprofit sector, Volume Two* (Bloomfield, CT: Kumarian Press, 2004).

6　The subject of social enterprises is covered in Chapter 5, "Social Enterprises: Fulfilling the promise of social enterprise," by Jon Huggett.

7　A loan guarantee is a transaction where a third party (in this case, the foundation) agrees to sign a letter of commitment stating they will guarantee a loan between a lender and a borrower who might otherwise not qualify for a loan on their own.

8　www.mcenterprises.org.

9　"PRI Financing: Trends and statistics 2000–2001," *The PRI Directory, 2003 Edition*, The Foundation Center, 2003, www.foundationcenter.org/gainknowledge/research/pdf/03pri_ex.pdf.

10　"Answers to some frequently asked questions about PRIs," Ford Foundation Economic Development Unit, 1997, www.tgci.com/magazine/Answers%20to%20Some%20Frequently%20Asked%20Questions%20About%20PRIs.pdf.

11　Stephanie Strom, "Nonprofits Paying Price for Gamble on Finances," *New York Times*, September 24, 2009, www.nytimes.com/2009/09/24/us/24debt.html?_r=1.

12　William Baue, "First and Largest International Microfinance Bond Issued," *Sustainability Investment News*, August 2004, available on Social Funds website, www.socialfunds.com/news/article.cgi/1498.html.

13　This term was coined for this chapter. It was suggested by Patsian Low of Serenity Consulting, who helped me with the research for the chapter.

14　"International Finance Facility for Immunisation," GAVI Alliance, www.gavialliance.org/vision/policies/in_financing/iffim/index.php; "Financial Innovation and the Poor," *The Economist*, September 25, 2009, www.economist.com/PrinterFriendly.cfm?story_id=14493098; "Advance Market Commitments (AMCs)," GAVI Alliance, www.gavialliance.org/vision/policies/in_financing/amcs/index.php.

15　"Social Impact Bonds: Rethinking finance for social outcomes," *Social Finance*, August 2009, www.socialfinance.org.uk/downloads/SIB_report_web.pdf.

16　"Global Development Bonds," Energy Future Coalition, www.energyfuturecoalition.org/What-Were-Doing/Clean-Energy-Development/Global-Development-Bonds.

17　Michael Eckhart, "Global Development Bonds and SolarBank," a presentation at the Sustainable Energy Finance Roundtable on October 27, 2005 in New York, www.sefi.unep.org/fileadmin/media/sefi/docs/documentation_roundtable/Michael_Eckhart.pdf.

18 Laura Howard, *Equity-like Capital for Social Ventures* (London: Bridges Community Ventures, 2004).

19 The subject of venture philanthropy is covered more fully in Chapter 9, "Venture Philanthropy: Venturing into entrepreneurial philanthropy," by Rob John.

20 Kim Alter of Virtue Ventures has described a social–business hybrid spectrum of entities that call themselves social enterprises. This is covered in Chapter 5, "Social Enterprises: Fulfilling the promise of social enterprise," by Jon Huggett.

21 www.cicassociation.org.uk/what-is-a-cic; www.cicregulator.gov.uk.

22 "The L3C: Low-profit limited liability company research brief," Council Wealth Ventures, July 2008, www.cof.org/files/Documents/Conferences/LegislativeandRegulatory01 .pdf; "L3C—Developments & Resources," Nonprofit Law Blog, March 17, 2009, www .nonprofitlawblog.com/home/2009/03/l3c-developments-resources.html.

23 Nina Schuyler, "Corporate Conscience: Attorneys seek to create a new business structure," *California Lawyer*, www.callawyer.com/story.cfm?eid=906576&evid=1.

24 www.bcorporation.net.

25 Ibid.

26 In December 2009, a lively discussion facilitated by Lindsay Clinton was held on the website Social Edge, on the pros and cons of hybrid structures. This was debated over the course of several weeks. The discussion may be found at www.socialedge .org/discussions/business-models/the-social-and-commercial-two-step?utm_sourc e=Social+Edge+Newsletter&utm_campaign=d6a2034547-Newsletter_Haiti_Equity_ Mission1_19_2010&utm_medium=email.

27 Edna McConnell Clark Foundation, Capital Aggregation Project: www.emcf.org/how/ growthcapitalpilot/index.htm.

28 Further discussion of the role to be played by both sustainable investing funds and traditional investment managers can be found in Jed Emerson, "Beyond Good versus Evil: Hedge funds, sustainable investing and capital markets," Blended Value, December 2009, www.blendedvalue.org.

29 In commercial markets, investment firms will often bring a set of funds together under a single investment vehicle called a "fund of funds." Such a structure allows one to invest in a given investment strategy, yet diversify across a wider set of fund managers, thereby decreasing potential risk. In the social capital markets context, one can envision how a similar approach might be used to offer impact investors with both diversification and exposure to a wider set of potential social/environmental impacts.

30 Jed Emerson and Jay Wachowicz, "Riding the Bleeding Edge: A framework for tracking equity in the social sector and the creation of a nonprofit stock market," REDF Box Set, 2000, www.redf.org.

31 Brazil's Social and Environmental Stock Exchange (BVS&A), www.bovespasocial .org.br/institucional/home.aspx; South Africa's Social Investment Exchange (SASIX), www.sasix.co.za; Portuguese Social Stock Exchange, www.gulbenkian .pt/section154artId2022langId2.html; Canada—Green Stock Exchange, www.greensx .com; London Social Stock Exchange, http://rockpa.org/impactinvesting/profiles/social-stock-exchange/; and the Kenya Social Investment Exchange, www.ksix.or.ke.

32 Global Giving, www.globalgiving.org/; KIVA, www.kiva.org; MixMarket, www .mixmarket.org/mfi.

33 For an orientation to the evolution and current responsibilities of fiduciaries, see Jed Emerson, Timothy Little, and Jonas Kron, *The Prudent Trustee: The evolution of the long term investor* (Oakland: The Rose Foundation for Communities and the Environment, 2005), www.blendedvalue.org, as well as publications from the United Nations' Principles for Responsible Investing website at www.unpri.org.

34 "Philanthropy Matters," The Center on Philanthropy at Indiana University, 17(1), 2009, www.philanthropy.iupui.edu/philanthropymatters/doc/philanthropy_matters_ 17_1.pdf.

35 George M. Overholser, "Nonprofit Growth Capital: Part one," Nonprofit Finance Fund, www.nonprofitfinancefund.org/docs/Building%20is%20Not%20Buying.pdf.

36 Keystone: Accountability for social change, www.keystoneaccountability.org; Centre for Effective Philanthropy, www.effectivephilanthropy.org/index.php.

37 While many have consistently pointed to the opportunity for collaborative action across the silos, this author first built a body of work around this opportunity in 2003, with the publication of the Blended Value Map, and has since written extensively on the power of this possibility. See www.blendedvalue.org for various papers on this theme.

Macro-Trends

Chapter 19

Global Civil Society

Rallying for Real Change

KUMI NAIDOO

Executive Director, Greenpeace International

The world has many problems, but civil society is rising to deal with them. While most of these civil society organizations are local and national, a growing minority are international and making waves.

Global civil society has its own set of problems. Some of these issues are similar to those it champions against in governments and businesses: accountability, the rich/poor divide, and self-interest.

However, the reformers understand the need for reform and are responding to the challenges. Three pragmatic solutions can help drive global civil society toward its ideal: multilateral institutions that work, multi-stakeholder campaigns that foster solidarity, and capacity building for nongovernment organizations.

Humanity is grappling with a perfect storm of convergent crises—the implosion of the global financial system, the escalating poverty pandemic, the threats of terrorism, trafficking and organized crime, rising concerns over energy security, and climate change. While some crises have given rise to agendas that bring greater global solidarity, others remain complex challenges which deepen social inequality and widen the chasm between the developed and developing nations.

Governments and multilateral institutions have demonstrated mixed results at meeting the needs and expectations of their citizens, sometimes falling victim to self-interests and political agendas. As a result, civil society[1] has emerged as a contender to fill the global leadership vacuum.

Yet, despite active citizen mobilization, there is still a shortage of solutions that is commensurate with the urgency and scale of the global challenges we face. Granted, the civil society space is not all about good and positive action. It, too, is a rich space of personalities, power, and personal agendas. The challenge is to find the way through this maze and sift out the good movements from the passive and potentially negative ones. This challenge remains even as civil society grows.

The Rise of Global Civil Society

It is hard to deny the numbers.

Worldwide, the civil society space is home to more than three million[2] nongovernmental organizations (NGOs).[3] These NGOs are a diverse mix of causes, approaches, and organizational forms. They are focused on as many different areas as there are issues in society: the poor, the environment, refugees, etc. Their approaches to solving these issues range from providing solace and services to those in need, to advocating for changes in policies and the law. Their organizational forms vary depending upon jurisdictions and purpose. Some are based on broad membership (of individuals and/or organizations), while others are founded and controlled by small groups of individuals. Each has its own geographical focus.

The scale of NGO activity across the globe is significant and growing. The Johns Hopkins Comparative Nonprofit Sector Project estimated an expenditure of US$1.9 trillion by NGOs in just 40 countries and a total workforce that is 48.4 million strong.[4] It also found that the average annual growth of the nonprofit sector was greater than the growth of the home economy; in five countries it was nearly double.

Most NGOs are domestic and focus on work in their particular countries. A growing minority operates across several countries. Today, there are about 21,000 international NGOs, up from just 32 in 1874 and slightly over 1,000 in 1918.[5] The majority of these international NGOs came into being only in the last decade.

The participation rate in international civil society movements has been impressive. Two global environmental networks, the Worldwide Fund for Nature and Sierra Club, have a combined membership of six million, the size of some small countries. The World Social Forum, an annual gathering on global civil society collaboration and centered in Brazil, gathered 155,000 participants in one location in 2005.[6] In some years, the Forum has been organized around several concurrent sessions in various cities around the world.

Over the years, global civil society has become a rich amalgam of causes and motivations. It started with anti-colonialism and self-determination in the early 20th century. From the 1970s, its campaigning dimension became more prominent as issues of feminism, peace, and human rights took hold. With the post-Cold War euphoria of the 1990s, humanitarian support rose to the fore. At the beginning of the 21st century, many groups have risen to tackle the negative side effects of globalization.[7] As the world becomes increasingly interconnected, new waves of globalization-related issues (migrants, terrorism, fair trade, etc.) are rising. The work of global civil society is far from done.

The work to date has achieved some of its intended effects. Its many successful campaigns against governments for unfair trade treaties (e.g. the stoppage of the Multilateral Agreement on Investment by the Organization for Economic Co-operation and Development (OECD) countries in 1998) and undesirable corporate activities (e.g. Brent Spar's planned disposal of a floating oil storage facility at sea, and the exploitation of child labor by Nike sweatshops) have made global civil society a force to reckon with.[8]

However, NGOs are also collaborating actively with governments and corporations who are recognizing the value of NGOs. For example, official development assistance from the OECD countries is increasingly being channeled through NGOs; NGO funding from such aid grew from 4.5 percent of total official development assistance in 1989 to 14 percent within five years. Many international policies formulated by UN agencies are increasingly the result of consultation with international NGOs.

The consultative rate for the UN Economic and Social Council, for instance, saw an exponential jump from less than 500 organizations in 1995 to over 2,500 in 2007.[9]

Challenges of Global Civil Society

Optimism for what global civil society can achieve is high. Back in the 1990s, Jessica Matthews, President of the Carnegie Endowment for International Peace, summed it up by speaking of a "power shift" that would lead to an explosion of democracy, with non-state actors taking on an active role in shaping government policy.[10]

However, global civil society is not without its problems. It continues to live with the challenges of limited resources. It is usually working against established ideas and the establishment. It often depends on governments and enterprises for funding and support even as it seeks to change them.

The greatest challenges that global civil society faces are, however, those that it actively champions against in governments and enterprises: accountability, the rich/poor divide, and self-interests.

Accountability

NGOs are best known for their advocacy and watchdog role over governments and businesses, but they have also been heavily criticized for paying lip-service to governance, accountability, and transparency.

Business and government leaders have pointed out that it is hypocritical for NGOs to push for compulsory accountability frameworks while their own sector relies on voluntary codes. Further, they argue that unlike elected governments, who are ultimately accountable to the electorate, and business leaders, who are accountable to their shareholders, NGO leaders are mostly self-appointed "do gooders" who are not accountable to anyone other than themselves and thus have no legitimacy.

Even among civil society players, the issues of legitimacy and accountability are widely acknowledged. Some NGO actors opine that these issues are the underlying cause of most of the other challenges faced by the civil society sector.[11] Alan Fowler, a civil society veteran, observes that it is not uncommon to see a "self-perpetuating, self-selected set of directors or trustees" in NGOs.[12] Compound this with the lack of resources—some say, the will—to have a proper and audited set of detailed reporting on NGO spending, and it makes it hard for NGOs to hold their heads high while asking governments and enterprises to be accountable.

Indeed, critics of NGO accountability have not sat still. Interest groups, known for their links with the conservative political faction in the US, have set up NGOWatch to "encourage transparency and accountability" in the NGO world.[13] Another group, the NGO Monitor, questions the political neutrality of the NGOs who are working on the conflict grounds of Palestine and Israel. Yet another watch group, Keystone, opts for a more constructive approach by cultivating both donors and NGOs on meeting expectations and understanding the limitations of the other.[14]

In response to the criticisms, several NGO leaders came together in 2003 to begin work to establish the INGO Accountability Charter, which was launched in 2006. The Charter seeks to provide recognized standards for good governance, including excellence, accountability, and transparency. Unfortunately, it still has a long way to go with its list of only 70 signatories.[15]

Unlike enterprises and even governments, who have clear accountability to their shareholders and electorate, the situation is much more complex for NGOs. To start, NGOs are accountable to their cause, the communities and beneficiaries for which they exist to serve; what can be referred to as "downward" accountability. Yet, NGOs are also "upwardly" accountable for their use of resources to their funders (e.g. donors, governments, and corporations) whose agenda may not necessarily be aligned with that of the beneficiaries.[16]

The challenge for civil society is to ensure that NGOs are fully accountable to the communities they serve—especially the vulnerable and marginalized communities that tend to be physically and figuratively distant from decision-making processes. Yet, at the same time, they need to be pragmatic and "play the game" to ensure a continuous stream of funds.

There is also "horizontal" accountability: the relationship with other civil society actors, making sure that they too can function effectively for the wider cause. This cultivation of peers reflects civil society's desire to distinguish itself from the culture of competition that exists in the business sector. This is where the NGOs will seek to put in place participatory mechanisms relying on peer pressure to regulate their conduct and implementation.

To be sure, global civil society can do better at being accountable. At the same time, the complexities of its relationships with its diverse stakeholders and its agenda of fomenting change in many of these stakeholders make the balance of accountability to the different groups a delicate one.

The Rich/Poor Divide

NGOs tend to champion the poor and the disadvantaged. They fight to narrow the rich/poor divide. Yet, the inequalities and inequities of the haves and have-nots in global governance are mirrored in global civil society.

International NGOs from developed countries seek to work with and through domestic NGOs in developing countries. However, the developed countries' NGOs possess much greater resources and clout compared to their poorer domestic NGO cousins. It is an unequal relationship. It has created what Ezra Mbogori, a prominent African civil society leader from Kenya, calls "a new dependency syndrome" that is not unlike the paternalistic rule of the colonial years.[17]

International NGOs tend to get better treatment from governments and major donors. Where governments and large donors from developed countries channel their funding, they tend to do so through the international NGOs who are from the developed countries. Even the governments of the poor countries frequently offer preferential treatment to international NGOs (over local ones) as an incentive to invest in their country. This hinders the development of an autonomous, indigenous civil society within the developing countries.[18]

At the same time, the NGOs of developed countries do not just bring their resources; they also bring their values and agendas. Civil society observers have lamented the predominance of international NGOs that do not execute local agendas. This, in part, is the result of the surge in foreign aid in the 1990s and the channeling of that aid to either NGOs based in the developed countries or local NGOs that are more compliant with the professed agenda of Western governments.[19]

Much aid is often directed at developing the human potential in the developing countries. However, the benefit may not always stay in those countries. The opposite can happen. The brightest doctors, nurses, teachers, and professionals in poorer nations—not just those who have been trained with aid money—are attracted to work in developed countries, either for better pay or in response to developed nations' bids to promote inclusiveness. This leads to the unintended consequence of depriving developing nations of the talent and leaders they so desperately need. For example, there are more Malawian specialist doctors in Manchester, in the UK, than in Malawi, where there is a severe shortage with just one doctor for every 50,000 people.[20]

Recent civil society efforts around foreign aid are urging for a move from a cycle of dependency to an agenda of empowerment. Steve Tibbett, formerly of ActionAid, said that "[t]here should be less focus on increasing aid and more focus on how that aid is spent and on re-writing the rules." He argues that civil society is not responding in this manner, largely because it is reluctant to criticize foreign governments.[21]

Self-Interest

Ideally, civil society actors are motivated by doing good for others—the fulfilling and meaningful sense of selflessness.

In practice, NGOs cannot escape the flaws of the humans that run them. As an NGO grows, the ambitions of the organization and its leaders come into play, self-interest rears its ugly head, and the organization can drift away from its mission.

Consider the competition for scarce resources. While such a spirit of rivalry can keep NGOs on their feet, it can also lead to a situation where they fervently promote the interests of their own organization at the expense of the overall cause they are championing. For example, a report on 21 elephant conservationist NGOs in 10 countries observed that the jostling for funds and publicity by the larger international NGOs (as opposed to local NGOs) "resulted[ed] in a divided movement that is not making the best use of its assets."[22] Aggressive marketing has also led to a situation where "overstating impact is widespread,"[23] hindering further the real progress of NGO efforts.

The trend of NGOs partnering businesses and governments is a double-edged sword. The latter have their vested interests. For example, the subcontracting of corporate social and environmental programs by corporations to NGOs has been said to be a case of NGOs being used as publicity fronts to cover for the corporations who continue inflicting long-term strategic damage on society.[24] Similarly, several European Commission-funded NGOs, despite their professed autonomy, have been alleged to be promoting "political messages that are congenial to the Commission."[25]

NGOs have also been accused of being established by parochial secular interests to foment certain agendas while overtly championing another. For instance, the earliest NGOs operating in post-colonial environments tended to be faith-based organizations motivated by a paternalistic desire to improve the lot of poor communities and perhaps to assuage the guilt of colonial misdeeds. Development aid usually consisted of material assistance—food, shelter, and schools—but these tended to come with a price: religious indoctrination and teaching locals to do things "our way."[26] More contemporary forms of sectoral interests can be found in nationalist and trade lobby groups.

Groundswell for Change

Despite many difficulties, global civil society is responding to the issues and opportunities to be more effective. It is learning to play its role better in various spheres of influence while working hard to ensure that its foundations are firmly rooted in mutuality and solidarity.

Three pragmatic solutions can help achieve this idealism:

- Multilateral institutions that work
- Multi-stakeholder campaigns that foster solidarity
- Capacity building for NGOs.

Multilateral Institutions that Work

Coalitions of civil society groups are often the only channel for the voices of developing countries to be heard in multilateral negotiations. Just as no single country or region can solve global challenges on its own, no single social movement, trade union, or NGO can deliver global justice alone. The sooner we recognize that, the more effective civil society will be.

It is important that NGOs coordinate their activities so that their programs are not duplicated, contradictory, or incoherent, especially given that divisions on the part of civil society are likely to be exploited by state policy. This is an area where national, regional, and global associations of NGOs such as CIVICUS (World Alliance for Citizen Participation), the Arab NGO Network for Development, Bond (the UK body for NGOs working in international development), and Dóchas (the Irish Association of Non-Governmental Development Organisations) have a vital role to play.[27]

These multilateral institutions can help to improve connectivity in both campaigning and discourse between the various movements that seek to address interconnected issues such as trade justice, debt cancellation, and more and better aid. These different interest groups already cooperate to some degree, but fail to coordinate at the levels that could exponentially improve overall performance.

If a coordinated approach were taken whereby human rights, human development, and human security were considered as interdependent tenets, other innovative constructs may be devised. And when global civil society proves that it can lead the way in breaking down the patterns of inequality between rich and poor countries, perhaps governments will be moved to act with the urgency that is needed to promote a genuinely interdependent world with much greater equality. One such attempt is the Global Call to Action Against Poverty alliance, which was launched at the World Social Forum in 2005.[28] The alliance straddles both northern and southern civil society groups and includes trade unions, faith-based groups, NGOs, and social movements. Additionally, its agenda includes gender equality, peace, and development, and covers a range of sectoral interests such as education, health, water, and sanitation.

The African proverb, "I am because you are" might have been formulated in a village context to underscore that human beings realize their full humanity through relationships with others. Yet, in our increasingly globalizing world, "I am because you are" is just as important and valid.

Multi-Stakeholder Campaigns that Foster Solidarity

The establishment of the Millennium Development Goals at the UN Millennium Summit in September 2000 was not without its critics—yet, it has become the rallying point and official forum for the disparate civic efforts on common issues to come together. The eight Millennium Development Goals have since sparked an unprecedented groundswell of attention at multiple levels, including innovations in social solutions and philanthropy across public and private sectors.[29]

One such common agenda is the eradication of poverty. The global financial crisis had affected people across many sectors of society, demonstrating all too clearly that citizens in rich and poor countries have much more in common than they thought. People have lost their jobs, homes, and pension funds, creating an urgent need for a system that is governed by equitable institutions accountable to the people.

The other uniting agenda is the threat of climate change, the impact of which cannot be underestimated. Past precedents tell us why. In the early 1990s, civil society groups promoted a global campaign against landmines, leading to the Landmines Treaty being adopted in Ottawa in 1997. In 2004, a coalition of Bulgarian civil society actors succeeded in getting the subject of fighting corruption incorporated into the curricula of Bulgarian secondary schools.[30]

Global civil society's access to global policy making has never been higher, considering its voice in global issues such as climate change and poverty alleviation. Although access does not always lead to influence, global governance bodies have recognized the role and significance of civil society. This was demonstrated by the rallies of the Global Call to Action against Poverty movement in October 2009, when more than 173 million people gathered at over 3,000 events in 120 countries, demanding that their governments "Stand Up, Take Action, End Poverty Now!" This set a world record for the largest mobilization of civil society in history and helped breathe life into the UN Millennium Development Goals.[31]

From within their national borders, civil societies in the developed world can do their part to shake any unsustainable policy practices at the global governance level. For example, they could promote lifestyle change to combat climate catastrophe, and further civil liberties, human rights legislation, and freedoms of association. Next, it is critical to spread the message far, wide, and deep among the ordinary citizens. For it is only through their vote that their country's negative and outmoded foreign policy decisions can be pressured to change.

Capacity Building for NGOs

In order to create real global partnerships, global civil society can do much more to promote mutual accountability, knowledge transfer, and two-way learning, to build up the capacity of NGOs.

In the Netherlands, Oxfam Novib has asked community leaders from developing countries to share their expertise with Dutch civil society groups working with marginalized and vulnerable communities in Holland. People in richer countries with stronger democratic traditions can learn from, as well as benefit, those from developing countries or those with weaker democratic traditions. Some in the NGO community in developing countries have established codes of conduct that have predated similar efforts in developed countries. For instance, SANGOCO, the South African NGO Coalition, adopted a code of ethical conduct in 1997. In Europe, a similar effort, albeit on a larger scale, is underway to urge the nonprofit organizations to self-regulate based on a set of transparency and accountability guidelines. We have seen some positive movements recently where, for example, the Council on Foundations in the US and the European Foundation Centre developed a set of standards that seek to enhance the grantmaking work of their members and, in so doing, to foster greater accountability to their grantees.

Conversely, NGOs from the developed world need to redress the imbalances in global power structures and facilitate the participation of NGOs from the developing world in the international arena. This will legitimize the efforts of NGOs from developed countries working in developing countries. It will also help empower the latter's civil society to have greater ownership over agendas, resources, and budget allocation to local authorities, communities, and organizations.

Leadership in the developing world's civil society will be strengthened, especially if it is supported by a rigorous process of self-evaluation that leads to stronger levels of trust while tackling problems of corruption and mismanagement. Similarly, civil society in the developing world needs to be committed to a robust framework to gain the support of its local citizens and to counter the corrupt elements in their own countries. Only then will the NGO voice be taken seriously in international forums.

There are already many positive examples of how civil society groups are working together more closely to build capacity. The OSANGO (Organizational Self-Audit for NGOs) tool developed by NGOs in South Asia and Latin America has been a positive step forward in building up an internal organizational culture that promotes the effectiveness of NGOs in achieving their mission.[32]

Real Change

In a global system that has been found wanting, people look to civil society for support and balance. This places a noble yet heavy responsibility on the shoulders of civic organizations. Yet, this weight may prove to be too much for some NGOs that succumb to self-interest and power.

A revolution is in order. The reformers need to be willing to be reformed. History and experience have taught the world that where social justice and equity is most wanting, the scene is most fertile for change. A never-before-seen groundswell of civic awareness and activism is now rising to the challenge.

But it is not seeking to topple an order. It is seeking rational and compassionate partners to set the system straight and it is sincere in setting itself right first.

Endnotes

1   The term "civil society"is used in this chapter to refer to the collection of nongovernment organizations (NGOs), trade unions, faith-based organizations, and other civic entities that are neither part of the market nor part of the state that are found in virtually every country. The term "global civil society" refers to the collection of these organizations across the world, including civic groups that operate within country boundaries as well as the international groups that operate across countries.

2   There are no official statistics on the worldwide number of NGOs. Estimates have ranged from 3 million to 10 million: (1) In "Civil Society—The third global power," *Info3*, 2001, the President of the Center for Alternative Development, Nicanor Perlas, estimates that there are over 3 million NGOs. (2) There are 8 million .org registrations in the Public Interest Registry, not taking into account the number of .net and .edu registrations, which could be NGOs. We should also bear in mind that there will be .org registrations which are not purely NGOs, www.pir.org/news/pr/2010/25years. (3) Author Dr. Timothy Schwartz mentions 10 million NGOs in his blog, "How to save the NGO sector from itself," http://open.salon.com/blog/timotuck/2010/03/10/part_i_how_to_save_the_ngo_sector_from_itself#_edn15.

3   The terms "nongovernmental organizations," "nonprofit organizations," and "civil society organizations" are often used interchangeably and while this chapter has focused on NGOs, it is important to note that NGOs are part of a much larger rubric, as described in endnote 1.

4   The figures of 48 million people and US$1.9 trillion budget are for an aggregate of 40 countries and are taken from a 2008 presentation made by Lester Salamon based on the Johns Hopkins Comparative Nonprofit Sector Project, a study of nonprofit activity across some 46 countries. Current information and data on the Johns Hopkins study is available online at www.ccss.jhu.edu/index.php?section=content&view=9&sub=3. The latest book summarizing the results of the study is: Lester M. Salamon, S. Wojciech Sokolowski and Associates, *Global Civil Society: Dimensions of the nonprofit sector, Volume Two* (Bloomfield, CT: Kumarian Press, 2004). Volumes One and Two of the publication deal with separate countries covered in the ongoing study.

5   Data for 1918 and 1874 can be found in Charles Chatfield, "Intergovernmental and Non-governmental Associations to 1945," *Transnational Social Movements and Global Politics* (New York: Syracuse University Press, 1997); "Data Programme—Union of International Associations, 2008/2009," *Global Civil Society 2009* (London: Sage Publications, 2009). *Yearbook of International Organizations 1998/99* (Brussels: Union of International Associations, 1998). According to this report, less than 10 percent of the transborder civic associations active in 1998 were more than 40 years old.

6   Francisco Whitaker, Boaventura de Sousa Santos, and Bernard Cassen, "The World Social Forum: Where do we stand and where are we going?" *Global Civil Society Yearbook 2005/2006* (London: Sage Publications, 2005).

7   Mary Kaldor, "Civil Society and Accountability," *Journal of Human Development*, 4(1), 2003.

8   Multilateral Agreement on Investment, www.oecd.org/document/22/0,3343,en_2649_33783766_1894819_1_1_1_1,00.html; Brent Spar, www.greenpeace.org/international/en/about/history/the-brent-spar/; Nike, http://depts.washington.edu/ccce/polcommcampaigns/Nike.htm, http://www.globalexchange.org/campaigns/sweatshops/nike/.

9   "Numbers of NGOs with Consultative Status with UN Economic and Social Council (ECOSOC) 1946–2007," *Global Civil Society 2009* (London: Sage Publications, 2009).

10 Jessica Mathews, "Power Shift," *Foreign Affairs*, 76(1), 1997.

11 Finn Heinrich, Jacob M. Mati, and L. David Brown, "The Varying Contexts for Civil Society Accountability: Insights from a global analysis of country-level assessments," *Civicus Global Survey of the State of Civil Society, Volume 2* (Bloomfield, CT: Kumarian Press, 2008).

12 Alan Fowler, *Civil Society, NGDOs and Social Development* (Geneva: United Nations Research Institute for Social Development, 2000).

13 Initiated by the American Enterprise Institute and the Federalist Society, NGOWatch has been closely tied to the agenda of the George W. Bush administration, www.globalgovernancewatch.org/ngo_watch.

14 NGOWatch, www.globalgovernancewatch.org/ngo_watch/; NGO Monitor, www.ngo-monitor.org; Keystone, www.keystoneaccountability.org.

15 www.ingoaccountabilitycharter.org.

16 I made this point in an address at the UN headquarters in New York on April 3, 2003, www.lse.ac.uk/Depts/global/Publications/PublicationsProfKaldor/CivilSocietyandAccountabilitybyMaryKaldor.pdf.

17 "Building Upon Community Assets Using the Community Foundation Model with Case Examples from Zimbabwe and Puerto Rico," Workshop Proceedings by Community Foundation for the Western Region of Zimbabwe and Synergos, November 10, 2000, www.synergos.org/knowledge/00/commassets.pdf.

18 For a fuller reading of the NGO–government relationship, please refer to Catherine Agg, *Trends in Government Support for Non-Governmental Organizations: Is the "Golden Age" of NGOS behind us?* (Geneva: United Nations Research Institute for Social Development, 2006).

19 Michael Edwards, *Civil Society* (Cambridge: Polity Press, 2004).

20 Judith Robertson, Head of Oxfam in Scotland, which has a specialized focus on Scotland, quoted in Eddie Barnes, "Big Chief Jack and Real Story of Malawi," *Scotland on Sunday*, May 29, 2005, http://scotlandonsunday.scotsman.com/famineinafrica/Big-chief-Jack-and-the.2630690.jp.

21 Kumi Naidoo, *Global Civil Society: The role of UK civil society in a rapidly globalising world* (London: Carnegie UK Trust, 2010). Available at http://democracy.carnegieuktrust.org.uk/civil_society/publications/global_civil_society__the_role_of_uk_civil_society_in_a_rapidly_globalising_world.

22 Paul Jepson and Susan Canney, *The State of Wild Asian Elephant Conservation: An independent audit for elephant family* (London, Oxford: Elephant Family, Conservation Direct, 2003).

23 Mary Kaldor, "Civil Society and Accountability," *Journal of Human Development*, 4(1), 2003.

24 For a more detailed explanation of this trend, refer to Mary Kaldor, ibid.

25 "A Rigged Dialogue with Civil Society—Charlemagne," *The Economist*, October 23, 2004.

26   Farah Stockman, Michael Cranish, Peter Canellos, and Kevin Baron, "Part 1: Bush "Brings Faith to Foreign Aid," *The Boston Globe*, October 8, 2006; Michael Kranish, "Part 2: Religious Right Wields Clout," *The Boston Globe*, October 9, 2006.

27   CIVICUS, www.civicus.org; Arab NGO Network for Development, www.annd.org/new/annd/index.php: Bond, www.bond.org.uk; Dóchas, www.dochas.ie.

28   www.whiteband.org.

29   United Nations Millennium Development Goals, www.un.org/millenniumgoals/bkgd .shtml.

30   Ottawa Treaty, www.clearlandmines.com/Ottawa_Treaty.cfm; Coalition 2000, www .anticorruption.bg/index.php?id=785.

31   "Press Info," CGAP, October 21, 2010, www.whiteband.org/media/press-info/world-record-shattered-by-citizens-across-globe-demanding-that-their-leaders-end-poverty.

32   www.osango.org/latinoamerica/index.htm.

Chapter 20

Social Innovation

Stepping on the Accelerator
of Social Change

GEOFF MULGAN
Director, The Young Foundation

The results of social innovation—new ideas that meet unmet social needs—are all around us. They include fair trade, open source software, restorative justice, distance learning, and microfinance.

Innovation is not just a matter of luck or inspiration. It can, and should, be managed, supported, and nurtured. There are hundreds of methods and tools for innovation, from developing the ideas to creating impact, some overlapping with those used in fields such as business and science, and some very different. These methods and tools can be grouped into a framework of six stages of social innovation.

More significantly, there is an increasing focus on accelerating social innovation through the development of a social innovation field, the creation of dedicated social innovation incubators and intermediaries, the emergence of "social Silicon Valleys" (districts dedicated to social innovation), and increasing cross-sector collaboration. Such acceleration of the accelerator of social change is needed in a world where there is a wide gap between the scale of the problems and the solutions offered.

Much of what we take for granted today in social policy and service delivery began as radical innovation, or as promising ideas and unproven possibilities. For instance, the idea of a freely available national health service was initially seen as a utopian dream; today, it is available in many countries around the world.[1] Examples of other social innovations that have improved lives include the creation of trade unions, cooperatives, collective insurance, and kindergartens.

Economists reckon that 60–80 percent of economic growth comes from innovation and new knowledge.[2] Social innovation is a part of this and it will be increasingly important for economic growth. Some of the barriers to lasting economic growth (such as climate change and aging populations) can only be solved with social innovation. There is also rising demand in many countries for economic growth to be reshaped so that it contributes better to social progress and human development.

Yet, surprisingly, little is known about social innovation compared to the vast amount of research into innovation in business and science. While insights gained into business innovation can be relevant to the social field, there are also important differences such as motives, resources, patterns of growth, and success criteria. Only in recent years has there been focused research that seeks to understand the engine of social innovation: its character, patterns of growth, and the methods for advancing social innovation.

Checking out the Social Innovation Engine

One starting point for a better understanding of social innovation is to have a clearer definition. There exist many views and definitions of what constitutes social innovation.[3]

In simple terms, social innovation refers to new ideas that meet unmet social needs. But the phrase is also used to refer to the tools used to meet these needs, to distinguish it from the development of a new pharmaceutical drug or a cheap car that meets needs. Given the many competing definitions, a simple definition for our purpose would be that social innovations are innovations that are social in both their ends and their means. In other words, not only do they meet needs more effectively than alternatives, but also leave behind a stronger capacity for cooperation and social action.

Distinguishing Social Innovation

What constitutes social innovation may be more readily understood by distinguishing it from similar but different concepts. Innovation overlaps with improvement and change but is not synonymous with them. Some innovations based on new insights can be incremental (building on what went before), while others are radical (providing entirely new models for thinking and doing). Radical innovations can be disruptive and generative in that they disrupt patterns of production, consumption, and distribution while generating further ideas and innovations (such as the move to a low-carbon economy or the creation of a preventative system of criminal justice).

Innovation is also different from creativity and invention, which are vital to innovation, but miss out the hard work of implementation and diffusion that makes promising ideas useful.

Social innovation should also be distinguished from business innovation, which is generally motivated by profit maximization and diffuses through organizations that are predominantly profit maximizing, even though many business innovations will meet the test of being socially beneficial. For instance, although the Google search engine has arguably created more value for society than the value that has accrued to its founders and shareholders, it would not count as a social innovation.

Social innovation is often mentioned in the same breath as social enterprise and social entrepreneurship. But there are key differences. Social innovation goes beyond the enterprise approach of social enterprises by embracing alternative models of implementation. It also goes beyond the individual social entrepreneur in order to address systemic change that is needed in many fields of social change. Some social enterprises and social entrepreneurs are both entrepreneurial and innovative, but many are not.

Recognizing Social Innovations

The 19th century German philosopher Arthur Schopenhauer pointed out that "all truth passes through three stages. First, it is ridiculed. Second, it is violently opposed. Third, it is accepted as being self-evident." In the same way, many social innovations may not be recognized as such because we now take them for granted, yet their benefits are all around us.

Over the last two centuries, innumerable social innovations—from distance learning to Wikipedia—have moved from the margins of society into the mainstream. Figure 20.1 provides of a list of what I would consider to be the 10 world-changing innovations of the last century.

Figure 20.1 Ten World-Changing Social Innovations

1. **The Open University** and the many models of distance learning that have opened up formal education across the world and are continuing to do so.

2. **Fair trade**—pioneered in the UK and the US in the 1970s and 1980s, and now growing globally.

3. **Greenpeace** (originating in Canada) and the many movements of ecological direct action that drew on much older Quaker ideas and which have transformed how citizens can engage directly in social change.

4. **Grameen**—alongside BRAC, Asa, and others whose new models of village- and community-based microcredit have been emulated worldwide.

5. **Amnesty International** and the growth of human rights.

6. **Oxfam**, Médecins Sans Frontières, and the spread of humanitarian relief.

7. **The Women's Institute** (founded in Canada in the 1890s) and the innumerable women's organizations and innovations that have made feminism mainstream.

8. **Linux software** (originating in Finland) and other open source methods such as Wikipedia and OhmyNews that are transforming many fields.

9. **NHS Direct** and the many organizations, such as the Expert Patients Programme, that have opened up access to health, and knowledge about health, to ordinary people.

10. **Participatory budgeting models** of the kind pioneered in Porto Alegre in Brazil and now being emulated, alongside a broad range of democratic innovations, all over the world.

Source: Geoff Mulgan et al., *Social Innovation: What it is, why it matters and how it can be accelerated* (Oxford: Saïd Business School, 2007).

Sources of Social Innovation

Social innovation is sometimes understood as resulting from the work of heroic individuals such as Robert Owen (cooperatives) or Muhammad Yunus (microfinance).[4] However, detailed studies of particular innovations usually show that many people were involved and that similar ideas spring up from different places at the same time. Most social innovations are better understood as the result of broader movements of change, such as feminism or environmentalism. Individuals play their part, but an overemphasis on them can be misleading. Innovations could also come from organizations, but not just from new organizations. Many come from existing organizations learning to renew themselves. The internet came from the military and the Defense Advanced Research Projects Agency, and the early understanding of climate change came from the US National Aeronautics and Space Administration (NASA).

A common feature of social innovation is that it is rarely either wholly top down or bottom up. Promising ideas need to find support at some point from people with money or power. The support that is needed to make an idea happen includes the passion and commitment of other people, the money of patrons or the state, and contracts or consumers.

Indeed, major social change depends on alliances between the top and the bottom, between what could be called the "bees" and the "trees." The bees are the small organizations, individuals, and groups who have new ideas, and are mobile, quick, and able to cross-pollinate. The trees are the big organizations—governments, companies, or big nongovernment organizations (NGOs)—which may be poor at creativity but have the power, money, and resilience to make things happen at scale.

Undertaking the Social Innovation Journey

Innovation is not just a matter of luck or eureka moments. Nor is it exclusively the province of brilliant individuals or great organizations. Innovation can, and should, be nurtured, supported, and managed. Anyone, if they want, can play a part.

A recent research project by the Young Foundation identified over 500 methods being used for social innovation around the world.[5] They range from ways of thinking, to very practical tools for finance or design. Some of these methods are specific to sectors—government, business, or charity. Some are specific to national cultures. But there are many patterns in common.

These methods can be grouped and organized into six stages of social innovation, as shown in Figure 20.2.

Figure 20.2 The Process of Social Innovation

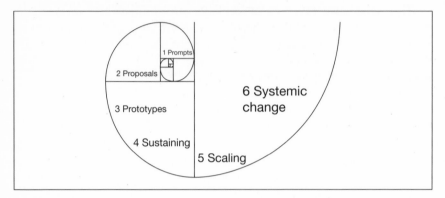

The diagram shows a linear model for social innovation from ideas to impact. It starts with prompts, moving through proposals to prototypes that then become sustained and scaled.

This framework is useful for thinking more rigorously about methods. Some innovations do develop in this way. But many do not develop in such a linear fashion. Some go quickly to scale—and then have to adapt quickly in the light of experience. Often the end use of innovation can be different from the one that was originally envisaged. Some innovations may evolve as solutions in search of problems. And always there is an iterative circling back as new insights change the nature of the innovation.

Nevertheless, these processes do indicate a trend in the development of an innovation. Hopefully, the spiral model provides a common language for thinking about how to support innovation more systematically.

A brief summary of the many methods used in each stage of development follows.

Prompts, Inspirations, and Diagnosis

The early stages of innovation involve creative leaps, new combinations of existing ideas and processes, and pressures to change. The triggers and prompts that lead to innovation vary from awareness of a need, to a crisis. But at the heart of many innovations is an idea that is both inspiring and backed by a compelling narrative about needs and possibilities.

Crises can trigger organizations to organize the prompts through research, engagement with the public, using crises creatively, and looking at the demand on resources caused by the failure.

Social science is another prompt. New knowledge—for example, the impact of parental support of a child's first three years on its future development—can spur social innovation, just as social science methods can be used to evaluate what works.

This stage also involves diagnosing the problem and framing the question in such a way that the root causes of the problem, not just its symptoms, will be tackled. Framing the right question is halfway toward finding the right solution. This means going beyond symptoms to identify the causes of a particular problem.

Proposals and Ideas

This is the stage of idea generation. Ideas come from many sources: users, citizens, communities and groups, other sectors, and even other countries.

There are many methods for developing more creative and powerful ideas. They include competitions such as reward-based contests (e.g. X PRIZE); open source soliciting of ideas for strategy, projects, and grantees (e.g. Ashoka's Changemakers); brainstorming approaches such as Thinkathon (which involves up to 10,000 people at a time); and the use of the community to solve problems (e.g. crowd sourcing).[6]

There are then many methods for choosing which ideas or innovations show most promise. They range from public voting (online or otherwise) and expert panels, to estimates of impact. At this stage, judgment is more of an art than a science; there will only rarely be any reliable data.

Prototypes and Tests

Once a promising idea has been picked, it then needs to be tested in practice.

There are many ways to test ideas. They range from simply trying things out, to formal pilots, prototypes, and randomized control trials.

Social entrepreneurs often dive into practice and hope to learn quickly without using formal evaluations or tests. A common theme of contemporary social innovation is that it often works best by moving quickly into practice, rather than spending too long developing detailed plans and strategies.

But testing and refining ideas is particularly important in the social economy because it is through iteration, and trial and error, that coalitions gather strength and conflicts are resolved. It is also through these processes that measures of success come to be agreed on and the ideas properly evaluated.

Sustaining

After testing, the next issue is how an idea can be sustained and put into everyday practice.

It often involves sharpening ideas, streamlining them, and identifying the organizational structure and income streams to ensure the long-term financial sustainability of the project or organization that will carry the innovation forward.

A wide range of financial tools is available at these early stages. These include grants, convertible loans, quasi-equity, prizes, direct commissions, and tendering.[7] The idea can then be sustained by embedding it in policy, public programs, a business model, or a venture.

Whatever the sector, there are critical decisions to be made about organizational form, governance, and accountability for sustaining an innovation. Is the new model best run by an existing agency, or does it need a new home to instill a distinctive culture? These decisions are critical not only for sustaining the innovation, but for moving it to the next stage of growing and spreading the innovation.

Scaling and Diffusion

There are many strategies for growing and spreading an innovation; they include organizational growth, licensing and franchising to federations, and looser diffusion.

Some of these strategies involve scaling, which means progressively, sometimes exponentially, increasing the level of activity and impact from one form. Other methods are better understood as more organic along the lines of a "cut and graft" model with ideas adapting as they spread, rather than growing in a single form.

Growing an innovation depends on effective supply and demand.

Effective demand refers to the willingness to pay; it is evidence that the innovation really works. To grow effective demand, there may be a need for diffusion through advocacy, raising awareness, and campaigning for change. Advocacy is key to creating a demand for services, particularly from public authorities: for example, making the case for public funding for drugs treatment or sex education.

Effective supply refers to the ability to provide the innovation at the right price point. Methods for effective supply include investment in evaluations and research data to demonstrate effectiveness and value for money, as well as adapting models to reduce costs or improve effectiveness.

As demand and supply come together, the options include organization growth, brand development, licensing, franchising, and federations. A good example of an organization that is able to achieve scale through a simple model at very low cost and with no assets is Pratham.[8] An NGO which seeks to provide quality education to underprivileged children in India, Pratham is able to reach millions of children through a range of interventions by relying largely on mobilizing corporate, public, community, and philanthropic support, as well as the Indian diaspora.

Systemic Change

Systemic change is the ultimate goal of social innovation.

Systemic change usually involves the interaction of many elements: social movements, business models, laws and regulations, data and infrastructures, and entirely new ways of thinking and doing.

Systemic change generally involves new frameworks made up of many smaller innovations. A car, for example, combines innovative modules such as engines, electronics, and materials, but it also needs a surrounding system of traffic management and regulation.

Systemic innovation commonly involves changes in all four sectors—the public sector, private sector, grant economy, and household sector—over long periods of time. It is a slow, cumulative process of change entailing changing infrastructures, behaviors, and cultures. By its nature, it is highly social, usually involving many leaders, many allies, and battles on many fronts. At this stage the individual hero story of social entrepreneurship is most misleading—success has many parents.

Strategies for systemic innovation include the formation of progressive coalitions; building up shared diagnoses and visions; growing a critical mass of demonstrated success; pre-empting inflexible conventional technologies that freeze disruptive forms of innovation; and accessing professional and other expertise for the contest of evidence.

Accelerating Social Innovation

The various methods of social innovation summarized above seek to speed up the process of social change. The ultimate goal is to accelerate the process of change so as to achieve systemic change—and better lives.

The last two decades have seen some focus on accelerating the process and results of social innovation itself; other words, accelerating the accelerator of social change. This has come about in several ways:

- The development of a social innovation industry
- The creation of dedicated social innovation incubators
- The emergence of social Silicon Valleys
- Increasing cross-sector collaboration.

The Social Innovation Industry

Social innovators, be they individuals or organizations, have existed for centuries. What is new in recent decades is the entry of players who are focused on understanding and developing the field.

Many of these are NGOs, such as the Young Foundation and the Lien Centre for Social Innovation. There are also public bodies, such as the NHS Institute for Innovation and Improvement in the UK. Some, such as the Stanford Center for Social Innovation, are driven entirely by academia. There is now even an innovation university: Finland's new Aalto University was launched in 2009 following the merger of the Technical University, the Business School, and the School of Arts and Design.[9]

With the emergence of more and more individuals and organizations who are dedicated to researching, educating, and fostering social innovation, the take-up of social innovation by other players in the social sector will be enhanced and accelerated.

The industry of social innovation is vibrant and growing. Many of the players have come together in the Social Innovation Exchange (SIX),[10] a global community of over 1,000 individuals and organizations who are committed to the cause of social innovation while growing its capacity. SIX was instigated by the Young Foundation but is governed by a group of global partners. It is an active network of people who come together virtually and physically for mutual learning and undertake joint initiatives, such as the planned establishment of the Global Academy for Social Innovation.

The interest created by the social innovation industry has led governments and grantmakers to provide funding and to create initiatives and programs that contribute to the industry, and to foster social innovations. There are, for example, new public programs, such as the nearly €4 billion (US$4.9 billion) EQUAL program in Europe, the £200 million (US$293 million) health innovation funds in the UK, and the nearly US$1 billion education innovation fund in the US to accelerate the development of higher impact models in public services.[11] Foundations have also provided funding for socially innovative projects. Examples include Case Foundation's public grants program on citizen engagement and the Nevada Community Foundation's flexible grants for community programs.[12] Foundations, governments, and nonprofits have also sought to spur the best of social innovation ideas through creating and funding competitions such as the X PRIZE, the Global Giveback Innovation Challenge, and NESTA's Innovation Challenges for Health and the Environment.[13]

Social Innovation Incubators

With the increased interest in social innovation, there is growing support for individual social entrepreneurs and nonprofits. Much of this takes the form of funding support, education, and limited assistance from grantmakers and academically-linked institutions such as the Skoll Centre for Social Entrepreneurship at Saïd Business School in Oxford.

Following the trend of the many incubators targeted at commercial start-ups, especially technology start-ups in the wake of the dot-com boom, there are now, increasingly, incubators of social ventures which provide funding, mentoring, and hands-on implementation support for new ideas. Examples include Social Fusion for social enterprises, the CAN mezzanine, and the worldwide The Hub.[14]

The Young Foundation's Launchpad program aims to take incubation a step further by taking a more active role in the identification of needs and the design of new organizations. From their incubation to launch, the program has maintained a focus on ideas that have the potential to be scaled up.[15] By 2010, Launchpad had nurtured many dozens of new social ventures such as new schools (Studio Schools), online ventures such as the School of Everything, radical new models for health care such as Neuroresponse for people suffering from multiple sclerosis, and new models of apprenticeship such as Working Rite. These ventures have generated far more investment—and nonfinancial resources.

MaRS, in Toronto, is an example of a nonprofit innovation center that links a business incubator, a university, and a hospital alongside a social innovation investment fund. They connect science, technology, and social entrepreneurs, and accelerate the creation and growth of successful Canadian enterprises.[16]

Social Silicon Valleys

In time, the social innovation industry will be at a stage where there will be a cluster of related institutions that are co-located, and that leverage and synergize with each other to mobilize resources and energies to tackle social problems. This will hopefully be comparable to the investments in technology made in Silicon Valley and its equivalents around the world.

The formation of these social Silicon Valleys will require major changes in how governments, foundations, civic organizations, and businesses strategize and prioritize creative connections and institutions that cut across boundaries.

Already, discussions are underway on the creation of social Silicon Valleys in Australia, New Zealand, Portugal, and Spain. The first is likely to be in Bilbao.[17] Called the Social Innovation Park, it will be a business park dedicated to innovation for the social sector and will house, among other facilities, three major resource centers:

- The Social Innovation Laboratory (G-Lab) to identify and conduct research on emerging social tendencies
- The Social Innovation Academy to provide onsite and online training to nonprofits and enterprises
- The Social Innovation Generator to incubate new social enterprises and to launch new projects based on the research work of G-Lab.

The Park is expected to house more than 50 national and international organizations. It is supported by national and local authorities with an initial budget of €6 million (US$7.3 million) and it will eventually cover some 775,000 square feet. Operations are expected to begin in 2011.

Cross-Sector Collaboration

Social innovation used to be considered the sole preserve of the nonprofit sector, or what we could call the grant economy. But more recent studies emphasize that it takes place in all sectors—ranging from the private market and the public sector to the nonprofit sector and ordinary households—and that particular innovations often move between sectors as they evolve.

The private market is responsible for ethical finance, corporate social responsibility, or new models of collaborative business. The public sector drives new policies and service models. Meanwhile, the household plays a critical role in the creation of social movements such as the Slow Food movement[18] or disability rights.

Each sector has different goals, institutional forms, and economic models. However, each is united by its focus on social goals and by the emphasis on ethics, social inclusion, empowerment, and solidarity. This is all the more significant given that the biggest economic segments are likely to be social ones, including health care, education, and environmental services.

The shaded area in Figure 20.3 represents those parts of the four sectors that are concerned with social innovation.

Figure 20.3 Social Innovation across the Four Sectors

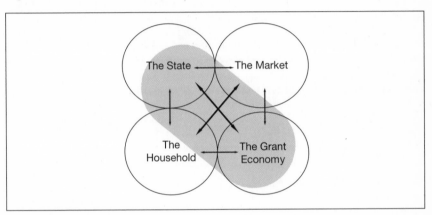

As the figure makes clear, innovations that begin in one sector can be taken up in others. According to the author of *The Medici Effect*, the greatest innovative breakthroughs often occur at the intersection of disciplines and cultures. Thus, the most exciting social innovations can occur when they cross sectors.[19]

One recent example of collaboration between the grant economy and the private economy occurred when a commercial organization (Danone) and a nonprofit organization (Grameen) produced and marketed healthy yogurt as a means of improving the health and nutrition of children in Bangladesh.[20]

Systematic cross-sector approaches to large-scale innovation are rare, but the UK health service may be becoming a good case study. The following box, "Innovation in the UK Health Service," describes how the key elements of health-care innovation became possible only through collaborative efforts by practitioners, policy makers, and social entrepreneurs to discuss and act on new possibilities and changing needs.

Innovation in the UK Health Service

With a turnover of around US$150 billion and some 1.2 million staff, the UK National Health Service (NHS) is a huge system by any standards.

It is already heavily involved in innovation through research, adoption of medical technology, and close links with premier research bodies.

However, in recent years, it has been recognized that these tools, while useful, do not go far enough in that they fail to exploit the potential for improving outcomes through nontechnological means such as service innovations. They also tend to encourage very costly solutions, rather than cheaper and lower-cost ones, and some of the greatest creativity can come from outside the high-status territory of clinical leaders, big business, and big government—for example, from patients groups, imaginative nurses and doctors, and social entrepreneurs.

The former chief executive of the NHS[21] predicts that wealthy countries will increasingly adapt innovations from the developing world, suggesting that these would be better suited to the needs of long-term conditions than the very costly, high-technology, clinical solutions that have dominated recent decades.

In response, NHS, in collaboration with the private and social sector, has sought to put in place comprehensive and pervasive innovation programs, covering many of the steps described in the social innovation process spiral. Some of the key elements of the emerging health innovation system include:

- Small grants for promising ideas coming from doctors, nurses, or social entrepreneurs

- A Social Enterprise Investment Fund (worth around US$150 million) to finance growth in these ideas

- Regional innovation funds (about US$350 million) to promote strategic service innovation both within the NHS and around it

- Whole-system demonstrators testing out new technologies to provide care in the home, showing not just that the technology works but also that the relevant social supports are effective

- New roles, such as Social Entrepreneurs in Residence, to speed up the development of new models while simultaneously backing innovators within the system and supporting others outside

- Prizes to encourage practitioners and in which the public can also participate

- Refashioning commissioning so that commissioners (the people who purchase services for the NHS) are performance managed according to how effectively they both promote and adopt innovations

- Schemes to promote adoption of proven innovations such as "adapt and adopt" funds

- New metrics to help frame assessment of innovations at different stages, including tools to judge the net present value of particular ideas

- Annual innovation reports for each geographical region to set out how well they have done in both commissioning innovation and adopting innovation from elsewhere.

These collaborative efforts have been especially impactful for solving issues of chronic illness, diet, fitness, and mental health, as these often require interdisciplinary innovation. Health-care professionals have now come to realize that health care is as much about lifestyles and influence as it is about treatments and medicine.

It is still too soon to know which of these alternative interventions is delivering the most impact in performance and productivity. But within the next two to three years, the results should be clear and provide insights to other countries seeking to implement comprehensive innovation programs in a public service.

Social Innovation at Top Speed

Understanding and accelerating the field of social innovation is still a work in progress. It has coincided with an economic downturn and a sharp squeeze in public spending. But if anything, this has given new urgency to the innovation agenda.

There is a wide, and probably growing, gap between the scale of the problems we face and the scale of solutions on offer. The new methods for advancing social innovation are relevant in every area, but they are likely to offer most in the fields where problems are intensifying, such as diversity, conflict, climate change, and mental illness; in fields where existing models such as traditional democracy and criminal justice are failing or stagnating; and in fields where new possibilities such as mobile technologies and open source methods are not yet fully exploited.

The good news is that the greater awareness, and application, of innovation to solve many of these social problems will help to raise productivity dramatically and create better results. More significantly, the many initiatives that are helping to accelerate the accelerator of social change will ensure that social innovation happens at top speed to treat, and even solve, the pressing social challenges of our time.

Endnotes

1   While universal health care is now available in many countries, it still eludes big countries such as China and Africa. Even the US has only recently, in 2010, passed the Health Reform Bill, which seeks to assure affordable, quality health coverage for all Americans.

2   Elhanan Helpman, *The Mystery of Economic Growth* (Cambridge, MA: Harvard University Press, 2004). Following on from Solow's work, Helpman estimated that differences in

knowledge and technology explain more than 60 percent of the income and growth rate differences between countries. This reference, and a significant part of the text in this chapter, is adapted from Geoff Mulgan with Simon Tucker, Rushanara Ali, and Ben Sanders, *Social Innovation: What it is, why it matters and how it can be accelerated* (Oxford: Saïd Business School, 2007).

3   Here are three definitions of social innovation:

(1) From J. A. Phills Jr., K. Deiglmeier, and D. T. Miller, "Rediscovering Social Innovation," *Stanford Social Innovation Review*, 2008: "A novel solution to a social problem that is more effective, efficient, sustainable, or just than existing solutions and for which the value created accrues primarily to society as a whole rather than to private individuals. A social innovation can be a product, production process, or technology (much like innovation in general), but it can also be a principle, an idea, a piece of legislation, a social movement, an intervention, or some combination of them."

(2) From Eduardo Pol and Simon Ville, "Social Innovation: Buzz word or enduring term?" *The Journal of Socio-Economics*, February 2009, the OECD LEED Forum on Social Innovation working definition of social innovation is that which "can concern conceptual, process or product change, organizational change, and changes in financing, and can deal with new relationships with stakeholders and territories. 'Social innovation' seeks new answers to social problems by: identifying and delivering new services that improve the quality of life of individuals and communities; identifying and implementing new labour market integration processes, new competencies, new jobs, and new forms of participation, as diverse elements that each contribute to improving the position of individuals in the workforce."

(3) The Lien Centre for Social Innovation uses a definition that seeks to define its scope of work: "Social Innovations are new ideas and insights implemented to create impactful social value. They take place within the social sectors, businesses, and government especially blossoming where these sectors intersect. The Centre aims to catalyze and cultivate these ideas to strengthen and empower civil society and the non-profit sector."

4   Described as a "utopian socialist," Robert Owen founded the New Lanark Mills in Scotland as an example of a viable cooperative factory community, www.spartacus .schoolnet.co.uk/IRowen.htm. Muhammad Yunus, winner of the Noble Peace Prize in 2006, popularized the microcredit movement for small entrepreneurs who are too poor to borrow from a bank, www.nobelprize.org/nobel_prizes/peace/laureates/2006/ yunus-bio.html.

5   These methods are collected, organized, and explained more fully in Robin Murray, Julie Caulier-Grice, and Geoff Mulgan's *The Open Book of Social Innovation* (London: Young Foundation and NESTA, March 2010).

6   X PRIZE, www.xprize.org/x-prizes/overview; Ashoka Changemakers, www.changemakers .com; Thinkathon, www.solutionpeople.com/thinkathon.htm; Crowdsourcing, www .crowdsourcingdirectory.com.

7   The subject of social finance is covered more fully in Chapter 19, "Social Finance: Changing finance, financing change," by Jed Emerson.

8   www.pratham.org.

9   Young Foundation, www.youngfoundation.org; Lien Centre for Social Innovation, www .lcsi.smu.edu.sg; NHS Institute for Innovation and Improvement, www.institute.nhs.uk;

Stanford Centre for Social Innovation, www.csi.gsb.stanford.edu; Aalto University, www.aalto.fi/en.

10   www.socialinnovationexchange.org.

11   European Social Fund Community Initiative Programme, www.equalmalta.org/
mfssequal/content.aspx?id=15545; UK Innovation Investment Fund, www.mynewsdesk
.com/uk/view/pressrelease/department-for-business-innovation-and-skills-200m-
boost-for-future-technology-sectors-375815; US Education Innovation Fund, www
./ed.gov/programs/innovation/factsheet.html.

12   Case Foundation, www.casefoundation.org/projects/make-it-your-own-awards; Nevada
Community Foundation, www.nevadacf.org/grant-process. It is useful to note that the
Nevada Community Foundation's grantmaking process is undergoing review with a
goal for greater impact.

13   X PRIZE is a US$10 million award given by the X PRIZE Foundation to the first team
to reach a specific goal that can benefit humanity, www.xprize.org/x-prizes/overview;
The Global Giveback Innovation Challenge, sponsored by Global Giving, InnoCentive,
and the Rockefeller Foundation, provides cash rewards to nonprofit leaders of up to
US$40,000 to find solutions to challenges facing their communities, www.innocentive
.com/landing/global-giveback.php; The NESTA Innovation Challenges is a £20 million
(US$29 million) initiative to encourage innovative solutions to the UK's social issues,
starting with health innovation and followed by the environment, www.b-a-n-k.co
.uk/article.cfm/id/161228.

14   Social Fusion, http://socialfusion.org/about.html; CAN Mezzanine, www.can-online
.org.uk/; The Hub, www.the-hub.net.

15   www.launchpad.youngfoundation.org.

16   www.marsdd.com/index.html.

17   Allison Benjamin, "Small is Powerful," *The Guardian*, January 7, 2009; Gorka Espiau,
"The New Social Silicon Valley," *DenokInn*, 2010, www.euclidnetwork.eu/data/files/
resources/the_social_innovation_park.pdf.

18   www.slowfood.com.

19   Frans Johansson, *The Medici Effect: What elephants and epidemics can teach us about
innovation* (Boston: Harvard Business School Press, 2006). See also Robin Murray,
Julie Caulier-Grice, and Geoff Mulgan, *How to Innovate: The tools for social innovation*
(London: NESTA, 2008).

20   www.grameencreativelab.com/live-examples/grameen-danone-foods-ltd.html.

21   Nigel Crisp, *Turning the World Upside Down: The search for global health in the 21st
century* (London: Royal Society of Medicine Press, 2010).

Chapter 21

The Phoenix Economy

Agenda for a Sustainable Future

JOHN ELKINGTON
Co-founder and Executive Chairman, Volans Ventures

Amid the economic discontinuity, a paradigm shift toward a more equitable and sustainable future is underway.

Leading the charge into what could be called the Phoenix Economy are 50 identified pioneering organizations. Many are leading social purpose organizations, some are mainstream companies, and a couple of them are governments.

These organizations share a common model for scaling change: from the recognition of an opportunity, to experimentation, and then achieving critical mass—first at the enterprise level, next at the ecosystem level, and finally at the economy level.

The Phoenix Economy can be more rapidly achieved with concerted action around an Agenda that comprises three building blocks: a Manifesto that drives necessary change in the public sector, a Prospectus that shapes investor and business decision making and strategy, and a Syllabus that informs future business education.

"**A**new economic order is rising from the ashes—and a new generation of innovators, entrepreneurs, and investors is accelerating the changes essential for delivering scalable sustainable solutions to the world."

This is the top-line conclusion of *The Phoenix Economy,*[1] a market intelligence report by Volans Ventures for the Skoll Foundation. The study seeks to gauge the thinking of leading entrepreneurs, investors, and businesses on today's economic, social, environmental, and governance challenges. Surveys and discussions conducted in 2008 and 2009 covered more than 500 of these thought leaders and practitioners in the field. What follows is an identification of 50 pioneering organizations and an agenda that can lead the charge toward the Phoenix Economy.

The Rise of the Phoenix

The backdrop to the study is the current economic discontinuity and an attempt to understand where that discontinuity might lead us.

Figure 21.1 is a wave diagram analyzing the underlying dynamics of sustainability-related pressures on governments, businesses, and financial markets since the 1960s.

Figure 21.1 Waves Model

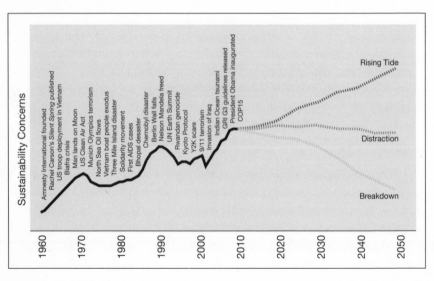

The vertical axis measures the levels of sustainability concerns—as expressed in media coverage about related issues in key regions around the world. Four waves can be observed:

- Wave 1, peaking between 1969 and 1973, focused on public policy and regulation.
- Wave 2, peaking between 1988 and 1991, focused on market dynamics, including the formulation of new management standards.
- Wave 3, which focused on globalization and two forms of governance—global and corporate—occurred in the last decade of the 20th century before the events of 2001 put these dynamics into reverse for a number of years.
- Wave 4, now building around the world, despite—and in some cases, because of—the economic discontinuity.

All this activity is driving toward a new global paradigm, one that has been evolving since the early 1960s. We are moving from the view of a Cornucopian world where the supply of resources is infinite, to a Gaian paradigm where a sustainable way of living on this fragile planet needs to be found. Unfortunately, the popular corporate citizenship and the corporate social responsibility models of change, while necessary and nice to have, are time-expired and are very unlikely to drive the shift to a sustainability-focused paradigm.

Because of these factors, change will likely come from higher-risk, more speculative initiatives whose outcomes are less certain. The iteration in the waves diagram in Figure 21.1 plots three possible scenarios: "Breakdown," "Distraction," and "Rising Tide." Elements of all three are playing out today, with the economic crisis distracting public, private, and citizen sector leaders alike, but with elements of the rising tide continuing to work through in areas such as clean technology.

Impending Shakeout

If the survey respondents agreed on one thing, it is probably that a paradigm shift is underway—with profound implications for politics, economics, and entrepreneurship. The thing about paradigms is that they persist for what seems like an eternity—and then turn inside out in what seems disconcertingly like an instant. As the older economic order begins to implode, the potential for a shift toward a more equitable and sustainable Phoenix Economy is emerging from conversations with leading innovators and entrepreneurs around the world.

While many respondents accepted that the near-term future seems dark, they also recognized that the resulting shakeout of the older order promises to create the conditions for the emergence of new thinking, new models, and a new landscape of opportunity—much of which underlies this framing of the Phoenix Economy.

The phoenix was a mythical bird with many-hued plumage. It symbolized longevity—sustainability—with a life expectancy of at least 500 years. At the end of its life cycle, it was consumed by flames, and a new bird rose from its ashes. Even today, in many countries the phoenix is considered a symbol of regeneration.

By extension, the Phoenix Economy symbolizes the various strands of social and environmental innovation and enterprise that could help create a more equitable and sustainable future.

The Phoenix 50

Leading the charge into the Phoenix Economy are numerous organizations that are operating freely, many across national borders, integrating the triple bottom lines of economic, social, and environmental value. The study spotlights 50 of these pioneers in the business of social innovation (see Figure 21.2).

As one would expect, the list contains a majority of social purpose organizations with many of the usual suspects: Ashoka (pioneer of the social entrepreneurship movement), Grameen Group (leader in microfinance and many other initiatives to uplift the rural poor), and the Population and Community Development Association (using humor and other means to deal with taboo issues of condom use and other national-level culture change in Thailand), to name a few.[2]

What might come as a surprise is the number of mainstream companies that made it into the list. They include General Electric with its "Ecomagination" initiative; Google for its focus on renewable energy and other sustainability issues; GlaxoSmithKline for its industry-consensus-shattering announcement that it would radically cut the cost of its drugs sold to the world's poorest countries; Novo Nordisk for its work with the Oxford Health Alliance (on the prevention and reduction of the global impact of chronic disease around the three risk factors of tobacco use, physical inactivity, and poor diet); and TNT for its work on providing the

Figure 21.2 The Phoenix 50 List

The Phoenix 50

Aflatoun (Netherlands)

AMEE (US)

American Council on Renewable Energy (US)

Apopo (Belgium)

Aravind Eye Care System (India)

Arup (UK)

Ashoka: Innovators for the Public (US)

Better Place (US)

Business and Human Rights Resource Centre (UK)

BYD Auto (China)

C40 Cities (US)

CellBazaar (Bangladesh)

Ceres (US)

Cleantech Group (US)

Climate Change Capital (UK)

E+Co (US)

Econcern (Netherlands)

General Electric's Ecomagination (US)

Generation Investment Management (UK & US)

GlaxoSmithKline (UK)

Global Footprint Network (US)

Global Impact Investing Network (US)

Good Energy (UK)

Google.org (US)

Grameen Group (Bangladesh)

Green for All (US)

Health Care Without Harm (US)

Himanshu Parikh Consulting Engineers (India)

Innocentive (US)

Institute for One World Health (US)

Interpeace (Switzerland)

J. Craig Venter Institute (US)

Kleiner Perkins Caufield & Byers (US)

Marine Stewardship Council (MSC)

MaRS (Canada)

Mothers2Mothers (South Africa)

Movimento Nacional dos Catadores de Materials Reciciaveis (Brazil)

MyC4 (Denmark)

Novo Nordisk and the Oxford Health Alliance (Denmark & UK)

Obama Presidency (US)

Participant Media (US)

Population and Community Development Association (Thailand)

Solarcentury (UK)

State of California (US)

Sustainable Asset Management (Switzerland)

TNT (Netherlands)

Virgance (US)

World Business Council for Sustainable Development (Switzerland)

World Resources Institute (US)

World Toilet Organization (Singapore)

---

logistics for disaster relief and other large-scale initiatives (including tree planting in East Africa).[3]

What may be more surprising is the presence of governments on the list, viz the State of California and the Obama Presidency. Barack Obama, the first African-American US President, is a symbol of new leadership for change. For example, his New Energy plan to make America the 21st century clean energy leader is remarkably ambitious.

Perhaps the one organization that sums up the Phoenix mindset and approach is Shai Agassi's Better Place.[4] Agassi has developed a business model that treats cars as if they were mobile phones, with drivers paying a monthly fee to charge their vehicles at easy-to-use battery stations. The aim is to convert cities and ultimately countries to electric vehicles. Already, Australia, Denmark, and Israel have signed up, together with states such as California and Hawaii, and cities such as Toronto. Their approach—mobilizing all levels of government, major companies (such as Renault), and investors—is a good example of what one might expect to see as the Phoenix paradigm takes hold and the relevant forms of innovation and entrepreneurship take flight.

Pathways to Scale

So, what are these pioneers trying to achieve? How are they scaling up for impact? The Volans research evolved a five-stage "Pathways to Scale" model of change (see Figure 21.3).

Figure 21.3 "Pathways to Scale" Model of Change

Stage 1 Eureka!	Stage 2 Experiment	Stage 3 Enterprise	Stage 4 Ecosystem	Stage 5 Economy
Opportunity is revealed via the growing dysfunctions of existing order.	Innovators and entrepreneurs begin to experiment. A period of trial-and-error begins.	Investors and managers build new business models to create new forms of value.	Critical mass is achieved through alliances and imitation.	The economic system flips to a more sustainable state to drive market and institutional transformation.

Each new business model will typically begin at Stage 1 with the early recognition of an opportunity for a new solution. In Stage 2, that initial idea is put to the test with prototypes and experimentation. Over time, successful experiments evolve into solutions around which new Stage 3 business models and enterprises are created. Stage 4 sees the focus shift to the evolution of broader ecosystems of change agents that involve a growing number of public, private, and citizen sector partnerships, followed by secondary waves of imitation.

Ultimately, if a truly sustainable and equitable future is to be achieved, entrepreneurial initiatives will need to scale up further to Stage 5 system change. This is typified by broad-based market and societal adoption of new mindsets, models, and technologies. Success in moving from Stage 4 to Stage 5 will involve the transformation of political priorities, governance processes, market rules, and cultures.

It is an uncomfortable fact that economic and social systems—like ecosystems—go through periods of convulsive change. Social and environmental entrepreneurs and intrapreneurs may be in the spotlight as never before, but we are seeing a shake-out that will hit both weak and strong organizations.

This should be of concern to leaders in the public, private, and citizen sectors alike, given that many socially conscious entrepreneurs spotlight and seek to address critical issues such as climate change, water scarcity, poverty, disease, corruption, and an expanding array of human rights concerns. These entrepreneurs are particularly worth watching because they are experimenting with new technologies and business models to underscore the potential for transformational solutions and change.[5]

Toward a Phoenix Agenda

In the course of the study, the surveyed entrepreneurs suggested ideas and actions that they would like to see from decision makers and policy makers to further the Phoenix Economy. These recommendations (the Phoenix Agenda)[6] can be grouped as follows:

- For political leaders and governments: the Phoenix Manifesto
- For business leaders: the Phoenix Prospectus
- For business and finance educators: the Phoenix Syllabus.

The Phoenix Manifesto

Entrepreneurs who are helping the Phoenix Economy take flight would like to see government leaders go beyond just saving ailing parts of the economy. They hope that governments will expand support for enterprises that create new forms of value, new forms of employment, and, ultimately, new landscapes of market opportunity. They want to see governments:

- *Collaborate:* More governments—and different levels of government—need to establish units and departments to provide effective interfaces between entrepreneurs and the government system, a process that has begun in the UK with the National Endowment for Science, Technology, and the Arts, and the Office of the Third Sector.[7]
- *Get the Targets Right:* To ensure effectiveness and accountability, governments must set, publish, monitor, and report on progress toward ambitious targets on key priority areas such as climate change. Partnerships will be crucial to help governments understand which targets to set. The Global Footprint Network[8] is working with governments around the world to build dashboards of metrics and management systems.
- *Simplify Regulatory Requirements:* Entrepreneurs have protested the complexity of registering new organizations, both commercial and nonprofit, in several countries. In the US, for example, there have been calls for government to federalize regulatory requirements for the social sector, instead of having separate filing requirements in each state.
- *Redirect Procurement:* All levels of government can help to drive the transition by adapting their policies in areas such as public purchasing. This approach has been trialed by initiatives such as C40.[9] Buying green—or more broadly, buying in ways that are "future-friendly"—by aggregating purchasing will inexorably drive market transformations.
- *Refine Market Governance:* Markets are social constructions. Sometimes they just happen; sometimes they are created by design. Public sector efforts are likely to be most effective where they learn from innovators creating a new generation of market governance rules and processes. Such players include the Extractive Industries Transparency Initiative, the Forest Stewardship Council, Health Care Without Harm, the Roundtable on Sustainable Palm Oil, the Roundtable on Sustainable Biofuels, and the Marine Stewardship Council.[10]

- *Design Better Infrastructure:* From public health spending to city blueprints, governments, at all levels, need to think beyond curative solutions and leverage the intelligence of entrepreneurs in the design of policies and interventions. This trend is illustrated by such examples as Better Place and the World Resource Institute's Embarq,[11] both working closely with governments around the world on the design of sustainable transport policies and infrastructures.
- *Grow Clusters:* Governments have a critical role to play in creating the necessary clusters of social enterprise and support services. This is something that MaRS is pioneering in Canada and Singapore's Economic Development Board is working toward.[12]
- *Foster Culture Change:* It is never easy to achieve cultural change, but the world will undergo a series of cultural transformations in the wake of massive, discontinuous economic upheaval. The success of productions such as *An Inconvenient Truth* (by Participant Media) and *Slumdog Millionaire* (by Celador Productions) has been inspirational in the use of mainstream media and entertainment to raise public social consciousness.[13]

The Phoenix Prospectus

When it comes to business, financial institutions, and business schools, the entrepreneurs surveyed want business to:

- *Partner:* There is a clear and growing appetite among the trailblazing innovators for new forms of partnership with business. This will involve funding relationships, of course, but leading entrepreneurs are also interested in gaining access to highly skilled, high-potential individuals in business. The Accenture Development Partnerships (ADP) program, which brings the organization's talents to work in, and improve, social organizations, is a leading model here.[14]
- *Build Market Intelligence:* Market intelligence is one thing, intelligent markets quite another. The entrepreneurs tend to have disparate needs in terms of market research, but as they grow, they know they will need better market intelligence. This is an area where new forms of partnership could be forged between constellations of entrepreneurs and market research providers, something the London Accord has been working on.[15]
- *Help Scale Solutions:* As they move from prototypes to proven business models, entrepreneurs need help in thinking through how

to consolidate, replicate, and scale their solutions. Business can help them think from the outset, as Novo Nordisk and TNT did with their respective partners.

– *Think Around Corners:* Again, easier said than done, but business federations need to be opened up to new thinking. An example is the World Business Council for Sustainable Development's growing interest in social entrepreneurs and its work with the Global Footprint Network to introduce mainstream corporate business to integrated Footprint metrics.[16] Companies might also improve their capacity to engage and understand the wider world by creating "social entrepreneurs in residence" programs.

– *Take the Lead and Lobby for Change:* Business has an increasing awareness of the risks that lie ahead and is quickly developing an interest in supporting change. It has a central role to play in building understanding of the need for new models and frameworks—and the related market opportunities. The work of the Ceres Investor Network on Climate Risk, the US Climate Action Partnership, and the UK's Corporate Leaders Group on Climate Change underscores the potential.[17]

The entrepreneurs would like financial institutions, in particular, to:

– *Invest in Phoenix Pioneers:* This may be an obvious one, but the stinger is that respondents also want to see the banks get back to sustainable models of lending and then to maintain and build credit lines for social enterprises, following the lead of banks such as ShoreBank and Triodos.[18]

– *Adopt New Metrics:* There is a need to support and adopt investment metrics that align financial investment more closely with long-term societal goals. Examples of leaders in this area are Generation Investment Management's model of equity management and the potential of the Global Impact Investing Network, which aims to pull together blends of private, public, and philanthropic funding in order to mainstream social impact investment.[19]

The Phoenix Syllabus

The surveyed entrepreneurs see business schools and educators as important drivers of change and want them to:

- *Rethink the Curriculum and Research Agenda:* The growing impact of the economic discontinuity suggests that it is time to question the very principles on which business educators base their curricula, where areas such as finance modeling, strategy, and marketing show little evidence of the integration of ethical, social, and environmental considerations.
- *Mainstream Social Innovation:* Most leading business schools have started to look at social entrepreneurship, but this has tended to be a marginal activity, with teaching and research kept in "social" silos within the schools. Now is the time to bring this teaching and research agenda closer to mainstream business education, looking beyond social enterprises to what Volans calls the "business of social innovation."
- *Reboot Case Studies:* There is a need to develop and adopt new metrics in business research and education (think triple bottom line or blended value). Universities and research institutions have an important role to play here, especially through the development of case studies with a focus on emerging Phoenix models. The coverage of the Aravind Eye Hospital in a recent Harvard Business School case study[20] should be emulated. New "living" case studies need to be developed to explore different types of solutions across a broader spectrum of organizational and sectoral models. One key area of focus should be on the strategies, alliances, and pathways to scale.
- *Unleash Students:* Student groups focused on social entrepreneurship have been remarkably successful and active in places such as the Haas Business School at Berkeley, the Fuqua School of Management at Duke University, Harvard University's Kennedy School of Government, INSEAD, and the Skoll Centre for Social Entrepreneurship at Oxford University.[21]

Riding the Phoenix

The year 2010 kicked off with the remarkable box office success of James Cameron's 3-D film *Avatar*. In it was a sequence where the hero Jake tamed a Toruk, a powerful flying creature that only five of the indigenous Na'vi people have ever managed to tame. That is the trick we now have to pull off with the sequence of economic recoveries that will gradually pull the global economy back on track. If, however, the net result is that we slip back into business-as-usual, we will have wasted a crisis.

The idea behind the Phoenix Manifesto, Prospectus, and Syllabus is that we have an unparalleled opportunity to shift the center of gravity of the global economy toward sustainability, although the outcomes of the 2009 UN Copenhagen Climate Change Conference and the 2010 World Economic Forum annual summit in Davos provide little comfort on that score.

Much of the change is going to have to come from the bottom up, from the outside in. That said, there is much that powerful political and market actors can do to speed the process, often simply by getting out of the way. As an illustration of the array of experiments now moving forward, Volans is currently developing the Pathways to Scale Program through a number of projects, including a year-long study of the ecosystem services marketplace funded by the Tellus Mater Foundation.[22]

Riding these great waves of change is never easy, but at this particular moment in our collective history, it is pertinent to recall what Ralph Waldo Emerson once said: "Once you make a decision, the universe conspires to make it happen."[23]

It is time to make the decisions that the future of our planet and our species require. And if this cannot be done top down, then it should be done any which way that yields results. The Phoenix Economy is going to be a wildly disparate affair, but the one thing it will inevitably build over time is momentum—and it will be our great task to steer it.

Endnotes

1   John Elkington, Alejandro Litovsky, and Charmian Love, *The Phoenix Economy: 50 pioneers in the business of social innovation* (London: Volans Ventures, 2009).

2   Ashoka, www.ashoka.org; Grameen Group, www.grameen-info.org; PDA, www.pda .or.th/eng.

3   General Electric's Ecomagination, which is a business strategy designed to achieve innovation and growth of profitable environmental solutions while engaging stakeholders, www.ge.com; Google, www.google.org; GlaxoSmithKline, www.gsk. com; Novo Nordisk's Oxford Health Alliance; www.novonordisk.com/sustainability/ values_in_action/advocacy/The-Oxford-Health-Alliance.asp; TNT, www.tnt.com.

4   www.betterplace.com.

5   *Growing Opportunity: Entrepreneurial solutions to insoluble problems* (London: SustainAbility, Skoll Foundation, 2007).

6   A draft of the Agenda was tested with a brains trust of entrepreneurs. The examples cited in the subsequent Phoenix Manifesto, Phoenix Prospectus, and Phoenix Syllabus are necessarily brief due to space constraints. More information on the Agenda and the examples cited can be found in the full report, the Volans website (www.volans .com), and the individual websites and references related to the specific examples.

7 The year-long Social Enterprise Access to Investment Facility, for example, is run by NESTA and co-funded by the Office of the Third Sector. www.nesta.org.uk/areas_ of_work/public_services_lab/social_enterprise/market_functioning/assets/features/ social_enterprises_offered_missing_link_to_access_investment_streams.

8 www.footprintnetwork.org/en/index.php/GFN.

9 www.c40cities.org.

10 Extractive Industries Transparency Initiative, www.eitransparency.org; Forest Stewardship Council, www.fscus.org; Health Care Without Harm, www.noharm.org; Roundtable on Sustainable Palm Oil, www.rspo.org; Roundtable on Sustainable Biofuels, cgse.epfl .ch/page65660-en.html; Marine Stewardship Council, www.msc.org.

11 www.embarq.org.

12 MaRS. www.marsdd.com; Singapore Economic Development Board, www.edb.gov.sg.

13 *An Inconvenient Truth*, www.climatecrisis.net; *Slumdog Millionaire*, www.slumdog millionairemovie.co.uk.

14 Started in 2003, the initiative was driven by Accenture employees who wanted to make a positive difference. www.accenture.com/Global/About_Accenture/Company_Overview/ Corporate_Citizenship/Time_and_Skills/ADP/Overview.htm.

15 www.london-accord.co.uk.

16 Global Footprint Network is developing a framework for the World Business Council for Sustainable Development in thinking about resource constraints and assessing if proposed pathways are enough to reach a one-planet economy by 2050. www .footprintnetwork.org/en/index.php/GFN/page/case_stories/#WBCSD.

17 Ceres Investor Network on Climate Risk, www.ceres.org/Page.aspx?pid=705; the US Climate Action Partnership, www.us-cap.org; UK's Corporate Leaders Group on Climate Change, www.cpi.cam.ac.uk/our_work/climate_leaders_groups/clgcc.aspx.

18 ShoreBank, www.shorebankcorp.com; Triodos, www.triodos.com.

19 Generation Investment Management, www.generationim.com; Global Impact Investing Network, www.globalimpactinvestingnetwork.org/cgi-bin/iowa/home/index.html.

20 Kasturi Rangan, "Aravind Eye Hospital, Madurai, India: In service for sight, *Harvard Business Review*, April 1, 1993, www.hbr.org/product/aravind-eye-hospital-madurai-india-in-service-for-/an/593098-PDF-ENG.

21 Haas Business School at Berkeley, www.entrepreneurship.berkeley.edu/students/ social.html; the Fuqua School of Management at Duke University, www .caseatduke.org; Harvard University's Kennedy School of Government, www .hks.harvard.edu/news-events/news/articles/center-for-public-leadership,-new-social-enterprise-fellowship-featured-in-the-new-york-times; INSEAD, www .insead.edu/home; and the Skoll Centre for Social Entrepreneurship, www.sbs .ox.ac.uk/centres/skoll/Pages/default.aspx.

22 *The Biosphere Economy: Natural limits can spur creativity, innovation and growth* (London: Volans, Tellus Mater Foundation and Business for Environment Global Summit, 2010), www.volans.com/pathways/projects/biosphere-economy.

23 Ralph Waldo Emerson was a 19th century American poet and known especially for his 1836 work, *Nature*.

About the Contributors

Editors and Authors

Willie Cheng is a former partner of Accenture, a global management and technology consulting company. He was the country managing director and the managing partner of its Communications & High Tech Practice in Asia before he retired in 2003. He remains active in the business and infocomm community. However, he spends the larger part of his time working with nonprofit organizations at the board and volunteer level. Among these, he is chairman of the Lien Centre for Social Innovation and Caritas Singapore. He is the author of *Doing Good Well: What does (and does not) make sense in the nonprofit world.* He first used the ecosystem concept to frame the charity world for a Lien Centre publication, *Social Space 2008. (Email: willie@doinggoodwell.net)*

Sharifah Mohamed is manager at the Lien Centre for Social Innovation, focusing on New Social Models. She currently manages projects and research in the areas of philanthropy, social entrepreneurship, and social innovation. She was part of the pioneering team for the Lien Centre's inaugural *Social Space* publication, a compilation of insightful articles by leaders and thinkers in the public, private, and nonprofit sectors. She also managed the recent Lien i3 Challenge, an Asia-wide competition for socially innovative projects. Outside of her job, she channels her energy toward addressing education and mobility issues of lower-income groups. She is a member of a nationwide youth self-help group making efforts in community enrichment. *(Email: smaisharahm@smu.edu.sg)*

Authors

Robert Chew is a former partner of Accenture where he focused on strategy work for clients in the infocomm industry. Since his retirement in 2007, he has remained active in the infocomm industry. He is chairman of the Information Technology Standards Committee, and a member of the National Grid Advisory Council, the Singapore Standards Council, and the Singapore Chinese Chambers of Commerce and Industry's Technology Committee. Chew is also currently a director of several commercial companies (OpenNet, Alexandra Health, and Integrated Health Information Systems) and nonprofit organizations (Lien Centre for Social Innovation, Dover Park Hospice, Singapore Hospice Council, TOUCH Community Services, TOUCH Youth, and TOUCH Family Services).

Chris Cusano is currently Change Leader, ASEAN, for Ashoka: Innovators for the Public. He joined Ashoka in 2000, after spending most of the 1990s working with refugees and displaced people along the Thailand–Burma border. Cusano managed Ashoka's global process for electing new Ashoka Fellows until 2005, when he returned to Thailand to help Ashoka develop its presence in Southeast Asia. As part of this program, Cusano is building the Ashoka Support Network in the region, enabling businesspeople and social entrepreneurs to combine forces for greater social impact.

Gerard Ee champions social service issues and rights in Singapore. The son of a prominent Singaporean philanthropist, Ee has inherited his father's mantle and is fondly known in Singapore as "Mr. Charity." A retired accountant, he has served in various nonprofit and national capacities. He was a Nominated Member of Parliament from 1997 to 2002. He was president of the National Council of Social Service from 2001 to 2006. He is currently chairman of the Public Transport Council, the Council for Third Age, and the National Kidney Foundation. He took over the challenge of turning around Singapore's National Kidney Foundation in 2004 after a scandal rocked the charity.

John Elkington is co-founder and executive chairman of Volans Ventures, co-founder of SustainAbility (1987), and co-founder of Environmental Data Services (1978). He is a world authority on corporate responsibility and sustainable development. He has authored or co-authored 17 books, including 1988's million-selling *Green Consumer Guide, Cannibals with Forks: The triple bottom line of 21st century business,* and *The Power of Unreasonable People: How social entrepreneurs create markets that change the world.* He has also written hundreds of articles for newspapers, magazines, and journals, as well as written or co-written some 40 published reports. He has spoken at hundreds of conferences around the world.

Jed Emerson has spent his career launching innovative nonprofit ventures and philanthropic funds. He is founding director of Larkin Youth Services, a homeless youth program in San Francisco, California, and founding director of REDF, a leading venture philanthropy fund. In addition to his work executing strategies, he is an internationally recognized thought leader, having written extensively about social entrepreneurship, metrics, and impact investing. He has had faculty appointments at Stanford, Harvard, and Oxford Universities. He framed the concept of Blended Value and has written extensively on both that and related topics. His work may be found at www.blendedvalue.org and www.redf.org.

Jonathan S. Huggett served as a partner with The Bridgespan Group in San Francisco and New York; and as a partner with Bain & Company in Johannesburg and Toronto. He is currently a Visiting Fellow at the Skoll Centre for Social Entrepreneurship, Saïd Business School, Oxford University, and advises social enterprise leaders worldwide. Earlier, he ran a US$75 million global health-care company, an economic development consultancy, and a venture-funded social enterprise. Huggett served as president of the STOP AIDS Project in San Francisco and is now serving on three charity boards: the Organization for Refuge, Asylum and Migration; One Inspire; and Khulisa UK. He has a BA and MA from Oxford University, and an MBA from Stanford University's Graduate School of Business, where he graduated as an Arjay Miller Scholar.

Dr. Rob John is an independent consultant specializing in venture philanthropy and social entrepreneurship. From 2005 to 2009, he was a visiting fellow at the Skoll Centre for Social Entrepreneurship at the University of Oxford's Saïd Business School. He was principal advisor to the European Venture Philanthropy Association during its start up and now advises the Asia Venture Philanthropy Network and the European Venture Philanthropy Fund. Following a career spanning 15 years in international development, including refugee assistance and microcredit, John directed a small Oxford-based venture philanthropy fund before becoming freelance in 2004. He is a Fellow of the Royal Society for the Encouragement of Arts, Manufactures, and Commerce.

Laurence Lien is CEO of the National Volunteer & Philanthropy Centre in Singapore. He previously served in the Singapore Administrative Service, rotating through different positions in the Ministries of Finance, Community Development and Sports, Home Affairs, and Education. He is also chairman of the Lien Foundation, deputy chairman of Lien Aid, and a board member of the Lien Centre for Social Innovation, and Caritas Singapore Community Council.

He has a Bachelor of Arts from Oxford University, an MBA from the National University of Singapore, and a Masters in Public Administration from the Harvard Kennedy School. He is an Eisenhower Fellow.

Stephen Lloyd is senior partner at Bates Wells & Braithwaite London LLP, the leading charity law firm in the UK. He acts for a great variety of charities and is also a trustee of five charities. He was the joint initiator of the idea that became the community interest company. He is also co-author of *Charities— The New Law 2006: A practical guide to the Charities Acts*; *Charities, Trading and the Law*; and *The Fundraiser's Guide to the Law*. He is also a former chairman of the Charity Law Association.

Paulette V. Maehara, CFRE, CAE is president and CEO of the Association of Fundraising Professionals (AFP), the professional association of individuals responsible for generating philanthropic support for nonprofit organizations. Prior to joining AFP, Maehara served as CEO of the Epilepsy Foundation. She has also held executive positions with several foundations and nonprofit organizations. She has been selected by *The NonProfit Times* as one of the Top 50 Most Influential People in Philanthropy for the last 10 years. Her work for Project HOPE led to a Best Direct Mail Program award from the Direct Marketing Association of America.

Dr. Maximilian Martin is a visiting professor at the University of Geneva and lectures at the University of St. Gallen. He is currently a senior partner and Global Head of Social Investments at IJ Partners, a Geneva-based wealth management firm. He was the Global Head and Managing Director of UBS AG's Philanthropy Services from 2004 to 2009. Prior to this, he was head of research at the Schwab Foundation for Social Entrepreneurship, senior consultant with McKinsey & Company, and Fellow at the Center for Public Leadership at the John F. Kennedy School of Government, Harvard University.

Dr. Thomas Menkhoff is Practice Associate Professor of Organizational Behavior and Human Resources at the Lee Kong Chian School of Business, Singapore Management University. He is the co-editor of *Chinese Entrepreneurship and Asian Business Networks* and *Governing and Managing Knowledge in Asia*. His recent research work aims to understand the antecedents of effective knowledge-sharing behavior in knowledge-intensive organizations. He is co-editor of a special 2010 issue of the *Journal of Asian Business* on *Chinese Philanthropy in Asia: Between Continuity and Change*. He is a Fellow of the Salzburg Seminar and a board member of the Lien Centre for Social Innovation.

Dr. Geoff Mulgan worked as head of policy and strategy in the UK Prime Minister's Office and Cabinet Office between 1997 and 2004. He is now director of the Young Foundation in London and visiting professor at several universities in Australia and the UK. His publications include: *The Art of Public Strategy*; *Good and Bad Power*; *Connexity*; *Life After Politics*; *Politics in an Anti-Political Age*; and *Communication and Control*. He has worked with several governments, including those of Australia, Canada, Denmark, France, China, and Russia.

Dr. Kumi Naidoo is the executive director of Greenpeace International and is based in Amsterdam. He also serves as the chairperson of the Global Campaign for Climate Action and is the co-chair of the Global Call to Action against Poverty. Prior to taking on his current role at Greenpeace International, Naidoo worked at CIVICUS where he was the secretary-general (1998 to 2008). He was active in the anti-apartheid struggle in his native South Africa and is an advocate for gender equality and labor rights. He has worked as a researcher, journalist, university lecturer, and youth counselor.

Sara Olsen is the founding partner of SVT Group (www.svtgroup.net), a San Francisco-based advisory firm that specializes in measuring, managing, and communicating social and environmental value and return on investment. To date, SVT has developed frameworks to measure the nonfinancial value of approximately US$2 billion in social and environmental investments and grants in over 20 countries. Olsen believes impact management is an emerging business discipline, and she works to promote its development and adoption. She is the co-author of *Social Return on Investment: A guide to SROI analysis* and co-founded the Global Social Venture Competition (www.gsvc. org) in 1999. Olsen holds an MBA from UC Berkeley, an MASW from the University of Chicago, and a BA from Dartmouth College.

Dr. Peter Shergold AC is Macquarie Group Foundation Professor at the Centre for Social Impact, which is headquartered in the Australian School of Business at the University of New South Wales. From 2003 to 2008, he was Secretary of the Department of the Prime Minister and Cabinet, Australia's most senior public administrator. He is a non-executive director of AMP and Corrs Chambers Westgarth, and is the chairman of a small venture capital start-up, QuintessenceLabs. On the nonprofit side, he is chairman of the Australian Rural Leadership Foundation and serves on the boards of the National Centre of Indigenous Excellence and the Monash Foundation.

Dr. Tan Chi Chiu is a gastroenterologist and managing director of Gastroenterology & Medicine International in Singapore. He has been deeply involved in the medical, youth development, and community service scene for several decades. He volunteers with several nonprofit organizations. He is a director of the Lien Centre for Social Innovation, SATA CommHealth, Make-A-Wish-Foundation

Singapore, and National Youth Achievement Awards. He is an elected member of the Singapore Medical Council and chairman of the Medical Ethics Committee. He was previously executive director of the Singapore International Foundation and has won numerous Singaporean and international military and civilian awards for his global humanitarian, community, and youth work. He is a keen observer of and commentator on the social arena.

Alan M. Webber is an award-winning editor, author, and columnist. In 1995, he launched *Fast Company* magazine (www.fastcompany.com), which became the fastest growing, most successful business magazine in history. He was also, for five years, the managing editor and editorial director of the *Harvard Business Review*. He is active globally in the social entrepreneurship movement, and describes his role as that of a "global detective." He has most recently authored *Rules of Thumb: 52 Truths for Winning at Business Without Losing Yourself*, which highlights the new practices and principles we need to adopt to create a better, more workable, sustainable future.

Dr. Stephen B. Young is the Global Executive Director of the Caux Round Table. His book, *Moral Capitalism* was written as a guide to the Caux Round Table ethical and socially responsible Principles for Business. Young was named by Professor Sandra Waddock as one of those who built the modern corporate social responsibility movement. He was a dean at the Hamline University School of Law, as well as assistant dean at Harvard Law School. He is the founding board chair of the Center of the American Experiment, and served as appointed Honorary Consul of Singapore in Minnesota for five years.

Index